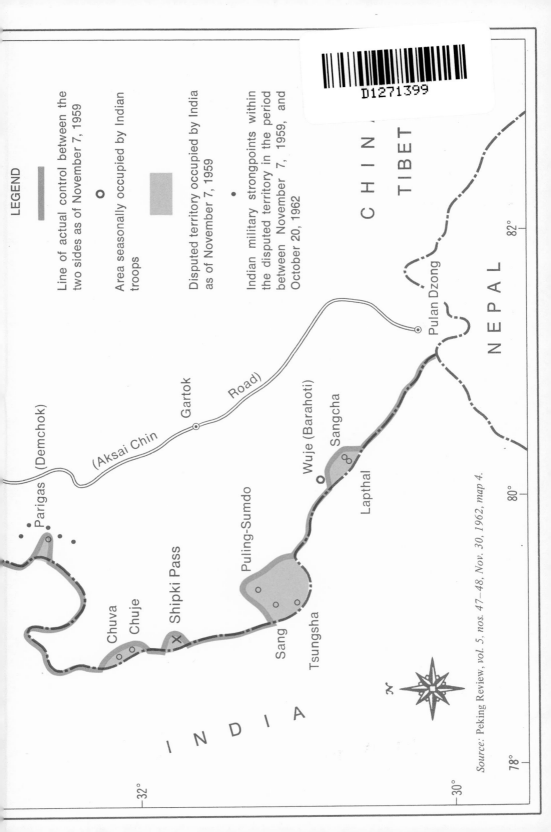

LEGEND

Line of actual control between the two sides as of November 7, 1959

○ Area seasonally occupied by Indian troops

Disputed territory occupied by India as of November 7, 1959

• Indian military strongpoints within the disputed territory in the period between November 7, 1959, and October 20, 1962

C H I N A

T I B E T

N E P A L

Pulan Dzong

Parigas (Demchok)

(Aksai Chin

Gartok

Road)

Chuva

Chuje

Shipki Pass

Puling-Sumdo

Wuje (Barahoti)

Sangcha

Lapthal

Sang

Tsungsha

I N D I A

82°

80°

78°

32°

30°

Source: Peking Review, vol. 5, nos. 47–48, Nov. 30, 1962, map 4.

Volumes previously published by the University of California Press, Berkeley, Los Angeles, London, for the Center for Chinese Studies of The University of Michigan:

MICHIGAN STUDIES ON CHINA

THE CHINESE CALCULUS OF DETERRENCE

Michigan Studies on China
Published for the Center for Chinese Studies
of The University of Michigan

MICHIGAN STUDIES ON CHINA

China's Economic Development: The Interplay of Scarcity and Ideology, by Alexander Eckstein
The Chinese Calculus of Deterrence: India and Indochina, by Allen S. Whiting

The research on which these books are based was supported by the Center for Chinese Studies of The University of Michigan.

The Chinese Calculus of Deterrence

INDIA AND INDOCHINA

ALLEN S. WHITING

Ann Arbor   The University of Michigan Press

Grateful acknowledgment is made to the following publishers for permission to reprint copyrighted material:

Allied Publishers Private Limited for material from Lieutenant General B. M. Kaul, *The Untold Story.*

Hoover Institution Press for material from J. Chester Cheng, *The Politics of the Chinese Red Army.* Copyright © 1966, by the Board of Trustees of the Leland Stanford Junior University.

Pantheon Books, a Division of Random House, Inc., for material from Neville Maxwell, *India's China War.* Copyright © 1970, 1972, by Neville Maxwell.

Thacker and Company, Ltd., for material from Brigadier J. P. Dalvi, *Himalayan Blunder.*

To Debbie, David,
Jeffrey, and Jennie

As a species mankind has the defect whereby one man simply despises others. A person with a little achievement looks down on one who still has no achievement. Big nations and rich nations look down on small nations and poor nations. Western nations used to have contempt for Russia. At present China still is in a position of being despised. There is a reason for people despising us. It is because we still have not progressed enough. Such a big country with so little steel and so many illiterates! But if people despise us, it is good because it forces us to strive and forces us to advance.

MAO TSE-TUNG (1961–62)*

*"Notes on the Soviet Union Textbook *Political Economy* (1961–1962)" in Mao Tse-tung ssu-hsiang wan-sui (Long Live Mao Tse-tung's Thought) [N.p., August 1969], p. 392.

Preface

My interest in the Sino-Indian border dispute grew out of a long fascination with China's border regions as arenas of international competition for influence and control. Among my earlier works, Mongolia loomed large in *Soviet Policies in China: 1917–1924*[1] while Japanese and Russian intrigue provided a leitmotif of foreign activity in *Sinkiang: Pawn or Pivot?*[2] As a member of the Rand Corporation I visited Nepal in 1960 to study Chinese activities in the sub-Himalayan region and conferred with Indian officials who were exchanging claims with their People's Republic of China (PRC) counterparts based on historical, legal, and cartographic evidence of ownership to disputed border territory.

In September, 1961, I joined the Bureau of Intelligence and Research (INR) in the Department of State as a member of a special studies group reporting to the director, Roger Hilsman. The next year I became director of the Office of Research and Analysis, Far East, INR, where I served until August 1, 1966. This office was responsible for collating and interpreting intelligence information for all countries in the arc of Asia extending from the Soviet border in the northeast to the Indian border in the southwest. Although its professional staff included only two dozen members, their professional competence and long experience brought rich returns from their access to personnel and information in the much larger offices of Defense, the Central Intelligence Agency (CIA), and the National Security Agency.[3]

The high caliber of the staff was exemplified by one senior analyst, Dr. Rhea Blue, who immediately upon my becoming office director on July 1, 1962, expressed her apprehension over possible conflict on the Sino-Indian border. Dr. Blue had served in INR since its establishment after World War II and as a specialist on China's minority regions was second to none in this country. Her meticulous memory, her painstaking research, and her devotion to such disciplines as history and geography made her an invaluable resource in this area.

The INR staff monitored growing tensions on the Himalayan front throughout the summer and, after Peking publicized its first casualties in September, we forecast that fighting would occur if India did not reverse its course.

The consistent escalation of warning manifest in Chinese statments, both diplomatic and propagandistic, paralleled the Korean War developments recounted in *China Crosses the Yalu.*[4] After the initial fighting occurred in October as predicted, a three-week pause in Chinese attacks led us to forecast a renewed offensive. Our ignorance about Indian military weaknesses and confusion of command led us to overestimate resistance and therefore to underestimate the ease with which Chinese forces would overrun all Indian positions, including the entire Northeast Frontier Agency.[5] However, we insisted the attack would not include any invasion of uncontested territory or air attacks on Indian cities. These views were contested elsewhere in the government but their accuracy was dramatically proven by the unilateral Chinese cease-fire of November 20, announced as the Harriman mission was to depart in response to Prime Minister Nehru's call for help. My participation in that mission brought the situation into close focus.

In lieu of a conventional narrative-memoir after leaving government service in September, 1968, I undertook a systematic reconstruction of the Chinese decisions which had led to war with India. Several factors dictated my course of action. I kept no notes, diaries, or papers in Washington and while I could recall major events, important details might have been omitted or in error. In addition, our view had been incomplete and partial. Our predictions had been right but they might have been based on incorrect reasoning. Only a rigorous reexamination of the evidence, together with a wider net of information than was available at the time, could test alternative hypotheses. Moreover only by presenting the full basis of analysis could others evaluate and replicate it.

A wider objective was the development of a conceptual approach and supporting research methods which could be applied elsewhere. In this regard, Kuang-sheng Liao provided brilliant, creative, and disciplined assistance in applying quantitative methods to content and interaction analysis.[6] In addition, we sought broader generalizations that would pertain both to Chinese behavior over time and to comparable situations across different states. Toward this end I examined Chinese participation in the Indochina war, from 1964 to 1968, so as to compare Peking's conflict behavior in Korea, India, and Indochina. While the Indochina portion relies more on intelligence data than was true for the analyzed Sino-Indian conflict, the essential facts were released by the United States Government in 1964–68 and therefore the conceptual framework of analysis could be applied without reliance upon intelligence data.

The acknowledgments for this book go well beyond the customary, as implied by its origins. Alexander George has played a recurring role of stimulus, critic, and friend, from his effort at the Rand Corporation to broaden my horizons beyond Sino-Soviet relations to his continual prodding for more conceptual and theoretical linkage between government analysis and academic research. Roger Hilsman introduced me to full-time intelligence analysis and supported our minority view of Chinese priorities and objectives ten years before the visit of President Nixon to Peking made it official policy. W. Averill Harriman deserves special credit for holding the line in October, 1962, against "worst case" analysis of Chinese intentions and defending the INR position despite public and private warnings to the contrary. His statesmanship and courage were an inspiration to middle-echelon experts whose views ran counter to Cold War orthodoxy. Less successful but equally courageous battles were fought by George W. Ball in defense of similarly expert but heretical views on Indochina. It was a particular privilege to work closely with these two men.

However, no single person in government functions solely on his own resources. Each is dependent on many others. In addition to Dr. Rhea Blue whom I have already mentioned, Mrs. Dorothy Avery and Paul Kreisberg were unflaggingly outstanding in their analytical roles in INR. Arthur C. Cohen has written the most comprehensive history of the 1962 conflict based on government sources; hopefully it will be made public eventually. Mrs. Evi Blake as my secretary, W. Bradford Coolidge, Richard T. Ewing, James M. Leonard as my deputies, and Mrs. Evelyn Colbert as colleague, critic, and friend all share in having made the INR analysis so successful. As a successor to Roger Hilsman, Thomas Hughes continued to lead the battle on our behalf while testing the analysts' mettle with his incisive mind and rapier wit.

An early version of this manuscript was commented on critically by the late Wayne C. Wilcox whose tragic death removed a vital, concerned, and stimulating scholar at the start of a promising policy career. Subsequent readings by Michel Oksenberg, Daniel Okimoto, Tang Tsou, Peter Van Ness, William W. Whitson, Jonathan Pollack, and David M. Lampton provided fresh perspectives and trenchant criticism.

Financial support for this study from the Center for Chinese Studies and the Horace H. Rackham School of Graduate Studies, both of the University of Michigan, as well as from the Social Science Research Council, is gratefully acknowledged. Needless to say, none of the individuals or organizations named above bear any responsibility for the views expressed herein. Finally I wish to express my deepest appreciation for the perseverance with which my wife Alice and my four children have tolerated the tensions and tribulations of simultaneously changing career in midstream and writing a book.

ALLEN S. WHITING

Introduction

General Focus

Compared with major wars of this century, the Sino-Indian conflict does not rank high in duration, scale, casualties, issues, or tangible consequences. The fighting lasted only thirty days, from October 20 to November 20, 1962. At most three Chinese divisions entered combat in the Northeast Frontier Agency (NEFA) at the eastern end of the border against an Indian force of approximately equal strength.[1] Engagements both here and in Ladakh, at the western end, rarely exceeded company or battalion size.[2] No air power was introduced by either side. While tanks were reported in the Chinese attack in Ladakh, they played a marginal role at best.

Official Indian figures admit to 1,383 killed, 1,696 missing, and 3,968 captured.[3] No Chinese figures were released but the People's Liberation Army (PLA) did not lose a single soldier to capture and its casualties were certainly less than those of the enemy, judging from Indian battle accounts. Virtually no civilian losses occurred, combat being almost wholly limited to unpopulated sectors of the Himalayan frontier claimed by both sides. The conflict ended with a unilateral cease-fire on the part of the People's Republic of China (PRC) and restoration of the status quo ante so far as its claims and armed presence were concerned, although all Indian posts in NEFA and throughout the contested part of Ladakh were eliminated.

Thus the Sino-Indian war might be readily dismissed as a classical border dispute which briefly flared into violence but otherwise is of little lasting importance. From this perspective it would seem to have already received sufficient study. A detailed narrative is provided by the controversial but illuminating work of Neville Maxwell, based on authoritative interviews and access to Indian government files during and after his coverage of the war as the *Times* (London) correspondent.[4] Against Maxwell's uniformly critical analysis of New Delhi and his implied exoneration of Peking stands a stack of Indian memoirs and analyses which attempt to document Chinese perfidy in detail.[5] At first most public comment attributed the war to Chinese aggression and expansionism.[6] Then gradually the balance shifted to hold New Delhi largely responsible for provoking the conflict. Even the former Indian military commander in NEFA conceded that his troops had unwittingly occupied Chinese territory across the McMahon Line which they refused to abandon in the face of PLA orders.[7]

An impressive array of scholarship has detailed the historical and legal bases of rival claims to territory while several accounts have argued differing views on Indian decision making.[8] However, the political significance of the war far transcended the actual border issue and thus raised further questions which remain unanswered. Moreover the details of Chinese decision making have never been systematically explored.[9] For the first time in history Chinese and Indian armies fought in the Himalayan heights. Peking's troops poured down one hundred miles of mountain valleys in NEFA only to stop within sight of the Assam plain and march back up to their starting point. 1. Why was the PLA unleashed against a weak, unaligned Asian neighbor whose military force posed no major threat? 2. Why did an obscure border dispute over largely uninhabited territory erupt at this time after dragging on for years without armed conflict? 3. Was the war planned long in advance or did it result from the ongoing diplomatic and military interaction between the two sides? 4. Was it an isolated occurrence or did it relate to other situations, foreign or domestic, confronting China? 5. How does this use of the PLA compare with its use in other conflict situations such as Korea and Indochina?

These questions enlarge our focus beyond the specifics of the 1962 conflict to an examination of the first twenty-five years of the People's Republic for patterns of conflict behavior associated with the use of force, deterrence, and risk taking. Thus, while the first two-thirds of this study reconstructs the policy process in Peking which resulted in war with New Delhi, the final third ranges more widely to span a broad spectrum of situations wherein the PLA moved beyond China's borders, from Korea to the 1969 Sino-Soviet border clashes. The study then concludes with speculations on elements of continuity and change in this area of foreign policy that appear likely to follow the departure of Mao Tse-tung from leadership and the acquisition of a major strategic nuclear capability.

Preview and Overview

This book is for laymen and specialists. The political scientist may choose to skip some chapters, so to help locate different areas of exploration an advance summary is in order, especially to highlight points of inquiry in the chronologically constructed sections. Chapter 1 presents the basic background factors which set the framework for Chinese decisions in the summer of 1962. Where ample details are available elsewhere, as for the historical and legal bases of rival territorial claims, the minimum information necessary to introduce the elements of controversy has been selected. However, where unexplored or seemingly unrelated phenomena pertinent to perceptions in Peking are slighted in other accounts, a fuller analysis is presented.

Foreign penetration of Tibet for subversive purposes was more visible to Chinese analysts than to outside observers and because of this provided important cues for perception of potential enemies and their intentions. However, it is virtually ignored in most analyses of the 1962 conflict. In the present study, the activity of United States and Chinese Nationalist agents in Tibet from 1949 to 1962 has been reconstructed from widely scattered sources, and while the account is necessarily incomplete it nonetheless contributes to filling a heretofore significant gap in understanding the premises of Peking's policy.[10]

Another dimension of Chinese concern in 1962 involved Nationalist activity which appeared to foreshadow an invasion attempt in the Taiwan Strait. Additional attention to this prospect, both in China and abroad, arose with the sudden exodus of more than 140,000 refugees into Hong Kong in May. Simultaneously but hidden from world view a similar exodus from Sinkiang crossed into the Soviet Union. A coincidence of threats may have been causally interpreted in Peking, particularly because of past Indian involvement with Tibetan exiles believed to be supported by United States–Nationalist agents and the contemporary delivery of Soviet aircraft which implemented New Delhi's "forward policy" against Chinese outposts in Ladakh, adjacent to Sinkiang. Accordingly, the Hong Kong and

Sinkiang developments are examined together with the Taiwan Strait crisis so as to set the scene in its full 180–degree perspective as seen from Peking.

Basic to all Chinese calculations was a domestic economic crisis that had persisted for three years as a result of failure in the Great Leap Forward experiment of 1958–59, and was compounded by the withdrawal of all Soviet economic assistance in 1960 and by successive natural disasters. This internal crisis aroused anxiety in Peking that external enemies would exploit PRC vulnerability, a fear that appeared justified by selected indicators of American, Nationalist, Indian, and possibly Russian intent. To appreciate the full dimensions of the crisis extensive use has been made of revelations contained in an official PLA publication, covering most of 1961, which was circulated only to regimental commanders and above and captured by guerrillas in Tibet.[11] Without an appreciation of the perceived linkages between internal and external developments as well as among the external events themselves, it is impossible to grasp the complete situation that confronted Chinese decision makers.

These decision makers remain largely shrouded in secrecy both as to their specific identity and their particular policy positions. However, the evidence does reveal a division between those who advocated muting confrontation with foreign opponents at this time of internal crisis and those who demanded a more defiant posture. This policy debate is fleetingly glimpsed throughout the year and is climaxed that fall by contradictory postures reflected in Chinese statements concerning Prime Minister Nehru.

While Cultural Revolution materials have been invaluable for domestic policy, unfortunately they do not document the foreign policy roles and relationships of key individuals, such as Mao Tse-tung, Liu Shao-ch'i, and Chou En-lai, or specific organizations such as the Ministry of Foreign Affairs, the PLA, and top party organs. Although this study speculates on possible linkages between individuals and groups in the Chinese policy process with alternative approaches to handling the crises of 1962, for the most part a rational actor model which treats the regime as a unified whole must be utilized.[12] Rationality in an initiatory policy is the pursuit of likely attainable goals through available means where perceived costs are outweighed by anticipated gains. In a reactive policy rationality is the attempt to deter an enemy with a credible counterthreat of costs which he will find unacceptable if he persists in conflictual behavior. The bulk of the focus is on reactive, deterrent situations, although in the final chapter initiatory actions in the Taiwan Straits in 1958 and Hong Kong in 1967 are also examined for clues to Chinese risk taking.

This approach follows that used in the author's earlier study, *China Crosses the Yalu*, subsequently characterized as a mediated stimulus-response model exemplified by the works of Robert North, Nazli Choucri, Ole Holsti, and others.[13] The primary focus of the present study is on the response of China to the stimulus of other governments' behavior as mediated by the perceptions of policy makers in Peking. The internal dynamics of policy formulation with the interaction of factions, organizational procedures, and bureaucratic politics are treated only as a secondary consideration.[14] The use of such terms as "Peking" and "the regime" does not deny the existence of differences among groups participating in the policy process but simply reflects the inadequacy of information on their interaction. Fortunately, as is evident from the concluding chapters, there is sufficient consistency in Chinese conflict behavior over time to justify use of this unitary model in forecasting PRC policy, with specific adjustment to allow for changes in factional and organizational influence.

A major concern of *China Crosses The Yalu*, miscommunication between states, also pertains to the 1962 conflict, albeit to a lesser extent. Although China and India had full diplomatic relations and could engage in direct, secret exchanges, deliberate signals were misread and unintended moves were mistakenly interpreted as signals. Chinese warnings were erroneously dismissed as either without serious basis or consequence while Indian statements designed for domestic purposes were taken in Peking as proof of belligerent intent. This phenomenon did not cause the final clash but it contributed to the escalatory process.

In chapter 2, examination of the June 1962 Taiwan Strait crisis reveals a more fundamental role of misperception and failure in communication which caused a direct Sino-American confrontation. In May, President John F. Kennedy sent an intended signal of interest in détente through a press conference response concerning the availability of United States wheat for China. Nevertheless this evoked an intransigent reply of defiance through a May 29 press conference held by Foreign Minister Ch'en Yi. The Kennedy signal was credibly contradicted by evidence from Taiwan of preparations for invasion, presumably with the support of Washington. Ch'en's response was delayed two months in transmission, and did not arrive until the crisis had passed. In the meantime a sudden PLA buildup opposite Taiwan puzzled American intelligence analysts until its purport was revealed by a Chinese demarche at the Warsaw ambassadorial talks which warned against invasion, simultaneous with a major propaganda attack in Peking against the "U.S.–Chiang plot." Actually the United States adamantly opposed a Nationalist attack, but it was only the failure to counter the PLA buildup with a responding increase of American force, an otherwise normal precaution, that prevented a mutual interaction of escalating tension and eventual conflict.

By contrast, the PLA buildup illustrated another type of communication which can heighten both the clarity and the credibility of signaling. This involves the intentional deployment of military units so as to be detected by a prospective enemy while remaining secret from public observation, thereby warning without provoking. Traditional academic analysis of "signals" focuses on propaganda, diplomatic exchanges, and open military demonstrations. However, improved technological capabilities for intelligence collection permit covert military activity, which is concealed from the view of all but a designated target audience, to add an important dimension to communication between nations. Knowledge of troop and aircraft movements, gained through the electronic interception of communications and through overhead reconnaissance, can serve the purposes of the detected as well as of the detector. This phenomenon which is first examined in the 1962 Taiwan Strait crisis becomes central to this study's later analysis of Chinese behavior in the Indochina conflict from 1964 to 1968.

Chapter 2 reviews the Soviet relationship with both India and China so as to highlight the mixture of positive and negative indicators that may have been argued in Peking as critical to policy. These included, on the one hand, the public stance of neutrality struck by Moscow in the 1959 Sino-Indian clashes, the sale of aircraft to New Delhi that transported troops into Ladakh, and the ongoing negotiations over India's acquisition and possible production of MIG jet fighters. On the other hand, friendly press gestures and a muting of polemics accompanied improved Sino-Soviet trade and diplomatic relations in the spring of 1962. Nothing in *People's Daily* hinted at serious tensions, nor does the available evidence reveal any official protest over alleged Russian connivance in the Sinkiang exodus until later that summer. Behind the facade of unity, however, the Soviet relationship with China proved to be both influential on and influenced by the Sino-Indian confrontation.

Chapter 3 covers the critical months of July through September, 1962, when Peking's reaction to New Delhi changed from concern to alarm in the aftermath of the June crisis in the Taiwan Strait. The coordination of military, diplomatic, and propaganda activity provides an impressive pattern of pressure designed to deter further Indian advances and to induce Indian concessions through negotiations. The gradual escalation of warnings verged on threats to retaliate in NEFA for moves in Ladakh, but domestic press attention was silenced while diplomatic probes in Geneva and New Delhi explored Indian hints of compromise. With the collapse of negotiatory prospects in late August, the PLA demonstrated a determined posture of preparation to oust Indian troops from Dhola, an outpost beyond the McMahon Line which Peking officially repudiated but observed in practice. Concurrently the PRC delivered an implicit ultimatum for negotiations to begin in mid-October. The ensuing clashes at Dhola resulted in the first fatalities on both sides, with a publicized funeral in Lhasa for fallen "frontier guards" signaling the imminence of war.

The degree of planning and coordination in the design and implementation of Chinese policy is fully revealed during the climactic period of October through November, covered in chapters 4 and 5. Moves to seize the political initiative and to drive the enemy from all disputed territory unfolded in an intriguing pattern of regularity, with strategic steps at monthly intervals and tactical moves scheduled at weekly benchmarks. Peking's diplomatic offensive expanded to include not only Moscow but capitals throughout the Afro-Asian world in a campaign calculated to isolate New Delhi. While this campaign developed outside China, no mass demonstrations occurred at home to exploit the Himalayan fighting for domestic political purposes. In this instance, the general hypothesis which posits external tensions as primarily linked to internal factors does not apply.

An important and persistent contradiction does appear, however, which suggests a lack of agreement over how hard a line of confrontation was to be advanced in the fall of 1962. Evidence from Chinese media and diplomatic notes indicates division between those who argued for defining Nehru as a personal and permanent enemy acting at the behest of "U.S. imperalism" and those who sought to limit the controversy, apparently in hope of avoiding a full break and major conflict. Inferentially the lines of division appear to place Mao Tse-tung and his associates in the public media, particularly those responsible for defining PRC policy abroad, in the former category, while the more moderate position emanated from the Ministry of Foreign Affairs and Premier Chou En-lai.

The unilateral cease-fire and withdrawal, unprecedented in modern history, is examined together with the October-November offensives in the context of alternative explanations advanced at the time and since, with special attention to the likely relevance of the Cuban missile crisis which occurred simultaneously. The nature of the evidence precludes confirmation but permits disconfirmation, thereby narrowing the range of plausible explanation. A recapitulation then attempts to determine the timing of key Chinese decisions and the extent to which they were affected by Indian behavior as well as by miscalculation.

The focus here is on Chinese perceptions in order to explain their origins and their consequences. There is no attempt to adjudicate the border controversy or to condemn or justify the actions of either side. The author does not impute wisdom or stupidity in the effort to understand how the two governments became locked in combat over uninhabited land in the Himalayan heights with such far-reaching consequences for the status and prestige of both sides. From this perspective, the particulars of which side fired first in one situation or another matter less than the postures both adopted which made that conflict situation possible and their reactions to it afterwards. Thus while the author has tried to reconstruct each event on the basis of partial and conflicting evidence, much of which may have been erroneous, the overall development of Chinese policy and behavior is more broadly based in this study and should be judged accordingly.

From Case Study to Generalization

Beyond the specific details of the Sino-Indian war, a larger body of data is necessary to generate hypotheses of prima facie plausibility concerning Chinese conflict behavior. Toward this end chapter 6 examines the Chinese military involvement in Indochina, 1964–68, as a case study in deterrence. Previous studies of China and the Vietnam war have focused almost exclusively on verbal evidence, but unlike the Korean and Indian conflicts this channel of communication proved highly misleading as an indicator of intent. More significant were covert military moves which were designed to be detected by the United States government but otherwise kept secret from general knowledge.

The United States threat of air attack against North Vietnam, first signaled in early 1964, was undeterred by subtle indicators of a potential Chinese air defense although it was partially contained to targets below the Sino-Vietnamese border and outside the central areas of Hanoi and Haiphong. Then in mid-1965, American combat troops were deployed to South Vietnam, posing the possibility of invading the north as their numbers expanded to more than 500,000 over the next three years. Peking thereupon covertly sent a comparatively small but detectable contingent of 50,000 troops to the Democratic Republic of Vietnam (DRV), demonstrating a token willingness to counter an invasion with massive intervention. In contrast with Korea, however, the American forces remained in the south, and the PLA eventually withdrew as quietly as it had come.

Chapter 7 combines evidence from the Korean, Indian, and Indochinese cases to construct a calculus of Chinese deterrence. Although objective differences distinguish the three situations, their subjective similarities as viewed from Peking facilitate comparison. In 1950, 1962, and 1967–68 internal tensions invited external exploitation. In all three instances a perceived enemy approached China's borders in hostile array by ground or air. Finally, this threat emerged over several months, and permitted a period for testing the enemy's intentions and attempting to change his course of action.

The Chinese deterrence calculus is inferred from behavior rather than from classical Chinese strategic writings such as Sun Tzu and Mao. While its postulates of early signaling, "worst case" assumptions, and deliberate timing, are illustrated from the three cases under examination, they have possible application in other instances in which the PLA was deployed against a perceived enemy, as in Laos, 1965–72, and the Sino-Soviet border in 1969. The earlier occasions where deterrence failed are compared with later occasions. This provides clues both to Chinese miscalculation and to adaptation through experience.

Heretofore deterrence analysis has been almost wholly confined to non-Asian states, primarily in the context of interaction between the United States and the Soviet Union as nuclear powers. To invite a wider testing of deterrence theory chapter 7 juxtaposes the construct of Chinese principles and practices against general propositions offered by Thomas Schelling and Alexander George.[15] The resulting convergence is reassuring evidence that comparative foreign policy need not exclude China as an idiosyncratic actor which is only susceptible to understanding through the esoteric analysis of Sinologues. In this regard chapter 7 is self-contained and may be read by the general specialist in strategic analysis independently of the preceding account of the Sino-Indian war.

Chapter 8 explores three phenomena that are central to the study of foreign policy and conflict behavior as manifested in China: the role of rationality, the use of force, and risk taking. In addition to drawing on the three case studies, additional evidence from the 1958 Quemoy blockade, the 1967 crisis in Hong Kong, and the 1969 Sino-Soviet border clashes is included for illustrative purposes. A pure rationality model requires modification to allow for elements of distortion in PRC perceptions of other political systems and for the possible intrusion of factionalism in the policy process, but otherwise has proven adequate for explicating past behavior and predicting future action. The relative priority of political versus military interests evidenced in the PRC use of force shows consistent emphasis on the former, but the degree of risk taking differs as between initiatory and reactive actions.

As a final point the author speculates on how the termination of Mao Tse-tung's leadership and the acquisition of a major strategic nuclear capability will affect these phenomena. The prospects of continuity and change are assessed with particular reference to relations with the United States, the Soviet Union, and Japan in specific conflict situations of northeast and southeast Asia. It is impossible to go beyond a few tentative observations, not only because of uncertainties in the post-Mao leadership composition but also because Chinese behavior will interact with that of the other major states and can only be abstracted for heuristic purposes. Despite these limitations it is possible to sketch the broad parameters of probability, at least for the near future.

Sources of Methodology

Wherever possible publicly available sources have been utilized in order to permit others to check the author's findings and to replicate his approach. Information from classified official sources is included infrequently in the chronological account of 1962 for both the Taiwan Strait crisis and the Himalayan conflict. In addition, details on the Sinkiang exodus are taken from interviews with Soviet officials who asked to remain anonymous. An understanding gained in government service is responsible for the 1967 Hong Kong crisis account and the examination of the 1969 Sino-Soviet border conflict. Such instances are appropriately footnoted and amount to less than one-tenth of the source material.

The principal material for the analysis of Sino-Indian interactions as mediated by perceptions in Peking comes from the voluminous compilation of diplomatic notes exchanged between the two governments and published in the official Indian *White Paper* series and in the two main Chinese publications, *Jen Min Jih Pao* (hereafter *People's Daily*) and *Peking Review*.[16] The People's Republic issued a small volume of selected exchanges down to May, 1962, which are identical with their counterparts in the *White Paper* and justify acceptance as authentic.[17] No additional documents appeared in Chinese. In contrast with the author's Korean war study, *Shih Chieh Chih Shih* (*World Culture*) carried little on the border conflict and merely echoed *People's Daily*. No other Chinese sources were found useful; however, monitored radio broadcasts in translation were valuable.

Certain data limitations remain to plague analysis, in particular ignorance of the total range of information that impacted on perceptions in Peking. For instance, the author does not know what intelligence was reported or with what accuracy on Chinese Nationalist planning for a mainland invasion or on Indian collusion with CIA subversion in Tibet. Agent collection on Taiwan presumably was facilitated by the common nationality between Peking and Taipei. However, the special United States–Taiwan relationship could give a degree of distortion to interpreting various Nationalist statements and actions directed against the mainland. Similarly, penetration of the Indian government and reporting of the Indian press would provide a mass of verbiage, much of which might be objectively worthless but subjectively appear credible in Peking.

A corollary problem lies in determining the "real" situation confronting Chinese estimators. The *New York Times* did not report on the clandestine airdrops of men and weapons into Tibet, and *People's Daily* remained silent on various indicators of United States–Nationalist military collaboration as they emerged in the spring of 1962. Often only long after the event is such information obtainable and then on a partial basis with little or no certainty of its having been known to foreign governments at the time. Therefore on both the subjective and objective levels, the author's reconstruction of external behavior and its perception is offered as no more than a minimum calculus of the developments which impacted on decision makers in Peking. If the author's conclusions are skewed, it is in a conservative rather than a radical direction. In sum, the situation was probably seen in a worse perspective than has been depicted here.

Another gap concerns the military details of Chinese behavior. While general descriptions of the deployments during the Taiwan Strait crisis in June are available, detailed information is lacking on PLA preparations for fighting India which would permit the pinpointing of this activity in space and time. Action is constrained by capabilities which in turn depend on communication and transportation nets as well as on the availability of manpower and firepower. Thus, the implementation of a decision to fight in the Himalayan heights on two fronts, separated by more than a thousand miles and distant from supply points outside of Tibet, involves a time lag between the estimate of need and the ability to meet it. In the absence of more specific information such time lags must be surmised and points of decision must be inferred from other evidence.

In this regard, reliance on Indian sources has been avoided except for eyewitness accounts by responsible participants. Especially useful descriptions of tactical situations in NEFA are offered by the local officer immediately responsible for the Dhola salient and the corps commander for the entire region.[18] Although their presentations suffer from recrimination and apologetics, they nonetheless credibly depict the state of Indian military disarray and the visible behavior of the PLA. Unfortunately this is less true for the then director of Indian intelligence whose lengthy memoir is wholly undocumented and replete with factual errors.[19] While he purports to prove the accuracy of his bureau's reports concerning Chinese preparations for war throughout the year, these exaggerated and repetitive alarms actually obscured reality. Although the bureau's premature assertions subsequently appeared validated, they lacked foundation at the time.

Finally, because perceptual analysis is central to this study's approach, its limitations must be stated at the outset. The author can only *infer* real perceptions from analysis of articulated perceptions communicated in the media and elsewhere. *People's Daily* and *Peking Review* transmit centrally derived and disseminated information and comment. The author does not know the level or tightness of control on specific items at a particular point in time. Presumably the reporting and analysis of foreign affairs receives close direction because of limited access to information on foreign developments. At times of potential crisis, the criticality of such reports adds to their importance. But taking this assumption at face value does not determine whether a particular communications posture is wholly manipulative or reflects actual perceptions, or perhaps is a mixture of both. To the degree it is manipulative, which domestic or foreign audiences are its target? If these audiences have conflicting interests, how can the message be confidently interpreted?

Silence or omission also raises problems of analysis. The failure to report an event or to react publicly to external threat may reflect uncertainty about its implications, fear of revealing anxiety before domestic or foreign audiences, or deliberate suppression to facilitate a surprise response. Chinese media reflected perceived threats quite differently as between the United States–Nationalist and the Indian situations, and reacted quite differently once combat with the enemy had begun in 1962 as compared with 1950. Sometimes an information overload may simply delay or screen out the reporting of events at the time, but they may subsequently be given considerable weight in policy review. For instance, one explanation for the low-key handling of Indian activity in June, 1962, contrasted with the seemingly sudden alarm of July was found to lie in the Taiwan Strait crisis.

Serious as these limitations are on content analysis of controlled media for inferring perceptions and policy at higher levels, two arguments favor the continual refining and developing of this methodology. First and fundamentally there is no better ongoing source of evidence on authoritarian regimes in general and the PRC in particular than that provided by the controlled press and radio. The inability to do archival research and oral interviews forces the scholar to the best available data that can be regularly acquired and systematically exploited. Up to now, that source remains the public media. Second, content analysis has had considerable success both in providing a credible explanation of past events and a correct forecast of future developments.[20] It deserves further attention as a means of understanding domestic as well as foreign political behavior.

At various points reference is made to the press treatment of events. To understand how summary statements were arrived at, some explanation is in order. This study surveyed the *People's Daily* from January 1 to October 20, 1962, for all news concerning the United States and India. This material shared three common characteristics. First, it reported actions carried out by the United States and India; second, it implied or explicitly stated that these actions were unfriendly or threatening to China in some way; and third, it publicly interpreted official Chinese reaction.

Each individual news item provided the unit of observation for analysis.

Three indicators were used for measuring articulated attitudes: the amount of attention, the priority of importance ascribed to the item, and the degree of threat suggested in describing the action. Each indicator in itself provides only a partial basis of measurement, but in combination the three define the parameters of expressed attitude. The purpose in aggregating these indicators is to measure change over time as well as to compare patterns of attention as between countries (United States and India) and behavior (military movements versus political statements). Since the inquiry is limited to change and comparison, the impossibility of interval scaling does not become a relevant liability.

The amount of space devoted to an item may reflect one of two decisions, or both: the amount of information to be released and the amount of attention the government wishes to be drawn to that particular item of news. To distinguish between these two factors, the importance given to each item is inferred from its location. In China, as elsewhere, the front page of a paper carries the most urgent news. Then, in the *People's Daily* at least, page 3 deals primarily with lesser items in foreign affairs, with pages 4 and 6 containing the least important items. Within these pages importance may be differentiated further by position; the top third of the page is the most prominent position, the middle portion comes next and the bottom section ranks last. As a final point of differentiation, the nature of the item may vary in importance, with official government statements and editorials ranking first and second, in that order, and above commentaries and wire stories. These locational aspects were combined into a nine-point scale.

The degree to which the Chinese articulated a particular United States or Indian action as manifesting threat can be measured by headline vocabulary. A random comparison of the *People's Daily* with two other major dailies, *Ta Kung Pao* and *Kuang Ming Jih Pao,* revealed that, for news items concerning the United States and India, headlines were identical in word and content, indicating that headlines, as well as the items themselves, emanated from a single authority. This permits far more significance to be attached to the wording of headlines in China than would be possible for the non-Communist press elsewhere. Thus, based on 182 items relating to United States actions and 93 relating to Indian actions, *People's Daily* headlines expressing differing degrees of threat were categorized into two series of nine groups, with each category reflecting the nuances of differentiation in the original Chinese:

Headline Expressions of Hostility or Threat toward China

By the United States	By India
1. Discrediting China	1. Distortion
2. Poisonously discrediting China	2. Discrediting China
3. Blackmail	3. Poisonously discrediting China
4. Anti-Communist	4. Blackmail
5. Anti-Chinese	5. Anti-Chinese
6. Attempts to intervene in the Vietnamese struggle or the Laotian war	6. Attempts to aggravate the Sino-Indian dispute
7. Preparation for war or aggression against China	7. Preparation for war or attack
8. Aggression against China or the Far East	8. Occupation of territory or aggression
9. Military provocation against China	9. Military provocation against China

These expressions of perceived hostility were ranked in terms of their intensity as articulated in standardized phrases and words. This was validated by two independent judges drawn from former members of the Chinese foreign service.* The training and experience of these two judges in interpreting overt communications for clues to policy makes their agreement an important argument for accepting the validity of the ranking.

Finally, a continuous "source" for this study has been the many profitable and pleasurable interactions with superiors, peers, and students during the author's successive assignments in the Rand Corporation, government, and academia. In particular, associates in government gave unstintingly and anonymously in a genuine group endeavor to solve problems and to improve policy. Without their helpful guidance in the author's growth and understanding, this study would be a shadow of itself.

---

*I am indebted to the assistance provided by the United States State Department which helped to contact Mr. Chao Fu and Mr. Miao Chen-pai.

Contents

Chapter 1

The Sino-Indian Border

Historical Background

A full recapitulation of the historical evolution of the Sino-Indian border and the respective positions adopted on it by Peking, Lhasa, New Delhi, and London, is not necessary here. Whole volumes have been written to elucidate the complex diplomatic and cartographic developments of the past century. This study focuses on the events of 1962 in the more immediate context of the interactions between Peking and New Delhi after 1958–59.[1] Only a brief overview of the earlier background is needed to clarify the main issues and to illustrate the various anomalies which made this border uniquely contentious at this time.

Political boundaries are officially justified by their physical, demographic, and historical attributes, but they basically result from the power relations between states at a given time. Borders are not immutable, as is amply evident by comparison of regional maps of Europe, Asia, and Africa at successive periods in the nineteenth and twentieth centuries. However, in theory political boundaries are assumed to be inviolate, having been negotiated between sovereign states, formally marked or delimited on mutually accepted maps, and physically demarcated on the ground. When change is forced on either side, usually by defeat in war, the new boundary is again legitimized by formal treaty, delimitation, and demarcation.

None of these basic attributes ever obtained for the Sino-Indian border. Central to its definition was the buffer area of Tibet around which evolved competing claims which culminated in the war of 1962. To begin with, Tibet, adjoining India on the north, had traditionally been part of the Chinese Empire but possessed a wholly distinct political, theological, and racial culture. Tibetan aspirations for independence waxed and waned in their assertion according to the changing power of Peking to enforce its claim to rule the fractious borderlands populated by Mongols in the north, Turki Moslems in the west, and Tibetans in the southwest. Externally the elusive concept of suzerainty was enunciated by foreign powers in order to combine symbolic recognition of Peking's claims and direct diplomatic relations with Mongolia and Tibet.[2] However, no government ever officially recognized Tibet as an independent country. On the contrary, in 1907 Britain and Russia formally agreed not to conclude any agreements affecting Tibet "except through the intermediary of the Chinese Government." Without Tibet's de jure independence, any international agreements concluded with Lhasa's officials lacked legitimacy in the absence of Chinese ratification. While this did not always prevent their negotiating such agreements, so long as these failed to win approval in Peking they remained ultra vires.

For their part British representatives acted out of two different offices which were less divided in their interests than were Tibetans and Chinese but which nonetheless coexisted in bureaucratic rivalry. Until its declaration of independence in 1947, India's government was subordinate to London. Understandably, the colonial government of India often saw its interests, especially in the northeast frontier area adjoining Tibet and Burma, quite differently from the Foreign Office in Whitehall. London formally negotiated with Peking for British prerogatives in Tibet and obtained a permanent representative in Lhasa, military escorts for trade officers at two other towns, and postal, telegraph, and telephone links among trading centers in southern Tibet. Informally and covertly, however, British representatives from New Delhi repeatedly tried to enlarge the Tibetan role from buffer to independent state, inter alia endeavoring to expand their jurisdiction in the northeast frontier area. These efforts were alternately advocated on the basis of alleged Russian or Chinese threats to the security of India, but their actual motivation appears to have been more the product of subjective perceptions than objective reality.

The only formal attempt at a multilateral definition of Tibet's status and boundaries was the abortive Simla Conference of 1913.[3] The collapse of the Chinese Empire in 1911 and its replacement by the shaky Republic seemed a propitious time to improve British interests. However, Peking looked to a better position in the future and refused to ratify its representative's initialing of the Simla accords, thus nullifying their legitimacy. British and Tibetan representatives later met secretly to agree on trade matters and to define the boundary. This was in violation not only of the

1907 Anglo-Russian treaty, but of the Anglo-Chinese Convention of 1906 wherein Britain had agreed "not to annex Tibetan territory." The definition of "Tibetan territory" obviously required Chinese sanction and could not be determined solely by British and Tibetan representatives.

It was at the Simla meetings that Sir Henry McMahon, Foreign Secretary of the Indian Government, produced a version of the boundary which later bore his name and which provided the basis for sharp dispute between India and China. Drawing a thick line on a small-scale map, McMahon advanced the Indian border sixty miles northward from the Himalayan foothills in Assam to the crestline running northward along Bhutan and eastward to Burma. Some 2,000 square miles below the watershed area adjoining Bhutan was included as Indian territory. This area was known as the Tawang Tract and named after the principal monastery and communal concentration of Tawang. McMahon, however, had exceeded his instructions which did not authorize boundary delimitation. Moreover the entire Tibetan-British agreement had to remain secret because of its violation of the two treaties. Under these circumstances neither London nor Delhi pressed to implement the accord with administration of the area. Two decades were to elapse before the McMahon Line was to achieve recognition even among British officials and it never won formal approval from China.

In the dozen years following the Simla conference, World War I moved British power and attention from Asia to Europe while the Peking government became the prize of shifting coalitions of warlords whose writ rarely extended beyond the Yellow River, let alone reach the high Himalayan marches. Finally in 1927 the Chinese Nationalist armies of Chiang Kai-shek founded a new capital at Nanking with a greater expanse of central rule, yet local warlords remained and the borderlands continued to be coveted by Japanese, Russian, and British expansionists. The vast area of Sinkiang, adjacent to Tibet, became a virtual Soviet satellite from 1933 to 1942 under its nominally Nationalist governor, General Sheng Shih-ts'ai. Sheng ceded to Russia mining rights, military bases, and secret police penetration as an adjunct to his personal dictatorship.[4] During these years of disruption, the government avoided formalizing its border claims through negotiations, but held them in reserve while attempting to cope with the main threat posed by Japanese invasion.

Although China's internal weakness favored Tibetan autonomy, formal independence still required outside help. But the heyday of British imperialist adventurism had disappeared with the exhausting victory of World War I. Not until 1935 was Foreign Office interest in the northeast frontier revived by a local incident which provoked a Whitehall maneuver that provided a spurious basis for legitimacy of the McMahon Line. Until then, the standard British definition of India's boundary, whether in memorandum or map, ran along the Himalayan foothills. The Simla agreements remained secret. Thus the official British compilation of all "Treaties, Engagements and Sanads relating to India and Neighboring Countries" issued in 1929 made no reference to the McMahon Line, much less argued for its legitimacy.[5] The 1931 volume of this compilation, concerned with Assam, specified that at least the northern portion of the Tawang Tract was administered by Tibet.[6] British cartographers, taking their cue both from precedent and from existing sources, likewise showed the Indian border at the Himalayan foothills.

Then in 1935 the Tibetan arrest of a British explorer and botanist, Captain Kingdon Ward, for alleged illegal entry through the Tawang Tract led to the rediscovery of the McMahon Line by Mr. O. K. Caroe, a Deputy Secretary in the Foreign and Political Department of the Government of India. Caroe subsequently recalled that "with considerable difficulty and almost by chance" he "unearthed the true position," i.e., the boundary agreements of 1914.[7] Caroe's persistent lobbying eventually persuaded the Foreign Office to acquiesce in a revision of Britain's public posture concerning the McMahon Line, albeit without moving so visibly as to arouse attention abroad, particularly in China. As a result a new printing of the key volume in the official treaty series, almost wholly identical with the original even to the inclusion of the 1929 date of publication on the flyleaf, was distributed in 1938 with a request that holders of the original volume return it for destruction.[8] The only change concerned the Simla accords. The new version revealed the secret agreements for the first time and specified the McMahon Line, including the Tawang Tract, as the actual frontier. As a consequence, the Survey of India maps thereafter showed the McMahon Line as delimited but undemarcated. In 1940, the authoritative *Times Handy Atlas* bowed to pressure from the Foreign Office with a similar change. However, British representatives failed to win fresh Tibetan confirmation of the 1914 agreement. Meanwhile officials in India cautioned that further pressure threatened to push Tibet back under Chinese protection by way of challenging Lhasa's jurisdiction over the Tawang Tract.

Suddenly Japanese expansion into Southeast Asia broadened the European conflict into World War II. The Himalayas again became the scene of foreign interest but now more as a potential conduit for supplies to beleaguered China than as an arena of foreign intrigue and influence. When American agents arrived to examine the logistics of alternative Tibetan routes, authorities in Lhasa asked for a transmitter station that would enhance their local political power. Washington, sensitive to Chinese claims of sovereignty, avoided encouraging Tibetan aspirations and cautioned Britain against challenging Chinese authority.[9]

In 1946–47 Nationalist power crumbled before Communist attack and this, in turn, encouraged Tibetan probes for greater recognition abroad. Trade and cultural missions emanated from Lhasa but failed to win formal acceptance of Tibet as an independent sovereign state.[10] Proclamation of the People's Republic of China on October 1, 1949, heralded the emergence of a new political and military power capable of reestablishing firm control over the borderlands. Following the collapse of British rule in the subcontinent and the establishment of an independent India, two entirely new governments confronted one another with a contentious heritage of claims and counterclaims compounded in their complexity by the prior absence of fully sovereign contiguous states. The anomalies of Chinese suzerainty, Tibetan autonomy, and British imperial rule had left a labyrinth of unilateral claims, secret bilateral agreements, and cartographic fakery.

This historic impasse could not be resolved by force. The actual power available to the various interested parties had proved to be ephemeral and in sharp conflict with the pretensions of power, whether expressed in Peking and Nanking, London and New Delhi, or Lhasa and Tawang. Since power is largely a function of recognized political authority backed by military force, before 1949 Chinese claims over Tibet could not be realized but neither could they be compromised lest this invite further foreign penetration of China's borderlands. Tibetan independence could not be achieved without foreign recognition and physical protection against a future Chinese reassertion of authority. This in turn meant that British efforts either to expand Indian territory or to prevent Chinese rule over Tibet required a more durable and lasting commitment than London was prepared or able to make.

Despite these realities, all three sides maintained their respective pretenses to one degree or another throughout the first half of the twentieth century. Yet the essential preconditions for fixing an international boundary, i.e., sovereign states existing in a sufficiently stable power relationship and willing to formalize the existing situation in treaty, did not exist prior to the establishment of the Republic of India and the People's Republic of China. The old seeds of conflict were to bear bitter fruit in 1962.

Ecological Factors: Physical and Human

In addition to these historical conditions, formidable ecological obstacles constrained delimiting and demarcating the Sino-Indian boundary.[11] For roughly two-thirds of its approximately 2,500 miles, the border marches along the Himalayan peaks and passes which rim the "roof of the world" extending westward from Burma. The remainder snakes uncertainly over mountains, valleys, and desert plains at altitudes ranging upwards from 12,000 feet. A readily discernible natural boundary rarely exists except as the summit of windswept passes, most of which lie above 10,000 feet. Agreement on acceptance of the watershed principle facilitated establishment of the boundary along most of the central area of Bhutan, Sikkim, and Nepal, but the eastern and western portions did not follow this convenient traditional definition.

The absence of mutually agreed surveys, the inadequate scale of such maps as were available, and the cavalier manner in which British officials unilaterally defined Chinese territory compounded the hazards of determining the propriety of conflicting claims by cartographic comparison. Even if the McMahon Line had been accepted as the general boundary instead of the Himalayan foothills sixty to one hundred miles southward, the crude map delimitation was wholly inadequate for determining the jurisdiction over particular promontories, ridges, and streams. Moreover the rugged terrain and severe weather posed serious problems for permanent demarcation on the ground.

Custom and usage did not facilitate resolution of the disputed boundary. At the western terminus the barren plateau of Ladakh known as Aksai Chin, central to the 1958–62 developments, was virtually uninhabited. At the eastern end, the area between the McMahon Line and Assam, termed the Northeast Frontier Agency (NEFA) under both British and Indian rule, was populated chiefly by tribes desiring no affiliation with any external authority. Despite being nominally under New Delhi, their ethnic and cultural attributes made them more akin to Tibetans and thus more liable to the assertion of Chinese than Indian rule.[12] At both ends of the boundary grazing needs prompted the intermittent flow of local peoples across presumed boundaries in search of pasture, sometimes on a seasonal basis and sometimes according to the vicissitudes of climate.

Under these cirumstances, the status quo or "customary practice" could and did mean different things to different people at different times, even with the best intentions on either side. But good intentions could not be assumed given the heritage of unresolved borders and expansionist pressures from the south which clashed with imperialist pretensions from the north. From the vantage point of Peking, a "century of shame and humiliation" required redressing past grievances suffered when foreign powers could take advantage of China's weakness. In this regard the difference between Chinese Nationalist and Chinese Communist behavior in Tibet was a function of capability and not of motivation. Thus Chiang Kai-shek spoke of "lost territories" in terms of China's needs, and claimed, "In the territory of China a hundred years ago, comprising more than ten million square kilometers, there was not a single district that was not essential to the survival of the Chinese nation."[13] In a similar vein, Mao Tse-tung informed Edgar Snow as early as 1936, "It is the immediate task of China to regain all our lost territories. . . .The Mohammedan and Tibetan peoples will form autonomous republics attached to the Chinese federation."[14]

Mao's words appropriately linked the two minority areas most able and willing to contest Chinese rule, whether Manchu, Nationalist, or Communist. The "Mohammedan peoples" of Sinkiang had repeatedly rebelled against Han domination, most recently in 1944 when the westernmost area adjoining the Soviet Union succeeded in establishing the so-called "East Turkestan Republic."[15] The revolt by Uighur, Kazakh, and Kirghiz militants threatened to overrun the entire province when Soviet mediation finally resulted in Nationalist agreement to full autonomy for the rebellious area. In 1949 the People's Republic extended its rule throughout Sinkiang and the established dissident leadership flew to Peking. However, according to the official New China News Agency (NCNA), they were killed in an airplane crash en route.[16] Whatever the actual circumstances, all local autonomy disappeared until 1955 when Peking established the Sinkiang Uighur Autonomous Region. This guaranteed complete control from the national capital, in sharp contrast with the situation which had prevailed from 1944 to 1949.[17]

Mao's linkage of "the Mohammedan and Tibetan peoples" not only recognized a common relationship among anti-Han minorities of potential rebelliousness but touched on an important strategic linkage as well. Whereas Chinese access to Tibet from the east and north is impeded by steep mountain roads and narrow defiles, a circuitous entry from the west is facilitated by lower, more level caravan trails which cross southern Sinkiang and western Tibet. According to specialists on this area,

> The almost forgotten bypass route through the Aksai Chin . . . is a serviceable winter route, as two invasions occurring in the early winter months have demonstrated—one in the early eighteenth century by the Dsungars when they took Lhasa from the rear and the other in 1950 by the Chinese Communists themselves. . . . Indeed, in the event of any serious weakening of the Peking Government, this area might well prove to be the key to the Chinese hold on Tibet.[18]

Although no Tibetan uprising threatened in 1950, Peking dispatched the PLA that year to "liberate" the area. The PLA advance halted in the eastern region of Chamdo in order to secure logistical and communications lines against remnant Nationalist troops and local armed groups, particularly the Goloks and the Khambas who were traditionally fiercer in their Tibetan militancy than the pacifistic groups around the Dalai Lama in Lhasa.[19] While Chinese officials sought to negotiate formal acceptance of Peking's sovereignty on conditions which promised considerable Tibetan autonomy, the young Dalai Lama fled to Yatung, near the Indian border. Failing to win any favorable outside response to Tibetan appeals for support, he returned to Lhasa while his representative in Peking concluded a 17-point agreement on May 31, 1951. The feebleness of Indian protestations and the unprecedented vigor with which Peking asserted Chinese claims ended once and for all the anomalous status of Tibet. Three years later Nehru formally agreed with Chou En-lai that Tibet was "an integral part of China."

These internal and external developments were no guarantee against further dissidence, and so in 1956 the PLA began construction of a road joining Sinkiang and Tibet. Nearly 750 miles long, it followed a traditional caravan trail through the Aksai Chin plateau which was claimed by India but which appeared on Peking's maps as Chinese.[20] This provided the only means of modern transportation in western China to facilitate troop movements between potentially dissident and otherwise remote regions. It was of prime strategic importance as subsequent Chinese behavior demonstrated. Although the area had been shaded as Indian since 1954 on New Delhi's maps, no Indian activity had sought to establish rule in this barren area, to which access required crossing the Ladakh mountains through a 13,000 foot pass. Details of the completed road were announced by the NCNA on October 5, 1957, and Indian patrols were dispatched the following summer to ascertain the facts.[21] One patrol confirmed that the southern portion of the road crossed territory claimed by India; a second disappeared in the northern sector. On October 18, 1958, New Delhi for the first time formally protested the Aksai Chin developments to Peking, whereupon the PRC acknowledged seizure of the patrol "on the Sinkiang-Tibet road in Chinese territory" and "deportation" through the Karakoram pass.

Nehru made no public mention of the dispute at that time. Potentially the most serious border controversy to have developed, it was actually the second such incident. The first concerned possession of the so-called "central sector," specifically Barahoti (Wuje).[22] In April 1954, Nehru and Chou had concluded an agreement on "Trade and Intercourse Between the Tibet Region of China and India." They enunciated inter alia the Five Principles of Peaceful Coexistence or "Panch Shila," which became a focal point of public rhetoric for both sides during the subsequent years of rapprochement and estrangement. Within a few months, however, charges and countercharges were exchanged privately over respective claims at Barahoti, with minor incidents occuring over the next few years. The circumstances of the unresolved dispute of Barahoti established a precedent for handling the more serious Aksai Chin dispute in which no clear basis existed for resolving the dispute in favor of either side. Unfortunately, only a mutual willingness to compromise or a mutual confrontation of force would determine the outcome.

In April, 1958 bilateral talks began in New Delhi on the central sector, wherein India proposed and China rejected a mutual withdrawal of troops and the cessation of any effort at enforcing control while negotiations were under way. In June the official *China Pictorial* published a map, already circulating in other Chinese publications, showing much of NEFA, part of Bhutan, and the disputed central sector and eastern Ladakh as PRC territory. New Delhi protested the maps, and provoked an evasive rejoinder from the Chinese Ministry of Foreign Affairs (MFA) in November. The reply noted that as Chou had pointed out to Nehru in 1954, the issue concerned "maps published in China before the liberation" and expressed confidence that "a new way of drawing the boundary" would emerge from surveys "and consultations with the various neighboring countries."[23] Nehru privately rejected this position in a letter to Chou, denying that nine years of PRC rule justified this rationale and insisting "there can be no question of these large parts of India being anything but Indian and there is no dispute about them."

Neville Maxwell's detailed analysis of the subsequent Chou-Nehru correspondence emphasizes: (1) Chou's apparent willingness to concede Indian rule over NEFA while remaining adamantly opposed to the legality of the McMahon Line per se, presumably because accepting the Simla accords would retroactively ratify Tibet's independence; (2) Chou's insistence that Aksai Chin lay in Chinese territory; and (3) Nehru's refusal to acknowledge any basis for contesting the McMahon Line while (4) demanding that China withdraw from all recently occupied territory which India claimed. Maxwell notes that the Nehru position emerged "some twelve months before the boundary dispute became a matter of public knowledge or political agitation in India," terming it a "collision course." If this is so, Chou En-lai either did not perceive it in this way or remained hopeful of changing Nehru's position, since in December, 1959, the Chinese Premier proposed a summit meeting which materialized the following April in New Delhi.

Chou's proposal and trip came after a steady deterioration in Sino-Indian relations during 1959. The revolt in Lhasa that March, climaxed by the Dalai Lama's flight to India, triggered an outburst of public polemics between New Delhi and Peking, with a rising chorus of Indian press and political and public opposition to Nehru's official posture of Sino-Indian friendship. By August, leaked details of the various border disputes, including information on the Aksai Chin road, fed the flames of controversy. This was followed by brief but bloody clashes between Indian and Chinese patrols at both the eastern and western extremities of the border. Few casualties resulted and no substantive changes in position occurred, but the fighting made explicit the threat of war.

In this context, Chou's gesture took on added significance as a possible move to break the impasse. A further indication of willingness to compromise appeared to be the Chinese agreement with Burma that their mutual boundary would follow the McMahon Line in its essentials without acknowledging its specific legitimacy. Following this announcement in Peking in January, 1960, Chou formalized the position in Rangoon en route to New Delhi in April. His public statements during the Indian visit implied that Chinese acceptance of Indian control of NEFA would accompany Nehru's agreement on Peking's possession of Aksai Chin.[24]

Nothing in Nehru's comments or in the general atmosphere attending Chou's visit signaled the slightest change in Indian policy. The Prime Minister agreed that individual instances of local disagreement might be adjusted to avoid such clashes as had occurred in the various sectors, but he insisted that neither the McMahon Line nor India's claim to the Aksai Chin was subject to negotiations. Moreover, any negotiations had to be preceded by Chinese withdrawal from the disputed area in the west, including all PLA outposts associated with the Sinkiang-Tibet road.

Under these circumstances, one might be tempted to dismiss the final conflict as inevitable. It would be "only a matter of time" before conflicting claims and local contacts caused major hostilities. However, there are two objections to this view. First, no serious incidents occurred between 1959 and 1962 when the problem remained virtually dormant with no significant military buildup by either side to strengthen its position. Peking steadily advanced its cartographic claims and moved PLA outposts accordingly to provide defense in depth for the Aksai Chin road. New Delhi was content to document its diplomatic position through extensive historical research and the publication of "white papers" containing the ongoing diplomatic exchanges.[25] Thus no progressive deterioration of the situation foreshadowed war. Second, the "inevitability" approach dismisses the central question: why did the war occur in 1962? Maxwell identifies the major cause of the war as India's "forward policy" of advancing patrols into the disputed Aksai Chin region, ostensibly following the PLA precedent whereby occupation was used to justify claims of ownership. But in itself this is insufficient to explain Peking's abandonment of many years of effort to strike a bargain while maintaining a firm but cordial relationship with New Delhi. Indeed, as Maxwell shows, Nehru did not believe that the "forward policy" risked war with China, at least during its inception. The incremental additions to India's miniscule military strength along the border, tenuously sustained over lengthy and arduous lines of communications, could hardly be viewed as a strategic threat to China. The answer to the question is to be found in an examination of the problem from Peking's perspective. To set the framework for Chinese behavior in 1962, our focus must be extended beyond Sino-Indian interactions for an investigation of how other external relations affected developments in Tibet and on the Sino-Indian boundary prior to 1962. These added dimensions, together with domestic political and economic considerations, provide a fuller array of factors whose relevance must be assessed in determining the Chinese calculus and behavior.

Foreign Activities and Tibet

It is impossible to recreate fully the foreign activities which Peking saw as affecting Tibet, particularly since public sources must be relied on for information about covert operations. The clandestine behavior of governments is rarely revealed, except for the publication of overturned or defeated regimes' documents and for the rare documentary "leaks" such as occurred with the "Pentagon Papers." Distorted reports of covert activity are commonplace in counterintelligence and counterespionage organizations, so that what the Chinese officials believed may or may not have reflected reality.

Fortunately, sufficient clues do exist concerning the clandestine activities of the United States and the Nationalist government in Southeast Asia generally and more specifically in Tibet to permit at least a partial reconstruction of the situation as seen from Peking in the years preceding the Sino-Indian war. An authoritative, if abbreviated summary of the Central Intelligence Agency sponsorship of Chinese Nationalist subversive activities appeared in the "Pentagon Papers," a voluminous history of United States decision making in the Vietnam War, prepared under the direction of former Secretary of Defense Robert S. McNamara and surreptitiously released to the *New York Times* by Dr. Daniel Ellsberg.[26] More detailed references appear in the somewhat sensational writings of George Patterson, a former Scottish missionary in East Tibet who had excellent contacts among the rebellious Khambas as well as with the Dalai Lama's entourage in Lhasa. Contemporary press reports occasionally provide corroborative detail, and of course, there are official charges from Peking concerning various activities allegedly in support of guerrillas in Tibet.

By reviewing this material, the basis for Chinese assumptions of external threat, particularly American, can be partially reconstructed. For example, foreign accounts of alleged Tibetan, American, and Chinese Nationalist efforts to undermine PRC rule presumably heightened Chinese Communist concern that such efforts might prove successful. To the degree that external evidence does validate this concern the reality of Peking's perceptions can be better evaluated.

In 1949 the crumbling rule of Chiang Kai-shek stimulated Tibetan hopes for American assistance. Although Tibetan aspirations for independence differed from Chiang's goal of a "return to the mainland," the two groups were joined in their anti-Communist objective through American actions. This coincidence of hostility to Mao's rule led to a series of mysterious and largely meaningless moves linking Tibetan insurgents, CIA operatives, and Nationalist agents. However marginal this activity to the actual effectiveness of Tibetan rebels, it did provide Peking with a credible record of American intentions which needed only opportunity and capability to pose a more serious threat to PRC control.

The first Tibetan probe invited the renowned American news commentator, Lowell Thomas, and his son to Lhasa in 1949. The son's account, published in 1950, quoted "two [Tibetan] Foreign Ministers" as asking directly, "If the Communists strike Tibet, will America help? And to what extent?"[27] Lowell Thomas denied he was an official representative and cautioned that such help would require congressional approval. His son noted, "The most important requirement is guerrilla forces. To create these, Tibet needs arms and advice principally from outside." Once back in Washington they "discussed the Tibetan problem with our government heads" but found no favorable response. Unaware of the position of the United States, Peking announced in 1950 that the PLA would "liberate Tibet" from "British and American imperialist influence."[28]

Up to this point it was "influence" and not "intervention." A letter from Lowell Thomas to the cabinet in Lhasa claimed that President Truman would not commit himself to the shipment of arms or military aid.[29] Despite Truman's express reservation, the letter was subsequently included in Peking's public display of evidence linking Tibet with "American imperialism." Tibetan efforts to enlist American support continued, however, and are described in George Patterson's *Tragic Destiny*. Published in 1959, this book provided fresh justification, if any were needed at that time, for Chinese apprehension. Partially corroborated by other sources, it bears summarizing here as reflective of information available to analysts in Peking.

Patterson told of meeting Takster Rimpoche (Thubten Jigme Norbu), elder brother of the Dalai Lama, in June, 1951, in Kalimpong, India,[30] Captured by the PLA the previous fall, Takster had agreed under duress to depose his younger brother and become head of Tibet. However, he reversed his mission upon arrival in Lhasa, warning the Dalai Lama to flee.

The young ruler went to Yatung, in Tibet, sending his older brother across the border with full authorization to seek foreign assistance. Patterson contacted American officials to facilitate Takster's escape from India where he feared capture or assassination by Chinese and Indian Communists. Among the steps undertaken on Takster's behalf was the securing of financial sponsorship in the United States by the Committee for Free Asia, widely (and correctly) suspected to be a CIA front organization.[31]

Before leaving Calcutta, however, Takster and Patterson negotiated a far-reaching agreement with American officials, "to the satisfaction of both sides," which reversed Truman's pre-Korean war statement to Thomas and linked Washington with Lhasa's independence aspirations. Coded communications with the Dalai Lama, still in Yatung, worked out arrangements whereby "the Dalai Lama's part was publicly to announce Tibet's rejection of the 17 Point Treaty forced on the Tibetan delegation in Peking the previous month, on which rejection the U. S. would take up the matter of Tibet's independence and Chinese aggression in the United Nations. On making the foregoing announcement the Dalai Lama would leave Yatung for India within seven days."[32]

Chinese knowledge of Takster's presence in Calcutta led to immediate personal calls by the Chinese ambassador from New Delhi as well as by the Tibetan-Chinese delegation en route back to Lhasa from Peking. Despite offers of clemency for having betrayed his earlier mission to the Dalai Lama, Takster persisted in the original plan, eluded his observers, and successfully flew to the United States. Patterson returned to Kalimpong for further negotiations with unnamed "American officials" to arrange for the Dalai Lama's escape. Suddenly word was received from the young ruler announcing a reversal of plans and his intent to return to Lhasa at the behest of the three abbots of the three chief monasteries.

The scheme was aborted. While its specific details may have been unknown in Peking at the time, Takster's CIA sponsorship and refuge in the United States probably alerted Chinese Communist security officials in Tibet to possible American support for resistance movements. In addition, according to reports he received at the time in Kalimpong, Chinese suspicions were focused on Patterson.[33] This center of international intrigue close to Tibet ultimately became the subject of official protests from Peking to New Delhi. Nevertheless, Patterson acting from Kalimpong continued to be the chief clandestine communications link between the Dalai Lama and his brother, with safe transit assured by use of the official United States diplomatic pouch from Calcutta to Washington.[34]

In 1952 another brother of the Dalai Lama traveled from Taiwan to Lhasa and returned that same year with accounts of fresh fighting in East Tibet.[35] Further details came to Patterson from an authoritative Tibetan of the Amdo area who claimed that the Goloks, together with remnant Chinese Nationalist forces and other local Tibetan groups, were waging guerrilla war against the PLA with "supplies dropped by Chinese Nationalist planes operating from Formosa."[36] According to this source the aircraft were guided by radios provided by former Kuomintang (KMT) troops who had taken refuge in the East Tibetan hills following defeat in the civil war.[37]

American involvement in this Chinese Nationalist activity could be presumed from the fact that on June 27, 1950, President Harry S Truman had reversed his policy of nonintervention in the Chinese civil war, proclaimed only six months previously, and had interposed the United States Seventh Fleet in the Taiwan Strait. Ostensibly acting in response to the June 25 North Korean invasion upon South Korea, the president's action revived the briefly suspended flow of American assistance to Chiang Kai-shek. In October, 1950, United Nations forces commanded by General Douglas MacArthur crossed the thirty-eighth parallel, overrunning all North Korea to the Yalu River bordering China. Then PLA "volunteers" made good Peking's earlier warnings against such an advance by driving United Nations forces back down the Korean peninsula.[38] These developments locked Peking and Washington in an armed confrontation which outlasted the three-year war, inter alia allying Washington with Taipei. In 1954 the alliance was formalized by a mutual assistance treaty.

However, Peking had more than ideological presumption to link clandestine Chinese Nationalist activity in Tibet with the CIA. According to a 1961 top secret memorandum from Brigadier General Edward Lansdale to General Maxwell Taylor, chief military adviser to President John F. Kennedy, the main commercial airline on Taiwan, Civil Air Transport (CAT), was actually "a CIA proprietary."[39] CAT furnished "air logistical support under commercial cover to most CIA and other U.S. Government agencies' requirements . . . by providing trained and experienced personnel, procurement of supplies and equipment through overt commercial channels, and the maintenance of a fairly large inventory of transport and other type aircraft under both China and U.S. registry."

More specifically, Lansdale claimed that down to 1961 CAT had undertaken "more than 200 overflights of mainland China and Tibet." CAT had no reconnaissance aircraft so presumably these overflights dropped men and supplies for espionage, sabotage, and insurgency. Its well-tested pilots and aircraft had ample experience from World War II both in flying the "Hump" to supply southwest China and in supporting guerrilla operations in the China-Burma-India theater. While the distance from Taiwan to Tibet precluded direct flight, intermediary bases in Thailand could meet the need. Thus, when an unscheduled CAT C-47 transport crashed in the Gulf of Siam near Bangkok in October, 1954, two Americans were aboard; no public explanation of the flight's purpose was forthcoming.[40]

Revolts in eastern Tibet recurred intermittently. In 1955–56 Chamdo was again the scene of the so-called "Kanting rebellion" where Peking estimated as many as 10,000 insurgents required PLA suppression.[41] While the local stockpile of arms left by warlords and remnant KMT forces more than sufficed to support the rebellion, Peking claimed to discover radio transmitters and airdrops from Taiwan of American weapons. Again in 1958, rebellion moved westward from Chamdo into Tibet proper, facilitated according to Peking by airdrops of American arms into Loda, southeast of Lhasa and abutting India.[42] Exhibitions later in Lhasa purportedly showed a full panoply of equipment dropped to insurgents, including wireless sets, maps, guns, ammunition, silver money, and a yellow parachute marked "24 ft. diameter, Aerial Delivery container canopy, load capacity 300 lbs. max. at 150 m.p.h."[43] Chinese briefers explained that yellow was helpful in permitting the agent to convert his parachute into a lama's robe after landing.

It is likely that Peking knew about the linkage between CIA and CAT, perhaps from its inception, given the relative ease of acquiring such information in Hong Kong and Taiwan throughout this period.[44] Moreover these covert United States–Chinese Nationalist operations were not limited in area but extended throughout Southeast Asia, as noted in Lansdale's summary. In 1954 Lansdale had personally trained paramilitary teams for sabotage and guerrilla activity. The teams were ferried into North Vietnam by "CAT [which] provided the Saigon Military Mission with the means for secret air travel between the North and South."[45] Lansdale also recalled that in 1958 CAT had furnished "complete logistical and tactical support for the Indonesian operations," an abortive CIA effort to overthrow Sukarno through an army rebellion in Sumatra, supported from Taiwan.[46] CAT subsequently gave way to a new CIA sponsored competitor, China Air Lines (CAL), which began charter operations in

Laos soon after its formation in 1960 and by 1962 had expanded into South Vietnam.[47]

At the time of the 1959 revolt, Chinese media made repeated references to "U.S. imperialism and Chiang Kai-shek agents" fomenting trouble in Tibet. However the airdrop issue achieved prominence in Sino-Indian relations through a curious sequence of events the following year. In 1960, Indian Defense Minister Krishna Menon protested to Peking "against repeated flights of Chinese planes over India's North East Frontier Agency" and declared in Parliament that "reports of forty-three air violations had been received so far that year."[48] Three weeks later Chou privately assured Nehru that investigation showed the aircraft were American.[49] Another Indian protest that August evoked a public denial from Peking which asserted that the aircraft "took off from Bangkok, passed over Burma or China and crossed the Chinese-Indian border to penetrate deep into China's interior where they parachuted weapons, supplies, and wireless sets to secret agents and then flew back to Bangkok again passing over the Chinese-Indian border."[50]

Peking's statement further revealed that the PRC was so confident there were no Chinese planes that Chou had notified Burma it was fully entitled to intercept any unidentified aircraft in its airspace, "either forcing them to land or shooting them down." In September, 1960, the Burmese hit a Chinese Nationalist PB4Y long distance patrol bomber, such as had been used by the United States Navy in World War II. Chiang Kai-shek apologized to Bangkok for the aircraft crash in Thailand, but Chinese Nationalist intelligence officers in Taiwan insisted the flights would continue.[51]

Chinese allegations concerning American efforts to subvert Communist rule in Tibet had some basis in fact, and Peking's protests to New Delhi concerning hostile activity in Kalimpong won support from other sources. Eight months before the Lhasa revolt, an official Chinese note declared:

> Since the peaceful liberation of the Tibetan region of China, reactionaries who have fled from Tibet to Kalimpong have been carrying on subversive and disruptive activities against China's Tibetan region under the instigation and direction of the U.S. and Chiang Kai-shek clique and in collusion with local reactionaries in Kalimpong. . . .According to reliable material available to the Chinese Government, the American—Chiang Kai-shek clique and local special agents and Tibetan reactionaries operating in Kalimpong have

recently stepped up their conspiratorial and disruptive activities. . . . They are actively inciting and organizing a handful of reactionaries hidden in Tibet for an armed revolt there in order to attain the traitors' aim and separate the Tibet region from the People's Republic of China.[52]

Patterson confirms that lengthy discussions took place between Tibetans allegedly representing rebel forces and unnamed American officials who promised to argue in Washington on behalf of a clandestinely organized revolt.[53] While relatively little material aid seems to have arrived before 1959, the Khamba rebellion of 1956–58 showed the potential for internal dissidence were outside help to become available.

According to L. Fletcher Prouty, a retired Air Force colonel who acted as "coordinator and expediter between the CIA and the Air Force," the Dalai Lama's flight in March, 1959, succeeded because of Washington:

> The CIA operation that enabled the Dalai Lama to escape to India . . . was one of the agency's most masterful performances. Aircraft from secret Southeast Asian bases, flying low among the Himalayan peaks to avoid detection, sought out pre-arranged rendevous [sic] areas. Tibetans who had received some training in operating directional radio beacons set them up to guide the planes. Once contact was made the CIA aircraft homed in on these signals, located the caravan in the snow-covered wilderness, parachuted supplies, and estimated the next day's rendezvous point.[54]

In May, 1959, it was decided to utilize the thousands of Khamba refugees fleeing Tibet for interdiction of two key roads over which PLA supplies and manpower entered the mountainous region. The longer route from Lanchow to Koko Nor crossed the 16,700-foot Tang Pass, while the 1,400-mile road from Chengtu traversed fourteen ranges at average altitudes of 13,000 feet. At best gravel but more commonly mud and rock, these critical roads were mostly one lane wide, often mere slits carved into the mountainside with tree trunks to shore up the grade. Crude bridges over torrential streams provided additional points of vulnerability.

Prouty recounts how C-130s were modified for the high Himalayan crossing while CIA crews trained in Okinawa. Meanwhile Tibetan volunteers were flown to a secret base in the Rocky Mountains:

> Army experts taught the Tibetans to operate military radios. They were shown how to use signal panels for daylight air drops and

shielded lights at night. CIA demolition specialists taught them how to place explosives along roadbeds and under bridges to do the most damage. Fire jumpers . . . taught the art of parachuting from low-flying planes into tree-studded mountains.[55]

Their destination was Lake Koko Nor, 1,350 miles from the jump-off base at Takhli in central Thailand but nearly twice that distance by the circuitous route adopted to avoid Chinese radars, via Burma and India's NEFA. After reconnaissance flights by the high altitude U-2, the first guerrilla team entered China in November, 1959. Prouty claims "between 200 and 300" Tibetans were trained in Colorado, and that "by May 1960 it was estimated that some 42,000 Tibetans were being armed and supplied" by the airdrops. The downing of another U-2 over the Soviet Union prompted Premier Nikita Khrushchev to cancel his summit meeting with President Dwight D. Eisenhower in May, 1960, and also resulted in the brief suspension of the training program. However, the program subsequently was revived and continued until at least December, 1961. Then an accident in Colorado involving a busload of Tibetans threatened to expose the operation, and President John F. Kennedy reportedly ordered its termination, although the flights out of Thailand apparently remained undisturbed.[56]

In addition to the evidence supporting covert linkages between Tibetan insurgents and Taiwan via the Central Intelligence Agency and bases in Southeast Asia, Chinese analysts and contingency planners could not have been unaware of the general increase of clandestine United States activities associated with Chinese Nationalists against Chinese Communist interests in the area. Washington's involvement with thousands of former Kuomintang troops, which were simultaneously seeking refuge and raising opium in the Burma-Thailand-Laos interlock, together with a heavy CIA investment in Laos, added to the potential importance of covert American operations in Tibet.[57] If the opportunity provided by the Tibetan revolt of 1958–59 had been missed or aborted by division among the Tibetans and prompt action by the PLA, another crisis might invite a more ambitious American intervention. It is against these considerations that the economic crisis generated by the collapse of Mao's Great Leap Forward provided a new context for a new United States threat to PRC security, possibly an attack coordinated from Taiwan with pressure from India or Tibet.

Economic Collapse, Political Crisis

Measured in scale and intensity,[58] the Great Leap Forward was the most massive economic experiment of modern times. More than 600 million persons experienced a year of total economic reorganization manifested in all aspects of daily life on farm and in factory. The regime consolidated collective farms into 25,000 communes, comprising virtually the entire agricultural sector with approximately 86 percent of the population. Backyard furnaces mushroomed throughout the country. In factories man and machine worked without surcease. Transportation was strained to the limit to meet new demands. Production and distribution systems collapsed under excessive pressures from both inputs and outputs. Statistical chaos compounded confusion at the top as the falsification of figures substituted propaganda for performance at the bottom.

Sector by sector, the Chinese economy declined under change and overload. Peasants reacted to the threatened loss of private livestock by slaughtering their animals. They resisted the abolition of private plots and free markets by consuming what they raised. Government demands for more industrial crops further depleted the supply of consumer foodstuffs. Meanwhile, industrial output peaked dramatically in 1959 only to decline precipitously as worker and machine fatigue triggered a chain reaction of breakdown and stagnation. To complicate matters still further, three years of bad weather hit major agricultural areas. Finally, the sudden withdrawal of all Soviet technicians and related assistance in 1960 brought key industrial projects to a standstill.

No statistics were issued by the government after 1959, but time has afforded some perspective for attempting a reconstruction of the economic decline. For the purposes of this study the most relevant sector of decline covers consumer commodities whose supply affected morale. In order to determine how Peking assessed the morale of the Chinese people and also how Peking saw its country's morale reflected abroad, two sources are valuable. The first is a classified PLA publication restricted to regimental army commanders and above.[59] Captured by United States intelligence in early 1962, it covers most of 1960–61.[60] It is an unusually authoritative document and as such reflects the information available to top officials, collected through the most reliable national instrument at the time, the PLA. The second source consists of refugee interrogations in Hong Kong. Long a staple for journalistic and foreign governmental information, these interviews received increasing attention abroad as dramatic eyewitness accounts told of mounting misery inside China. A massive refugee exodus of more than 140,000 persons suddenly poured across the Hong Kong border in May, 1962.[61] This unprecedented outflow won worldwide publicity, inter alia raising speculation over the prospect of revolt or collapse on the mainland. These two sources provide unique access to developments during the critical period of mid-1961 to mid-1962. This coincides with the important interval within which Chinese assessments of domestic and foreign threat led to policies pertinent to this inquiry.

The annual fall harvest estimate, essential to consumer and industrial needs, is initially undertaken in August and revised in late September after the worst weather has usually passed. Final figures based on confirmed barn storage only emerge in the late fall. Thus, the regime cannot count on the total yield before mid-summer. However, consumer demand becomes increasingly critical through the spring as the previous year's stockpile draws down before the new crops can be gathered. This is an especially tense period if emergency reserves are depleted by successive bad years, as in 1959–61. In sum, the government's best approximation of the harvest is in August and its first respite from consumer demand comes in July.

While isolated economic catastrophes occur frequently in a country as large and poor as China, the scope and duration of this crisis was unprecedented since the founding of the PRC. Equally important, it was accompanied by two political blows. First, the collapse of Mao's vaunted scheme had triggered a high level confrontation with his colleagues in mid-1959, resulting in the dismissal of P'eng Teh-huai, Minister of Defense and Long March veteran, together with the Chief of Staff and other officials.[62] Second, the sharp deterioration of Sino-Soviet relations, accelerated by an ideological polemic initiated by Mao in April, 1960, had prompted Nikita Khrushchev to terminate Soviet technical assistance that August.[63] No economic program had been launched with such propagandistic fervor or promise as had the Great Leap Forward. No single foreign policy theme had saturated Chinese media with such intensity and consistency as had the Sino-Soviet alliance.

These two major shocks were felt throughout the political system at both the elite and mass levels,[64] and continuing economic tensions became an especially worrisome concern to the leadership. The captured military documents give ample evidence of the linkages between economic and political tensions, with emphasis on border areas, particularly in Tibet and adjacent provinces.

One significant report included in the PLA documents came from Hsiao Hua, then Deputy Secretary-General of the Military Affairs Commission (MAC) of the Chinese Communist Party (CCP) and Deputy Director of the General Political Department of the PLA.[65] Dated May 20, 1961, it was addressed to MAC Vice-Chairmen Lin Piao, Ho Lung, and Nieh Jung-chen on the basis of a special inspection of PLA units in the Nanking Military Region. Hsiao warned, "Family problems exert a great influence upon the thinking of the men in the Army. If a relative at home falls ill or dies, if the labor force is insufficient, or there is not enough grain . . . if disaster affects the home district or there are difficulties about the working conditions . . . all such problems can seriously disturb the peace of mind of the soldier." He noted that "letters from home are at present fairly numerous . . . on the average of five or six for each soldier [per month] or at the most fourteen. Family members coming to visit the soldiers are also more frequent and numerous than before." In short, PLA morale was suffering because of empathy with depressed conditions in the countryside.

Worse, the PLA itself was suffering directly, as revealed in explicit detail by Hsiao:

> The Tank Sub-unit of the 0100th Army Unit had had meat only twice in their meals from Spring Festival (February) until the May 1st Festival. The reason given was that the supply of supplementary foodstuffs was short and the men did not have the food needed by such tank units. . . .Because their food does not have enough nutrition for them the drivers of tanks are losing their physical energy. Many times when a man has driven a tank for more than an hour he becomes dizzy or nauseated. . . .
>
> . . . At present infectious diseases are becoming a serious problem, especially inflammation of the liver. The Chekiang Provincial Military District has sixteen responsible cadres of whom seven are ill. In other places many leadership cadres are ill too, together with their families, all of whom are affected by inflammation of the liver [hepatitis]. The 0937th Army Unit has a Political Department the Secretarial Section of which are all suffering from parasitic diseases of the blood. Some cadres with large families do not get enough to eat so that they are directly affected by a lowered living standard.

Conditions did not improve in mid-1961. A report by the General Rear Services Department of August 4 to the MAC frankly itemized the wide range of shortages confronting the PLA.[66] Its opening paragraphs which summarized the positive side as "better than last winter" noted that "from January to May, in most Army units . . . each person had a monthly diet of forty-five catties of vegetables, nine to fifteen ounces of meat, and nine to ten ounces of edible oil, which is close to or has reached the standard ration." However,

> . . . some problems still remain. Except for naval and air personnel, as well as the wounded and the sick, the state has stopped the supply of meat to most districts. At present the supply of edible oil and beans has been reduced. In the latter part of this year, it may be further reduced. The supply of food to Army units remains short. Approximately 5 to 10 percent of the persons in a company do not have sufficient food to eat. Besides they have to transfer part of their food to solve the problem of food needed by their families. . . . At present, the heart of the problem, in terms of the living conditions in Army units, remains the supply of food.

While an army may march on its stomach, material inputs are essential to its fighting capabilities and here the report was equally blunt:

> In the first half of this year, only 23 percent of the planned amount of steel was delivered . . . only about 10 percent of the planned amount of lumber was delivered. In the second half of this year, the state could not possibly deliver more materials than in the first half. . . .During the period from January to May the state delivered less than 10 percent of the goods [automobile parts] ordered. The supply of steel plates accounted for only 4.9 percent of the amount ordered, that of tires only 17 percent. *In the first half of this year, state factories accomplished only 15.9 percent of the planned target in the manufacturing of weapons, equipment, accessories, and parts.* [Italics added.]

Although no planned target figures were included in this report, the awareness of declining production in 1960 presumably focused attention on 1961 goals and adjusted them downward in advance to logically realistic targets. Thus, the reported shortfalls provided a grim warning to the leadership. Finally, health worsened in the PLA as the cumulative effects of malnutrition became manifest:

> The rate of infectious diseases in the first season of this year increased by 30 percent, as compared to the same period of last year. . . .What is particularly worth our attention is the fact that

typhus, typhoid, paratyphoid, malaria and other diseases which were formerly under control and close to extinction have become increasingly common again this year. Infectious diseases which rarely occurred in our country before, such as brucellosis and parrot disease (which was discovered in our country for the first time), have also begun to appear.

The crisis was clearly communicated to higher levels throughout 1961, as documented in these secret reports with specific examples and detailed surveys. Chief of Staff Lo Jui-ch'ing personally examined selected regions, noting, "In some units a large proportion of the soldiers' families are in disaster areas. According to comrades in the Wuhan Military Region, the proportion . . . ranges from 16 to 71 percent in some companies. Of the 600 soldiers in the engineering battalion of Army Unit 9354, 300 have families in the Hsin-yang Special District, 100 in Shantung, and 80 in Kansu."[67] Even grain-rich Szechuan was hit, as shown by one survey wherein 60 soldiers from that province included "twenty-four from places which suffered serious disasters last year [1960]. From last May to the end of last year, 16 persons in 10 soldiers' families died, and 9 of them died of dropsy resulting from the famine."[68] The disaffection of these troops emerged in recorded questions and complaints such as, "Where did the food go? Is it true the state has held back food from the people? After the communes were established, why have the crops become worse than before?" The report laconically noted, "Some soldiers whose relatives died because of the disasters wept, became depressed, and refused to talk." One more daringly articulate than the rest bluntly declared, " 'At the time of my discharge, I shall not want anything but a rifle.' Someone asked him: 'Why a rifle?' He replied, 'To fight the Party!' "[69]

This shocking state of economic collapse and political disaffection showed no significant alleviation down to August, 1961, the last period covered by these PLA studies. Other sources do not indicate any improvement during that winter. On the contrary, subsequent estimates show 1961–62 as the trough of economic decline (table 1). The comparison with earlier years of similar output acquires added significance when juxtaposed against intervening population increases. As for the political impact on public morale and perceptions, however, the most relevant comparison is with the immediately preceding years of soaring productivity manifested by the Great Leap Forward (GLF) (table 2).

Table 1

Selected Estimates for PRC Economy, 1961[70]

(Bracketed Year Indicates Previous Comparable Level)

GNP (in billions of dollars)	GNP per Capita (in dollars)	Agricultural Production (1957=100%)	Grain Output (millions of metric tons)	Population (mid-year, millions)
72 [1955]	103 [1952]	78 [1951–2]	160 [1954,1960]	701 [NB: 596 in 1954]

Food production worsened qualitatively more than is indicated by these estimates because subsidiary foods of high nutrient and protein value, such as vegetables, fruits, and livestock, had come primarily from the private plots which were abolished under the communes. Thus, under-nutrition from an insufficient supply of calories consequent from grain shortages was accompanied by malnutrition associated with the loss of vitamins, minerals, and protein. The only palliative lay in greater reliance on outside sources to which the government turned in a major way, as indicated by the following figures which show the trimming of food exports together with a major expansion of food imports (table 3).

In addition, the regime made little effort to censor communication abroad to overseas Chinese families, probably calculating that some additional relief would eventuate from that source. Letters and refugees told of rampant illness and near-famine conditions, with the peasants reverting to traditional methods of cooking leaves and bark, usurping fodder normally used for pigs, and ultimately resorting to infanticide, especially of girls. In response, the number of food parcels sent by Hong Kong Chinese alone rose from less than one million in 1959 to almost 12 million in 1961.[71]

In desperation, the regime restored the private plots which had been confiscated during the Great Leap Forward, but this came too late to bring in significant yields before the 1962 harvest. Meanwhile press admonitions warned against "spontaneous capitalist tendencies" manifest in black markets, profiteering, and the neglect of industrial and state-designated crops

Table 2
Estimated GLF Peak Output and 1961[72]

Item	Base Line 1957	Leap Forward High Amount	Year	Post-leap Collapse Amount	Year
GNP (billions)	$ 82	$95	1958	$72	1961
GNP per Capita	$128	$144	1958	$103	1961
Grain (millions of tons)	185	200	1958	160	1960–61
Steel (millions of tons)	5.35	13	1960	8	1961

Table 3
PRC Imports and Exports of Major
Agricultural Commodities, 1960–61 [73]
(Thousand Metric Tons)

	Imports			Exports		
	Wheat	Rice	Sugar	Rice	Sugar	Soybeans
1960	60	28	203	1,174	16	996
1961	6,200	62	1,534	444	127	335

in favor of salable consumer commodities. Privately, PLA reports warned of serious tensions between the local militia and the populace, stemming from armed attacks on individuals and storeplaces in search of food. [74] In Honan, this led to the complete removal of weapons from the 20,000,000 militia members. [75]

More significant from the vantage point of this inquiry are revelations pertaining to actual insurgency, especially in border areas. Here "an outline of the 1961 plan for the work of building up national defense" issued by the MAC on January 16, 1961, contains a section specifically linking internal disorder with external enemies:

E. Continue to fight the rebels and aim to destroy them.
    In Kansu, Chinghai, Szechuan, Tibet, and Yunnan, and in some other places armed rebels, after we spent the whole of last year to destroy them, have already been reduced to submission. There are still, however, about 3,000 scattered and roaming about. . . .Most of them are leaders of the most rabid of the rebels, familiar with the terrain, equipped with combat experience against us. . . .The counterrevolutionaries outside were still in communication with those inside, and there is in some places the danger of repeated uprisings and new uprisings. In addition, rebels who had escaped abroad may return for further action. [76]

While there undoubtedly was a downgrading in the numerical estimate of those engaged in overt rebellion, the identification of insurgent areas is plausible in its coincidence with traditionally rebellious minority groups "still in communication with counterrevolutionaries outside." The most serious anxiety concerned Tibetan guerrillas, as evidenced by an entire paragraph devoted to the handling of problems in the Himalayan region which included express permission to cross the border in pursuit of rebels:

> In places near to the border of neighboring countries, such as the Sino-Indian border, the Sino-Nepalese border, and the Sino-Sikkim border, we must strictly respect the ruling not to exceed the limit of entry into the neighboring country beyond 20 kilometres. Regarding bandits returning from abroad to fight, we must also strictly observe the principles contained in the Southwest Region Border Defense Regulations promulgated by the Military Affairs Commission, together with the rulings of the eight documents.[77]

The linkage of internal dissafection with rebellion which might culminate in international crisis was implicit in the section that immediately followed:

> 1. We must work hard to make our Southwest and Northwest regional borders peaceful and secure. This is the best way to settle the problem of our border regions. . . .
> 2. In the neighboring countries (including fraternal nations and nationalistic countries) if and when in these border regions there occurs any international incident, it is required to report quickly to superiors and await the decision and orders, if any. Under no circumstances should an officer upon his own personal responsibility take steps to carry out an unauthorized decision.[78]

The clear concern to avoid escalation through a strict command and control over local military responses to "incidents" is particularly interesting in view of the euphemistic references to the "fraternal" (Russia) and "nationalistic" (India) nations. This reluctance to identify Moscow and New Delhi as specific sources of subversion and aggression contrasts with the next section which called for being "ready to deal with the sudden attacks of the armed forces of American imperialism, the remnant bandit Chiang and the servile nations of American imperialism." It is also worth noting the juxtaposition of "rebels, bandits, and counterrevolutionaries" with concern over the "Southwest and Northwest regional borders."

The Enemy Without and Trouble Within: Hong Kong and Sinkiang

Throughout the winter of 1961–62, foreign press accounts raised increasingly serious questions over the regime's viability. The most dramatic and widely disseminated of these reports came from the columns of Joseph Alsop. A senior China specialist among journalists, Alsop was known to enjoy access to American officials in Hong Kong and Washington and therefore was a presumed mirror of United States intelligence estimates, at least in the eyes of Chinese analysts. His view merits attention:

> ... The most reliable data obtainable in Hong Kong this spring [1962], derived from great numbers of refugee interrogations and collected and analysed with extreme care, showed an average food intake for mainland China of 1,300 to 1,600 calories per person per day, according to the individual's labor category.... The figures include the supplements to the peasants' diet provided by the private plots. They are so low that one cannot imagine the Chinese masses surviving, at this wretched diet level, for three years on end.
> ... The existence of a descending spiral is seen to be undeniable. Each year has been worse for China than the year before, and all the self-reversals, concessions and tergiversations of the Communist leadership have thus far failed to halt the downward movement.[79]

Alsop pointed to the regime's sense of desperation as reflected by Chou En-lai's reported announcement at the March, 1962, National People's Congress that 30 percent of China's urban population would be returned to the countryside. While Alsop acknowledged this program had been quietly in effect for eighteen months, he nonetheless saw this announcement as evidence of a "downward spiral" whereby successive shortfalls in agricultural productivity would trigger increasingly desperate moves to quell the dissent that would in turn accentuate problems of control throughout the country.

He then drew parallels with ancient China and contemporary East Europe that suggested dire prospects as a result of a third disastrous year of harvest in 1962. Alsop discounted the likelihood of a major population decrease "by something like a quarter or a third" because he thought "something will give somewhere else, in the army, in the police, or in the regime itself." The development he regarded as most likely was "a breakdown of the entire Chinese Communist system." This would be a virtual certainty "if the army rallies to the people."

Alsop's prognosis, while expressly dependent on the 1962 harvest, coincided uncomfortably with much of the data available in Peking concerning PLA morale. Indeed, the leadership may have suspected more than coincidence since it is possible that some officials knew of the classified PLA reports having fallen into the hands of United States intelligence. If so, they had even more reason to take Alsop's columns as reflecting awareness in Washington, and inter alia Taipei and New Delhi, of the full extent of China's economic and political crisis.

Alsop's persistent bias against the PRC and his penchant for purple prose gave his forecasts of disaster somewhat less credibility abroad than might have been thought in Peking, but his analysis won new respect with the unprecedented exodus of more than 140,000 refugees into Hong Kong during the first three weeks of May, 1962. This key event is an important part of the context for subsequent analysis of Sino-American and Sino-Indian interactions. It merits discussion at this point as the culmination of developments associated with economic crisis and political disaffection both as seen by the Chinese leadership and as believed to be determining decisions in Washington, Taipei, New Delhi, and Moscow. Moreover, Moscow's knowledge of a simultaneous movement across the Sinkiang border added a further dimension of apprehension to perspectives in Peking.

The exact details of how the exodus into Hong Kong began remain somewhat confused, shrouded in secrecy at the time and complicated by post hoc "revelations" in the form of Cultural Revolution accusations against T'ao Chu, then regional party boss of South China.[80] Apparently the pressures to migrate were multiple. In part, of course, they stemmed from food shortages; however, another important motivation was resistance to the sending of large numbers of the urban populace—especially able-bodied males—to the countryside. This was done to relieve the pressure on municipalities to provide food, shelter, and employment and to provide additional labor in the countryside. The latter goal included substituting manpower for bullocks in plowing, as much of the livestock had died or been slaughtered during the previous years of disruption and disaster. In addition, the rumored confiscation of private plots and the feared retaliation for "capitalist" or corrupt practices prompted "rightists" to seek refuge in Hong Kong. Finally, the sheer uncertainty of future conditions in China contrasted with the incomparably more serene life in Hong Kong and abroad. Knowledge of this better life was readily communicated in Kwangtung province by the many who frequently crossed the border for business and family reasons, as well as through letters from relatives and friends, both in Hong Kong and throughout the overseas Chinese communities of Southeast Asia.

For their part, local authorities faced increasing problems in curbing illegal migration. The transfer of people, estimated in Canton as 800,000 out of a population of 2,000,000, simply shifted a multitude of problems from the city to the countryside. This action met with resistance not only from the transferred, but from local villagers who did not welcome more empty stomachs and idle hands, especially since many transfers were not only contemptuous or ignorant of peasant life but were outsiders who had drifted south from northern, Mandarin-speaking regions. From the viewpoint of all concerned, the migration of this portion of the populace to Hong Kong provided an expedient alternative to forced settlement in already hard-pressed rural areas. At the very least, should British authority deny the refugees permission to stay in the colony, resentment might be diverted from inside Kwangtung to outside targets.

Whatever may have been the mixture of motivations on the part of the refugees and of the local authorities, Kwangtung officials suddenly eased border controls in late April. Without the previous physical constraints that limited legal crossings to fifty persons a day, tens of thousands suddenly streamed across the frontier into Hong Kong. At first, British guards sought simply to stop the refugees, but they soon had to resort to increased security fences and temporary internment camps as the flood swelled. Thousands were returned within days of crossing. By mid-May these measures began to take hold and news of their effectiveness deterred many still on their way from Kwangtung. On May 21, in response to British protests, Chinese officials formally closed the border following triangular communications between London, Peking, and Canton. However, evidence of the remaining refugee pressure emerged on June 1 when several thousand persons demanded access to the train in Canton. Denied permission to board, they caused a sufficient disturbance to require the presence of police, troops, and the mayor.[81] Those who remained after an all-night demonstration were forcibly moved to a detention center, with normal train travel being restored several days later.

Hong Kong's role as the peephole for "China-watchers" assured full press coverage complete with photographs of the exodus and its aftermath.[82] This provided dramatic support for Alsop's analysis and a damaging blow to the PRC image abroad. Despite the absence of overt anti-Communist sentiment among the refugees and the implicit demonstration of Chinese authority in both the easing and the tightening of border controls, American analysts interpreted the exodus as symptomatic of a deep-seated disaffection which could foreshadow a loss of Communist control on the mainland.

Wholly shielded from such foreign attention but remarkably similar in its implications was the simultaneous exodus of between sixty and eighty thousand persons from Sinkiang into the Soviet Union. The details are even more obscure than in the case of Kwangtung since the area was closed to outside observation and neither the Russian nor the Chinese press reported the events at the time. From accounts by the two sides and occasional refugee interviews, it is possible to reconstruct the basic situation and to infer its importance for Chinese policy perceptions in 1962.

Sinkiang's population, 80 percent non-Chinese people of Turki background and Moslem faith, contains large numbers of Kazakhs who fled Soviet collectivization in the early 1930s. Clustered in the western regions, these nomadic herdsmen traditionally visited freely with their kinsmen in the Soviet Kazakh Republic across the border. In addition, pockets of White Russians and Uighurs remained from previous migrations, including those following the turmoil of the Russian Revolution. Sino-Soviet agreements facilitated registration and repatriation of these groups during the mid-fifties, but apparently the departure of approximately 170,000 between 1957 and 1959 caused concern in Peking and the program was stopped.[83]

Meanwhile the flow of Chinese into Sinkiang, initially begun as a frontier development program, increased markedly after the failure of the Great Leap Forward. This resulted in the shipment of hundreds of thousands, principally male youths, to the region, taxing the local economy and threatening the position of non-Chinese groups. Attacks against "local nationalism" in 1959–60 foreshadowed the Sinicization of Sinkiang and prompted increased efforts to migrate across the border. These efforts, which peaked in 1961–62, may have been encouraged by Moscow. According to later accounts by White Russian refugees from Sinkiang, the Soviet consulates distributed thousands of Russian passports clandestinely, predating them for credibility, to permit holders to apply for Chinese exit visas.[84] This appears to have been the basis for the official Chinese charge of September 6, 1963:

> In April and May 1962 the leaders of the CPSU (Communist Party of the Soviet Union) used their organs and personnel in Sinkiang, China to carry out large-scale subversive activities in the Ili region

and enticed and coerced several tens of thousands of Chinese citizens into going to the Soviet Union. The Chinese Government lodged repeated protests and made repeated representations, but the Soviet Government refused to repatriate these Chinese citizens on the pretext of "the sense of Soviet legality" and "humanitarianism."[85]

The Chinese charges are not wholly credible. The coincidence in timing with the Kwangtung exodus suggests an initial permissiveness by local Chinese officials, almost certainly authorized by Peking. The scale of movement further suggests official stimulus since the population density is so much sparser and more widely scattered than in Kwangtung. Whether designed to alleviate local shortages or to shift discontent into neighboring states, second thoughts in Peking prompted by late May a reimposition of restrictions paralleling those enforced at Canton. The repercussions too were similar to what happened at Canton. On May 29, angry Kazakh demonstrators protested in Kuldja against the suspension of exit permits. Precisely what happened next is uncertain, but at some point the PLA opened fire with automatic weapons, killing or wounding several dozen demonstrators who ransacked municipal offices and beat Chinese officials.[86] News of the incident triggered similar outbreaks in other towns, whereupon the PLA reinforced its local garrison and began turning the border into a depopulated security zone.

According to informed Soviet sources, Chou En-lai immediately dispatched a note of apology to Moscow, accepting responsibility for the local difficulty.[87] Not until July did Peking impose new restrictions on travel and communication that forced closure of the two Soviet consulates.[88] Subsequently Chou accused Moscow of attempting to subvert and separate Sinkiang from Chinese rule; this posture did not emerge at the time, although it may have been advanced by one group in Peking. The parallel with past precedent is interesting. Soviet consulates had played an important role in organizing and arming the "East Turkestan Republic" uprising in Ili in November, 1944, and again in mediating between the rebels and local Chinese officials the following summer.[89] Moreover the 1944 uprising had maintained its hold on western Sinkiang because of leadership and recruitment which drew upon Turki groups that straddled the border and migrated freely across it. Thus, without attempting to assess the accuracy of various particulars in the 1962 crisis, it seems likely that some policy makers in Peking saw Sinkiang tensions as inviting Soviet intervention. Coupled with the Hong Kong exodus, these developments could heighten anxiety over how Chinese vulnerability might invite hostile action on the part of both Moscow and Washington.

Chinese Perceptions of the International Environment

In completing this survey of the larger context of the specific interactions of 1962, it is important to establish, to the extent possible, Chinese preconceptions of the main actors in the international environment. Preconceptions can act as filters for selecting relevant evidence of intention as well as determinants of bias in assessing the degree of threat to be anticipated. Careful analysis of the captured secret PLA materials provides a more authoritative definition of policy judgments than might be inferred solely from public speeches and press materials. While it is still possible that the innermost calculations within the leadership, especially those of particular individuals such as Mao or Chou, diverged from these classified documents, they nonetheless offer a reasonable approximation of high-level perceptions down to mid-1961.

A general review of the world situation, distributed in May of 1961, by the General Political Department of the PLA, bore the express admonition, "This material is for the study and reference of cadres at and above the regimental level. It is not allowed to spread knowledge of the contents outside or to quote or copy the same in public. Under no circumstances can this be lost or misplaced!"[90] While its contents did not diverge markedly from open propaganda, they did include details of strategy and tactics not found in public media. For instance, in acknowledging that "our enemies have felt happy about the natural disasters that descended upon our country" the writer added elliptically, "Some of our friends do not really understand us and we must be patient with them, not reckoning our accounts with them too exactly."[91] Since the statement occurred under a subhead, "The unity of the Socialist camp depends on work done," the allusion to "some friends" would seem to fit the Moscow leadership, despite assertions here and elsewhere that "after the issuance of the Moscow declaration last December [1960] a new era in the friendship of China and the Soviet Union began."

No such indirection marked the Chinese analysis of President Kennedy. Written after the abortive Bay of Pigs invasion and the final crisis in Laos when Washington had decided against intervention in favor of negotiations, this analysis drew a harsh profile of the new administration:

> . . . The smell of gunpowder is more evident in Kennedy's administration than in Eisenhower's, for it is more reactionary, treacherous, elusive and deceitful. There was a kind of saying during Kennedy's presidential campaign and after his election that he was comparatively realistic, loving peace, and desirous of relaxing the world situation. But facts have proved that the cards he played in Laos, Cuba and the Congo did not show any indication of relaxation. . . .Kennedy wants to walk on two legs: on the one hand to raise American technology to the highest degree of perfection in order to reduce the missile gap and on the other hand to enlarge the standing army, develop conventional weapons and prepare actively for a limited and sublimited war.
>
> . . . It is better to maintain a frozen relationship between China and the United States with a continued impasse for many years. . . . Some people criticize us for being too stiff and unbending, but this is not correct. . . . The unbending attitude is found on the side of the United States, and not on the side of China. . . .Generally speaking, the United States, thinking of itself as a large, strong and advanced country, does whatever it likes without justification, and considers that China is a weak country and China ought to yield to it. There has been no fundamental change in Kennedy. . . . We must be very watchful of this smiling tiger, which looks "relaxed externally but tense internally."

Six weeks later, following the opening of the Geneva Conference on May 12, 1961, a somewhat more confident tone emerged in a lengthy analysis of the American, British, and French positions on Laos, but the posture of the United States was still depicted as one of strategic confrontation, mixed with concessions forced by weakness and continued treachery:

> . . . The United States has always considered as important the geographical position of Laos . . . is trying hard to make this into a military base like South Korea and Taiwan. . . .If the United States controls Laos, then it can make Laos allied with Vietnam and Thailand, surrounding Cambodia and affecting Burma in order to force them to give up their peaceful neutralist policy. . . .
> . . . It is worth serious consideration that the United States, because it wants to get at the conference table what it cannot get on

the battlefield, while the conference is proceeding, is again preparing to carry on a new military venture. . . . .Especially serious is that under the scheming of the United States, the Laotian rebel forces-are just in the process of becoming entangled with the troops of South Vietnam and Thailand, preparing to attack suddenly the army of the lawful government and the combat units of the Patriotic Front of Laos. . . .From the conditions of the Geneva Conference during the first week, it was very obvious that the United States would not easily give up its policy of aggression and interference. Therefore, in the conference, with every step carefully planned in advance and the procuring of every success, a bitter fight must be waged with American imperialism.[92]

Again, it is not the purpose of this study to evaluate the accuracy of Chinese charges, although it is worth noting they were consonant with past practices of the United States in Laos. Rather the intent is to note the consistency with which authorized interpretations of American policy depict hostility, if not actual threat, toward Chinese interests.

The last such document in this PLA series was issued August 1 and concerned United States–Japanese relations subsequent to Prime Minister Ikeda's visit to Washington in late June. As might be expected, a pernicious collusion between nascent "Japanese militarism" and "U.S. imperialism" keynoted the analysis:

> . . . Their [Ikeda-Kennedy-Rusk] aim was to carry further their evil association, add strength to the strategical position of the United States in the Far East, and use their energies to treat us as an enemy. . . .Japan has for a long time harbored an aggressive attitude toward the territories of South Korea and Taiwan, and it is likely that its activities will be promoted by the support of the United States. Its aggressive steps will probably be, first, economic penetration into South Korea, then establishment of diplomatic relations before a gradual strengthening of its control; another step is continually to prevent us from liberating Taiwan and simultaneously to penetrate from the political, economic and cultural sides into Taiwan in order to cultivate a pro-Japanese influence, overthrow the rule of Chiang Kai-shek and urge an "independent Taiwan." At present Japan wants the United States to "cooperate" with it to organize a "Northeast Asian Alliance" with Japan in the principal role and then gradually to put the above-mentioned areas into the sphere of influence of Japan. . . .[93]

The article interpreted Japanese "peace corps" plans as designed to penetrate Southeast Asian countries. In collusion with Washington Japan would use economic trade and aid with Laos, Cambodia, and Burma as part of an overall design "to accelerate expansion toward Southeast Asia, to struggle for buffer zones, and resist the influence of our country." While the writer foresaw ultimate success in "mobilizing the people of Japan and Asia to rise and struggle against American and Japanese imperialism," the general tone of the analysis was one of moderate concern over short-term prospects.

No immediate alarms were sounded in any of these documents. Nehru was dismissed lightly, his "nonviolence policy acting as an escort for American imperialism."[94] Differences with Moscow were inevitable and understandable, since "as there is no exact identification between the circumstances of China and the Soviet Union, it is impossible for the two countries to have an exactly identical point of view on every problem." More specifically, "The policy of our country towards the United States must also be different from that of the Soviet Union. But this difference will not hinder the transition from Socialism to Communism or the overall opposition to imperialism." Even Laos posed no threat to Chinese security according to these analyses. In sum, their tone was one of defensive vigilance, documented with credible evidence of external hostility, given the premises of Communist confrontation with "U.S. imperialism" and Washington's reciprocal stance of "containing Chinese aggression."

These explicit foreign policy analyses parallel the handling of the Soviet Union and India as discussed earlier in connection with the MAC outline for national defense in 1961. Neither country was portrayed as threatening imminent invasion or subversion, although both posed general problems which required PLA attention in suppressing rebellion and strengthening border defenses. Similarly while the overt enemy, the United States and its allies, was consistently addressed in terms of major war, no sense of imminent danger was expressed.

The continued economic crisis and its attendant impact on domestic disunity apparently evoked a review of foreign policy as the winter of 1961–62 showed increasing strain from the cumulative effects of three years of deteriorating production and consumption. On February 21–22, 1962, Liu Shao-ch'i reportedly convened an enlarged session of the CCP Politbureau Standing Committee.[95] According to a later Cultural Revolution document, Liu recalled that "a certain comrade . . . advocated a policy of three reconciliations and one reduction [*san ho yi shao*]." As amplified elsewhere, this proposal urged a lessening of tension with "the imperialists [the United States], the reactionaires [India], and the revisionists [the Soviet Union]." In addition, "reducing aid to the world revolution" was advocated in this general posture of lessening external tensions and costs at a time of increasing domestic problems.

While the documentation does not describe the full policy discussion or identify all the participants and their respective positions, two main points make this report plausible. First, the PLA documents suggest a debate over assessment of and policy toward the United States as early as the spring of 1961. For instance, President Kennedy's press conference of March 9, 1961, "concerning Sino-American relations" was described as "pompous and somewhat bewildering."[96] This was not a wholly inaccurate description, given the rambling and contradictory nature of the president's remarks. In contrast with his usually precise performance, Kennedy vacillated as he bridged the traditional "hard-line" posture with a hesitant indicator of "soft" possibilities. After reminding his audience that the Chinese "have been . . . extremely belligerent towards us, and they have been unfailing in their attacks upon the United States," he added, "Of course, I think part of that has been because they recognize that the United States is committed to maintaining its connections with other countries, committed to its own defense and the defense of freedom." He then noted, "I would like to see a lessening of . . . tension . . . but we are not prepared to surrender in order to get a relaxation of that."

With no more specific reference than these remarks, the PLA analyst continued, "Recently . . . from 'two Chinas' the United States has changed to seeing 'one and a half China.' It has virtually admitted that China has suzerainty over Taiwan, making Taiwan into a 'semi-independent' state. . . . Some people are saying that [if] half of Taiwan is conceded, China may stop there!" The writer hastened to warn that " 'One and a half China' is in reality a crystallization of the plot of 'two Chinas'; it is a cup of poisonous wine, sweet in taste but strong poison, which we can never drink." Whether "some people" were inside or outside China was not made clear. Nevertheless the identification of an express concession by Washington in 1961 could be linked with the conciliatory posture of the United States in the Geneva negotiations over Laos and could justify a "reconciliation" in early 1962.[97]

Second, "reconciliation" with Moscow remained a distinct possibility, as evidenced by the official *People's Daily* editorial on February 14, 1962, commemorating the twelfth anniversary of the Sino-Soviet Treaty of Friendship, Alliance, and Mutual Assistance.[98] Despite the bitter confrontation between Chou and Khrushchev in Moscow the previous fall, principally over Soviet pressure against Albania, the editorial continued to praise the alliance for among other things, the two countries' mutual policy to "assist, support, and cooperate with each other in the fields of economy, science, and culture. . . . In the course of their socialist construction the Chinese people have received tremendous assistance from the Soviet Union, and we will always be sincerely grateful for this." *Pravda's* reciprocal editorial pointedly called attention to cultural exchanges scheduled for 1962, the "large number of Chinese students" studying at universities and technical institutes throughout the U.S.S.R., and the presence of Chinese scientists in the Joint Institute of Nuclear Research at Dubna.[99] Moreover it revived a celebrated but rarely quoted statement issued by Khrushchev during the 1958 Taiwan Strait crisis, "An attack on the Chinese People's Republic—which is a great friend, ally, and neighbor of our country—is an attack on the Soviet Union."[100] This exchange was followed by a muting of polemical attacks and responses in the early spring.[101] In short, the handling of the United States and the Soviet Union provides credibility to the reported Feburary proposal for a lessening of tension.

As a final observation, Liu's alleged reference to "a certain comrade" implies that someone other than he, perhaps Chou En-lai, advanced the *san ho yi shao* line. During the 1967 Cultural Revolution attacks Liu was initially called "China's Khrushchev" and was later identified by name. Chou's proximity to Mao precluded attacking him directly for all but a few exceptionally daring Red Guard groups.[102] Chou's domination of foreign affairs, first as foreign minister and after 1958 through his successor and close deputy, Ch'en Yi, together with his past posture of moderation and diplomacy abroad, makes him a likely proponent of a more conciliatory line.

This tantalizing glimpse of a foreign policy debate dictated by domestic crisis cannot be examined further because of insufficient evidence. At this point, however, the debate is worth noting for several reasons. First, it suggests a keen appreciation of internal weakness as a constraint on foreign policy, especially with regard to the three perceived opponents, the United States, India, and the Soviet Union. Second, it suggests that divisions may have existed, not only among individuals but also among groups and perhaps even between coalitions within the regime. While these divisions cannot be documented with the available evidence, they can reasonably be hypothesized as remaining in dynamic interaction through the year. Their respective influence on policy and behavior also can be assumed to depend, at least in part, on the perceived intentions and behavior of the three opponents. Thus, while analysis is compelled to "black-box" the decision makers and their respective groups under the general rubric of "Peking," "the Chinese," and "the government," the probability must be recognized that different perspectives and positions characterized various bureaucratic leaders and that their respective roles and influence also varied over time.

The Stage is Set

Depending upon one's vantage point and time frame, quite different backgrounds might be depicted as setting the stage for Sino-Indian confrontation in 1962. A distant observer could see the absence of authority and bilateral agreement on the border through the first half of the century as both natural and mutually tolerable to the interests of India and China. When each consolidated its modern state power, some jockeying for position at the frontier was predictable, but reason and goodwill could produce an eventual compromise without any serious difficulty.

An Indian analysis, however, would focus on the Chinese construction of a road in Aksai Chin and the forcible ouster of New Delhi's patrol in 1958 as initiating an expansionist policy which sooner or later had to be met with countermeasures. The border clashes in 1959 and further cartographic claims in 1960 presaged Chinese pressure along the entire frontier extending from Ladakh through Nepal, Bhutan, and Sikkim and terminating in NEFA. Weak as it was, the Indian military capability had to demonstrate a determination not to acquiesce passively in an arbitrary, unilateral definition of disputed territory. Because China was inherently weak and had manifested no overt bellicose posture toward India, this "forward policy" of firmness would redress the balance for bargaining over the border and eventual negotiations could resolve the dispute peacefully.

A Chinese view differed from both these perspectives. In the first place the issue was not a minor border question over ownership of marginal land. It involved the vital question of national security. Tibet had once attracted British intervention with relatively little consequence so far as Chinese claims of sovereignty were concerned. Since 1950, however, Tibet had become the target of American subversive efforts in collusion with Peking's civil war enemy on Taiwan. Although the goals of Tibetan insurgents and Chinese Nationalist agents might ultimately diverge, their ability to join forces against Chinese Communist control threatened national security, as vividly demonstrated by the 1959 revolt. In this context, the Aksai Chin road was a vital military communications route that could not be jeopardized by any potential hostile presence nearby.

Second, while China's overall strength had developed at a rapid rate between 1949 and 1959, the disastrous Great Leap Forward had shaken the regime's economic foundations and seriously weakened its sense of control over the populace. The depth and duration of the crisis triggered debate and division at high policy levels while causing widespread malnutrition and unrest among the populace at large. The Hong Kong exodus of May, 1962, only dramatized to the world a situation which had confronted the regime with increasing severity over the previous three years.

In its most sober internal analysis, the regime's estimates specifically linked the problems of economic discontent, border security, and relations with neighboring countries. To be sure, far more guarded language characterized discussion of the Soviet Union and India as compared with the United States and its Chinese Nationalist ally. In no case was the joining of external and internal threat made an urgent concern down to the winter of 1961–62. Nonetheless the potential for trouble existed from at least the Taiwan and Tibetan fronts, and evidence of hostile intent would be accorded particular attention. It was amid this unique sense of vulnerability in Peking that New Delhi activated its long declared but little implemented "forward policy." To compound the problem, Taipei manifested a fresh willingness to prepare for "counterattack against the mainland" while Sinkiang again flared with unrest potentially involving the Soviet Union. Each of the three points of external activity was independent of the other, but all were perceived from the single vantage point of Peking.

Chapter 2

Precrisis Interactions: November, 1961 – June, 1962

Specific interactions between China and India divide the year of November, 1961 to October, 1962 into two periods, precrisis and crisis. The precrisis phase ended in June and is differentiated from the remaining months by the absence of armed clashes. This phase provides the immediate prelude to the 1962 war as distinct from the longer historical setting discussed in chapter 1. In addition it provides a basis for analyzing change in Chinese perceptions of the Indian threat. In this regard, consideration of third country threats, manifested in the Taiwan Strait and Sinkiang crises, enlarges the focus to include the total perspective as seen from Peking within which Indian behavior was assessed.

Chronology

1961

Fall	India implements "forward policy" in Ladakh and NEFA
November 30	China notes that crossing of McMahon Line would be justified by Indian moves in Ladakh

1962

February 26	India claims Chinese crossing of McMahon Line will be regarded as "aggression"
April 13	China publishes twenty-two notes exchanged between December and March
April 30	China issues "strongest protest" over Indian moves in previous two weeks, alleging threat to PLA in Chip Chap valley; warns PLA guards will "defend themselves" if necessary; announces limited resumption of border patrols suspended since 1959

May 1–25	More than 140,000 refugees enter Hong Kong; 60–80,000 flee Sinkiang to Soviet Union
May 11	China charges Indian troops fired near Spanggur on May 5
May 19	China demands India vacate Longju; warns China "will not stand idly by"
May 21–26	China curtails Hong Kong and Sinkiang exodus
May 29	Ch'en Yi press conference depicts United States contemplating landing Chinese Nationalists on mainland or causing "trouble" on Sino-Indian border; warns "Himalayas not fit for waging war"
June 3	*People's Daily* editorializes on "Peaceful Coexistence" with India; expresses confidence disputes will "sooner or later" be solved
June 1–20	PLA moves more than 100,000 troops to reinforce garrison opposite Quemoy
June 25	China warns United States at Warsaw not to back Chinese Nationalist invasion; United States assures China it is opposed to use of force in Taiwan Strait

Because this is a less intensive phase of interaction than the crisis months from July to November, there is no need to attempt a detailed reconstruction of all inputs of Indian behavior which may have affected decisions in Peking, such as parliamentary debates and press opinion. The degree of Chinese attention to such materials is problematic, given the preoccupation with domestic problems and the marginal sense of threat communicated in the Chinese press and diplomatic notes until late April.

A more intriguing question concerns the degree to which Chinese intelligence was able to gain information on secret policy deliberations and to intercept military radio communications. The laxity of Indian security was strikingly revealed during the invasion of the Portuguese colony of Goa in December, 1961. According to General B. M. Kaul who coordinated and led the attack,

> The news of our 'D' Day leaked out to Salazar who in his last telegram to Governor General D'Silva at Goa on the 13th warned that India would attack Goa on the 15 December (which was correct as on [the] 13th). This leakage must have taken place from one of our high Government sources in Delhi. Later the 'D' day was changed to

18 December. Thanks to our lack of security, some officers and other ranks had divulged the 'D' day in their private mail, some of which was intercepted by the Army Headquarters censors.[1]

Whether Chinese knowledge of Indian planning was similarly successful cannot be determined, but the possibility is worth noting as another input to Peking's perspective.

By contrast there is good reason to believe that the PLA was able to intercept Indian military communication at some point during the year. Signal intelligence is a common means of locating foreign military units by radio directional findings focused on communication with their head-quarters. In addition the volume of messages exchanged can provide patterns for interpreting extraordinary preparations for action. On occasion messages are sent in plain text to facilitate rapid exchange, in which case they can be read by the interceptor. Finally, of course, there are situations in which the breaking of military codes permits a full reading of the traffic. The Chinese Communists developed their first signal intelligence capability in 1931.[2] Because of the terrain, some local weaknesses may have existed in the early stages of the border dispute, but this was probably overcome by mid-summer when armed clashes became a serious threat. Thus an awareness of Indian military movements could be obtained by such means well before actual contact occurred between rival patrols.

One final source of information must be mentioned although little evidence is available on its contents. Although the two governments published volumes of diplomatic exchanges between the two foreign ministries, no material was released concerning diplomatic conversations or communications involving third countries. It is highly unlikely that the published documents exhaust the record of all that transpired between Peking and New Delhi, and indeed there are indications to the contrary, both with respect to third country channels in the spring and direct diplomatic contacts in the summer. Speculations on these developments will be included when appropriate but these interactions cannot be traced in the same detail provided by published exchanges.

1961: Preliminary Diplomatic and Military Maneuvers

1960 had brought an end, at least temporarily, to Chinese efforts at direct negotiation of the border dispute. Chou En-lai's abortive trip to New Delhi in the spring was followed by the completion of technical talks between the two staffs in December.[3] The PLA had stopped patrolling the disputed western sector, but it continued to advance its posts in Ladakh, and Peking tabled new maps which advanced its claim in exchanges between the technical staffs.[4] With the domestic situation worsening, however, Chinese strategy persisted in seeking to persuade India to accept the Aksai Chin road while suggesting that compromises in other aspects, including map claims, might be negotiated.

Toward this end, in 1960 the Chinese concluded border settlements favorable to Burma and Nepal.[5] In January General Ne Win signed a preliminary agreement in Peking whereby the PRC ceded the Namwan Assigned Tract to which it had laid claim in 1956. Surveying began in July, with the final accord signed in October by U Nu and demarcation completed by October, 1961. As noted earlier, Peking accepted the McMahon Line's location for the trijuncture of China, India, and Burma at the Diphu pass.[6] Although New Delhi protested the settlement as predetermining the trijuncture without its participation and in addition claimed the actual point lay five miles to the north through another pass, the agreement clearly implied a willingness to legitimize the entire McMahon Line. Meanwhile negotiations with Nepal, begun in March 1960, abandoned the previous map claims that China's boundary included the summit of Mount Everest. In October, 1961, the final agreement was announced in Peking during a visit by King Mahendra, together with a PRC proposal to construct a highway between Lhasa and Katmandu.

These moves could signal compromise or they might merely mean additional pressure to isolate India and force Nehru into negotiations on Peking's terms. In New Delhi the latter reasoning prevailed as evidenced by the protest over the Sino-Burmese accord. Until Chinese troops evacuated all disputed land, there would be no negotiations. In Peking, however, the moves seem to have been designed more as an inducement to compromise. This was a period of increasing domestic discontent and rising regime concern over rebellion and border security, as shown in the PLA documents. Moreover unconfirmed reports in April and May of 1961 claimed an effort to involve Burma in facilitating Sino-Indian negotiations, beginning with acceptance of the trijuncture at the McMahon Line.[7] But concession by China would have required a reciprocal concession by India, and there was no indication of any inclination to cede Aksai Chin.

On the contrary, Indian determination increased with the strengthening of PLA capabilities ordered in the January, 1961, outline of border defense needs.[8] In the summer of 1961 reconnaissance discovered new feeder roads to the westernmost PLA positions, including a new outpost in the Chip Chap valley.[9] A meeting of high level civilian and military officials concluded this signaled Peking's intention to occupy the entire claimed area unless challenged by an Indian presence. On November 2 an important directive formalized the "forward policy" in language which was further strengthened in official Army directives of December 5 to commanders of the eastern and western sectors:

> *[In Ladakh]* we are to patrol as far forward as possible from our present positions towards the International Border as recognized by us. This will be done with a view to establishing additional posts located *to prevent the Chinese from advancing further and also to dominate any Chinese posts already established in our territory.* . . . This "Forward Policy" shall be carried out without getting involved in a clash with the Chinese unless it becomes necessary in self-defense.[10] [Italics added.]

The italicized words sowed the seeds of conflict, despite the subsequent admonition against armed clashes except as "necessary in self-defense." This order allowed considerable discretionary authority to Indian patrols, in contrast with the strict PLA injunction against any response to local incidents without a full report to and reply from higher headquarters.[11] Such discretion not only relied on the judgment of troops remote from a support base and moving under extremely hazardous conditions of terrain and weather, but it left the fuller interpretation to subordinates in a military system that was badly divided on how forward a policy should be adopted under circumstances of military inferiority. Moreover such divisions were compounded as between military and civilian authority, as amply documented in the recriminating memoir of General Kaul and the insightful history by Maxwell.[12] Kaul claimed that "Nehru framed this policy principally for the benefit of the Parliament and the public and also perhaps as a 'strategy' of beating the Chinese at their own game. . . . He saw in it one reply to his critics."[13]

However political may have been the decision, its implementation had to be military in consequence, as revealed by Kaul:

> By the end of the year we had established over fifty posts in Ladakh and NEFA and hence our occupation rights in some 200

square miles of Indian territory. These posts were not set up for the purpose of administration, as there was no population there, but to ensure that the Chinese did not repeat the Aksai Chin story in NEFA or even in Ladakh.[14]

Essential to the November decision to "dominate" PLA outposts was the assumption that the PLA would remain passive and disciplined, avoiding either deliberate retaliation elsewhere or localized resistance. This was coincidentally challenged by an MFA protest of November 30, just prior to the enabling orders to Indian command headquarters. Referring to earlier activity, near Demchok and Spanggur Lake, the note denied New Delhi's claim that the new posts were "within boundary lines unilaterally claimed by India and that therefore whatever actions the Indian side may take, these do not constitute intrusions into Chinese territory."[15] The note warned that "such logic" was "untenable and also most dangerous." It continued:

Taking the case of the Eastern Sector . . . the Chinese Government has always held that this sector of the boundary lies along the Southern foot of the Himalayas and that the so-called "McMahon Line" is totally illegal. *If the Indian Government's above logic should be followed, the Chinese Government would have every reason to send troops to cross the so-called "McMahon Line"* and enter the vast area between the crest of the Himalayas and their Southern foot. But the Chinese Government has never done so and all Chinese military and administrative personnel, acting upon orders, have not crossed the so-called "McMahon Line." [Italics added.]

India did not reply until February 26, 1962, at which time it explicitly alleged a perceived threat of a Chinese "tit for tat" response in NEFA for Indian activity in Ladakh:

It seems preposterous . . . to argue that because the Government of India continued to exercise lawful jurisdiction over the territories that traditionally belong to them, the Government of China would be justified in crossing the so-called "McMahon Line." . . . The Government of India takes strong exception to the Chinese attempt to reply to the Government of India's protest against Chinese aggression in the Western Sector by threatening aggression elsewhere. If the threat materializes and Chinese forces attempt to cross the "McMahon Line," the Government of India would regard it as a further instance of aggression, and take such action as may be necessary to meet this further aggression.[16]

The Chinese reference to the "Eastern Sector" was seen as bluff or blackmail in New Delhi, while it was more likely designed as a debating point in Peking. So flagrant a move as occupying NEFA just as China was entering its second winter of discontent would not seem a credible effort to force negotiations. In fact, the PLA documents of 1961 and the February, 1962, policy debate argued for a low posture of "reconciliation with the reactionaries." Notwithstanding New Delhi's interpretation to the contrary, this introduction of the "Eastern Sector" as a potential offset to the "Western Sector" was almost certainly not intended as a threat. This point is important to establish because in the crisis context of July, 1962, Peking did threaten a response in NEFA if New Delhi did not desist in Ladakh, but under wholly different circumstances of posture and context. For New Delhi, however, the later threat merely amplified perceptions of Chinese designs on NEFA already signaled in the note of November 30, 1961.[17]

An additional dimension to calculations in New Delhi paradoxically paralleled those in Peking which downgraded the threat latent in the opponent's capability to make good his declared intention of holding claimed territory with force if need be. Just as Chinese statements at this time showed no serious alarm—logically enough, given extant limitations on Indian military force in the Himalayas—so the evidence suggests that perceptions in New Delhi discounted a Chinese capacity and will to stand firm because of internal conditions. In fact, Kaul attributes to Nehru views strikingly similar to those reflected in the captured PLA documents, perhaps reflecting knowledge of their contents as communicated by American officials in New Delhi or Washington:

> Nehru believed—on seeing reports by some of his Ambassadors, the assessment of his Foreign Office, the advice of some of his political and other confidants—that the Chinese were really not so strong, as they were made out to be, and had many of their own troubles; they had internal disorders due to food shortage, floods, and an unpopular dictatorial regime; that there were revolts in Tibet, and on the whole, the morale of the Chinese people and their Armed Forces was cracking up; and that if we dealt with them strongly, we should have the better of them.... Nehru felt that due to this background, the Chinese were in no position to divert their attention to anything except putting their own internal matters right.[18]

Public governmental reactions to Chinese statements highlighted their aggressive intent, while privately the "forward policy" was justified as a no-risk action which would not meet any serious Chinese resistance. Both postures interlocked to keep momentum behind the policy, on the one hand proving governmental determination and on the other hand facing no perceived constraint from the enemy. By the time this private perception changed as a result of actual clashes that summer, the public posture had made policy a hostage of nationalist and opposition politics. The result was war.

Winter stopped virtually all activity in the Himalayan highlands and nothing further occurred there to cause Chinese concern. However, the year ended with an unprecedented display of Indian militaristic nationalism elsewhere, with explicit reference to the border dispute. In mid-December New Delhi's forces quickly overran and occupied the Portuguese colony of Goa.[19] Despite the obvious dissimilarity between the power which China, as compared with Portugal, could bring to bear on India, Nehru responded to a post-victory press query on ousting the PLA, "The use of force is, of course, open to us and should be used by us according to suitability and opportunity."[20] The following February, his Home Minister, Lal Bahadur Shastri, declared, "If the Chinese will not vacate the areas occupied by her, India will have to repeat what she did in Goa. She will certainly drive out the Chinese forces."[21]

One final conciliatory gesture by Peking closed out 1961. On December 3 the Ministry of Foreign Affairs noted that the 1954 "Agreement on Trade and Intercourse between the Tibet Region of China and The Republic of India" would expire in June, 1962.[22] Referring to the famous Five Principles, the MFA "with a view of consolidating and developing the traditional friendship between the peoples of China and India and promoting the economic and cultural interflow between the two countries" proposed that a new agreement be negotiated. New Delhi lost little time in replying, in contrast with its three-month delayed response to the November 30 demarche which linked NEFA with Ladakh. On December 15, the Ministry of External Affairs, in a note three times the length of Peking's proposal, flatly refused negotiations until there was a "reversal of the aggressive policies followed by the Government of the People's Republic of China during the last few years." This rebuff was replete with accusations of Chinese encroachments "at first insidiously and later openly" on Indian territory to the extent of having "actually occupied by force over 12,000 square miles" through "aggressive military activity."[23] Thus 1961 ended with public postures of Chinese flexibility and Indian intransigence. However, nothing had basically changed the military balance wherein the PLA clearly prevailed in both the west and the east.

Spring, 1962: Moves and Countermoves

The "forward policy" moved into high gear in 1962, triggering a succession of developments that culminated in war. To summarize, a flurry of Chinese protests was followed by the full publication of their contents in *People's Daily*. Increasing concern was evidenced in April and May, but events elsewhere preempted attention in June. However, beginning in July armed incidents changed concern to anxiety and prompted China to a dual posture of public threats and private negotiations. With the failure of these negotiations in August, Peking increased both military and political deterrence warnings in September. After more serious clashes and the final Indian rejection of negotiations, the PLA forced a major military showdown in October and November.

The gradual stiffening of Chinese responses to India's "forward policy" moves is easily traced during the spring of 1962 when better weather and improved Indian logistic capabilities accelerated implementation of the November, 1961, directives. At the outset in January, *People's Daily* inconspicuously reported three items concerning Nehru's election pledge to recover Indian territory together with accusations against China by his finance minister and the Indian press. Refusing to answer in kind, Liu Shao-ch'i and Chou En-lai cabled congratulations on India's national day, January 26, while Ch'en Yi publicly reaffirmed the Five Principles the next day.

Privately Peking combined its rejection of Indian charges with countercharges and a renewed proposal for negotiations. In a lengthy note of February 26, the MFA reaffirmed its 1959 policy of suspending patrols "within twenty kilometres on its side of the boundary" while noting that "In the past year and more, [India] has shifted its emphasis in occupying China's territory to the western sector of the Sino-Indian boundary, where Indian troops have steadily pushed forward, continually set up new checkposts, and extended their scope of patrol on China's territory. Indian aircraft have intruded into Chinese air space again and again to carry out willful reconnaissance and harrassment [*sic*]."[24] Returning to the November 30 note which linked the McMahon Line's status with the western boundary, the MFA explicitly stated that the point was solely one of principle and not of threatened action:

> ...Although the Chinese Government does not recognize the so-called McMahon line ... yet ... it has strictly restrained all its military and administrative personnel from crossing this line. If, like the Indian Government, the Chinese Government had also taken unilateral actions to violate the status quo of the boundary, what would the relations between the two countries have been like? The Chinese Government has not done so and considers that it should not do so.

The last sentence went beyond the November 30 note by communicating express policy, at least for the near future. By coincidence, on the same day this was sent India dispatched its rejection of threatened "aggression" allegedly communicated in the earlier note.

The February 26 statement closed with a regretful recollection of Chou's abortive visit to Nehru in 1960 but declared, "Premier Chou En-lai still hoped that negotiations would continue between the two sides. As far as the Chinese side is concerned, the door for negotiations is still open." It noted a Nehru speech of February 11 which "indicated that India wanted to settle the Sino-Indian border dispute through peaceful means and not to create an everlasting enmity with China. The Chinese Government hopes that this indicated desire will be translated into action." A paragraph echoing the Five Principles ended the note.

The February 26 message apparently implemented the "reconciliation with the reactionaries" line proposed earlier that month. Nevertheless, New Delhi's reply of March 13 adamantly restated its standard position, " ... the withdrawal of Chinese forces from Indian territory into which they have intruded since 1957 is an essential step for the creation of a favorable climate for any negotiations."[25] At this point Chinese policy makers decided to increase their pressure on New Delhi by making their case public. Previously successive Indian "White Papers" had published verbatim texts of notes exchanged between the two capitals, beginning in 1959. In February, 1961, the entire six-hundred page report of the 1960 technical staff meetings was presented in Parliament. Now on April 13, 1962, Peking released its translation of the report, together with twenty-two notes exchanged between December and April.[26] Publication was ostensibly necessary for consideration of the dispute at the Third Session of the Second National People's Congress. However, the lack of any immediate urgency for policy decisions on the one hand and any genuine legislative power by the Congress on the other suggest this was an excuse to justify the release of confidential materials.

In this context of anticipated publication the Chinese note of March 22 is significant. Its unusual length had little to do with recent incidents but the note itself provided a good recapitulation of China's position for the public record. In addition, its restatement of earlier arguments served to remind India of essential rather than secondary concerns. Finally the actual timing of the note, as well as the decision both to compete and to communicate with New Delhi through public media, seems responsive to the Indian statement of March 13 which was correctly interpreted as foreclosing any possible negotiations in the near future. In this regard, it is interesting that exactly one month separated this statement from the April 13 release of documents, an interval that will be subsequently seen as repeatedly coinciding with important steps in Chinese policy planning and implementation.

To speculate further, the MFA February 26 note with its emphasis on negotiations may have been seen in Peking as eliciting one of two responses, either a willingness to negotiate or renewed Indian intransigence. Contingency planning for the latter eventuality could have included compiling a record for public revelation which would improve Peking's image at home and abroad. In addition to the February note, various reports claim that at this time the Chinese privately indicated their willingness to abandon their maximum map claims and to compromise on the actual line of occupation. Thus, the instructions to prepare a public record within a month of the March 13 response could have made final release contingent upon any negative indicators of New Delhi's position, including its response to the March 22 protest.

In this regard, the MFA protest made a particular point of noting, "It was especially unexpected that the Indian Government, in its note of March 13, 1962, took a negative attitude towards the Chinese Government's friendly indication for a peaceful settlement of the boundary question through negotiations."[27] After citing the Indian condition for talks quoted above, it summarized the entire record concerning the Aksai Chin road:

> . . . To say nothing of the remote past, after the founding of the People's Republic of China it was by the traditional route running

through this area that Chinese troops in 1950 entered the Ari District of Tibet from Sinkiang. From 1954 to 1957, China surveyed and constructed the 1200 kilometre-long Sinkiang-Tibet Highway which traverses this area. Before the summer of 1958 the Indian Government had never questioned or objected to the exercise of sovereignty in this area by the Chinese Government. The Indian Government stated in its note that it was in 1958 that the Chinese Government began to enter the Aksai Chin area. This statement is a distortion of the fact and does not merit any attention.

The detailed treatment of this portion of the dispute, in contrast with only passing reference to the McMahon Line and the so-called "middle sector," strengthens the plausibility of implied concessions communicated through other channels. However, Nehru's insistence on a complete Chinese withdrawal before any negotiations constituted a fundamental impasse since such a withdrawal would leave the Aksai Chin road defenseless and dependent upon the outcome of negotiations. Easy access would be provided by such Indian outposts as Demchok in the south, Khurnak Fort, Daulat Beg Oldi at the Karakoram Pass, and the Chip Chap Valley.

The weakness of Indian forces in the area together with poor logistical support from lower areas did not yet pose a serious threat to the PLA in the Aksai Chin plateau. Maxwell summarized the situation:

> . . . The towering, naked ridges kept the [Indian] troops to the valleys, a necessity confirmed by the need to have flat dropping zones on to which the Air Force could parachute their supplies. The general altitude was in the region of 14,000 feet, and passes took the patrols up as high as 16,000 feet. The temperatures were frigid, and the troops' winter clothing was inadequate and in short supply, the rarified air meant that the troops could carry only small loads themselves; mules were not much use at those altitudes and there were few of these in any event, and no yaks which were the only reliable pack animal in such conditions. All supplies, often including water, had to be airdropped. When the forward policy began to be put into effect the Leh-based 114 Brigade still had only three battalions in command—one regular, two militia. These troops were between them responsible for a front of more than two hundred miles, stretching from the Karakoram Pass to a few miles beyond Demchok.[28]

Under these circumstances, Peking was neither willing to concede nor threatened by a superior enemy. Therefore it closed its lengthy statement with its standard offer to negotiate all differences without any withdrawals by either side.

The document's brief reference to possible threats from the Taiwan Strait area is notable as precedent for more substantive anxieties two months later. It said, "To date China's Taiwan is still under armed U.S. occupation and China's security is continuously threatened by U.S. imperialism. How is it thinkable that China in turn should commit aggression against Indian territory?" This is more a rhetorical response to Indian accusations than a genuine argument against the plausibility of Chinese escalation in the face of possible attack from a second front. Nevertheless the coupling of the United States–Chiang Kai-shek threat with the border dispute suggests an additional dimension of concern in Chinese thinking already present at this time.

On April 13, *People's Daily* headlined on page one its publication of the Sino-Indian diplomatic exchanges and staff study, inaugurating a new pattern of publicity for the conflict. Thereafter Chinese protests appeared in print within three days of their transmission. All aspects of the relationship won public attention, as indicated in this first release which included twelve notes alleging Indian air and ground intrusions, seven dealing with general boundary questions, and three concerning the trade and exchange agreement scheduled to expire in June. On April 22, "Observer" writing in the *People's Daily* reintroduced the long dormant issue of subversive designs on Tibet, linking New Delhi with Taipei under the heading "It Is Vain and Futile To Try To Interfere in Tibet."[29] He recapitulated a January 26 dispatch by the Indian *Statesman* alleging that a "Tibetan Welfare Association" in Darjeeling, "organized by the secret agents of the Chiang Kai-shek gang," had reopened to distribute funds to refugees. An Agence France Presse dispatch of April 6 from Taiwan was quoted to the effect that "on the basis of a plan advanced by an 'influential Tibetan leader now in India,' the Chiang Kai-shek gang contemplates training in Taiwan 2,000 Tibetan youths as 'future leaders' of Tibet." The writer warned:

> Obviously, U.S. imperialism and the Chiang Kai-shek gang are actively planning to help Tibetan serfowners to stage a comeback riding once again on the backs of the people of Tibet. But apart from them, it appears that there are also many others who want to make use of the Tibetan rebels sheltering in India. The *Statesman* has gone even further; it openly proposes that support for the Dalai

Lama and for the "Tibetan refugees" be made part of Indian policy towards China. It was amidst this clamouring that the Dalai Lama inspected the "Tibetan refugee camps" in March and met the Indian President, the Vice-President and Prime Minister Nehru. Nehru, according to a London *Times* report, took the initiative in meeting the Dalai Lama and took Defense Minister Krishna Menon along with him. It is not without reason that the *Times* should mention the Dalai Lama as "a significant factor" in the Sino-Indian "border dispute."

Peking's decision to intensify its public pressure on New Delhi, inter alia alerting domestic audiences to increasing tensions on the Himalayan border, brought no slackening of New Delhi's "forward policy." On the contrary, April saw a significant increase in the implementation of that policy to which Peking responded with an important change in its military and political posture. Indian patrols, moving from their base at Daulat Beg Oldi near the Karakoram Pass, advanced down the Chip Chap river valley to occupy a commanding height in the vicinity of a Chinese outpost while intensifying aerial and ground reconnaissance in the general area. On April 30 Peking issued a "strongest protest" which detailed fifteen alleged "provocations" between April 15 and April 27 in the sharpest language employed since the armed clashes of 1959:

> ... What is more serious, both to the southwest and northwest of the Chinese post, Indian troops have established aggressive posts with fortifications which are obviously meant for prolonged entrenchment. This shows that Indian troops are pressing on the Chinese post and carrying out provocation and would not scruple to create another [*sic*] incident of bloodshed. The Chinese Government ... demands that the Indian Government immediately withdraw the Indian military posts and intruding Indian troops from Chinese territory. *Should the Indian Government refuse to withdraw its aggressive posts and continue to carry out provocation against the Chinese post, the Chinese frontier guards will be forced to defend themselves.* The Indian side will be wholly responsible for the consequences arising therefrom.[30] [Italics added.]

After accusing India of taking advantage of China's suspension of patrols, the note declared:

> ... In these circumstances, *the Chinese Government,* exercising its sacred right to defend China's territory and maintain the tranquil-

lity on the border, *has ordered Chinese frontier guards to resume border patrols in the sector from Karakoram Pass to Kongka Pass,* where recently the Indian side has made repeated intrusions and harassments. . . . If India continues to invade and occupy China's territory and expand the area of its intrusion and harassment on China's border, the Chinese Government will be compelled to consider the further step of resuming border patrols along the entire Sino-Indian boundary. [Italics added.]

The Pace Quickens, Tensions Rise

The threat to resume patrolling along the entire border, suspended since 1959, together with the references to possible "bloodshed" and Chinese guards being "forced to defend themselves," signaled a major change in Peking's position from its February 26 note. One stimulus to a stronger posture was the increase in Indian capability manifested by increased air activity, both for reconnaissance and for the dropping of supplies. According to PLA reports, between March 6 and April 30 sixty-seven airspace violations occurred "with the intrusions over the western sector the most serious . . . in direct co-ordination with the setting up of new military strong points on Chinese territory and other recent Indian activities of intrusion and provocation on the ground."[31] The rate increased in May, allegedly reaching fifty-nine sorties in one month with "all intrusions . . . concentrated in the western sector." Specifically, "about 80 parachutes were dropped on May 23, over forty bales of supplies were dropped on May 25, and over thirty bales of supplies were dropped on May 27."[32]

If supplies could be dropped, so could troops. Previous PLA calculations based on the tortuous land routes now were challenged by New Delhi's growing ability to support operations in the high Himalayan plateau. This could interdict supply lines to PLA outposts and force their eventual withdrawal. In addition the Aksai Chin road could be cut. Without an adequate air defense system complete with radar and fighter bases, western Tibet lay vulnerable to a combined air and ground penetration.

This qualitative change in Indian capabilities triggered an appreciably higher level of articulated threat perceptions in *People's Daily* associated with reports of air intrusions as compared with other actions. The greater sensitivity to air than to ground movements became even more marked during the subsequent crisis period that summer and fall, but its appearance in the spring suggests apprehension of the new activity. Nor were

Chinese concerns allayed by the political climate in New Delhi. Rising apprehension over the border evoked disquieting reports in April and parliamentary discussion in May.[33] On May 2 Nehru declared that "India does not want, and dislikes very much, a war with China. But that is not within India's control," adding that the government was prepared for any contingency. The next day he admitted the Chinese were "rather annoyed" because Indian posts had moved behind the PLA, but "there is nothing to be alarmed at, although the [April 30] note threatens all kinds of steps they might take. If they do take those steps we shall be ready for them."[34] This claim was reinforced by orders on May 1 to 1,800 troops in Srinagar for movement to Ladakh and the Chip Chap area. The next day General Kaul dispatched them with a "fight to the death" speech whose contents seemed a direct response to the April 30 resumption of limited patrolling by Chinese border guards.

According to Maxwell, in "early May" one of the two Indian outposts in the Chip Chap valley was threatened by a PLA advance "in assault formation, giving every indication that they meant to wipe it out."[35] The local commander reportedly requested permission to withdraw but Nehru believed the Chinese were "making a show of force to test India's resolution" and refused permission, instead ordering that the garrison be reinforced. When the PLA did not attack, he appeared to be vindicated and the "forward policy" was seemingly shown to be without risk. No record of the incident exists in the published exchanges and it may have resulted from confused reporting since nothing in the PLA posture at this time makes it credible.[36]

At approximately the same time, however, another reported incident illustrated the risks of localized behavior, remote from command and control, that could provoke armed clashes. A Chinese protest of May 11 alleged that on May 5 two Indian guards in the Spanggur Lake area fired three shots at a Chinese outpost.[37] The MFA noted that had the outpost not held its fire "very serious consequences" could have resulted, and accused New Delhi of trying "to create incidents of bloodshed." The protest repeated verbatim the April 30 demand for Indian withdrawal lest Chinese frontier guards be forced "to defend themselves." This was the first recorded charge of actual firing by either side. The six-day delay in Peking's response suggests extra care in verifying the incident, perhaps also permitting a review of other areas to determine whether it was isolated or part of a deliberately more aggressive Indian posture.

Suddenly Peking shifted its emphasis to the eastern end of the border, using singular deterrence language reminiscent of the Korean War but masking this from public view. The point at issue was Longju, scene of an armed clash in August, 1959. Claimed by both sides through a disputed interpretation of the McMahon Line, it had remained unoccupied by joint agreement. In April New Delhi alleged Peking had violated this agreement in January. On May 15 the MFA rejected the charge on two grounds: there had been no Chinese visit, and the area was indisputably Chinese.[38] Moreover "there is reason to believe that the aim of the Indian Government . . . is to seek pretexts for India's further violations of the status quo of the boundary and precipitation of new armed clashes in this area. The Chinese Government cannot but regard this with gravity and is closely following the development of events."

This note had hardly arrived in New Delhi when a more ominous tone emerged in a protest of May 19, alleging that "at noon on April 28, 1962, ten fully armed Indian military personnel intruded into Chinese territory at Longju . . . and did not leave till they had carried out military reconnaissance there.[39] After repeating the accusatory language of May 15, the note concluded:

> The Chinese Government demands that the Indian Government desist immediately from its intrusion into Longju; otherwise *the Chinese Government will not stand idly by* seeing its territory once again unlawfully invaded and occupied, and the Indian Government must bear the responsibility for all the grave consequences arising therefrom. [Italics added.]

The salient phrase "will not stand idly by" had not appeared previously in 1962. It had first achieved political prominence in the abortive effort to deter United Nations Commander General Douglas MacArthur from occupying North Korea. On October 10, 1950, the MFA warned, "Now that the American forces are attempting to cross the thirty-eighth parallel on a large scale, the Chinese people cannot stand idly by with regard to such a serious situation created by the invasion of Korea . . . and to the dangerous trend towards extending the war."[40] Two weeks later the "Chinese People's Volunteers" attacked forty miles below the Yalu River.

Not only did the phrase have an historic and alarming precedent, but it had originally followed two private warnings communicated through the Indian ambassador in Peking, K. M. Panikkar. On September 25, 1950, the acting PLA Chief of Staff had informally remarked at dinner that the PRC would not "sit back with folded hands and let the Americans come to the border."[41] More pointedly, on October 2 Chou summoned Panikkar to a midnight meeting, declaring that should American forces invade North Korea China would intervene.[42] Thus, New Delhi had played a crucial role linking Peking with Washington.

Peking's awareness of these impressive antecedents may explain the decision merely to summarize the May 19 protest in *People's Daily*, instead of reprinting it verbatim as was the custom down to and including the May 15 note, with no public reference to the implied ultimatum or to the phrase "will not stand idly by." Thus, neither domestic nor foreign audiences were alerted to the full implications of this heightened deterrence signal.

Yet the two notes in tandem, together with the exceptional phraseology and treatment of the second, suggest a further qualitative change in the Chinese posture. Earlier references to the eastern sector had explicitly raised it as a hypothetical rejoinder to the western developments, coupled with assurances the status quo would continue. It is possible that Chinese perceptions were singularly sensitive to Longju because of the clash there in August, 1959. However, the note provided no evidence of a continued Indian presence after April 28, fully three weeks before its issuance, nor is there independent evidence of any strategic or tactical change in the respective forces in the area at this time. In fact, Longju did not reappear as a point of serious confrontation, diplomatic or military, until the fall.

On balance, it seems more likely that Chinese concern was aroused to this particular peak of protest not because of events in Longju but because of the larger context of Indian behavior. Nehru's belligerent posture in Parliament, the continued increase in air activity, and the movement of nearly 2,000 additional troops toward Ladakh added new elements of seriousness to the situation. Having so recently escalated its deterrence warnings in the western sector, the MFA may have felt compelled to find any pretext for capping the new posture with the May 19 thrust. If so, the "will not stand idly by" signal was preplanned and independent of specific situations so long as Indian behavior remained generally consistent with the "forward policy."

No change in the PLA posture followed this unusual statement. Contrary to the implications of the April 30 note, patrols remained limited to the short western sector between the Karakorum and Kongka passes. This apparent ambivalence over how hard a line to adopt was reflected in the press handling of Sino-Indian affairs. Measured in terms of placement, space, and the level of threat articulated in headlines, a marked ebb in *People's Daily* coverage appeared during May 23–31 followed by an unprecedented peak on all scores for June 1–7. Then the dispute virtually disappeared from its pages, except for two days, until July. The thrust of different media also varied. On June 3, when the Sino-Indian treaty of trade and intercourse expired, *People's Daily* ran its first editorial of the year, "The Radiance of the Principles of Peaceful Coexistence Can Never Be Obscured," on the relationship. The Five Principles had been first enunciated in treaty form in the 1954 accord, and expanding this theme, *People's Daily* declared, "The Chinese Government and people will never change their stand of safeguarding Sino-Indian amity . . . through negotiations on the basis of the Five Principles of Peaceful Coexistence. . . . The disputes between the countries will sooner or later be solved in a fair and reasonable way."

No such confidence was reflected in *Peking Review,* however, with its cover-page headed, "India Plays a Dangerous Game."[43] After recapitulating various past charges, the writer dealt at length with New Delhi's suppression of material disseminated by the Chinese embassy, including a news bulletin and copies of *Peking Review,* both of which had been burned by demonstrators outside the embassy on May 25. Preceding his article was a report on "Democratic Reform in Tibet" while immediately following was a *People's Daily* editorial and an MFA note, both rejecting New Delhi's protest over the announced intention of China and Pakistan to negotiate a provisional boundary agreement involving Kashmir. In short, the principal medium reflecting Chinese policy abroad made confrontation with India its prime focus of attention while the main domestic medium sounded a more optimistic line.

As between the two postures, that of *Peking Review* more truly reflected the MFA which dispatched three stiff notes on June 2 to the Indian embassy in Peking. One dealt with a six-month-old running exchange concerning the PRC Consulate-General in Calcutta and its prerogatives over a Chinese school in Kalimpong allegedly shut down because "Indian local authorities had . . . connived with the scheming activities of Chiang Kai-shek elements."[44] A second argued at length over India's responsibility for violating the Five Principles and allowing the trade agreement to expire.[45] The third and most pointedly worded responded to New Delhi's sole concessionary move of this period. On May 14, India had rejected the April 30 threat of resumed patrols as proof "the Chinese Government propose to adopt further aggressive measures and precipitate clashes."[46] However, ostensibly to avoid undesirable incidents, the note restated Nehru's proposal to Chou of November 16, 1959, whereby both sides would withdraw from all territory in the western sector claimed by either party. "The Government of India are prepared, in the interest of a peaceful settlement, to permit, pending negotiations and settlement of the boundary question, the continued use of the Aksai Chin road for Chinese civilian traffic."

The MFA response of June 2 was contemptuous of the offer, noting, "Why should China need to ask India's permission for using its own road on its own territory? What an absurdity!"[47] Unmentioned but undoubtedly noticed was the attendant restriction limiting the road to "civilian" and not "military" traffic. As for the withdrawal proposal, Peking reminded New Delhi of Chou's initial response of December 17, 1959, "that it is unfair and that, though 'equitable' it may appear, it in fact would require China to make a one-sided withdrawal." To prove the point Nehru's own remarks in Parliament of May 14, 1962, were cited: "In the Ladakh area, it meant a very small withdrawal for us—a few villages—and it meant a large withdrawal for them." Finally, the exclusion of the eastern sector as a balancer was interpreted to mean that the Indian Government was not serious.

The June 2 note warned that "a border clash may be touched off at any moment," and charged "that what the Indian Government now seeks is to provoke bloody conflicts, occupy China's territory, and change the *status quo* of the boundary regardless of consequences." It concluded:

> However China will never submit before any threat of force. What is imperative now is for the Indian Government to stop its military provocations and withdraw Indian military strong points and troops from Chinese territory. The Chinese Government renews its protest and demand made on April 30 and May 28. This is a serious test as to whether the Indian Government has the sincerity to settle peacefully the Sino-Indian boundary question and improve Sino-Indian relations.

The note was an exercise in futility, however, as must have been seen in Peking. If "reconciliation" had been a notable failure in February and March, none of the deterrence signals, beginning in April, had slackened the "forward policy." On the contrary, public and private Indian behavior suggested increasing intransigence and determination to turn the tables on the PLA by a systematic military buildup in the western sector. To be sure, Peking's options were limited, as Nehru had correctly surmised. The PRC had already escalated its political posture by publishing the notes and raising the seriousness of its warnings. The PLA had announced on April 30 a limited resumption of patrols, but improving the capability of its logistical network in Tibet was a slow yet absolutely necessary prerequisite to deploying larger forces in the area. New Delhi observed that "Chinese troops are daily intruding into Indian territory, pushing forward on trucks and jeeps, blasting the mountainside with heavy explosives, constructing new military bases and extending military bases already set up."[48] However, the relative increase in local capability was rapidly favoring the Indians, especially in the westernmost portions of the disputed area.

To force a confrontation at this time might have committed the PLA beyond its capacity, not only because of tactical limitations in Tibet but because of responsibilities, actual or potential, associated with domestic problems and perceived external threats elsewhere. Indeed, both the rapid rise in expressed Chinese anxiety over Sino-Indian relations and Peking's failure to maintain a consistent posture may be better understood in the larger context of economic and political problems which beset the regime with unprecedented difficulties beginning in mid-May. On the one hand these problems made the risks of even small clashes on the remote Himalayan frontier particularly worrisome. On the other, they diverted time and energy from Sino-Indian relations to more immediately urgent matters. The effect, in sum, was to interrupt the dialogue between Peking and New Delhi.

Other Problems, Other Areas

The general economic crisis of 1961 continued into 1962, with slight improvement hampered by bad weather. Severe drought hit North China during the first half of the year while excessive rain inundated much of the south.[49] Rainfall along the Yangtse River was forty percent below normal, necessitating "comfort visits" by provincial officials in drought-stricken areas during May. On April 15 *Honan Daily* reported that drought and wind had retarded summer crops and delayed the sowing of autumn crops in the "fourth year of natural adversity for Honan." In Szechwan sixty-seven counties and urban areas faced a near total loss of crops; other areas suffered serious pest infestations. Shantung reported 1.7 million fewer acres under the winter plough because of heavy autumn rains. There is no documentation available to show the degree of local disorder that may have occurred, but the attendant refugee flow from Sinkiang and Kwangtung into Russia and Hong Kong suggests the likelihood of similar tensions elsewhere.

The Hong Kong exodus in particular damaged the regime's image abroad and, in turn, its sense of security from attack. From May 2 to May 26 daily press reports told of thousands streaming across the frontier into emergency camps, with dramatic photos of women and children forced back across the border by British authorities. Chinese Nationalist propaganda organs depicted the country as ripe for revolt. President Kennedy announced an easing in the Chinese immigration quota while the United States, Canada, and Great Britain rushed food relief to Hong Kong.[50]

On May 29 a particularly full summation of the situation as seen in Peking was given publicly by Foreign Minister Ch'en Yi to Japanese journalists. Ch'en ranged widely and authoritatively over Sino-American relations, American policy in Southeast Asia, and the linkage of threats facing China from the United States, Taiwan, and India, omitting only the Soviet Union and Sinkiang in his specific inventory of problems. The May 29 interview merits quotation at length for its perspective on the interlock of domestic and foreign threats:

> . . . The Pentagon generals . . . may support Chiang Kai-shek in starting a "counter-offensive on the mainland" along the coastal areas of Fukien and Chekiang provinces. . . .Or they may be planning to raise trouble on the western border area of China by utilizing the China-India border dispute. . . .As for the China-India border dispute, the question is whether others want to be utilized by America. The Himalayas are not fit for waging a war.
>
> The first possibility is to create an incident in the Taiwan Strait. Thinking particularly that the Chinese economic situation is difficult they may attempt to have Chiang Kai-shek land on the mainland and start a civil war. . . .America is aiming to kill two birds with one stone. If Chiang Kai-shek should succeed in landing operations on the coast of Fukien and Chekiang provinces, America intends to participate and expand the victory further. . . .
>
> On the one hand we must overcome the economic difficulties due to the three years of natural calamities and, on the other provide against the provocations of a Chiang Kai-shek supported by America.

Also we must provide against incidents that may occur on other borders. . . .

We must intend to endure this test. It is an opportunity to test whether we can fight back in case American imperialism and its vassal forces come on us. This summer's harvests will not be very favorable. We are faced with two tests: to overcome the internal economic difficulties and to cope with the external aggression of imperialism. . . .Chiang Kai-shek's logic is that the mainland people will rise in revolt or are already rising in revolt, but this is not the case in my view. . . .

We cannot say that the Chinese population of more than 600 million does not include opponents of communism. We cannot say all are in support of socialism. Those opposed are small in number. In the 600 million population, however, they may amount to several million. . . .Some oppose by utilizing economic difficulties, but struggles against them are always under way. A disturbance by Chiang Kai-shek would mean another reason for an attack on the government by them. . . .We cannot definitely deny that no elements trained by Chiang Kai-shek are hiding in the mainland. In case Chiang Kai-shek drops paratroops and lands on the mainland with American support, these elements will come out of hiding.[51]

Ch'en's remarks are uniquely revealing in their repeated coupling of internal "economic difficulties" with the threat of external attack by the United States, the Chinese Nationalists, and India, implicitly including the Soviet Union by reference to "incidents . . . on other borders." This preoccupation with war was not based solely on the recent exodus and its possible effect abroad. In addition two separate developments, one on Taiwan and the other in Thailand, commanded the attention of analysts in Peking responsible for responding to threats against the People's Republic.

Beginning in March, a series of high level United States officials had conferred with Chiang Kai-shek, including Admiral Harry Felt, commander of American forces in the Pacific; Roger Hilsman, director of intelligence for the State Department; W. Averill Harriman, assistant secretary for Far East affairs in State; General Lyman L. Lemnitzer, Chairman of the Joint Chiefs of Staff; Elvis J. Stahr, Secretary of the Army; and other key Pentagon officials. At the end of March, Chiang made a more direct call for invasion preparations than he had issued in many years, declaring, "Either subjectively or objectively we can no longer vacillate or hesitate to perform our duty to deliver our people, our nation, and the whole world from catastrophe. . . .We can no longer passively wait and see if something will happen. . . .There is no doubt that we can annihilate the Communists, reunify our country, and restore freedom to the people on the mainland in the nearest future."[52]

Privately Taipei's long-standing invasion plan was revised with instructions to make it operational in the shortest possible time.[53] Negotiations were undertaken with American firms to secure additional naval vessels, amphibious craft, and hundreds of heavy-duty outboard engines.[54] While these moves took place secretly, recurrent Chinese Nationalist discovery of Communist agents, some at high levels, suggests such planning may have become known in Peking. Overtly Nationalist legislation made Chiang's words seem authoritative as a March 31 decree banned all political activity which interfered with "the sacred task" of preparing the invasion and on May 5 an "invasion preparation tax" levied a 20–25 percent tariff on most industries.[55] Peking subsequently noted a "conscription mobilization decree" of early March calling up recruits a year ahead of schedule, the indefinite extension of terms for those due to be demobilized, and the placement of ships, fishing boats, and all vehicles into "mobilization groupings."[56]

Beyond these posture indicators were action indicators that presaged possible attack. As summarized later in *Peking Review,*

> . . . In February U.S.–Chiang naval and ground forces undertook a joint "offensive-defensive exercise." In March, U.S.–Chiang naval and air forces staged a "combined submarine-detecting exercise" and a "mixed exercise" for naval mine-laying and mine-sweeping. Between April and May there was an exercise in the emergency embarkation of troops by merchant and civilian vessels. Recently a joint air-sea-ground landing operational manoevre [*sic*] was carried out in southern Taiwan. There have been very many busy movements of troops and war material along the coast of Taiwan and in the Penghu, Quemoy and other islands.[57]

Unmentioned but certainly noticed was a sharp increase in raids from the offshore islands during May and April coinciding with visits to Quemoy by American officers touring the west Pacific. Perhaps most symbolic, in early May Washington announced the appointment of Admiral Alan G. Kirk as ambassador to the Republic of China. Kirk had had considerable experience with amphibious warfare in World War II.[58] While he was chosen to persuade the Nationalists to face the realities which made an invasion suicidal, his appointment was probably seen quite differently in Peking.

At precisely this time, a sudden flare-up in Laos triggered American military reactions which created still another crisis on China's periphery. On May 2, 1962, the year-old cease-fire ended with firing around the Royal Lao defenses at Nam Tha.[59] On May 3 Communist forces seized Muong Sing, the last remaining air field in northern Laos, twenty-five miles to the west; on May 6 Nam Tha fell to a force estimated at more than four battalions. Although no further action followed immediately, Washington reacted vigorously, interpreting this as a probe to test American responses in the final stages of concluding a peace agreement at Geneva. On May 12 the United States announced dispatch of the Seventh Fleet to the Gulf of Siam. On May 15 President Kennedy ordered the buildup of American troops in Thailand to 5,000; on May 16, American jet bombers landed in Bangkok; on May 17, 1,800 Marines arrived.

Peking's initial response explicitly linked Taiwan and Laos. "Commentator" writing in *People's Daily* of May 16 declared, "The Chinese people cannot remain indifferent to U.S. imperialism's threat to embark on direct military intervention in Laos and to its increasingly flagrant collaboration with and use of the remnant Chiang Kai-shek bandits to extend the civil war in that country. They cannot but watch closely the development of the situation and take a serious view of it." Citing a Voice of Laos broadcast, "Commentator" claimed that at Muong Sing more than one hundred "Chiang troops" had taken part along with other KMT troops encountered in the general area. Another 2,000 allegedly stood ready for joint operations with Royal Laotian forces along the northern border of Thailand.[60] The article called attention to the May 14 visit of Prince Boun Oum to Taipei and the Taiwan *Central Daily News* pledge that "every possible positive assistance will be given to Laos."

On May 19, *People's Daily* editorialized, "U.S. aggressive moves in Southeast Asia are a serious threat to the security of China. The Chinese people cannot remain indifferent to this. . . .The Chinese people firmly oppose U.S. imperialist armed intervention in Laos, and absolutely cannot tolerate the establishment by U.S. imperialism in areas close to China of any new military bridgeheads directed against this country. . . .We must serve a fresh warning to the Kennedy Administration that it shall be held fully responsible for all grave consequences arising from its policy of playing with fire."[61] By the time of his May 29 press conference, Ch'en Yi could treat the crisis in a lower key since it had already become clear in Southeast Asia and at Geneva that neither side wanted any further escalation. Nonetheless he twice stated that the United States move into Thailand was aimed at China.

It is worth noting that Ch'en did not treat all potential threats alike, differentiating among them as to the likelihood of an actual crisis erupting. This was exemplified by Korea, where he noted that "according to our estimates they [the United States] may by some chance employ the forces of the reactionary South Korean Government to start an attack on North Korea . . . [but] they will not lightly try such a venture because they once failed."[62] Since the People's Republic was bound by a treaty of "mutual assistance" to Pyongyang, its interests were inextricably linked with peace on the peninsula. *Peking Review* vigorously attacked the current talks between Seoul and Tokyo as portending "a carefully planned U.S. scheme to pull together a so-called Northeast Asia military alliance composed of Japan, South Korea, and the Chiang Kai-shek gang in Taiwan, with militarist Japan as its backbone."[63] Ch'en's remarks, however, placed Korea in perspective by identifying it as a point of concern, but without according it the seriousness of attention given to Taiwan, India, and Thailand.

The Perceived Threat from Taiwan

Of these three situations, Ch'en clearly singled out Taiwan as the most serious. In fact, portions of his remarks in the May 29 interview struck a surprisingly anxious note concerning the possible support such an invasion might win: "This summer's harvests will not be very favorable. . . .Those opposed [to Communism] are small in number. In the 600 million population, however, they may amount to several million. . . .We cannot definitely deny that no elements trained by Chiang Kai-shek are hiding on the mainland. In case Chiang Kai-shek drops paratroops and lands on the mainland with American support, these elements will come out of hiding."[64] A foreign ambassador in Peking privately described the leadership's state of mind as "panicky" over the prospect of an attack from Taiwan.[65] According to a later Cultural Revolution document, Ch'en Yün, a former top economic planner recently restored to favor, advised a special meeting to disband the communes and revive private land ownership so that the peasants would have a stake in resisting the Nationalists.[66]

Thus, Ch'en Yi's press conference probably reflected a comprehensive assessment of the United States–Chiang threat, with a decision to deter it by major military and political moves. During the first three weeks of June, a massive PLA redeployment moved more than 100,000 troops to Chekiang and Fukien provinces along the Taiwan Strait.[67] The region was already heavily garrisoned so this emergency transfer imposed severe burdens on the local economy, displacing large numbers of persons and tying up rail lines for two weeks. News of these dislocations quickly spread to nearby Hong Kong, exciting further press attention as evidence of disruption on the mainland.[68]

The troop redeployment was deliberately conducted in such a way as to be easily detected by United States intelligence, thereby enhancing the credibility of deterrence.[69] Only upon its completion did Peking reveal the full sense of crisis to domestic and foreign audiences by means of a lengthy NCNA story. The June 23 dispatch claimed its "correspondent has learned from authoritative sources that the Chiang Kai-shek gang entrenched in Taiwan, with the support and encouragement of U.S. imperialism, is preparing for a large-scale military adventure, an invasion of the coastal areas of the mainland."[70] After summarizing the indicators of a forthcoming attack, the writer mixed confident assurances of victory with cautious admonitions to prepare for defensive difficulties:

> The majority of the Chiang Kai-shek bandit troops will be sent over to their doom under compulsion, but there will also be some diehard counter-revolutionaries who will be coming to the mainland to put up a desperate fight or to loot the mainland coast for ill-gotten gains. . . .Military men and civilians in the provinces along the southeast coast and in their rear areas, especially, must heighten their vigilance and be fully prepared in every way to smash an invasion of the Chiang Kai-shek gang at any time . . . and smash in good time the disruptive activities of underground and air-dropped special agents of the Chiang Kai-shek gang. . . .

Having marshaled its forces and mobilized its populace, the PRC moved to formalize its deterrent warning by summoning a Sino-American ambassadorial meeting in Warsaw on twenty-four hours' notice. On June 23 Ambassador Wang Ping-nan pointedly alluded to the Korean War in warning that the United States would bear the responsibility and suffer the consequences should Chiang invade the mainland.[71] Ambassador John Moors Cabot responded, as instructed, that the United States would not support any Nationalist invasion nor did it associate itself with any such proclamations of intent on Taiwan.[72] Four days later President Kennedy publicly confirmed the American position at his press conference, declaring "our basic position has always been that we are opposed to the use of force in this area."[73] He further recalled Secretary John Foster Dulles's remarks of 1955 to the effect that treaty agreements with the Republic of China "make it quite clear that it is in our mutual contemplation that force shall not be used." The assurances were credible; Peking eased its propaganda alert, and the crisis passed.

PRC experience and behavior in the Taiwan Strait bear in various ways on our understanding of the Sino-Indian confrontation. In addition to the pre-June indicators of Nationalist intentions to invade the mainland, continued evidence appeared to validate an alarmist view of external threat. General Peng Meng-chi, Nationalist chief of staff, visited the northern offshore island of Matsu and declared that the attack would be mounted "in the near future."[74] Meanwhile an official in Taipei claimed "the mainland is a powder keg on the verge of explosion" as proven by alleged uprisings in Fukien, Hupei, and Kwangtung.[75] Heightened Nationalist propaganda exploitation of the Hong Kong exodus explicitly linked the refugees with potential revolt.

These developments proved that an external threat genuinely existed so far as Nationalist intentions were concerned. Since Chiang Kai-shek could not invade without American support, this raised the larger question of "U.S. imperialism and its running-dogs" seeking to exploit China's vulnerabilities. In this regard, the continued CIA-Nationalist activity in Tibet could be logically linked with increased Indian activity on the Himalayan border as part of an overall design to increase pressure on the mainland from two fronts.

Such "worst case" analysis often occurs among organizations responsible for safeguarding national defense, but may be even more frequent where Communist assumptions of omnipresent conflict with capitalist foes are compounded by a Chinese preoccupation with "encirclement." However, pure speculation need not be relied upon for inferring that a linkage between the Indian and Nationalist threats was perceived in Peking. Precisely at this time a prominent Indian newspaper explicitly raised the specter of "war on two fronts." As noted later by *People's Daily:*

> ... It should be pointed out that in particular the number of invasions and provocations by Indian troops has increased steadily in the past few months and this is by no means fortuitous. The *Hindustan Times,* in an article on June 8, revealed that the recent

intensified Indian intrusions into China were connected with the Chiang Kai-shek gang's preparations, with the support of U.S. imperialism, to invade the mainland. This paper had the effrontery to declare that China must be made to understand that it "might have to face prospects of war on two fronts simultaneously."[76]

Whatever interpretation may have been given to Indian behavior before June, 1962, subsequent evidence would be likely to receive particularly hostile treatment.

In addition to linking India with the "U.S.-Chiang" threat, the June events also served to undermine the argument for adopting a posture of "reconciliation with imperialists, revisionists, and reactionaries." The decision to confront Washington directly both by local military deployments and with an unprecedented diplomatic demarche at Warsaw appeared to prove successful. No further indicators of an intended Nationalist invasion appeared; on the contrary, the United States gave both private and public assurances it was opposed to any such venture.

It is not certain how much attention Peking may have given to indicators before the June 23 confrontation that Washington actually was opposed to Chiang's plans. One clear hint of differences on this issue was given by Nationalist Premier Chen Cheng who declared, "It is a grave mistake for anyone not to want us to counterattack or even disapprove our preparation for the counterattack."[77] An important Taipei newspaper editorially called on "President Kennedy . . . to change a blind fear of war . . . and give us timely support in changing the situation on the mainland."[78] Friction over the invasion became so serious that younger Nationalist officers threatened to resist invasion orders unless Washington backed the attack.[79]

Radio Peking showed some sensitivity to these tensions in broadcasts to Taiwan which claimed the United States wanted to oust Chiang Kai-shek, citing in particular an Associated Press dispatch which quoted "foreign" opinion in Taipei that a Nationalist invasion would be "suicide."[80] This appears to have been only a tactical ploy, however, because at a more prominent level there was no effort to exploit differences between Taipei and Washington. Instead, the PRC explicitly rebuffed a subtle American effort to improve relations in the wake of the Hong Kong exodus.

On May 23, President Kennedy responded to a press query with an oblique offer to consider sending food to China should Peking request it.[81] This was promptly attacked by Ch'en Yi in his May 29 statement which interpreted it as a hostile move:

> American traders, Rusk, and President Kennedy say they will supply China with food if China makes such a gesture. But we will never make any gesture in reply to this bid. The Americans are attempting to take mean advantage of China's difficulties and to make China withdraw its anti-imperialist slogans and Marxist principles. . . .The *People's Daily* and the *New China News Agency* make no mention of this problem. America is angry, questioning why China does not heed Kennedy's gesture when the Chinese people are hungry in contrast to their holding the olive branch in one hand and the atomic bomb in the other, their having plenty of money and food. But we can overcome our difficulties. Even if we receive aid from somewhere, we will refuse American aid. The American plan to "utilize food for peace" is a "plan for subversion" designed to open the way for American occupation.[82]

Ch'en Yi's remarks showed an unwillingness to accept at face value Washington's effort to relax its rigid China policy. This rebuff of President Kennedy's probe is not surprising. In itself the gesture was so light and unspecific as to seem without serious purpose. Moreover, in any overall assessment of United States intentions it was far outweighed by contrary indicators of hostility. Worse, in this larger context it could actually be interpreted as a cunning probe to reveal PRC weakness.

Analysis of PRC strategy and tactics is impeded by the fact that several days elapsed between the appearance of foreign press accounts, which aroused worldwide attention to the PLA buildup, and release of the initial NCNA statement on the situation. Conceivably, no revelation was intended at that time; a covert military deployment detectable by United States intelligence may have been seen as sufficient deterrence. Even the ambassadorial meeting could have occurred without public knowledge of its proceedings, as was customary for most of the previous sessions. Had Washington then forced Taipei to back off, there would have been no need for a public confrontation unless it served other political purposes.

Mainland media postures are suggestive in this regard, although they are by no means conclusive. During the first week of June the PLA went on alert and prepared to move its special reserve divisions to the Taiwan front.[83] Yet aside from some increases in references to Taiwan and tension in the area between June 7–17, no nationwide attention to the crisis explicitly alerted audiences at home or abroad to the pending confrontation.[84] In regional broadcasts to Fukien, special commentaries began on June 8 to stress the miserable life of various groups on Taiwan but sounded no specific alarm over threat of attack by either the National- ists or "U.S. imperialism." This overall low-key posture continued until June 23 when NCNA offered the first PRC comment on the crisis simulta- neous with the summoning to Warsaw of the American and Chinese ambassadors.

It is worth noting that the Taiwan Strait developments fail to confirm the hypothesis that expressions of external threat under circumstances of internal crisis represent an artifice to divert domestic attention and to mobilize the populace.[85] Two facts pertain here. First, mainland media did not report the growing indications of Nationalist invasion preparations during the spring or the less direct evidence of American encouragement. Peking's attention to the crisis quickly subsided in the aftermath of the Warsaw meeting and President Kennedy's press conference. Second, there is no reason to doubt the genuineness of alarm manifested in the sudden, massive deployment of forces toward the Taiwan Strait and the unprece- dented use of the Warsaw channel for a diplomatic demarche which specifically recalled the Korean War collision between Chinese and Ameri- can forces. Combined, these two moves provide maximum credibility to China's expression of concern. This in turn suggests that public expressions of concern over Indian intentions were not primarily aimed at a domestic audience for political or economic reasons.[86] Such goals would have been better served by exploitation of the Taiwan crisis.

The Soviet Puzzle

Whatever the debate over the proper assessment and handling of the United States, it seems certain that important divisions of opinion sur- rounded discussion of the Soviet Union and its relationship with both China and India. The earlier deterioration of Sino-Soviet relations in 1959 covered a wide range of issues which, according to later revelations by both sides, included the precise terms of nuclear sharing, Khrushchev's summit meeting with President Eisenhower at Camp David, Soviet atti- tudes toward the communes and the Great Leap Forward, and suspicions of collusion between Chinese opponents to Mao's policies and the leader- ship in Moscow.[87] Additional fuel for the fire came from Moscow's "neutral" posture in 1959 after a shooting incident on the Sino-Indian border. The casualties were few (nine Indian and one Chinese dead), but the consequences were serious for the triangular relations of Moscow-Peking-New Delhi. In the subsequent exchange of polemics, *People's Daily* recounted a detailed chronology of events following the first incident of August 25, 1959, including a futile Chinese effort to prevent Soviet release of a TASS statement on September 10 which deplored the clash and which declared, "Friendly co-operation between the USSR and India is successfully developing in keeping with the ideas of peaceful co-existence,"[88] Despite further Chinese objections Khrushchev publicly expressed "regret" and "distress" over a second incident in late October.[89]

The Chinese later claimed that their leadership met six times with the Soviet ambassador between December 10, 1959, and January 30, 1960, to protest the "strict neutrality" of Moscow's position. There was no modification in the Soviet public posture, and privately the Chinese views were allegedly rebuffed as both factually and politically wrong.[90] Soviet policy had already shown a willingness to support India's economic development. However, in the context of Sino-Indian clashes a further expansion of Russian aid, with $500 million pledged by mid-1960 to the Third Five Year Plan, underscored Moscow's opposition to Peking on this issue.[91]

More directly relevant to the border dispute was the emerging military component in Sino-Indian relations. In April, 1961, Moscow sold to India eight Antonov-12 four-engine turboprop transports which New Delhi revealed were intended for use in Ladakh.[92] The aircraft were accompanied by forty Russian pilots, navigators, and mechanics whose presence eventually prompted questions in Parliament concerning the risk of military secrets leaking to Soviet training missions in Ladakh.[93] Nehru's reassuring response quieted his local opposition, but it was unlikely to have a similar effect in Peking.

The AN-12s were followed by two dozen Ilyushin-14 transports. Equally important were Mil'-4 helicopters, capable of lifting men and supplies to altitudes of 17,000 feet.[94] Less pertinent for Himalayan warfare but relevant to assessment of Moscow's intentions were prolonged parallel negotiations over jet engines and fighter planes. In mid-1961 New Delhi purchased six Soviet jet engines to test in an aircraft under development, and in the spring of 1962 American Congressmen voiced concern over reports that India intended to purchase two squadrons of the latest MIG jet fighters.[95] During May, Indian statements claimed these squadrons were intended to offset the equal amount of F-104s which Washington had promised to Pakistan, but in June talk switched to the eventual manufacture of MIGs in India on the basis of Soviet-provided factories. In this context the anticipated purchase of planes was justified as preparation for the manufacture and use of aircraft to be available two or three years later.

The publicity and political furor attending these developments assured their winning attention in Peking on two counts. First, the transports and helicopters provided a growing capability to sustain troops in Ladakh and to interdict Chinese communications in western Tibet, including the vital Aksai Chin road. Second, the Soviet origin of these and other planes raised the possibility of an eventual joint Russo-Indian threat on the Sinkiang-Tibet fronts, paralleling joint United States—Nationalist—Indian threats on the Taiwan-Tibet fronts.

As of June, 1962, however, there was more shadow than substance to the specter of joint Russo-Indian actions. The MIG negotiations had not yet culminated in agreement, much less the acquisition of aircraft by India. Many months were still required to train Indian crews and troops for the hazards of airdrop operations at high altitudes under difficult climatic conditions. Meanwhile in the immediate cirumstances those in Peking who favored "reconciliation" with Moscow could point to contrary indicators of Russian intent. It has already been noted how *Pravda* marked the twelfth anniversary of the Sino-Soviet military alliance in February by recalling Khrushchev's celebrated pledge from the 1958 Taiwan Strait crisis, "An attack on the Chinese People's Republic is an attack upon the Soviet Union." In mid-April Ambassador Liu Hsiao returned to Moscow after a long absence, both sides agreed to mute the polemical dispute, a new Sino-Soviet trade protocol pledged modest increases over 1961, and a substantial expansion occurred in the exchange of delegations and public messages between the two countries.[96] On balance, the relationship continued to be strained with a particular potential for trouble over India but the decisive point of no return remained in the future.

Initially the Sinkiang exodus does not seem to have caused any immediate difficulty in Sino-Soviet relations. As previously noted, no anti-Soviet attacks appeared in Chinese media and Chou En-lai reportedly apologized for the inconvenience it caused Soviet border control. Nevertheless, simultaneous with the dispatch of emergency reserves to the Taiwan front in early June, indicators of heightened military attention to the Sinkiang and

Tibet fronts appeared.[97] This attention resulted in a strengthening of communications facilities with both areas and an alert posture in mid-June. No further developments occurred on this front during the month the Taiwan Strait crisis peaked. However, it is likely that evidence bearing on Soviet intentions as manifested both directly across the Sinkiang border and indirectly by way of India was subject to continuous close examination and argumentation.

The Month in Review

The events of June impacted on China's handling of India in several mutually reinforcing aspects. First, convictions about external hostility seeking to exploit internal vulnerabilities appeared confirmed by Nationalist behavior. Second, the "encirclement" hypothesis won renewed life, supported by Indian press speculation over China facing a "war on two fronts." Third, forceful military measures proved effective in ending a perceived threat from Taiwan and the United States. Finally, the ending of that threat freed the PLA and its relatively few reserve divisions to cope with more distant threats on the Himalayan front.

In short, a qualitative difference emerged in the framework within which Indian moves were evaluated and responded to during the summer of 1962 as compared with the earlier spring. Although nothing changed in the pattern of Indian military behavior and public pronouncements, Chinese reactions to them occurred within an atmosphere of heightened crisis. Against the backdrop of the June events, this appears to be the result of two phenomena. One, Indian actions were increasingly interpreted as a function of encouragement from other sources, either Washington or Moscow, or both. Two, having deterred the worst threat of invasion from Taiwan, Peking could act with increased freedom and self-confidence against the remaining threat from India.

While these conditions raised the risk of war if both sides remained intransigent, several countervailing circumstances continued as a constraint. The relatively marginal size of Indian forces engaged in the "forward policy" and the substantial logistical difficulties confronting both sides in strengthening their Himalayan positions argued for patience and caution. Peking had not exploited the Taiwan Strait crisis as a major domestic campaign. On the contrary a relatively restrained propaganda posture together with firm but quiet diplomacy at Warsaw had pushed the crisis quickly out of public attention. This suggested there was no compulsion for an open confrontation operating within the Chinese leadership. Thus, while the events of June qualitatively changed the environment within which Indian actions would be perceived by policy makers in Peking, they did not make conflict inevitable.

Chapter 3

July, 1962 – September, 1962: PRC Deterrence and Diplomacy

The PLA Applies Pressure

In early July, the Chinese ambassador to India, Pan Tsu-li, returned to New Delhi after a six-month absence. His return marked an increase in PRC diplomatic probes for negotiations while Peking's propaganda posture and PLA activity signaled a stiffening in Chinese resistance to Indian advances. This heightened stance followed the easing of tensions in Sinkiang and on the Taiwan front. The following chronology reveals the nature of the buildup.

Chinese Diplomatic, Media, and Military Moves: July, 1962

July 9 *People's Daily* declares "sanguinary clashes may occur any time"; warns India "to rein in on brink of precipice"

July 10 PLA surrounds Indian post in Galwan valley but avoids clash

July 21 "Observer" in *People's Daily* hints at retaliation in NEFA for Indian moves in Ladakh

July 22 MFA protests July 21 armed clash in Chip Chap Valley; warns China "can by no means sit idle while its frontier guards are being encircled and annihilated by aggressors"

While the Chinese press played down the Indian imbroglio during most of June, New Delhi's forces continued to push forward, permitting high officials to boast of "a general advance over a wide front of 2,500 square miles."[1] Three battalions in Ladakh were joined by a fourth, with the resultant manning of approximately sixty outposts in this sector.[2] Against them, however, was arrayed at least one full PLA division. Not only did

Peking enjoy a five-to-one manpower superiority it also showed a full complement of weaponry including heavy mortars, recoilless guns, and automatic rifles. In contrast the Indian forces had only a few machine guns, three-inch mortars, and pre-World War I rifles.

The asymmetry of strength did not dismay Nehru, who assured Parliament that the western sector situation "was more advantageous to India than it was previously."[3] In NEFA the Indian Army established a new outpost at Dhola, near the trijunction of India, Bhutan, and Tibet.[4] Located south of Thag La, Dhola was almost sixty miles west of Tawang, the nearest Indian road-head, while the PLA terminal at Leh was less than ten miles north of Thag La. Meanwhile in Ladakh, a platoon of Gurkhas spent all of June traversing the difficult ridges between Hot Springs and the Galwan valley; on July 6 the Gurkhas finally set up positions that cut off a small Chinese post down the valley and challenged the main PLA base at the valley head.

In marked contrast with the pre-June period official reaction was immediate. Whereas earlier MFA notes usually followed five to ten days after alleged incidents, this one arrived within forty-eight hours on July 8, indicating an improved communications capability between western Tibet and Peking as well as a higher state of attention in the Chinese capital. Peking's second "strongest protest" of the year, the previous one having been issued on April 30, alleged that "by seizing that place they [Indian forces] obviously intended to cut off the only rear route for the Chinese post . . . and to launch an attack on that post."[5] The note hinted worse things might come, claiming "a serious incident [was] averted only because the Chinese patrol exercised self-restraint throughout, repeatedly advised the Indian troops against a clash and withdrew a certain distance on their own."

The next day *People's Daily* editorialized on the incident beneath an alarming headline, "The Indian Government Should Rein In On the Brink of the Precipice."[6] This reaction of July 9 contradicted the first editorial of June 3 which had optimistically proclaimed, "The Radiance of the Principles of Peaceful Coexistence Can Never Be Obscured." The authoritative journal now bluntly worded its concern in the opening sentence, "Sanguinary clashes on the Sino-Indian border may occur at any time as a result of the continuous intrusions into and the provocations along China's borders by Indian troops in defiance of the repeated warnings of the Chinese Government."

This unprecedentedly pessimistic prognosis appears to have been as much intended to alert audiences in New Delhi as in Peking, judging from the subsequent admonition:

> . . . .It seems that the Indian Government takes China's restraint as an indication of weakness. But .the Indian authorities would be making a big mistake if they thought that the Chinese frontier guards would submit to the armed Indian advance, that they would renounce their sacred duty of defending the frontiers of the motherland, and give up the right of self-defense when subjected to unwarranted attacks. . . .It is quite clear that if the Indian Government refuses to withdraw immediately its troops which have already penetrated into Chinese territory and refuses to cease immediately all its provocative activities on the border, India will be held fully responsible for all the consequences arising therefrom. It is still not too late for India to rein in on the brink of the precipice. The Indian authorities had better think twice on this matter.

The July 9 *People's Daily* warning to "rein in" and "think twice" was promptly reinforced by the PLA on July 10 when a full company of approximately 375 Chinese surrounded the Gurkha platoon of approximately twenty troops.[7] On the same day another MFA protest accused New Delhi of developing "aggressive strong-points which . . . form a threatening encirclement of the Chinese posts" in the Chip Chap valley, and two more which "form a pincer thrust on the Chinese post in the Spanggur Lake area."[8]

The juxtaposition within four days of a "strongest protest," a *People's Daily* editorial, and a major PLA countermove is in marked contrast with the pattern of Chinese behavior earlier in the spring. Moreover the specific content of the editorial, totally reversing the position of one month earlier, suggests a deliberate design of escalated pressure. That the PLA was able to respond so promptly with so superior a body of force indicates the situation did not seriously threaten its positions in the area. In short the evidence implies an earlier decision to exploit the Gurkhas' move, perhaps anticipated by scouting or other means of detection, for unveiling a new posture employing diplomatic, media, and military means.

The timing of this change is significant. One month previously *People's Daily* had adopted a benign interpretation of Sino-Indian relations while *Peking Review* had expressed a belligerent tone of confrontation. In the interim an anticipated threat from Taiwan had been countered by military

movement and a diplomatic demarche. If this mixture had proven successful with "U.S. imperialism," why not apply it to "Indian reactionaries"?
It has been seen how a less serious estimate of Indian intentions and of the
possible foreign interests behind them may have been dominant before the
coincidence of crises in Sinkiang and the Taiwan Strait. Reassessment in
the June context could have resulted in a felt need to deter the Indian
threat before it became critical, just as the Chinese Nationalist invasion
plans had been countered in advance of their being ready for implementation. To speculate further, the qualitative change in China's posture may
reflect the ascendancy of a "hard-line" faction in Peking, opposing the
earlier advocates of a soft approach toward New Delhi.

The concatenation of protest, editorial, and PLA movement evoked
sudden alarm in New Delhi over the fate of the beleaguered Gurkhas.
Ambassador Pan was summoned to the Ministry of External Affairs (MEA)
and bluntly warned that the Gurkhas would shoot if the PLA advanced
any closer.[9] Moreover if they were attacked India would retaliate elsewhere.

Apparently flexibility as well as firmness was introduced into the
Indian position at this time, as reflected in an important message sent via
Ambassador Pan. According to Chou En-lai in an interview many years
later, "On July 13, 1962, when our ambassador paid a farewell call on
Nehru, Nehru told him our two sides could hold discussions on the basis of
the report of the meetings of the officials of the two sides."[10] This
seemed to signal a major change in the Indian position which heretofore
had steadfastly demanded withdrawal from contested territory as a precondition for negotiations. Assuming that Chou's term "farewell call" is
correct, Pan appears to have returned to Peking for a short period because
he was subsequently in New Delhi through most of August. His return
presumably explored the implications of this new Indian posture which
was reaffirmed later in July, publicly in New Delhi and privately in
Geneva.

Exploration was indeed required. Were "discussions" tantamount to
negotiations? If so the hardening of China's military and media postures
would seem to have been successful both in halting Indian advances and in
bringing Nehru to the conference table. Under the circumstances further
inflammation of the border was both unnecessary and perhaps unadvisa-
ble. The PLA did not press closer or attack the beseiged Galwan outpost,
but neither did it lift the seige, forcing supplies to be air-dropped until the

unit was finally overrun in the general fighting of late October. Partly because of this, Indian air activity increased sharply with the unprecedented total of 124 alleged intrusions, mostly in the western sector, protested by Peking as having occurred in the first twenty-seven days of July.[11] Diplomatic activity also accelerated with a flurry of seven protests and exchanges between July 8–16, arguing respective rights and mutual accusations concerning patrols and posts on a line extending roughly north-south from below the Karakoram Pass to Spanggur Lake. Regardless of the risks, each side expressed by word and action its determination to maintain and strengthen troop positions in the contested territory as proof of ownership.

On July 13, an MFA spokesman declared that the "menacing" and "ever closer encirclement of the Chinese frontier post and patrol in the Galwan Valley . . . had developed to a point where an explosion might be touched off at any moment."[12] One week later *Peking Review* recapitulated events with a detailed map under the heading, "Sino-Indian Border Worsens."[13] The fullest public expression of the new deterrent posture, including revival of the "tit for tat" threat against NEFA, came in an authoritative "Observer" article in *People's Daily* on July 21.[14] The article deserves extended quotation because of its pointed threat against NEFA and its previously cited linkage of New Delhi's "forward policy" with alleged Chinese Nationalist preparations to invade the mainland:

> If the Indian troops, according to the logic of the Indian side can launch at will large-scale intrusions into Chinese territory, occupy what they regard as their territory and change by force the status quo along the border, then, it may be asked, have not the Chinese troops every reason to enter and station themselves on the Chinese territory south of the "McMahon Line" which has been encroached upon by India? If the Indian side unreasonably insists that China relinquish its own territory as a prerequisite to the avoidance of conflicts and the holding of negotiations, then has not China every reason to demand that the Indian side should first of all withdraw from the 90,000 square kilometres of Chinese territory south of the "McMahon Line" which it has occupied?
>
> . . . Everybody knows that India, taking advantage of the fact that the People's Republic of China during the early period after its founding was too busy to pay attention to the Sino-Indian border, did what even British imperialism had not dared to do in the past, forcibly pushing India's northeastern boundary up to the so-called "McMahon Line," a line invented by British imperialism with a view

to grabbing Chinese territory, thereby seizing 90,000 square kilometres of Chinese territory on the eastern sector of the Sino-Indian boundary. The Chinese Government has all along maintained an attitude of restraint towards this matter, calling for a settlement by negotiation and not by force. Orders have been given to all Chinese military and administrative personnel not to go beyond the so-called "McMahon Line."

... The Indian authorities have been betting on the basis of a wrong assessment of the situation: they take the attitude of the Chinese Government in setting great store by Sino-Indian friendship and trying its utmost to avoid a border clash to be a sign of weakness and think it possible to bring China to her knees by the use of force. It should be pointed out in particular that the number of invasions and provocations by Indian troops has increased steadily in the past few months and this is by no means fortuitous. The *Hindustan Times,* in an article on June 8, revealed that the recent intensified Indian intrusions into China were connected with the Chiang Kai-shek gang's preparations, with the support of U.S. imperialism, to invade the mainland. This paper had the effrontery to declare that China must be made to understand that it "might have to face prospects of war on two fronts simultaneously."

... We must tell the Indian authorities in all seriousness that they had better not miscalculate. If the Indian authorities insist on gambling despite the risk, then it is certain that they will gain absolutely nothing but will simply be picking up a rock only to drop it on their own feet.

This attention to NEFA would appear to be purposeful, particularly against the past pattern of this issue. As was noted earlier, it had first surfaced through a rhetorical query in an MFA note of November 30, 1961, which evoked an adamant Indian reply the following February. At that time Peking had explicitly reassured New Delhi it had no intention of altering its orders which prohibited "all military and administrative personnel [from] crossing this line." No such assurance was offered by "Observer" in July, however, as he merely restated existing orders against such movement. By resurrecting the question of NEFA after months of silence on this area, Peking subtly raised the stakes. Curiously no mention was made of the new post at Dhola although it was to become a point of sharp contention later in the year.

The "Observer" article received dramatic reinforcement on July 21, the day of its appearance, with the outbreak of actual fighting between Indian and Chinese troops in the Chip Chap valley. New Delhi claimed two wounded; Peking announced no casualties.[15] The skirmish may have resulted from cautionary shooting, but in any event Maxwell claims that following the Galwan incident Indian military orders were altered from "fire only if fired upon" to "fire if the Chinese press dangerously close to your positions."[16]

Peking's response to this development combined a low-key treatment of the affair with a uniquely sensitive warning reminiscent of the Korean War "will not stand idly by" demarche. A prompt but short MFA protest of July 21 alleged Indian troops had "suddenly launched an armed attack" on frontier guards and "as their lives were under direct threat the Chinese frontier guards were compelled to resort to self defense."[17] The note claimed the post was "still under the Indian troops' attack" yet went to extreme lengths to avow peaceful intentions while reintroducing a variant to the historic formulation:

> The Chinese Government has repeatedly stated that *China is not willing to fight with India* and the Sino-Indian boundary question can be settled only through routine negotiations. It has all along exercised the greatest forbearance and self-restraint towards Indian armed intrusions and provocations on many occasions. *However the Chinese Government can by no means sit idle while its frontier guards are being encircled and annihilated by aggressors.* At this critical moment the Chinese Government demands that the Indian Government immediately order the Indian troops to stop attacking the aforesaid Chinese post and withdraw from the area lest the situation be further aggravated. [Italics added.]

The timing of this incident with the "Observer" article is probably pure coincidence, but the content of the "Observer" analysis is consistent with the exaggerated reference to "frontier guards being . . . annihilated by aggressors" and the allusion to "can by no means sit idle." The inconsistencies lie in the brevity of the note, its deemphasis in the media, and its assertion that "China is not willing to fight with India." It seems likely that this ambivalence resulted from ongoing efforts by Ambassador Pan in New Delhi to win agreement for resuming discussion of the problem. Thus, PLA pressure on the border and Pan's presence in the Indian capital combined deterrence with diplomacy, signaling Peking's intention to stand firm and to risk war while offering to resolve the conflict at the conference table if New Delhi so wished.

Diplomatic Interlude: July–August

Whether because of Pan's probing or Peking's posture or both, Indian policy made a half-turn away from its previous position and edged toward negotiations. In its response of July 26 to the MFA protest of July 21, the Ministry of External Affairs offered two oblique concessions. First, its protest against PLA advances along a so-called "1960" line beyond that initially claimed in 1956 implied a possible acceptance of the earlier boundary which Chou had said "correctly shows the traditional boundary between the two peoples in this sector."[18] As the MEA now put it:

> Even if the Government of China are inclined to contest this boundary, the Government of India fail to understand why the Government of China do not restrain their forces from going beyond even their 1956 Chinese map claim line which is capable of easy and quick verification. It is true that the Government of India contest the validity of the 1956 Chinese map claim line but the Chinese local forces should not go beyond their own claim line confirmed by Prime Minister Chou En-lai.

More significantly, however, the note abandoned India's standing demand that Chinese troops withdraw from disputed territory as a precondition for talks. Instead, it adopted an ambiguous formula in proposing the resumption of "discussions":

> The Government of India are prepared, as soon as the current tensions have eased and the appropriate climate is created, to enter into further discussions on the India-China boundary question on the basis of the report of the officials as contemplated during the meeting of Prime Minister Chou En-lai with the Prime Minister of India in 1960. The Government of India hope that the Government of China will give a positive response on the concrete suggestions made by the Government of India for relaxation of the current tensions and for creation of the right climate for negotiations.

The ambiguities of the July 26 note magnified those communicated by Nehru to Pan on July 13. What preconditions for "discussions"—later referred to as "negotiations"—were embodied in the phrase "as soon as the current tensions have eased and the appropriate climate is created"? No "concrete suggestions" were offered in this message to which Peking could "give a positive response." Yet the thrust of the statement seemed sufficiently changed from previous notes to warrant an interpretation of intended concession.

This interpretation was reinforced in Geneva where, according to Chou in a later interview, "On July 23, Comrade Ch'en Yi who was attending the Geneva Conference on Laos, proposed to Krishna Menon that the ministers of the two sides would hold negotiations on the prevention of border conflicts."[19] Menon replied that there was not sufficient time at the moment but proposed that after he returned to New Delhi such a statement could be issued by the two governments. However, Chou continued, "After Menon returned to Delhi nothing came of it."

An additional, albeit minor, dimension to these diplomatic moves appears to have been Soviet involvement. Maxwell claims that "the Russians were urging negotiations" and calls attention to the coincidence in timing between the July 26 note and the presence in New Delhi of Anastas Mikoyan, first deputy premier of the Soviet Union.[20] Although the evidence is slight it has sufficient plausibility to warrant examination for the possibility of Moscow moving to support Peking's position in the border dispute so as to strengthen its potential advocates in current policy discussions involving the top CCP leadership. Particularly if this coincided with a predisposition on the part of Nehru to modify his stance in view of more serious Chinese military and diplomatic signals, additional Russian support for negotiations without preconditions would risk little in New Delhi while perhaps winning credit in Peking.

The earlier discussion of "reconciliation" with "imperialists, revisionists, and reactionaries" has already been noted along with its apparent eclipse in the "panicky" assessments of threat during May and June.[21] Advocates of both "reconciliation" and of confrontation could mobilize a number of new facts to serve their case. On the one hand, China now faced fewer foreign threats to its interests than at any time in the recent past. The Geneva Conference on Laos successfully closed on July 23, thereby eliminating the prospect, at least in the near future, of a major power conflict on China's borders. Whether the formula for a three-part "neutral" government would survive the presence of continued clandestine operations by Washington, Bangkok, Peking, and Hanoi was doubtful but the risk of formal United States ground or air intervention had been removed for the present.

Meanwhile the Taiwan Strait crisis had ended with credible assurances from Washington that it had no intention of supporting a Nationalist invasion, and the PLA had reinforced the Sinkiang border to control cross-border movement in either direction. Thus, those favoring a relaxed posture could point to the absence of a need for vigilance while those who wished to toughen the stand against India could cite the absence of serious risks elsewhere.

On the other hand, domestic conditions, while improving, remained difficult. Better weather and the cumulative effects of crisis management in agriculture augured for a better harvest, with mid-year estimates already indicating a possibility of the first good crop since 1959. However, the badly depleted reserves of grain required more than one season for replenishing, and the debilitating effects of three years' malnutrition left significant portions of the populace vulnerable to disaffection.

Cutting across all such considerations was a fundamental division within the Chinese leadership over basic policy goals and the means of pursuing them. Throughout 1962, particularly in the months prior to the Tenth Plenum of the Eighth Central Committee of the CCP in September, a wide-ranging controversy over these matters affected policy discussions at all levels and included State Chairman Liu Shao-ch'i and Party Chairman Mao Tse-tung.[22] The central points of controversy involved such domestic issues as the degree of eminence and omniscience to be accorded Mao, the role of scientists and intellectuals, the relationship between "the masses" and the cadres or bureaucrats, the function of criticism and its limits, and the implications of Great Leap Forward disasters for economic policy and planning. These issues were aired through esoteric and disguised allusions in literary works, particularly plays, and through more direct discussions, such as a two-week meeting of prominent literary bureaucrats at Dairen in August, and a CCP leadership conference in Peitaiho in late July.[23]

Issues of foreign relations were raised at least by implication and in one or two instances directly debated when Teng T'o, editor of *People's Daily* and director of the ideological and cultural activities of the Peking Party Committee since 1959, wrote a series of essays over eighteen months which appeared in the three main Peking newspapers, including *Chien-hsien* (Frontline), the theoretical journal of the Peking Party Committee. At several points he argued for emulating Soviet models in modernizing China, warning that "If a man with a swelled head thinks he can learn a subject easily and then kicks out his teacher, he will never learn anything."[24] In another piece he advised it was "important to make friends with others, especially with those in a competitive position" so as to learn from them. A third piece, "Who Were the Earliest Discoverers of America" claimed it was the Chinese who had discovered the United States by way of the Aleutian Islands and Alaska, concluding pointedly, "We can be sure that there has been a close association between the Chinese and the Americans as early as the fifth century. This long tradition of Chinese-American friendship is an important historical fact."[25]

On August 1, the annual celebration of the PLA founding, *Red Flag* and *People's Daily* published a newly revised version of Liu Shao-ch'i's 1939 classic, "How To Be a Good Communist." At the PLA ceremonial reception that same day, Minister of Defense Lin Piao failed to appear. Instead, Chief of Staff Lo Jui-ch'ing together with Foreign Minister and Army Marshal Ch'en Yi did the honors. Lo's address made no reference to "the thought of Mao Tse-tung" which had been so prominent in Lin's speeches of 1959 and 1960.[26]

Later Cultural Revolution accusations against Liu and Lo, both of whom were purged, alleged close relationships with Khrushchev and the Soviet leadership. It is possible that Moscow acted in New Delhi to strengthen its supporters in Peking at a time when Mao appeared to be increasingly subject to attack. With the Russians urging India to negotiate without preconditions, the PLA could remain in place throughout the disputed area. If this indeed was Moscow's design, the results were short-lived.[27]

The July 26 MEA note aroused sharp opposition in New Delhi. The *Hindustan Times,* under the heading "The Road to Dishonour," declared:

> The Government of India in its infinite wisdom has deemed the time opportune for a complete reversal of its China policy. It has all but sanctified the illegal gains of Chinese aggression in Ladakh as the price for the opening of a new round of negotiations with the overlords of Peking. In so doing it has broken faith with the people of India—the people and its Parliament.[28]

China's reaction was guarded. On August 4 the MFA informed New Delhi that the PRC "approves of the suggestion put forth by the Indian Government in its note for further discussions on the Sino-Indian boundary question on the basis of the report of the officials of the two countries."[29] However, the note immediately continued, "There need not and should not be any pre-conditions for such discussions. As a matter of fact, if only the Indian side stops advancing into Chinese territory, a relaxation of the border situation will be effected at once." Inasmuch as the Indian proposal had made no mention of withdrawal by either side, referring elliptically to easing of "current tensions" and "the appropriate climate" for discussions, Peking's choice of words seems gratuitously provocative and unnecessary. This is particularly true in view of the sensitivity of the issue in India and Nehru's vulnerability to domestic political opposition. Nevertheless, the August 4 reply closed optimistically:

> The Chinese Government proposes that such discussions be held as soon as possible, and that the level, date, place and other procedural matters for these discussions be immediately decided upon by consultations through diplomatic channels. The Chinese Government hopes that the Indian Government will give positive consideration to this proposal and kindly reply at an early date.

Three days later, *People's Daily* prominently headlined its page-one publication of the note, "China Agrees with India's Suggestion to Discuss Question Based on 1960 Official Report."

While diplomacy moved to the fore, deterrence did not fall far behind. On the same day the MFA issued its positive response to the July 26 proposal, it also revived the matter of NEFA and alleged Indian movement around Longju in a lengthy protest which recapitulated events between May 18 and June 22.[30] Two points are of interest. First, considerable delay marked the protesting of Indian troops "crossing the so-called McMahon Line and intruding into the Migyitun area in China's Tibet." Second, previously stated arguments were reiterated without pretense of urgency or importance at this time. This suggests that the statement was deliberately designed to balance the simultaneous move toward negotiations with a reminder of the consequences for NEFA were there to be no compromise in Ladakh.

At this point China's diplomatic and propaganda posture was lowered to a point of near invisibility so far as Sino-Indian affairs were concerned. Only one protest against alleged Indian shooting emerged from Peking during the three-week period August 5–26, in contrast with the five that occurred from July 15 to August 4. More significantly, Peking suspended its policy of publicizing the issues and kept secret all of the thirteen protests on various matters sent in August, offering no further editorial comment on the border dispute. As a result, spatial attention to Sino-

Indian relations in *People's Daily* fell to the lowest point since March. This relaxed atmosphere, in contrast with July, seems intentionally designed to deemphasize the controversy in public media so as to facilitate private exchanges that might defuse the border confrontation itself.

However, while a curtain of secrecy fell over whatever exchanges might be occurring concerning the proposed discussions, rising opposition in New Delhi evoked a statement from Prime Minister Nehru that hardened the July 26 position. Speaking from a prepared statement in Parliament on August 13, he declared that no discussions could occur "unless present tensions are removed and the status quo of the boundary which existed before and which has been altered by force is restored."[31] This literally returned the precondition for negotiations to the standard Indian position which had been expressly rejected by the Chinese note of August 4, i.e., a withdrawal by the PLA from all posts in disputed territory. Nehru further diluted his earlier proposal for "discussions" by dividing them into two stages:

> The Government of India is prepared to discuss what measures should be taken to remove the tensions that exist in this [western] region and to create the appropriate climate for further discussions. This would be preliminary to any further discussions on the basis of the report of the officials with a view to resolving the differences between the two Governments on the boundary question.[32]

The PRC response to these remarks, while indirect, subtly blended the tough tone of deterrence with the softer shading of diplomacy. An extended *Peking Review* commentary publicly reviewed developments since 1959, stressing the negative aspects of Indian behavior and noting inter alia, "Although the Indian Government has lately expressed its readiness to discuss the boundary question further on the basis of the report of the officials of the two countries, it nevertheless still clings to its unreasonable pre-condition, namely, that China should withdraw from large tracts of Chinese territory on the western sector."[33] Since no such demand had been formally communicated to China in the past month, this allusion referred to Nehru's parliamentary remarks but stopped short of attacking him directly.

Privately Peking communicated stronger warnings. On August 17 the MFA issued its only protest of this period that alleged the occurrence of Indian troop firings, a minor incident of August 13 wherein "four separate shots" were reportedly fired in the Galwan valley without consequence. [34] On August 18, rejecting an Indian claim of Chinese firing in the Pangong Lake area on August 14, the MFA denied the action had occurred and then pointedly remarked, "At a time when the Governments of the two countries are exchanging views for holding discussions as soon as possible on the Sino-Indian boundary question, the Indian Government has invented an exchange of fire between the troops of the two sides. . . .This cannot but be deemed as done with ulterior motives."[35]

Neither protest appeared in the Chinese press. Whatever the "exchange of views" contained, apparently a formal reply from New Delhi was still awaited. On August 22 New Delhi finally responded to Peking's August 4 acceptance of the Indian proposal for "discussion." Two additional notes on the same day dealt with earlier Chinese protests and gave a detailed accounting of "no less than eighteen new aggressive military posts deep inside Indian territory" which allegedly had been established since the last such summary protest of July 12. The main message dealt with proposed discussions and used language identical to that employed by Nehru in Parliament: "These discussions cannot start unless the status quo of the boundary in this region which has been altered by force since 1957 is restored and the current tension removed."[36] The note concluded:

> . . . An essential preliminary to the holding of further discussions on the basis of the report of the officials of the two sides . . . is a definition of measures that should be taken to restore the status quo of the boundary in this region . . . and to remove the current tensions in this area so as to create the appropriate climate for purposeful discussions. The Government of India would be glad to receive a representative of the Government of China to discuss these essential preliminary measures.

Diplomacy had failed to prevail over domestic politics in India. Chinese military pressure and political behavior, both secret and public, had— perhaps in combination with Soviet advice—brought Nehru to a position of potential compromise on July 26. However, his public retreat in mid-August, formalized in the August 22 note, seems to have been wholly a function of press and parliamentary reaction, both within and outside his own party.

To be sure, Peking alleged and may well have believed that Nehru had other inducements for intransigence. As the August 17 *Peking Review* analysis noted, "Since India's anti-Chinese campaigns began, U.S. 'aid' has been pouring into that country. . . .Between 1947 and 1959 . . . when India started its anti-Chinese campaigns, 'aid' from the United States and U.S.-controlled international institutions amounted to less than $2,000 million, but in the short span of the ensuing three years and more this 'aid' registered a sharp increase of about $4,000 million."[37] In June, Senator John Sparkman, acting chairman of the Senate Foreign Relations Committee, had declared, "We know right now that India is pressing very hard against Communist China upon her northeastern frontier," and had urged that proposed cuts in aid be defeated "at the very time she is moving in the direction that we have been wanting her to move for a long time."[38] But the critical determinant appears to have been Indian political opposition to the implied compromise of July 26, opposition which the explicit rejoinder against "preconditions" in the MFA reply of August 4 may have exacerbated.

Without access to the unpublished exchanges between Pan and Nehru or other Indian officials, it is only possible to speculate as to the reasons for Peking's failure to answer the July 26 note in kind. Making explicit the exclusion of withdrawal as a precondition instead of leaving ambiguous how "the appropriate climate" would be achieved was likely to embarrass Nehru, if not make his new position untenable. Perhaps secret talks revealed the ambiguity was meaningless.[39] Perhaps councils in Peking were divided on how far to compromise at this point and also remained insensitive to Indian domestic politics. Finally, Soviet mediation may have become suspect. In sum, a harder position may have been felt to be necessary if negotiations were not to break down as they had in 1960.[40] Whatever the explanation, the Indian position of July 26 disappeared on August 22 and with it the only period of serious negotiatory prospects in 1962. Ambassador Pan returned quietly to Peking, and within a month the first serious casualties were to occur on the Sino-Indian border since 1959.

PRC Resumes Political Pressure, Escalates Deterrence Warnings

A critical change occurred in Chinese behavior following the collapse of negotiatory prospects in late August. This was manifested in fresh diplomatic protests to New Delhi after a hiatus of several weeks, sharpened warnings over the consequences of Indian activity, and actual military clashes on the border. The following chronology highlights this month of activity which bridged diplomatic defeat with armed fighting and casualties on both sides.

Increased Hostile Interactions, August, 1962–September, 1962

August 27	PRC resumes protests against alleged Indian "provocative firing"
September 4	PRC protests July 18 entry into Longju
September 5	PRC warns India "whoever plays with fire will burn himself" in alleging "ambush" without casualties
September 8	PLA crosses Thag La ridge to threaten Dhola Post in NEFA
September 13	PRC warns "he who plays with fire will eventually be consumed by fire"; proposes discussions begin October 15 without preconditions; accuses Nehru of "using peaceful negotiations as cover for plans of nibbling Chinese territory"
September 16	Chinese protest activity near Dhola
September 19	India rejects September 13 proposal for discussion on border but accepts October 15 for talks to "define measures to restore *status quo* in western sector"
September 20	Clash at Dhola post results in Chinese dead and wounded; PLA resumes border patrolling in eastern and middle sectors
September 21	Peking warns "flames of war may break out" in NEFA
September 24	Three more Chinese killed at Dhola, two wounded
September 28	Lhasa Radio broadcasts funeral ceremonies for five "frontier guards" killed on border

As indicated at the outset, information about actual troop behavior on both sides is extremely partial and imprecise, based almost wholly on what each chose to reveal or to allege in the exchanges of protests. It seems safe to assume, however, that a generally consistent pattern prevailed throughout the summer as the opposing sides brought additional men and material into the contested area, built new outposts to prove possession, and threatened the opponent's position both by directly confronting and indirectly isolating him from his rear base.

However, one major difference distinguished Chinese from Indian military activity during the summer months. There is ample documentation from Indian sources and also the evidence of subsequent defeats to prove that New Delhi made no preparation for the contingency of serious warfare. It appears, however, that Peking translated its threat estimates into actions that would assure victory in combat should deterrence and diplomacy fail in halting the "forward policy" and bringing Nehru to the conference table. Unlike the Taiwan Strait crisis, this did not require a massive transfer of manpower. While estimates vary, the PLA strength in Tibet only changed from 125,000 troops in early summer to approximately 140,000–150,000 by fall.[41] Not only was this more than ample superiority against the likely enemy dispositions, but troop increases were limited by the need for transfer over long, hazardous roads of virtually all living and combat supplies.

Indeed, while the concept of "regional defense" provided adequate security for Tibet based on its permanent garrison, anticipated combat called for the stockpiling of ammunition, weapons, gasoline, and spare parts.[42] This would protect against unexpected needs as well as against the possible interdiction of supply routes by guerrillas supported from external sources. Although there is little direct evidence on the PLA buildup, it presumably progressed steadily while the diplomatic probes and responses of July and August tested Indian intentions. After the collapse of diplomacy on August 22, Peking further improved its communications, logistical, and combat capabilities on the Sinkiang-Tibet fronts as well as in NEFA. A later Indian reconstruction claims that in Ladakh, "on August 29 . . . they started building up of ammunition dumps all along the line astride which the Indian and Chinese troops faced each other. Day and night convoys of 3-ton and 5-ton trucks ran up and down bringing support and ammunition. As the ammunition dumps grew in volume simultaneously the number of Chinese outposts increased."[43]

Since neither side is known to have altered its posture at the front during August, fluctuations in the frequency and intensity of diplomatic protests and press attention more likely reflect a tactical change in posture on the part of the protester than an actual change in behavior on the part of the accused. During August 4–22 when New Delhi's reply was being awaited, Peking alleged the occurrence of only one instance of Indian firing. By contrast twelve such incidents were claimed to have taken place during the previous two weeks. Again, from August 27 to September 13, Peking claimed fourteen shooting incidents occurred. The delay of protesting developments of August 21, 22, and 23 until a summary note of August 27 indicates an intentional manipulation of events. The August 27 note was presumably delivered as the initial riposte to New Delhi's adamant stand of August 22 and presaged Peking's return to public pressure.

An alternative explanation posits Indian action as deliberately restrained during the first three weeks of August while negotiatory prospects were being weighed, with all constraint lifted once the decision was made to press forward. However, no supporting evidence can be found in the various Indian memoirs or in Maxwell's authoritative account. Moreover the greater restraint was manifest in Chinese, not Indian, media. While Peking muted the issue in *People's Daily*, New Delhi maintained a determined public posture through Nehru's parliamentary statements and officially inspired stories in the press.

Peking's return to protests and press discussion of the border conflict appears to have been a deliberate signal to alert home audiences and to deter Indian policy makers, rather than a reflection of more frequent reports of conflict from the border. In September a freshet of notes accused Indian patrols of firing on Chinese positions, albeit without any casualties. The majority of these incidents reportedly involved only a few rifle shots, although on some occasions machine-gun and mortar fire were reported.[44]

Some confusion attends differing versions of one potentially serious clash on September 2 in the Chip Chap valley. According to Peking, six rear service personnel were "ambushed by a large number of intruding Indian soldiers [who] unwarrantedly opened up fierce fire at the Chinese non-combatants with machine-guns and rifles . . . shooting a total of nearly 200 rounds."[45] The MFA protest, claiming this marked a "new peak" in "provocative activity," warned, "The Chinese Government seriously urges the Indian Government to give careful consideration to the grave consequences that may arise from such acts of playing with fire by the Indian side. One should be aware that whoever plays with fire will burn himself." Despite this alarming description of the incident, Peking did not claim any casualties. Maxwell, however, reports that an incident in the same area at this time resulted in several Chinese killed at point-blank range when they menaced an Indian post by their advance.[46] The Chinese charge d'affaires was requested by the MEA to "arrange for collection of the Chinese dead" and, while the incident was kept quiet by New Delhi, press leaks at the time reported its occurrence. This appears to be the same event alluded to in Peking's note. New Delhi's protest, while making no reference to casualties, was unprecedentedly delivered at midnight on the same day the incident had taken place and was so hastily drafted that it lacked routine details of specific location and troop size. This suggested an unusual situation existed.[47]

Whatever may have actually occurred, the September 5 warning represented a deliberate escalation of deterrence language in its allusion to "playing with fire." On September 13 this language was further strengthened. The MFA warned: "Taking only the cases of provocative firings at Chinese frontier guards, apart from the daily increase of shooting incidents (as many as four such incidents occurred on September 5 alone), even the use of artillery shells has been started. The Indian Government should be aware that shooting and shelling are no child's play; and he who plays with fire will eventually be consumed by fire." The September 5 figure of speech merely alluded to being "burnt"; now the threatened consequences included being "consumed by fire." In closing, the MFA declared that should shooting continue against "Chinese border defense forces who are duty-bound to defend their territory and thereby arouse their resistance [the Government of India] must bear the responsibility for all the consequences arising therefrom."[48]

A new diplomatic initiative accompanied this warning. On the same day, Peking replied to the Indian statement of August 22 which had made withdrawal a precondition for border discussions. After summarizing recent Indian activity and rejecting any preconditions, the MFA accused Nehru of bad faith and then restated its desire for negotiations, proposing that they begin on October 15. The mixture of deterrence threat and diplomatic initiative is worth examination:

> . . . One can hardly avoid the conclusion that the Indian Government has no desire to solve the boundary question peacefully through negotiations but is using peaceful negotiation as a cover for its plans of nibbling Chinese territory and altering the *status quo* of the boundary. In his speech at the Rajya Sabha on August 22, 1962 Prime Minister Nehru stated outright that on the Sino-Indian boundary question the Indian Government is following a "dual policy" and intends to gain from China what it seeks to gain "by political pressure, military pressure, or other pressures." To adopt one policy or another is India's own business. *But the Chinese Government wishes to point out that China will welcome negotiations if seriously intended, but will resist, whenever attacked, and that it will bring*

India no good to pursue a policy of "sham negotiations and real fighting."

. . . The Chinese Government still considers that the Chinese and Indian Governments should quickly hold further discussions on the Sino-Indian boundary question on the basis of the report of the officials of the two countries without setting any pre-conditions.

. . . *It formally proposes that the two Governments appoint representatives to start these discussions from October 15 first in Peking and then in Delhi, alternatively.* [Italics added.]

Among other things, Peking repeated its earlier proposal for a mutual withdrawal of armed forces for twenty kilometers along the entire border. Chinese media did not release the note until October, adding to its credibility as a serious initiative.

This was the first time either side had suggested a specific date for talks. In the context of Peking's charges and warnings, the proposal, although not worded like an ultimatum, could be seen as one. Taken in conjunction with a small but significant change in PLA behavior in NEFA, the note signaled a major turn in Peking's posture. To appreciate the import of this turn more fully, the NEFA situation must be examined in greater detail as it soon proved to be the flashpoint for the first known casualties of 1962.

As we noted earlier, the establishment of an Indian post at Dhola in June did not arouse any visible reaction at that time. This was unusual because it lay in territory which was shaded as Chinese even on Indian Army maps; in addition, in May a Chinese sign had been found (translated two months later) that claimed, "This is our river and our mountain."[49] The general area had come into contention in 1959 when the Indians set up a post at Khinzemane, north of the McMahon Line, claiming that in the absence of a watershed, McMahon had intended to follow the highest ridge rather than the line at which he inadvertently drew the boundary.[50] This made the Thag La ridge, four miles north of the McMahon marking, the proposed boundary. The PLA had reacted by "physically pushing back" the Assam Rifles from Khinzemane, but two days later they returned after the PLA had vacated the post. After exchanging protests Peking agreed to New Delhi's proposal that the post be left alone while the PLA remained back of Thag La ridge, provided that no further changes in troop disposition occurred.

The total area concerned was only about twenty-five square miles, but it did lie above the McMahon Line which had not been agreed to by China in 1914. In addition the Thag La ridge had strategic significance since it provided access to the Chinese base at Leh through a 14,500-foot pass. The Indian post was actually north of Dhola, close to the south bank of the Namka Chu, a river which ran along the base of the Thag La ridge slope. Occupied by only a platoon under a junior commissioned officer, it posed no serious threat and possibly went unnoticed for some time in Peking, in view of the Taiwan Strait crisis and the prominence of the western sector in early July.

However, the systematic strengthening of Chinese positions opposite NEFA apparently occurred during the summer, focusing in particular on the contested triangle containing the Dhola post and Khinzemane. According to Brigadier J. P. Dalvi, commander of Indian forces in this area, the PLA built up forward supply dumps at Leh and other points, moving up at least two divisions and 150 artillery pieces behind Thag La ridge and opposite his Seventh Brigade headquarters at Tawang to the southeast. [51] This buildup was facilitated by the dry period from May to August and the generally flat terrain on the Tibetan side of the ridge.

The tactical advantage lay entirely with the PLA. It enjoyed a seven-ton road-head at Marmang only three hours from the ridge as against the Indian line which ran from a three-ton road-head at Misamari, twenty-one days distant, through a one-ton terminal point at Tawang, five to six days away. Moreover heavy monsoon rains beginning in late August turned the narrow, steep dirt roads of NEFA into mud and slush, requiring supplies to be air-dropped at Tawang and all points forward. Uncertain weather, limited equipment, and a paucity of drop zones made this a poor substitute for ground transportation. As a result the garrison at Tawang was limited to a ceiling of 2,400 men instead of full brigade strength of 3,500, with the remainder stationed at Misamari. Moreover, actual combat strength was only two half-strength battalions totaling approximately 800 with one battery of mountain guns that could not be moved forward. [52]

In short, the Dhola post was virtually defenseless from both a political and a military standpoint. As such it offered the optimal point for pressure to counter Indian advances in the western sector and to make credible the threatened consequences of refusing to negotiate without preconditions of withdrawal. In early September a patrol reportedly encountered Chinese troops who warned that the post would have to be vacated or it would be eliminated. [53] On September 8, sixty Chinese soldiers crossed Thag La ridge in broad daylight and advanced near the post, cutting one of the log bridges on its supply route and threatening its water supply.[54] While the troops did not attack, their continued presence signaled every intention of adopting tactics similar to those employed in the western sector to contest the location of Indian posts in disputed territory.

The timing of PLA pressure on the Dhola post, established in June but still not formally protested by Peking, combined with the changes in deterrence language and the proposal that discussions without preconditions begin October 15 indicate a major Chinese decision had occurred in the aftermath of New Delhi's August 22 note. The decision was to leave open for one month the possibility for gradually escalated military and political pressure to force acceptance of unconditional negotiations, after which major military action would force New Delhi to abandon its "forward policy" once and for all. The mixed pattern of "soft" and "hard" lines manifested in diplomatic, media, and military postures since early July gave way to an unprecedented tough posture in early September that ended in the October–November war.

To understand what evoked the one-month negotiating proposal at this time, the tactical considerations must be reviewed. Three factors appear relevant. First, diplomatic probes under lesser pressure had to exhaust their potential before moving to the alternatives of escalation and possible conflict. This had required most of July and August. Second, the PLA capability in Tibet needed reinforcement for offensive action. Logistical limitations combined with weather to confine such strengthening to the summer months. Finally, if extensive combat were to result, it would have to be completed before the December storms engulfed the Himalayan heights with fierce winds and deep snow.

Within these considerations which forced the timing of final confrontation, causing the conflict to arise in early fall, was the additional requirement to prepare a political justification for major military action. If reservations over the use of force remained within Chinese decision-making circles they could be allayed by the one-month period permitting a reversal of the Indian position. During this time the Tenth CC Plenum would take place and the decision to attack could be fully reviewed. In addition, audiences outside China, particularly in the neutral countries of the Afro-Asian world, might be better persuaded through the proposal that Peking had exhausted all alternatives before reacting to "Indian aggression and provocations." Not only did the one-month notice facilitate these political goals, but Indian intransigence may well have been calculated upon in advance as a likely asset should it manifest itself in extreme verbal or military behavior during this period.

The initial Indian reaction was one of concern and determination to counter the Chinese move.[55] The Dhola post was ordered to hold its ground while a battalion from Seventh Brigade, together with the Assam Rifles, moved to reopen the supply route from Tawang along the Namka Chu river. Within two days the developments had been leaked to the Indian press, stirring up a predictable storm of demands to expel the Chinese "from every inch of sacred Indian soil." Peking continued the pressure, however, and on September 16 made its first formal protest over the Dhola post. Ignoring the June move, it charged that "Indian troops recently again crossed the so-called 'McMahon Line' . . . and constructed barracks and defense works in preparation for prolonged entrenchment."[56] It also charged "Indian aircraft repeatedly intruded into the air space over the Leh village and circled over there for reconnaissance purposes on August 29, September 9, and September 10." These actions "show that the Indian side is actively extending the tension to the entire Sino-Indian border."

Meanwhile the PLA dug in on the Thag La ridge slope in full view of Indian observation, with three tiers of defense positions from the river bank to the crest of the ridge, complete with machine guns, automatic weapons, and presumably mortars on the reverse slope.[57] Further downstream a company of Chinese troops crossed one of the five rough log bridges spanning the river, stationing itself on the south side and shouting in Hindi that Indians and Chinese were brothers ("Hindi Chini bhai bhai") and that the Indians should leave since this was Chinese land. In conversation the troops claimed to be only frontier guards, not regular PLA forces, and proposed that local civil officials meet to discuss the exact location of the border so as to prevent bloodshed.[58]

New Delhi was undaunted. It promptly responded the following day to Peking's September 16 protest with identical countercharges, holding "the Chinese Government responsible for any untoward incident that may occur."[59] On September 19 India rejected the September 13 proposal for discussion of the border on October 15 but accepted that date for talks, first in Peking and then New Delhi, to "define measures to restore the *status quo* in the western sector which had been altered by force in the last few years and to remove the current tensions in that area." Only after this would there be "discussions to resolve the differences . . . on the boundary question." Paralleling the September 13 accusations of bad faith, the note charged that the Chinese, "while repeating their professions for a peaceful settlement, are determined to do all they can to continue their aggressive activities . . . using talks and discussions between the two Governments only as a cloak to further their aggressive and expansionist aims." After inveighing against the "use of undiplomatic language or holding out threats of force," the MEA declared that "no amount of casuistry or threats of force will deter [the Government of India] from their resolve to maintain inviolate the territorial integrity of India." On September 18, a senior Indian civil servant informed the press that Army orders were "to drive away the Chinese from our territory in NEFA."[60]

Negotiations were clearly out of the question at this point. Even as New Delhi's reply was being transmitted to Chinese officials, a minor clash near Dhola evoked the first casualties in what was to become a series of military encounters that climaxed with the massive PLA assault of October 20.

Clashes and Casualties in NEFA

Sometime after 9 P.M. on the night of September 20, firing broke out at the Namka Chu bridge held by Chinese troops. It recurred intermittently until daybreak by which time Peking claimed to have suffered one dead and one wounded while Indian accounts told of two Chinese killed and two wounded. Neither side reported any Indian dead although differing Indian versions reported three or five wounded.[61] It is impossible on the basis of available information to determine precisely why the clash oc-curred. However, it is worth attempting to reconstruct the event as a possible reflection of deliberate initiative by one side or the other. Con-ceivably it was wholly spontaneous, resulting from an accidental detona-tion in the dark to which opposing forces, operating under tense condi-tions of confrontation, mutually responded. While allowing for this possibility, alternative logical constructs can still be examined to assess the plausibility of a deliberate attack.

The accounts differ, not only as might be expected between the two sides, but also among various Indian sources. Peking claimed "a sudden armed attack on Chinese frontier sentries" occurred at midnight. New Delhi alleged that around 9:30 P.M. "two Chinese sentries crept up to an Indian patrol post" and "threw two hand-grenades, injuring three Indian soldiers" whereupon the post fired flares that revealed "a substantial number of Chinese soldiers massed some distance away." This force reportedly opened fire at that point. Dalvi placed the action near 10:30 P.M. when a single sentry "threw a grenade at our sentry post which was a few yards away. Our post opened up and thereupon firing started from opposite sides of the Namka Chu." General Kaul asserted that at 10:40 P.M. the sentry's grenade wounded three Indians, one of whom opened up his light machine gun on the enemy position "from where fire was returned."

Dalvi had just completed a tour of Indian positions together with the local battalion commander, and his grave doubts as to their viability went so far as to prompt his flat refusal of official orders for action at that time.[62] The initial command was to "capture Thag La . . . by 19th September" but this was amended to read "capture the Chinese position one thousand yards northeast of Dhola and contain them south of Thag La." Dalvi instructed the local commander to ignore these messages and do nothing until he personally ordered it. He meanwhile informed higher levels he would not accept any further orders until he had completed his reconnaissance and had prepared a detailed assessment of the local situation.[63] His analysis is worth extensive quotation, not only with respect to the September 20 incident but for an appreciation of the striking asymmetry of forces in the area:

> The Chinese had deployed more than two companies opposite us and a prudent estimate would indicate that the rest of the battalion would be near at hand . . . [we] did not have the necessary superiority to dislodge the Chinese. . . .The terrain made it impossible for an attack to be mounted between bridges one to five. The precipitous slopes would have caused our troops to be massacred. . . .They would have to wade the roaring, boulder-strewn river as they had no bridging equipment before attacking the mountains head-on, while a comfortably entrenched enemy, watching them through-out from a vantage point, could pick them off as he pleased. . . .
>
> The men had no rations and were short of ammunition and porters. They had come on hard scales and pouch ammunition. Every precious round had to be carried by the men for several miles over a 13,400-foot pass. For the defending Chinese there would be an abundance of everything. We had no fire support except for the two mortars and a few bombs. A Chinese infantry battalion has a great deal more firepower. We had no digging tools or saws to cut logs for bunkers, or defense stores (mines and wire). If we attacked the Chinese and gained ground we could not consolidate and hold

such ground against a counterattack. There were no reinforcements within fifteen days' march of the Namka Chu. If we precipitated a hasty, major skirmish and lost, the Chinese could advance.[64]

Dalvi communicated these points to New Delhi in his formal assessment on September 25. Their forceful exposition together with his flat refusal of orders to attack make incredible the hypothesis that Indian troops deliberately initiated the September 20 action.

On the other hand, Peking's posture had stiffened still further earlier that day with a formal notification to New Delhi that active patrolling had been ordered to resume on the eastern and middle sectors, as had occurred earlier in the western sector.[65] The note specifically singled out the existing confrontation at the bridge to justify this return to patrolling, claiming "The Chinese Government . . . cannot remain indifferent to the intensified aggressive activities of the Indian side." Moreover Peking's September 21 note over the "sudden armed attack" voiced "the most serious and strongest protest," reserving "the right to ask for an apology and compensation." Yet no such action is known to have followed, despite the unprecedented PLA casualties.

On balance, the logic of the situation and circumstantial evidence points to the PLA as having initiated the firefight of September 20–21. Its occurrence one week after the September 13 proposal is suggestive of an increasingly evident pattern wherein important Chinese actions occurred at regular rhythmic intervals within a larger framework of preplanning. The primary temporal benchmarks were monthly, within which weekly timepoints separated tactical moves. In this regard, the September 20 incident is also of interest, coming one month before the massive PLA attack of October 20.

Peking's September 21 protest bluntly declared, "The situation in the Che Dong [Dhola] area is extremely dangerous and flames of war may break out there." *People's Daily* tempered this language only slightly in its most emotionally worded editorial to date, "The Chinese people are extremely indignant at the frenzied criminal provocations of the intruding Indian troops in the Che Dong area. . . .We must tell the Indian authorities in all seriousness that the situation is most critical and the consequences will be serious. Let the Indian authorities not say that warning has not been served in advance."[66]

It was the PLA "frontier guards" who had taken the initiative in early

September by advancing on a small, isolated outpost established three months earlier and threatening its supply line by crossing one of five small log bridges across the Namka Chu river. Even if the Chinese did not initiate the September 20 fight the close proximity of hostile forces increased the probability of an incident immeasurably beyond that which would have obtained had they remained dug in on the opposite slope. Later their withdrawal to this slope after the clash would not have impaired defense of the Thag La ridge, much less the plateau behind it. Moreover the river became easily fordable in early October, removing all importance from the bridge.

Inaccurate reporting presumably distorted the situation for decision makers in Peking. Thus, the September 25 protest alleged artillery fire when no such Indian capability seems to have existed at this point. In addition this note claimed only "four casualties" resulted from subsequent fighting on September 24, but four days later the MFA corrected this to "three soldiers killed and two officers wounded."[67] Even allowing for faulty reports, however, does not make credible the image of a serious threat to local PLA superiority. The gross asymmetry of forces described by Dalvi, coupled with the lack of logistical preparations throughout NEFA for rapid deployment of well-equipped reinforcements, should have been readily ascertained by Chinese intelligence. Not only did the Chinese enjoy easy surveillance over Indian movement in and around Dhola, but agent reports were facilitated by the close ethnic relationship between NEFA tribes and the Tibetan population. In particular, the Monpas, who acted as guides for Indian army units, crossed freely into Chinese occupied areas in pursuit of their cattle and for social intercourse.[68]

In sum, the Chinese reaction to this first clash reinforces the conclusion that a decision had been made to use Dhola as the testing-point of Indian intentions, with ample "warning . . . served in advance" that "flames of war may break out there." Thus, far from disengaging in order to defuse the volatile situation, Peking moved to exploit it publicly in such a manner as to confront New Delhi with the prospect of serious hostilities should it not withdraw. On September 28 five "frontier guards" were given a ceremonious funeral in Lhasa, attended by 4,000 mourners and with addresses made by both the local PLA commander and the ranking religious leader, the Panchen Lama. By broadcasting full accounts to overseas and home audiences, the regime virtually committed itself to avenging the martyrs' deaths. In the Panchen Lama's words, "We should turn our sorrow into strength, resolutely retaliate for our martyrs, strengthen the unity among the people of all walks of life in Tibet, raise [our] vigilance and be cautious of the Indian reactionary elements' two-faced trick of undertaking false negotiations and launching attacks. . . .If the Indian side wants to negotiate, we will welcome this; if they want to fight, we will resist."[69]

The mass meeting adopted a resolution which left no room for doubt that the issue had been drawn:

> We will never tolerate the occupation of our territory by Indian troops, nor shall we sit by with folded arms and let them shoot at our compatriots or let them kill our frontier fighters. Should Indian troops dare continue their intrusion, the Tibetan people, together with the people of all nationalities throughout the country and the PLA, and frontier guards in the Tibet region, will resolutely smash the Indian troops armed provocations and aggression and strive to safeguard the territorial integrity of our fatherland, the happy livelihood of the people of all nationalities, and the fruits of the victory of the revolution of the Tibetan people.[70]

This signaled to Chinese audiences as had no previous development the likelihood of much heavier fighting, barring a major change in Indian behavior. The traditional symbolic significance of guarding China's borders against foreign intrusion, the implicit humiliation manifest in the loss of five soldiers without comparable casualties for the other side, and the sensitivity of Tibet as an established point of subversion and insurgency combined to make the NEFA developments a watershed in Chinese perceptions and behavior.

Between September 21 and 30 *People's Daily* unleashed a flood of articles on the border crisis. Measured in space, location, and content this far surpassed any previously comparable period in 1962. Coinciding with the Tenth CC Plenum, September 24–27, and the arrival of officials from the entire country to celebrate National Day on October 1, this brought the crisis to the attention of key figures on a nationwide basis. Maps pointedly showed Dhola on the Chinese side of the McMahon Line. Front-page publication of MFA protests highlighted the situation. The Plenum communiqué, while not explicitly mentioning Sino-Indian relations, struck a militant defense posture that could not be mistaken in its application amidst the attendant publicity about the border:

The Chinese People's Liberation Army and the public security forces are strong and reliable armed forces of the people. Our country has also a heroic military force of vast numbers. They have performed well their glorious task of defending the motherland, the people's labor, and the socialist system. At all times they are vigilantly guarding the frontiers of our great motherland and protecting public order, and stand ready to smash the aggressive and sabotage activities of any enemy. . . . Our people have resolutely smashed and will continue to smash every one of these scheming activities, be it intrusion, provocation or aggression or subversion within our state or the party.[71]

The "scheming activities" alluded to fit the formula ritualistically applied to Indian behavior, typified by one domestic broadcast which concluded, "It is absolutely unreasonable for the Indian Government to force China to accept the Indian-proposed boundary line, and to repeatedly violate the boundary *status quo* and to perpetrate armed provocation and aggression. The Indian authorities are clearly mistaken in thinking that China will succumb to the armed threat of India."[72]

China also began to argue its case internationally with a detailed exposition of NEFA developments, focusing in particular on the Dhola salient. *Peking Review,* in discussing the clash at the bridge, noted, "The firing was no accident. It had been heavy and prolonged. Up to September 25 [Indian troops] had killed five Chinese frontier guards (including one officer) and wounded five others. What is more, the Indian troops are continuing their bloody attack."[73] After stressing the "great restraint" by frontier guards, the writer warned, "But there is a limit to China's patience and self-restraint. The Chinese people cannot allow their land to be wantonly encroached upon by India; *nor can they stand idle while their frontier guards are being mercilessly killed."* [Italics added.] An international broadcast commentary ended on an equally ominous note: "When China's territory has been invaded and when the Chinese frontier guards are suffering increased casualties, the Chinese side has no choice but to fire back resolutely in self-defense. At present fighting is still going on in the Che Dong area and the situation has worsened. The Chinese authorities are keeping a close watch on the development of events."[74] Both accounts now revealed the Dhola post had been established in June, but the broadcast alleged PRC knowledge came only "in August" via "reports from local inhabitants."

This barrage of publicity stopped short of fully mobilizing the populace for war. No mass rallies or demonstrations were reported outside of Tibet, as was customary in past crises concerning Korea and the Taiwan Strait. Moreover the wave of anti-Indian articles subsided markedly after September 30, and was not resumed until October 10. However, within these limits the media treatment of Sino-Indian relations in the last ten days of September sharply escalated the signals of alert to home audiences and deterrence to observers abroad, particularly in New Delhi.

The month ended with the situation deadlocked and with heightened fighting at Dhola. On September 29 the Indians demonstrated their newly acquired mortar capability in the area and the next day reported seeing "fourteen corpses and some 'walking wounded' being carried away by the Chinese."[75] That same day in New Delhi Defense Minister Krishna Menon informed top army officers that "Government policy was to make an impact on the Chinese in NEFA before they settled down for the winter."[76] The die was cast.

Chapter 4

October, 1962:
The War Begins

From Words to War

During October, PRC political, diplomatic, and military measures culminated in the first PLA offensive of October 20. The events leading up to and immediately following that attack are outlined here.

Chinese Moves on and after the Eve of Attack

October 3   MFA replies to New Delhi's September 19 counter-proposal, warns "Whenever India attacks, China is sure to strike back"; repeats October 15 deadline for "discussions"

October 10   Fighting near Thag La ridge kills 7 Indians with 33 PLA dead and wounded

October 11   MFA warns "Indian side [must] rein in before the precipice [or] continue to spread the flames of war"

October 14   *People's Daily* declares "massive invasion of Chinese territory . . . seems imminent"; calls on PLA to "redouble vigilance . . . be well-prepared . . . to defend our territory and . . . to deal resolute counterblows to any invaders!"

October 20   PLA attacks Indian positions at Thag La and in Ladakh in coordinated offensive; NCNA and Ministry of National Defense charge India with "large-scale, all-out attacks"

October 22   Ministry of National Defense announces "Chinese frontier guards need no longer restrict themselves to the limits of the illegal McMahon Line"

October 24   PRC proposes (1) twenty kilometer mutual withdrawal and disengagement from "the line of actual control," (2) res-

107

toration of status quo ante in NEFA provided Indians do
not reestablish lost posts in NEFA and Ladakh, and (3)
Peking or New Delhi as meeting place for prime ministers

October 27   PLA offensive ends; *People's Daily* publishes 15,000 word
attack, "More on Nehru's Philosophy"

Peking did not reply to New Delhi's September 19 note until October
3. This delay is striking since the Indian response had countered the PRC
proposal for discussions beginning October 15. It is possible that the Tenth
Central Committee Plenum, then in progress, argued this matter at some
length or simply preempted attention to other affairs. As will be seen,
evidence of different tactics, if not different strategies, for handling the
political side of the Sino-Indian dispute persisted well into October. More
likely, however, the reply was intended as little more than an exercise to
influence foreign opinion and to set the stage for subsequent fighting.
Hence, urgency was unnecessary.

The Indian note had in effect rejected the Chinese position, attaching
the express precondition that China agree the October 15 meeting would
"define measures to restore the status quo in the western sector which has
been altered by force in the last few years and to remove the current
tensions in that area." Implementation of these measures would "alone
make possible" discussion on the general boundary problem.

The MFA response combined toughness and flexibility in a frank appeal
to world opinion that left open only two prospects: either a last-minute
reversal in Indian policy or a major conflict. The tough wording was
bluntly put, "It is clear that the Indian Government is determined to
answer the Chinese Government's peace proposal with rifles and guns. . . .
Whenever India attacks, China is sure to strike back. The Indian Government must bear responsibility for all the serious consequences arising from
this."[1] The flexibility of the message emerged somewhat more elliptically.
On the one hand, the MFA flatly rejected all "preconditions for the
discussions on the boundary question" specified in New Delhi's September
19 note. On the other hand, it agreed "that during the discussions
questions concerning the middle and eastern sectors of the boundary must
be discussed as well as those concerning the western sector, in a word, that
neither side should refuse to discuss any question concerning the Sino-
Indian boundary that may be raised by the other side."

To confuse the issue still further, the MFA note concluded, "As regards the concrete arrangement, the Chinese Government has noted that the Indian Government has agreed to the proposal for holding discussions from October 15 first in Peking and then in Delhi alternately. The Chinese Government is prepared to receive on October 15 the representative to be sent by the Indian side." This directly contradicted the opening paragraphs which correctly noted that "the Indian Government has once again refused [China's] proposal for speedily and unconditionally holding discussions on the Sino-Indian boundary question on the basis of the report of the officials of the two countries."

The two-week delay in replying to New Delhi's counter-proposal rules out the possibility of simple confusion or misreading of the Indian note. Instead the ambiguities and contradictions in the Chinese position were deliberately calculated to serve two purposes. First, they permitted a final testing of Indian intentions. By simultaneously rejecting any "preconditions" and pretending that New Delhi had "agreed to the proposal for holding discussions," it might be possible to finesse the impasse without an undue loss of face for either side. The shooting at Dhola and the consequent Chinese casualties, prominently publicized in Lhasa and Peking, had occurred after the Indian note of September 19. These developments together with the Chinese reply might provoke a policy reversal in New Delhi to make the October 15 meeting acceptable despite refusal of the specific Indian terms. Second, the ambiguities and obfuscations permitted Peking to prepare a public case for its position before further escalating its military pressure. This tactic was signaled by the statement, unprecedented in previous MFA notes, "It is not difficult for the Asian countries and all peace-loving countries to see from this that the Chinese Government is sincerely working for a peaceful settlement of the Sino-Indian boundary question." Apprehension over the likely reaction to an anticipated PLA offensive, regardless of the degree of self-justification behind such a move, appears to have determined this allusion as the opening move in what was to become a major part of Peking's diplomatic and propaganda posture.

New Delhi's swift reply on October 6 suggested it was acutely aware of the threat to its international position represented by the Chinese allusion to "Asian and all peace-loving countries." It ignored the MFA formula for talks without preconditions or prearrangements as to their context and content, asserting, "No useful talks and discussions can take place in the absence of a precise agenda."[2] It repeated verbatim the key paragraph from the September 19 note concerning the western sector as the first problem to be resolved, after which the general boundary could be discussed. Finally, New Delhi added a new demand, namely withdrawal behind the Thag La ridge:

> . . . The Government of India will not enter into any talks and discussions under duress or continuing threat of force. The latest Chinese intrusion must be terminated first. . . .
>
> . . . The Government of India are prepared to make necessary arrangements for starting discussion in Peking or in Delhi from a mutually convenient date as soon as the latest intrusion by Chinese forces in Indian territory south of the McMahon line has been terminated as requested in Government of India's note of 25th September 1962, and the Chinese Government indicate their acceptance of the proposal made in that note. . . .

This ended the exchange on the possibility of discussions beginning October 15. Peking did not reply to this note before the deadline, and chose instead to use the PLA to communicate China's posture through intensified military action.

Fighting at Thag La Ridge

The Indian troops near Dhola required a major increase in supplies particularly with winter weather threatening, if they were to drive the Chinese behind the Thag La ridge. The only suitable airdrop zone in the immediate vicinity was Tsangdhar, a small area approximately 120 by 50 yards, some 3,500 yards south of the ridge and in clear visibility of PLA outposts.[3] Beginning September 21, an increased number of flights dropped tons of blankets, clothing, guns, and ammunition, most of which missed the designated area and was lost in the steep ravines and thickly wooded slopes.[4] However, as Dalvi subsequently remarked, "These feverish drops, under the noses of the Chinese, naturally gave the impression that we were 'building up.' "[5]

On October 4, Lieutenant General B. M. Kaul was named commander of a newly created "IV Corps," immediately headlined in the Indian press:

> Special Task Force Created to Oust Chinese
> General Kaul Leaves for NEFA
> To Assume Command; Indian Army
> Poised for All-Out Effort[6]

Actually the "IV Corps" did not exist in any conventional military sense but was merely a paper designation to cover the congeries of forces responsible for defending the 350 miles of NEFA frontier. At the time this totaled some 6,000 troops or two brigades, instead of the normal corps complement of six to twelve brigades.[7] Nevertheless, the publicity attending Kaul's appointment and flight to the front committed New Delhi to action in the near future. The Chinese press duly reported his appointment and movements in this light.

The Indian forces steadily strengthened and expanded their positions. Dalvi claimed that "by the 30th of September I was able to provide them with three first lines of ammunition and 21 days' rations. . . .The Punjabis were well dug-in and reasonably well-stocked. They were exchanging fire, round for round, with the Chinese every day and getting the better of these fire-fights."[8] While this did not redress the overall balance of forces in the area which still remained favorable to the PLA, it provided the basis for planning an offensive to press Chinese troops behind Thag La ridge as ordered.

Accordingly, on September 29 reconnoitering probed the western approaches to the ridge in order to flank and ultimately to dominate the PLA positions.[9] On October 4, as a first step toward this end, one company of the Punjabis moved to Tsangle. The Indian apprehension that this move would alert the Chinese proved correct as the PLA quickly erected blocking positions.[10] The Chinese were excellently positioned to observe virtually all forward movement, and were able to intercept Indian tactical communications through monitoring the radio telephone "in continuous wireless touch" with the advancing company.[11]

The proximity and visibility of the two sides facilitated PLA tactics in still another way. Broadcasts in excellent Hindi to the Indian troops professed friendship and predicted high level talks in the future.[12] Chinese claims were supported by details and assurances of peaceful intent. Meanwhile, New Delhi's intelligence reported increases in the PLA strength from the single battalion estimated on September 22 to at least a full brigade as of October 5.[13] Two days later New Delhi warned Kaul of a major buildup behind Thag La approximating divisional strength, including heavy mortar and artillery.

Kaul arrived at the Namka Chu late on October 6, spending the next three days surveying the area and meeting with local officers. On October 8 he ordered two battalions from the drop zone at Tsangdhar to take up positions at the bridges, preparatory to a further move.[14] The next day Kaul unveiled his plan to occupy Yumtso La, a 16,000-foot pass one mile west of Thag La. Indian troops would thus be positioned behind the PLA, just as in Ladakh where Indian forces had moved behind the Chinese outposts to contest Peking's claim to de jure ownership by de facto occupation. Unlike Ladakh, however, the NEFA deployment came amidst express statements in New Delhi vowing to drive the PLA back from its present positions and not merely to contest ownership by countermoves.

An advance patrol of some fifty Punjabis crossed the Namka Chu at noon on October 9 and by evening established its initial advance base at a hut known as Tseng Jong (Chitung). Shortly after dawn on October 10, fierce fighting broke out between the Punjabis and a Chinese force estimated at between 500 and 800 troops supported with heavy mortars.[15] Despite the extreme disparity in strength, the Indians inflicted the greater casualties by splitting their force in two without detection and firing on the advancing PLA from higher flanking positions. The PLA regrouped, attacked from three sides, and soon overran the Indian positions. Perhaps embarrassed by the defeat, New Delhi made no immediate official protest although Kaul listed Indian losses as six dead, eleven wounded, and five missing.[16]

In contrast, Peking sent three notes, on October 10, 11, and 13, claiming thirty-three Chinese guards were "killed and wounded" and warning New Delhi in successive formulations that sounded identical deterrence threats of more serious fighting:

> ... If the Indian side does not immediately stop its armed attacks and withdraw from the Che Dong area but keeps creating new incidents of bloodshed the Chinese side will surely act resolutely in self defense and the Indian Government must bear full responsibility for all the consequences. (October 10)

> ... Should the Indian side still not rein in before the precipice but continue to spread the flames of war, the Indian Government must bear full responsibility for the resulting casualties on both sides and all other consequences that may ensue. (October 11)

> ... Should the Indian side disregard the repeated protests and warnings by the Chinese Government and persist stubbornly in

expanding its scope of aggression and continuing its attacks on the Chinese frontier guards, the latter will surely continue to strike back resolutely.[17]

(October 13)

The Chinese account agrees with Kaul in noting that the Indians "left behind them six corpses," which the PLA ceremoniously buried in full view of the opposing side "with full military honors." On all other aspects, however, the two sides offered wholly contradictory accounts of the fighting except as to its location and intensity.

As with the September 20 clash, it cannot be ascertained definitively who fired the first shot. However, several inferences about the likely context of the event can be made. First, the PLA observed the Indian resupply and deployment and interpreted it to mean that New Delhi had decided to take the initiative in an attempt to force the Chinese back. The obvious Indian weakness posed no serious threat to local security, but the move was both provocative and inviting. Second, the alacrity with which the PLA reacted in strength against the advance patrol suggests ample preparation for hostilities in the immediate area. Indeed, so great was the disparity of firepower that Brigadier General Dalvi chose not to support his beleaguered unit with mortar and machine-gun fire after the fighting began because he calculated his entire main force would be quickly overwhelmed.[18] Third, the timing of the clash, exactly one week after the October 3 MFA demarche had distorted New Delhi's position as having "agreed to the proposal for holding discussion from October 15," raises the possibility that Kaul inadvertently stumbled into a preplanned PLA trap. In this regard it is worth noting that on October 8, "a Chinese leader told the Soviet Ambassador that China had information that India was about to launch a massive attack along the Sino-Indian border and that should India attack we would resolutely defend ourselves."[19] The unnamed official also "pointed out that the fact that Soviet-made helicopters and transport planes were being used by India for air-dropping and transporting military supplies in the Sino-Indian border areas was making a bad impression on our frontier guards." So far as is known this was the first such representation from Peking to Moscow. It is conceivable that Peking grossly misperceived Indian capabilities, hence the "massive attack" prediction. More likely, however, deliberate exaggeration served to prepare the record for anticipated combat.

The limited nature of the Chinese military action, together with the ostentatious burying of Indian dead, suggests the attack was carefully designed to serve as a deterrent signal rather than a major punitive blow or a strategic offensive. No PLA troops crossed the Namka Chu and no firing was reported on Indian forces stationed at the bridges, although, according to Dalvi's description, troops there were "milling about trying to find cover" and could "have been mowed down, in the open, by the Chinese machine-guns across the narrow Namka Chu."[20] Moreover Dalvi noted that Indian casualties "came directly . . . under the noses of the Chinese who had evidently decided to allow us to use a route which they were controlling."

After the clash, General Kaul concurred with the plea of the local brigade and division commanders to "go to Delhi and ask the Army Headquarters and the Government not to press us to 'expel' the Chinese from this area, a task which was far beyond our capacity. . . .The fact that they had suffered more casualties than us that day was no yardstick by which to judge the situation."[21] He specifically ordered "that the instructions to drive the enemy back were to be held in abeyance till I returned from Delhi." However, on October 12 Nehru publicly declared in a press interview "that the armed forces had been ordered to throw the Chinese aggressors out of NEFA. Our instructions are to free our territory."[22]

Peking's Propaganda Offensive

Chinese media immediately publicized Nehru's statement together with other Indian views, whether official or unofficial, in order to contrast New Delhi's "aggressive plans" with Peking's proposals for discussion. An unusually virulent *People's Daily* editorial kicked off a new press campaign on the same day as the October 10 clash. After recapitulating the developments at Dhola and the conflicting proposals for talks, the editorial declared:

> . . . All these facts show that "peaceful negotiations" on the lips of the Indian ruling group headed by Nehru is nothing but a smokescreen to hoodwink the Indian people and to hoodwink world public opinion. This total lack of any sincere desire on the part of the Indian Government to settle the Sino-Indian boundary question by peaceful means has laid bare the Nehru government's intention to pay lip-service to talks while actually launching invasions. . . . The

Indian Government harbours an extremely malicious design, namely, to provoke serious clashes in the border areas and stir up a new anti-Chinese campaign in conformity with the needs of the imperialists and their lackeys. However the Indian Government has gone too far and is too barefaced in its scheming. . . . India's aggression and provocations against China and its truculent, preposterous attitude on the Sino-Indian boundary question cannot but arouse the boundless indignation of the Chinese people. . . .[23]

The polemical tone of this attack, as implied by its references to "world public opinion" and "the needs of the imperialists and their lackeys," was heightened in republication by *Peking Review*'s subheads, "Chinese and Indian Stands: A Glaring Contrast"; "Who Has Intruded?"; "Who Is Responsible for Border Tension?"; "Who Is Attempting Blackmail?"; and "Who Is Using Threats of Force?" A sketch map accompanying the editorial purported to show three different locations of the McMahon Line as located in Indian maps or proposals with Dhola (Che Dong) clearly above the "Original Map of 1914" location.

The international audience had become a salient target for Chinese exploitation of the border crisis. This was intimated by the October 3 reference to "Asian and all peace-loving countries." The October 10 editorial coincided in its timing with a one-week interval following the note as well as with the standard time delay of three to four days following a significant external stimulus which was, in this case, the Indian reply of October 6. Therefore, while the cause of the editorial cannot be clearly inferred, its implications are revealed in the pattern of Chinese media over the next week.

Within hours of the outbreak of fighting at Thag La ridge Radio Peking broadcast abroad an initial account which claimed "eleven casualties" among "Chinese frontier guards" with "the battle still continuing."[24] This followed an earlier item the same day alleging Nehru had ordered the Indian Air Force to "go into action in the 'Northeast Frontier Agency' if necessary 'to oust' the Chinese troops" and adding the original United Press comment to the effect that the situation "could turn into a major battle at any time."[25] By the time this selected quote was being beamed overseas, Chinese officials knew the clash had progressed well beyond any previous incident.

Two days later Peking broadcast a résumé of six Indian newspapers for the period October 8–10 to show that "Indian capitalist papers have clamored for an immediate attack on China in the eastern sector of the Sino-Indian boundary and have revealed that the Indian authorities decided long ago to refuse negotiations and launch military attacks."[26] While the accompanying quotations supported this allegation, it was not the first time that year the charge could have been made since such items had appeared frequently. The decision to offer this evidence to support Chinese charges against New Delhi further suggested preparation for greater hostilities.

As a counter theme, relations with India's neighbors received special emphasis at this time. On October 6 the first anniversary of the Sino-Nepalese boundary treaty was celebrated in Peking with a reception at which Minister of Foreign Affairs Ch'en Yi declared, "The Indian reactionaries are trying by force to impose on China a plan of occupying Chinese territory which even British imperialism failed to realize. All countries stressing Asian unity are opposed to this practice by the Indian reactionaries."[27] Going beyond the limits of any known agreement, he vowed, "The Nepalese people can rest fully assured that should any foreign power dare to attack Nepal, the Chinese Government and people, along with all countries and people upholding justice, will stand forever at the side of Nepal." This pledge could only apply against India and as such was well calculated to extend Peking's protection below the Himalayan crest while denying New Delhi this avenue of approach to Tibetan guerrillas.

More revealing of Peking's diplomatic strategy and more provocative from New Delhi's standpoint was the announcement on October 12 of a Sino-Pakistani agreement reached that day in the PRC capital "on procedural matters concerning future discussions . . . on the question of the boundary between China's Sinkiang and contiguous area, the defense of which is under the control of Pakistan."[28] This sudden climax to exchanges which had dragged on between the two sides since January, 1961, was a tribute to Chinese maneuvering in the week before war with India and as such deserves brief review.

A full understanding of the complex and conflicting border claims involving Pakistan, India, and China requires more detailed background, particularly on the Kashmir dispute, than is necessary for the purposes of this study.[29] It is sufficient to note that the dispute opened up a twofold possibility for Peking. Geographically a Pakistani presence in northern Kashmir could provide a two-hundred mile buffer between the Sino-Indian border terminus at the Karakoram pass and the Sino-Soviet-Afghan trijuncture in the Pamir mountains adjoining Sinkiang. Politically China could offset Soviet collusion with India by adopting a parallel posture with Pakistan.

The potential for conflict with Pakistan was far less than with India since no territory of strategic value to China was in question. Until mid-1962, the Chinese did not push a settlement, perhaps out of deference to India's claims over Kashmir and the hope of avoiding further inflammation of New Delhi's sensitivity so long as some prospect of negotiating the Sino-Indian boundary was in view. Thus, while Pakistan proposed formal negotiations with China on the border as early as March 28, 1961, the PRC did not reply until February 27, 1962, at which time it noted that any agreement could only be provisional until the Kashmir dispute was formally settled.[30]

Even then events moved slowly. Although Pakistan agreed to the Chinese provision on March 19, a joint commission did not start to exchange views until May 3, 1962. Its deliberations went unreported through the summer but the appointment of General Raza as Pakistan's first ambassador in Peking suggested serious intentions, especially in view of his having negotiated the border agreement with Iran. Thus the October 12 announcement of forthcoming border talks was well-timed for securing the tacit cooperation of Pakistan in the imminent Sino-Indian hostilities.

Finally, on October 13, the first anniversary of the Sino-Burmese boundary protocol was celebrated in Peking with the claim that it "demonstrated to the world that any complicated problem between countries left behind by history, can be settled if the countries wish to settle them and if they adhere to the principle of equality and mutual benefit."[31] The contrast with Sino-Indian relations did not need more specific reference.

Meanwhile *People's Daily* increased its coverage of the crisis to peak proportions. This included the most bluntly worded editorial up to that time, one which merits quotation at length both for its alarmist rhetoric and for the date of its occurrence—October 14, the deadline for discussions. Entitled, "Mr. Nehru, It Is High Time For You To Pull Back From the Brink of the Precipice," the editorial declared:

> *A massive invasion of Chinese territory by Indian troops in the eastern sector of the Sino-Indian boundary seems imminent.* Indian Prime Minister Nehru declared on October 12 that he had issued instructions to the Indian armed forces "to free Indian territory in the Northeast Frontier Agency of Chinese intruders." . . . So *it*

seems that Mr. Nehru has made up his mind to attack the Chinese frontier guards on an even bigger scale. . . .They have reached out for a yard after taking an inch, proceeding from the western sector of the Sino-Indian boundary to its eastern sector, from nibbling to large-scale invasion, from minor provocations to big joint attacks by regular ground and air forces.

How could the Chinese possibly be so weak-kneed and faint-hearted as to tolerate this? It is high time to show to Mr. Nehru that the heroic Chinese troops with the glorious tradition of resisting foreign aggression, can never be cleared by anyone from their own territory. History has furnished repeated proof that not the Chinese troops, but the Japanese imperial army and the Yankees were cleared out of Chinese territory. This has been the fate of all foreign aggressors on Chinese soil and this will be so in the future. If there are still some maniacs who are reckless enough to ignore our well-intentioned advice and insist on having another try, well, let them do so. History will pronounce its inexorable verdict.

All comrade commanders and fighters of the People's Liberation Army guarding the Sino-Indian border, redouble your vigilance! Indian troops may at any time attempt to carry out Nehru's instructions to get rid of you. Be well-prepared! Your sacred task now is to defend our territory and be ever-ready to deal resolute counterblows at any invaders!

At this most critical moment in the development of the Sino-Indian border situation, we still want to appeal once more to Mr. Nehru: pull back from the brink of the precipice and do not use the lives of Indian troops as stakes in your gamble. . . .[32] [Italics added.]

This was a major change from the earlier deterrence warnings as manifested by its mobilization appeals to the PLA, its admonition against being "weak-kneed and faint-hearted," and its personal accusations directed against Nehru. The allusion to "some maniacs who are reckless enough to ignore our well-intentioned advice" was gratuitous in view of the consistent indicators amply cited by Radio Peking that New Delhi had no intention of halting its forward policy either in NEFA or Ladakh. Beyond deterrence, the main purpose of this editorial appears to have been a final alert to Chinese audiences of the impending war and a last "warning" for the record to make certain that "history will pronounce its inexorable verdict" against New Delhi.

China Attacks: The First Phase

As the first snow began to fall on Indian positions at Tsangle, Dalvi's detailed account of the conditions which his troops faced provides a graphic description of the local superiority enjoyed by the PLA on the eve of the battle:

> . . . The efforts of our troops to cut logs with entrenching tools and shovels were pathetic and openly derided by the Chinese who could see us. They had a lavish scale of mechanical saws and could build defense and bunkers at an incomparably faster rate.
>
> . . . By 16th October we had a total of 450 Border Roads Pioneers to assist us in carrying loads and collecting air-drops at Tsangdhar. . . .They had come without rations and winter clothing. . . .I had barely two days rations for my command.[33]
>
> . . . The tempo of air drops at Tsangdhar reached a climax between 15th and 19th October. . . .Only 30 per cent of stores reached the troops. . . .It was impossible to drop supplies on so small a dropping zone . . . without a large number of canisters going astray . . . bouncing down a precipitous slope. . . .Tsangdhar was also in full view of the Chinese positions on the Thagla slopes. . . .Four para-field guns were dropped, but were damaged beyond local repair.[34]
>
> . . . Throughout we were in full view of the Chinese and no surprise was possible, nor hopes of purposeful camouflage. The Chinese could also be seen clearly, which fact did not do our morale any good. With their superiority and preparedness they made no attempt to conceal their movements or activities. They almost openly dared us to make this first move . . . At night they lit bonfires to keep themselves warm.[35]
>
> . . . [Chinese] groups were seen receiving orders, and artillery personnel were brazenly taking bearings on our positions for silent registration of targets. They brought guns and mortars across Thagla Ridge on ponies. . . .They even brought a jeep to Thagla. . . .I had deployed 25 observation posts to watch the Chinese build-up. . . . These posts were actually able to count the number of mortar bombs and shells dumped. On 19th October one of the observation posts actually counted 1,978 armed Chinese soldiers concentrated at Tseng-Jong.[36]
>
> . . . On 18th October the Chinese were engaged in last minute preparations for a night advance and a dawn attack. We could see their marking parties and guides moving to forming-up places. . . .On the evening of 19th October, 7 Brigade was squarely in the Chinese

trap and it was a matter of hours before it was sprung. Through the day Chinese units could be seen moving to battle locations, which they had reconnoitered during the preceding three days.[37]

Dalvi aptly concluded, "We were mute witnesses of our own impending destruction." The situation could not have escaped notice in Peking, either for its lack of immediate threat or for its invitation to a swift and relatively cheap victory.

Precisely at 5 A.M. on the morning of October 20, two flares burst over the Namka Chu.[38] As Dalvi describes it, "This signal was followed by a cannonade of over 150 guns and heavy mortars, exposed on the forward slopes of Thagla [on] our positions at bridges three and four, Tsangdhar, log and temporary bridges, and brigade headquarters, which was some one thousand yards from the river bank." The PLA simultaneously attacked in the Galwan and Chip Chap valleys as well as other points on the western front.

Within four days the Chinese had overrun Khinzemane, Dhola, and Tawang, while in the west more than a dozen Indian posts fell with others hastily evacuated. According to Kaul, "We had given up the whole of northern Ladakh within forty-eight hours."[39] There were no large-scale battles; most engagements were fierce and brief. No aircraft or armored units were involved, although the PLA fired upon Indian pilots attempting to drop supplies at Tsangdhar. The combination of shock at the Chinese attack and the overwhelming material and manpower superiority of the PLA quickly broke Indian resistance at all points.

Despite the PLA's clear advantage its offensive was limited in scope and duration. No attempt was made to pursue the Indian troops at Tsangle, and they escaped into Bhutan. Despite press reports to the contrary, it was not "human wave" attacks but standard military tactics which characterized the Chinese offensive. In this regard Dalvi noted that "the most impressive display of Chinese training was their uncannily accurate artillery barrages. . . .Their attacks were preceded by supporting fire of pin-point accuracy. . . .The real Chinese success can be attributed to their high command. They had maneuvered the Thagla incident with cunning; and the Chinese soldier had delivered the *coup de grace* with skill and fanaticism."[40] The initial assault on the central river positions was followed by flanking and enveloping thrusts around the remaining Indian forces in the Namka Chu and Nyam Jung Chu valleys. Forty-eight hours after the attack began, all positions forward of Tawang were wiped out or in jeopardy and New Delhi ordered the evacuation of its main supply base without a fight.

The PLA entered the abandoned base of Tawang on October 25. Further east on the same day probing attacks around Walong encountered stiff resistance and soon subsided to minor shooting. Meanwhile on the western front the Indian withdrawal outpaced Chinese attacks, beginning with the evacuation of Daulet Beg Oldi before any assault occurred. However, the PLA did not occupy it since it lay beyond the Chinese claim line. Then one week after the initial attack a three-week lull settled over both ends of the boundary, and the first phase of the Chinese military offensive was ended.

Peking's political posture displayed some curious anomalies at this time, perhaps reflecting uncertainty at some levels as to how the situation might evolve. The initial news of the fighting came from NCNA which accused Indian forces of having attacked Chinese frontier guards, first in NEFA and then in Aksai Chin. This announcement came approximately two hours after the actual outbreak of hostilities.[41] Such speed suggests a preplanned release. The Ministry of Defense matched NCNA's alacrity when, later that day, it declared that "large scale, all-out attacks" in NEFA and the western sector had resulted in "Chinese frontier guards [being] compelled to strike back resolutely."[42] Although ostensibly acting in "self-defense" the PLA had already "recovered Khinzemane, Che Dong [Dhola], and Kalung" in the east and had "cleared away some aggressive strongpoints" in the west. Despite these admitted gains, the Ministry of Foreign Affairs dramatically summoned the Indian charge d'affaires at 4 A.M. the next morning to deliver "the most urgent, most serious, and strongest protest" over "the massive general attacks against the Chinese frontier guards in both the eastern and western sectors of the Sino-Indian border simultaneously."[43] Replete with accusations of "fierce artillery fire" near Dhola and "heavy casualties" (unspecified) on the Chinese side, the note bluntly concluded, "China has no choice but to rebuff these frenzied attacks resolutely. The fight is still going on. The Indian Government must bear full responsibility for all the serious consequences arising therefrom."

Apparently two versions of the MFA protest existed. Radio Peking broadcast internationally one text which included the customary diplomatic ending, "The Ministry of Foreign Affairs avails itself of this opportunity to renew to the Indian Embassy the assurances of its highest consideration."[44] A scant half-hour later NCNA instructed domestic recipients to correct the already transmitted text by deleting this sentence.[45] The official version reprinted in the Indian *White Paper* does not contain this expression, but curiously enough it does appear in the text printed by *Peking Review* on October 26.

The contentious phrase was included in the next protest filed by the MFA, on November 6, and all successive notes. This raises the question as to why it should have become so sensitive at this particular moment. Unlike low level reports for radio or newspaper release, the MFA protest would presumably be carefully reviewed at the highest levels of government. Given the coordinated nature of the PLA offensive, it is likely that the timing and general content of the protest were agreed upon in advance of the attack. Under these circumstances, only last-minute reservations or divided views could explain the changes in wording and the attendant confusion.

The inclusion of the customary closing sentence implies the expectation that normal diplomatic communications would continue regardless of how acrimonious their content at the moment. On the one hand, this may have been seen by some in Peking as an anomaly in view of the alleged egregiousness of Indian behavior. On the other hand, knowing the specific charges were false and becoming aware of the PLA advances as additional reports reached the capital, some may have feared that New Delhi would break relations and move to a formal state of war. Such an Indian initiative would further complicate China's already difficult internal and external affairs by increasing the defense burden of a long, tortuous frontier amidst a rebellious populace while providing India with more leverage on Russian, American, and Afro-Asian support. These competing considerations may have elicited divided views on how hard a posture to adopt during the opening days of the PLA attack, resulting, among other things, in different versions of the MFA protest.

The suddenness of the Indian collapse amid Chinese protestations of purely "defensive" action prompted a second defense ministry statement on October 22. Somewhat belatedly in view of the rapid advance in NEFA, it declared the McMahon Line had become wholly irrelevant for PLA movements. It argued that because "the Indian Government has finally broken the limits indicated by this [the McMahon] line, the Chinese side now formally declares that in order to prevent the Indian troops from staging a comeback and launching fresh attacks, the Chinese frontier guards fighting in self defense need no longer restrict themselves to the limits of the illegal McMahon Line."[46] This served formal notice for the first time that the PRC would not limit itself to reacting against Indian posts established under the "forward policy" but was prepared to pursue the attack to whatever length policy and circumstances permitted. At the very least, this raised the prospect of all NEFA being overrun; at worst, it could mean an advance into the Assam plain.

Close on its heels came a major PRC statement designed for maximum international effectiveness, accompanied by a private letter from Chou to Nehru which evidenced the softer side of Peking's posture. On October 24, Radio Peking broadcast an "appeal to the Indian Government . . . to the governments of Asian and African countries . . . to all the peace-loving countries and people" which, as this verbiage suggests, was aimed at mobilizing opinion behind the Chinese position.[47] It termed "serious armed clashes" as "most unfortunate," claiming "that China and India should cross swords on account of the boundary question is something the Chinese Government and people are unwilling to see. It is also what the peace-loving countries and people of the whole world are unwilling to see."

After a lengthy recapitulation of the diplomatic exchanges since 1959, the statement repeated the accusation that "on October 20, Indian forces started a massive general offensive in both the eastern and western sectors." It then asked, "What issue is there between China and India that cannot be settled peacefully? What reason is there for bloody clashes to occur between China and India?" There followed a concatenation of themes recalling "the Five Principles of Peaceful Coexistence," "the spirit of the Bandung Conference," the "struggle against imperialism," and "Asian-African solidarity." Following this revival of references long muted in Sino-Indian relations, the statement made three formal proposals. First, both sides should agree to "respect the line of actual control . . . along the entire Sino-Indian border and the armed forces of each side withdraw twenty kilometres from this line and disengage." Second, provided that New Delhi accepts the first point, China "is willing . . . to withdraw its frontier guards in the eastern sector of the border to the north of the line of actual control; at the same time both China and India undertake not to cross the line of actual control, i.e. the traditional customary line, in the middle and western sectors of the border." And third, talks should be held between the two prime ministers, either in Peking or New Delhi depending on the convenience of Nehru.

So important a diplomatic document was undoubtedly drafted in advance of the October 20 offensive with release scheduled soon after the initial hostilities. Its significance was underlined by its transmission, over Chou En-lai's personal signature, to ten Afro-Asian leaders who had recently been circularized by President Gamal Abdel Nasser of the United Arab Republic for consultation on Sino-Indian tensions. Among the leaders representing Indonesia, Cambodia, Ghana, Guinea, Mali, Morocco, Ceylon, Burma, Algeria, and Afghanistan were several key figures of potential influence as likely patrons of Peking's cause, such as Sukarno, Nkrumah, and Ben Bella.

Basically the terms offered nothing new, but for those audiences less than attentive to past diplomatic exchanges between Peking and New Delhi, it was adroitly phrased. Its ambiguities and assertions provided a ready riposte for the anticipated criticism that attended China's resort to open military force. In addition, the proposal to evacuate all NEFA territory occupied in the attack in exchange for Indian abandonment of all posts established in Ladakh over the previous two years offered a modicum of compromise should second thoughts on talks be entertained in Delhi.

To encourage such thoughts, Chou sent a personal letter to Nehru together with the proposal which diplomatically eschewed the more provocative language of the government statement:

> It is most distressing that border clashes as serious as the present ones should have occurred between our two countries. Fierce fighting is still going on. *At this critical moment, I do not propose to trace the origin of this conflict. I think we should look ahead, we should take measures to turn the tide.* . . . We have a major responsibility for Sino-Indian friendship, Asian-African solidarity, and Asian peace. Driven by a deep sense of this responsibility I sincerely appeal to you that you may respond positively to the above three proposals. Please accept, your Excellency, the assurances of my highest consideration.[48] [Italics added.]

Two points are worth attention in connection with Chou's letter. First, it remained secret until November 7, thereby avoiding the appearance of pressuring Nehru or trying to embarrass his response publicly. Second, Chou's lack of personal invective and recrimination was in sharp contrast with the *People's Daily* editorial of October 20 which had repeatedly accused Nehru of having "lied" and "slandered," concluding that "whatever Nehru feigned to be, he is in fact bellicose to the bone."[49]

Behind the contradiction between *People's Daily* and Chou's letter is the possibility that the PLA attack was calculated to awaken Delhi to the true facts of power, with the consequent abandoning of the forward policy once and for all. For this to be a realistic prospect, however, China would have to exercise some restraint to avoid provoking a wholly nationalistic and militant response. Seen in this light Chou's letter was well written. Moreover should nothing change, its subsequent release would strengthen the record of Chinese reasonableness.

In this regard, the general media treatment of the fighting strengthens the hypothesis of deliberate restraint in order to limit the consequences of attack. Little attention was given to Chinese victories and advances. Instead the media focused defensively on the alleged record of Indian provocations and preparations for attack. Front-page maps in the Peking press showed the McMahon Line with Indian positions beyond it, but omitted the customary arrows depicting PLA movements behind these positions. In fact, the PLA was seldom identified with the fighting which was described as involving only "frontier guards."

Not only was there no systematic effort to publicize victory or to mobilize the populace for war but, by the end of the week, Chinese media shifted their attention to support for Premier Fidel Castro and Cuba in the wake of the United States—Soviet missile crisis which had erupted on October 22. Large rallies, reportedly involving more than five million persons by November 7, took place throughout the cities.[50] The initial mass meeting in Peking on October 28 was attended by Chou, Ch'en Yi, Chief of Staff Lo Jui-ch'ing, and CCP General Secretary Teng Hsiao-p'ing, with the main speech by Politbureau member and mayor of Peking, P'eng Chen. Even in Urumchi and Lhasa, mass rallies pledged the "support" of Uighurs and Tibetans to the remote "socialist" ally in the Caribbean, but beat no audible drums over nearby "aggression" on the Himalayan border.

On the rare occasions where reference to India crept into statements addressing other issues, Chinese officials emulated Chou's "low posture." For instance, in commemoration of the "Chinese People's Volunteers" entry into the Korean War on October 25, Chief of Staff Lo resisted the obvious temptation to draw a parallel between the two situations. Instead he placed his main emphasis on "the ferocious aggressive countenance of

United States imperialism," pledging "the Chinese people will always support the Cuban revolution and fight to the end together with the Cuban people against the U.S. imperialist policies of war and aggression."[51] By contrast, he summarized India's "successive armed provocations and . . . large scale armed attacks" in one sentence, noting "the Chinese Government still upholds its usual position and continues its efforts to find ways to stop the border conflicts, reopen peaceful negotiations, and settle the Sino-Indian border question."

Following the initial surges in east and west, PLA pressure waned and Peking's political posture struck a judicious mixture of diplomatic offensive and restraint. But whatever hope there may have been for changing Indian policy quickly proved misplaced. Responding privately to Chou's letter on October 27, Nehru rejected the latest proposal for joint disengagement, withdrawal, and talks.[52] His position had already been foreshadowed by an official government statement made public on October 24 in response to press agency reports on the Chinese statement, but Nehru's more formal reply was authoritative and final. Charging that "the current clashes" arose "out of what is in effect a Chinese invasion of India," Nehru professed to be "not able to understand the niceties of . . . talk about 'lines of actual control.' " He counterproposed that both sides "revert to the position as it prevailed all along the India-China boundary prior to 8th September 1962. . . . We will, thereafter, be glad to welcome you or a delegation from your country at any level that is mutually acceptable to discuss and arrive at further agreed measures which can facilitate a peaceful settlement of our differences on this border question, in one stage or in more than one stage as may be necessary."

Nehru had moved somewhat from his previous position. He no longer insisted on a total Chinese withdrawal from all territory occupied since November, 1959, before any substantive discussion could begin. By agreeing to a possible "one stage" settlement, he in effect reverted to the position of July 26 which had proposed "further discussions . . . as soon as the current tensions have eased and the appropriate climate is created." However, his "September 8, 1962" line more than offset this apparent concession since it would restore the Dhola post and force the PLA back behind Thag La ridge. Moreover, despite all the intervening developments, forty-one Indian positions which had been eliminated in the western sector could be restored. In short, Nehru's reply, though of a generally temperate tone and privately transmitted, signaled a complete impasse and assured the continuation of confrontation on the Himalayan front.

Military Lull, Political Offensive

On October 27, exactly one week after the initial attack, *People's Daily* devoted its main space to India with a mixture of honey and vinegar that clearly subordinated the "sweet" to the "sour." Under the title "Fair and Reasonable Proposals," an editorial echoed the October 24 statement, declaring "The Chinese Government would welcome the Indian Prime Minister to Peking. If this should be inconvenient to the Indian Prime Minister, Premier Chou En-lai would be ready to go to Delhi."[53] At the same time it rejected Delhi's immediate public reaction, noting "China stands firmly opposed to the restoration of the situation of the entire boundary line before September 8," but made no threat, express or implied, of punitive action should the three-point proposal fail. The alarmist warnings of earlier editorials were wholly absent.

However, it was impossible to conceive of any imminent discussions, much less a meeting of prime ministers, given the simultaneous publication in *People's Daily* of a 15,000-word essay, "More on Nehru's Philosophy In The Light of the Sino-Indian Boundary Question."[54] This unmitigated personal attack on Nehru as a man bent on expansion and aggrandizement appeared concurrently with Chou's avowed willingness to meet with Nehru in Peking or Delhi—a paradox further heightened by attributing the article to the editorial department of *People's Daily*.

Its title identified the essay as an express sequel to a similar article of May 6, 1959, issued when Sino-Indian relations had sharply worsened after the Tibet revolt. The article went well beyond the 1959 analysis of Nehru's writings and speeches in order to demonstrate not only his personal perfidy but also the pernicious influence of capitalism in India and the replacement of British with "U.S. imperialism." It asserted, "A rough count shows that in the past three years Nehru has made more than 300 speeches on the Sino-Indian boundary question . . . [and] used the most malicious language in attacking and vilifying China." The prime minister was variously described as acting "obstinately" and "haughtily," trying "in the most despicable and sinister way to sow dissension between China and other countries," displaying "fickle and erratic behavior," and "dreaming of a great Indian empire . . . [whose] sphere of influence would include a series of countries from the Middle East to Southeast Asia and far surpass that of the colonial system set up in Asia in the past by the British empire."

The far-ranging analysis included the role of foreign—particularly American—investment, peasant landholdings and indebtedness, statistics on internal violence, as well as Delhi's policy positions on Korea (1950), Hungary (1956), Lebanon (1958), Japan (1960), Cuba (1961), and the Congo (1961). Quotations taken from American political figures and journals showed favorable comment on Indian developments with the general role of "U.S. imperialism" magnified to unprecedented proportions. The tie with Washington now became the central factor explaining the border crisis: "In a word, in the effort to satisfy their own needs and meet the demands of U.S. imperialism, the Indian ruling circles headed by Nehru have become pawns in the international anti-China campaign. This is the root cause and background of the Sino-Indian dispute."

The alleged dependency on Washington was argued statistically with figures showing the proportion of Indian imports from the United States increasing "from 16 to 27 percent (not including grains)" between 1948 and 1960–61, while United States aid "extended or promised" during this time totaled $4.7 billion. The analysis continued, "If to this is added the 'aid' extended . . . by international financial organizations controlled by the United States, the grand total will reach U. S. $6,598.2 million." Nehru personally had become "a lackey of the imperialists," having "practically thrown away the banner of opposition to imperialism and colonialism in international affairs, suited himself to the needs of U.S. imperialism, become a busy spokesman for U.S. imperialism, and even openly made Indian troops serve as an international policeman for U.S. imperialism in its suppression of national liberation movements."

This language was so wholly incompatible with Chou's private letter to Nehru as to completely nullify its contents. The article's complex and lengthy analysis precluded the possibility of its having been drafted as a response to New Delhi's public rejection on October 24 of Peking's latest proposal; moreover, Nehru's private response could not have arrived before the article was published. Finally, the virulence of the attack was unique at a time when all Chinese media were treating Cuba as the primary foreign policy issue, giving scant heed to the prospects of war with India.

These considerations raise the possibility that the essay originated outside the normal decision-making framework responsible for handling Sino-Indian relations. As such it may have represented a wholly different perspective on the crisis, its implications, and the best means of handling it. If so, this evidence of policy divisions could explain some of the lesser contradictions in Peking's posture previously noted.

Both the style and content of the essay provide clues to its origin and purpose. Stylistically, "More on Nehru's Philosophy" is dominated by ideological vocabulary which had characterized the Chinese polemic with Moscow initiated by "Long Live Leninism" in April, 1960.[55] Whereas previous analyses of the border crisis ritualistically focused on historical documentation, maps, speeches, and the respective "control" exercised by both sides in contested territory, this statement claimed to "lay bare the essential truth of the matter and elucidate the root cause" of the dispute within a Marxist—Leninist framework of economic determinism. As the opening section put it, both India's earlier "interference in China's Tibet" and its recent "large-scale armed invasion of China" were "determined by the class nature of India's big bourgeoisie and big landlords whose interests are closely connected with those of the imperialists."

The analysis elaborated on the inherent "contradictions" in the interests and behavior of "the national bourgeoisie of the colonial and semi-colonial countries," citing Lenin's views on "bourgeois nationalism." These "contradictions" were manifested both internally in the struggle against "feudalism" and externally in the drive for "independence" while remaining dependent on "monopoly capitalism and imperialism." Nehru's personal vacillation was documented by his writings and by his political record, which had received increasingly unfavorable comment as time progressed.

A further clue to the import of the essay lies in its treatment of two issues, both of which bore directly on Soviet policy. Having identified "the Indian ruling circles headed by Nehru" as "revealing their policy of reactionary nationalism" as early as 1958–59, the article asked, "What stand should the Marxist-Leninists take on this policy of reactionary nationalism followed by Nehru?" A three-part answer followed. First, an analogy was drawn with Chinese Communist policy during Soviet-Chinese hostilities over the Chinese Eastern Railway in 1929. Second, the "Yugoslav modern revisionist" position on the border was attacked as a negative example. Third, the Indian Communist party was addressed with specific reference to "progressives" as opposed to "self-styled Marxist-Leninists."

The use of history and surrogate targets for attacks on the Soviet leadership had become common practice by this time, particularly with the agreement in the spring of 1962 to suspend open polemics. For example, a series of *Red Flag* articles from March through May had examined critically the errors of such long gone heretics as Edward

Bernstein, Karl Kautsky, and the Economists, in what were transparent attacks on Khrushchev and contemporary Soviet practices.[56] The "Tito clique" and "Yugoslav modern revisionists" had been prominent substitutes for Moscow in earlier commentaries of 1959 and subsequent diatribes following the abortive efforts to end the dispute in 1960–61.[57] The mending of relations between Belgrade and Moscow, accelerated in mid-1962 and climaxed with Leonid Brezhnev's visit to Yugoslavia as chief of state in late September, made the Soviet Union more obviously the real target of Chinese attacks.

The 1929 analogy posed by the essay is of special interest. Earlier Sino-Soviet relations were discussed in terminology so precisely parallel to Peking's contemporary prose that it was unnecessary to spell out the full implications for 1962. Such phrases as "whipped up a frantic anti-Soviet campaign," while "the Soviet Union repeatedly showed forbearance and proposed the holding of a meeting to settle the question peacefully" were followed by the reminder that "in October . . . the army of the Kuomintang reactionaries attacked the Soviet border . . . thus the Soviet Union was compelled to act in self-defense."

It was laconically noted that "Sino-Indian relations today bear certain similarities to Sino-Soviet relations of more than thirty years ago." Beyond this, however, the text invited the comparison of the CCP's posture in the first instance with that of Moscow in the 1962 crisis. This point became clear in the section immediately following a written attack upon "the Yugoslav modern revisionists, renegades to Marxism-Leninism and lackeys of the imperialists" for having "openly shielded and supported the outrageous anti-China policy of the Nehru government." The article at this point asserted:

> . . . Moreover, Tito said that the Soviet Union should play a "pacifying" role in relation to China on the Sino-Indian boundary question. Does the Tito clique think that when a socialist country is invaded by the bourgeois reactionaries of a foreign country, another socialist country should stand by the bourgeois reactionaries and play a "pacifying" role in relation to the invaded socialist country? By this fallacy, the Tito clique has further exposed itself as a group of renegades betraying socialism, hating socialist China and sowing dissension among the socialist countries.

This allusion to the proper "socialist" behavior touched on a long-standing issue in the Sino-Soviet dispute. In September, 1959, as noted earlier, a TASS statement which "deplored" violence in the border controversy aroused anger in Peking for its neutral position on a matter that carried obligatory support for the Chinese side. As recently as October 8 Peking had officially drawn Moscow's attention to an impending Indian "massive attack" inter alia voicing its objection to the Soviet supply of transport aircraft and high-altitude helicopters.[58] According to the Chinese account, "On October 13 and 14, 1962, Khrushchev told the Chinese Ambassador . . . their information on Indian preparations to attack China was similar to China's. If they were in China's position, they would have taken the same measures. A neutral attitude on the Sino-Indian boundary question was impossible. If anyone attacked China and they said they were neutral, it would be an act of betrayal."

In the absence of any documentation or Soviet account it cannot be ascertained whether this is accurate and complete. However, subsequent Russian behavior largely confirms it. Within hours of the Chinese attack of October 20, a letter from Khrushchev was delivered to Nehru which voiced concern over reports of Indian plans for military action and urged acceptance of earlier Chinese proposals for talks.[59] The day following the October 24 statement *Pravda* reprinted the three-point proposal, calling it "constructive," and editorially gave the first significant Russian support for China to be publicly announced since the dispute began in 1959. It included an oblique call on the Indian Communist party to take Peking's side:

> The fanning of the conflict . . . serves not only the interests of imperialism, but also of certain reactionary circles inside India which have tightly bound their destiny with foreign capital, with imperialist forces that are hostile to the Indian people. *A peaceful settlement of the conflict demands more active efforts on the part of progressive forces in India.* . . . *Common sense demands that in settling disputes mutual desire should be shown and no preliminary conditions dictated.* As to the Soviet people, they see in the statement of the Chinese Government a manifestation of sincere anxiety over relations with India and a desire to put an end to the conflict. *The proposals made by the Chinese Government are constructive,* in our opinion. Without damaging the prestige of either side, they are *an acceptable basis for the beginning of talks and a peaceful settlement* of disputed questions with due account given for the interests of both the CPR and India. [Italics added.][60]

Beyond disavowing the "notorious 'McMahon Line' which was never recognized by China," the editorial affirmed that "the Soviet Union and the CPR are bound by an old inviolable friendship . . . based on an identity of aims . . . the economic base of a similar type, a state system of a similar type, and a joint ideology, Marxism-Leninism." It even recalled "the warning of N. S. Khrushchev . . . four years ago in 1958, when the Chiang Kai-shek clique started a provocative bustle in the Taiwan Strait in collusion with the American brass." Significantly, the editorial did not reiterate the express words, "An attack on China is an attack on the Soviet Union" in the Sino-Indian context.

The editorial stopped short of condemning Indian "aggression" as charged by China's official statements and did not address the specifics of Chinese territorial claims in Ladakh or NEFA. Nevertheless its promptness suggested prior communication with Peking, and it did call on New Delhi to abandon its insistence on Chinese withdrawal from territory occupied since 1959 before beginning talks as advocated in Peking's latest proposals. Meanwhile Soviet officials hinted privately to the Indian Embassy in Moscow that their agreement to supply MIG fighters might not be fulfilled.[61]

These developments went unnoticed in the Chinese press. Later, when the Sino-Soviet dispute publicly intensified in 1963, Peking charged:

> . . . During the Caribbean crisis, they spoke a few seemingly fair words out of considerations of expediency. But when the crisis was over, they went back on their words. They have sided with the Indian reactionaries against China all the time. As facts show, the stand taken by the leaders of the CPSU on the Sino-Indian boundary question is a complete betrayal of proletarian internationalism. . . .[62]

While this could be post hoc rationalization for a polemical point, it more likely reflects the current judgments of those whose involvement in the dispute had convinced them that, regardless of surface appearances, no good could be expected of Moscow. Moreover the gesture on India came amidst increasing acrimony on other matters. The improvement in Soviet-Yugoslav relations had triggered heightened indirect polemics in September, as did continuing Soviet hostility toward Albania.[63] Then in late September separate reports from Moscow and Peking claimed China had requested the closure of all remaining Russian consulates.[64] In this context the allusion to "subversion within our state or our Party" in the Tenth CCP Plenum communiqué of September 24, clearly implicated Moscow and its representatives, reflecting suspicions held personally by Mao and his closest associates.

Equally important so far as the degree of trust which could be placed in the safeguarding of mutual interests while dealing with third parties was the question of a partial halt to nuclear tests. According to later Chinese revelations, the Soviet Union informed the PRC on August 25, 1962, "two days before the United States and Britain put forward their draft treaty," that Moscow had agreed to an American proposal whereby non-nuclear countries "should undertake to refrain from them [nuclear arms], from seeking them from the nuclear powers or from accepting technical information concerning their manufacture."[65]

As might be expected, this evoked sharp protests, first on September 3 and again on October 20, 1962, warning the Soviets not to "infringe on China's sovereign rights and act for China in assuming an obligation to refrain from manufacturing nuclear weapons."[66] In Peking's words, "We solemnly stated that we would not tolerate the conclusion, in disregard of China's opposition, of any sort of treaty between the Soviet Government and the United States which aimed at depriving the Chinese people of their right to take steps to resist the nuclear threats of U.S. imperialism."

Against this record of conflicting interests and mutual hostility, the specific Soviet words and actions with respect to Sino-Indian relations which emerged in mid-October may have been largely discounted both in advance and at the time as inadequate or purely tactical. Once the Cuban missile crisis emerged on October 22, such doubts would have been strengthened, further justifying the October 27 essay on "Nehru's Philosophy" as part of the ongoing dispute with Moscow in the "struggle against modern revisionism."

The essay's import carried beyond the Sino-Soviet dispute. By linking India with "U.S. imperialism" and the dispute as well, it elevated the border controversy to a major political struggle of prolonged duration, regardless of developments on the frontier. At no point did the essay refer to the October 24 statement or its three proposals. No mention appeared of a possible meeting of prime ministers. On the contrary, the essay implicitly called on the Indian army to revolt and the people to rebel, in language which could not be misread in Delhi. After claiming that "how India should solve its economic and political problems is entirely the Indian people's own affair, and China has never interfered," the essay declared:

... We note with profound concern that since the Nehru government has ignored the sufferings of the Indian people and has aggravated the tension on the Sino-Indian border and extended the armed clashes, the Indian people will have to shoulder heavy military burdens in addition to the exorbitant taxes which are weighing down on them. *Indian soldiers are being used as pawns by the selfish ruling circles; they are making meaningless sacrifices in the border clashes, while India's big capitalists and big landlords are taking the opportunity to feather their own nests.* The Chinese people have the greatest sympathy for the broad masses of India's working people who are facing such sufferings. *The Chinese people sincerely hope that the Indian people will free themselves* from this lot, that India will soon become prosperous and strong, and that the Indian people will be able to lead a happy life. We hope to see a progressive, democratic, and strong India on the continent of Asia. [Italics added.]

The retrospective and prospective implications of the October 27 analysis are intriguing. If Nehru and New Delhi had been so obviously and hopelessly captive to United States imperialism for so long, what sense was there in attempting "reconciliation" as had been advocated in January and February or "discussions" as in July and September? Admittedly the essay included routine rhetoric on the Five Principles, "peaceful negotiations," and "Sino-Indian friendship which dates back to the immemorial past ... [and] will tower forever like the Himalaya and the Karakorum." Yet sprinkled amidst these closing paragraphs were more militant arguments, warning, "the Nehru government" should "not want to bruise its head against a stone wall in further expanding the border clashes to the advantage of the imperialists," and asserting that "those people ... who whipped up anti-China campaigns ... will only expose their reactionary features and meet with utter defeat.'

This analysis implicitly cast doubt on the wisdom of the soft or diplomatic approach manifested in Chou's letter and particularly on the express willingness to meet with Nehru at the latter's convenience. It is possible Chou's signature was a mere formality and his own views were actually in consonance with the anti-Nehru attack. He had shown pique after the abortive meeting with Nehru in 1960 and reportedly expressed shock in private over Nehru's adamant stand, describing him as "being both unreliable and impenetrable."[67] Yet in view of his subsequent role and longstanding diplomatic posture it seems more likely that Chou still attempted to minimize the escalatory possibilities and maximize the prospects of a settlement then or later. The general halt to PLA attacks, the lack of publicity for Chinese victories, and the low-key posture in official references to the border fighting all suggest a basically consistent, coordinated policy, agreed upon and implemented through the State Council of which Chou was chairman.

Apparently a contrary line advocated a strong attack and defined the relationship in basic ideological terms of confrontation. This was suggested by the tampering with the initial MFA protest of October 20 and the *People's Daily* editorial of that date, culminating in the October 27 analysis. It is conceivable that the dual policy came from a single source whereby diplomacy and deterrence could be implemented through official government channels while militancy and mobilization of opinion would be pursued through the media, particularly *People's Daily*. Ostensibly this would relieve Chou of any responsibility for the hard-line posture, including the personal attacks on Nehru, and would leave open the possibility of the two men meeting once again as they had in 1960.

Alternatively, however, a differing policy thrust may have emanated from another source, namely the party, or more precisely the office of its chairman, Mao Tse-tung. His imprimateur, regardless of the actual authorship, would guarantee the dissemination of a document even if it were not implemented throughout the government. This would be particularly true in the aftermath of the Tenth CCP Plenum wherein the Chairman succeeded in reinstating his authority over various opponents who had been maneuvering against his views throughout the year.[68]

As has been noted, weekly benchmarks in Chinese behavior appear to reflect a regular rhythm of planning. Thus "More on Nehru's Philosophy" could have been designed to follow the October 20 attack with a new political offensive should nothing intervene to make it unwise or unnecessary. New Delhi's prompt public rebuff of the October 24 statement and proposal foreshadowed continued intransigence despite defeats. Seen from this perspective, the essay could be part of a centralized, coordinated strategy.

Yet dissemination of the essay by Chinese media at home and abroad with its challenge to all Nehru and his government stood for is in marked contrast to the dominant Chinese political and military postures up to that time and indicates that it represented a competing policy rather than a coordinated one. Its contents and contingency use were probably known to top officials, who realized that should the situation remain the same after the attack and the diplomatic demarche, Sino-Indian relations would be put on an entirely new footing. But this is not the same as if these officials had initiated the qualitative escalation of the political conflict which facilitated open Indian dependence on Moscow and Washington to support its military needs.

A question remains as to whether the consequences were fully anticipated by those who wrote the essay, but at the very least Peking apparently anticipated sharply renewed fighting in the near future, if not because of Indian reaction then by Chinese initiative. Chinese media subtly shifted from quoting Indian statements that merely pledged greater military effort at some unspecified time to terse reports of alleged shelling of PLA positions. Before the essay's publication, Defense Minister Menon was quoted, "We will, if necessary, regroup ourselves and fight again." Nehru's selected words suggested a prolonged crisis without any immediate hostilities: "We have to prepare for military conflict on a large scale in the field of war. . . . The whole industrial machinery of the state has to grow in order to feed and sustain that war effort."[69] After October 27, however, fresh shelling at Walong and Tawang was reported while a summary of November 4 claimed "more than 170 shells" had fallen in the Pangong Lake region of Ladakh since October 29. Two more items on November 5 reported "more than 600 shells" fired near Tawang since October 30 inflicted "heavy casualties on Chinese forces" while "more than 200 shells" had fallen near Walong since October 28.[70]

Indian sources separately confirmed some of these reports. On October 30 the Defense Ministry announced its forces had "moved to the offensive along the northeastern frontier" and Delhi radio claimed the first Indian use of artillery and mortar fire near Tawang and Walong.[71] Clearly the PLA halt offered only a temporary lull unless one side or the other instituted a major unilateral withdrawal. October ended with the Cuban missile crisis all but over; however, the outcome of the Himalayan war hung in suspense as both armies prepared for further fighting.

Chapter 5

November, 1962:
The Chinese Attack and Cease-Fire

The Politics of War

Three weeks separated the first and second phases of the Chinese military offensive. During this time Peking worked to strengthen its military position at the front and its political position in the international arena. This interval afforded policy makers the opportunity to determine the necessity as well as the potential gains and risks of further military action. The ending of the Cuban crisis released Moscow and Washington from a confrontation that could have escalated to nuclear war, and left them free to focus on the Sino-Indian crisis. Although their actions were unlikely to change the Himalayan situation materially before winter set in, they could serve as a harbinger of things to come should the conflict not be resolved one way or another.

During the lull, Indian troops in forward positions below Se La ridge in NEFA could hear intermittent blasting day and night as the PLA built a road from Bum La on the McMahon Line over the old trade route to Tawang.[1] Construction progressed at roughly a mile a day, soon permitting trucks to reach Tawang, whereupon the Chinese began improving the next stage to Se La. Working in full view of Indian aerial and ground observation, the PLA demonstrated its intention to hold and probably to expand the positions already gained. As subsequent developments revealed, secret Chinese deployments also penetrated down the crests of NEFA which straddled the narrow valleys and defiles through which Indian reinforcements trudged upward to the front. This covert deployment permitted the PLA later to cut off the main avenues of retreat without costly fighting.

The Indian decision to abandon Tawang as indefensible carried parallel implications for Chinese strategy, and compelled the PLA to move either forward to Se La or backward to a more secure vantage point. Under these

137

circumstances road-building could only imply a new attack in the near future. Peking authorities may have seen this as still another signal to New Delhi of the need to negotiate or to abandon forthwith the claimed positions in NEFA as they had been abandoned in Ladakh. However, Indian behavior communicated the intention to muster whatever force was available indigenously and from foreign sources, particularly American and Russian, for a counterattack at the earliest opportunity.

In this regard, Chinese media promptly reported each development between New Delhi and Washington that related to American military assistance, beginning with Nehru's October 26 letter to President Kennedy which allegedly requested "speedy U.S. delivery of all kinds of arms and military equipment, including aircraft, heavy-duty automatic weapons, helicopters, trucks, and tank parts."[2] Two days later an affirmative reply from Kennedy was reportedly sent through Ambassador John Kenneth Galbraith, with initial shipments of infantry weapons scheduled for airlift from American bases in Thailand by the end of that week.[3] Meanwhile a British spokesman was quoted as pledging fulfillment of an Indian request for "small arms," with another official interpreting this to mean "anything less than field guns."[4] By November 4, NCNA could describe a worldwide network of air shipments from North America to India via Europe and the Middle East as well as through Asia and Thailand.[5] Soon eight flights a day delivered twenty tons each of automatic rifles, heavy mortars, and other weapons.

This made the October 27 analysis of Indian-American relations more plausible than it had been at the time. Chou's next letter to Nehru accordingly abandoned some of the diplomatic niceties and was released by Peking three days after its dispatch. Unlike the earlier message, this was long, argumentative, and at times provocative in its insinuations. The Chinese premier noted that his offering "the 1959 line of actual control and not the present line of actual contact between the armed forces of the two sides is full proof that the Chinese side has not tried to force any unilateral demand on the Indian side on account of the advances gained in the recent counter-attack in self-defense."[6] Lest the point be missed, he added, "As Your Excellency is surely aware, in concretely implementing this proposal the Chinese armed forces will have to withdraw much more than twenty kilometres from their present position in the eastern sector."

Chou castigated the Indian proposal as containing "humiliating conditions such as forced on a vanquished party." After this dismissal of

Nehru's demand that the September 8, 1962, line be restored, he moved to the real purpose of his letter:

> Since the unfortunate Sino-Indian border clashes began, many Asian and African countries have appealed to our two countries, expressing the hope that we may stop the clashes and resume negotiations. They say that imperialism and colonialism are the chief enemies of us newly-independent Asian and African countries, and that the Asian and African countries should settle their mutual disputes peacefully on the basis of mutual understanding and mutual accommodation. I am convinced that their intentions are good and their viewpoint is correct. We should not disappoint their eager expectations.

Thus, one month after the first such reference in the MFA note of October 3, the PRC made its appeal to Afro-Asian governments a primary function of statements on the border crisis with Indian responses only a secondary consideration. Since bilateral deterrence and diplomacy had proven futile, multilateral maneuvers to isolate and discredit India became of prime importance. On November 7 Peking published the entire Chou-Nehru exchange.

The MFA joined in this effort with a November 6 note. Ostensibly in reply to New Delhi's of October 26, it was more in accord with public propaganda practices than diplomatic communication in its recitation of Indian perfidy and aggressive planning. After detailing recent developments it declared:

> While still refusing to stop the clashes and reopen negotiations on a fair and reasonable basis, the Indian Government is even now actively preparing for attacks on a larger scale. . . .The Indian side is stepping up nation-wide anti-China mobilization. The Indian President proclaimed on October 26 a "state of emergency" throughout the country. The Indian Prime Minister declared that the fight with the Chinese will go on for a long time to come. The Indian Ministers of Defense and Home Affairs personally flew to the frontiers to make inspections and dispositions. The Indian side is organizing new army units and moving large numbers of troops and transporting huge quantities of arms and ammunition to the eastern and western sectors of the border. What is especially serious, the Indian side is relying on the United States for the supply of large quantities of arms. Indian troops have never ceased bombarding and attacking Chinese frontier guards. Indian airplanes are continually intruding

into China's air space for the purposes of reconnaissance and harrassment. Indian troops, declared a spokesman of the Indian Defense Ministry, have already made a series of "probing attacks." In a word, the Indian side is using every means to create a war atmosphere, stir up anti-China waves, persecute Chinese nationals in India, preposterously close down the branches of the Bank of China in Calcutta and Bombay and step up military dispositions in preparation for fresh attacks on China on an even larger military scale.[7]

Prompt publication of the note in *People's Daily* and *Peking Review* placed it with Chou's letter in the stockpile of political ammunition to be used in a worldwide offensive against New Delhi.

Foreign Minister Ch'en Yi slightly amplified the unexplained claim that the United States' "supply of large quantities of arms" was "especially serious." Speaking at the Russian Revolution anniversary reception on November 7, he charged Washington with "openly clamoring for an expansion of the Sino-Indian border clashes so as to attain its vicious aim of dominating India and using Asians to fight Asians."[8] *People's Daily* expanded on this theme in an authoritative "Observer" article, "The Pretense of 'Non-Alignment' Falls Away."[9] It claimed that "Nehru's acceptance of U.S. military aid is the most significant of all recent developments." The implications of this for Afro-Asian neutrals was spelled out:

> ... Because it suppresses the people at home and fawns on imperialism abroad, the Nehru government must necessarily follow a line which runs counter to the national interests of India and to the cause of the Asian and African peoples opposing imperialism and colonialism and defending world peace. The Asian and African peoples have noticed that at the conference of non-aligned countries last year, Nehru took the lead in opposing the anti-imperialist, anti-colonialist stand taken by the heads of the majority of the countries attending, and also that over a number of questions such as the Congo, south Viet Nam and Cuba, the Nehru government has invariably helped U.S. imperialism and hampered and undermined the just anti-imperialist struggles of the Asian, African, and Latin American peoples. The Nehru government, in effect, has long stood opposed to the large number of young countries which take an active part in the struggle against colonialism and for world peace. The growing isolation of India among the neutral countries of Asia and Africa ... is a logical result of the Nehru government's sell-out to imperialism and its betrayal of the anti-imperialist and anti-colonialist stand of the Asian and African peoples.

After detailing the most recent evidence of linkage between United States encouragement and Nehru's "massive general attacks" against China the article concluded, "This shows that in effect, the United States and India have for a long time now been in an alliance though it has not been definitely formalized."

In contrast with other lengthily documented diatribes against American military assistance, there was no direct commentary on a development of potentially equal significance, namely the resumption of Soviet military aid to India. While Ch'en Yi's attendance at the November 7 reception given by the Soviet embassy maintained a facade of good relations, a barrage of thinly veiled Chinese attacks against Khrushchev's withdrawal of missiles from Cuba had brought the dispute to its sharpest point since the Russian removal of technical assistance in 1960. In response, the temporary Soviet support for Peking voiced by *Pravda* on October 25 quickly faded with its next statement on November 5. Balancing fraternal relations with China "based on the common fundamental aims of building socialism and communism" against ties to India bound "by good friendly relations which we prize highly," the editorial said "the Soviet people could not remain indifferent" to the blood being shed by "our brothers and friends, the Chinese and the Indian peoples."[10] It urged both sides to "sit down at the conference table as quickly as possible" to find "a mutually acceptable solution" lest continued clashes "lead to a prolonged bloody war."

This returned Soviet policy to the "neutral" position first enunciated in 1959. A more serious change from October, however, was revealed by Nehru's announcement on November 9 "that the Soviet Union has promised to stand by its agreement to supply India with MIG-21 fighter planes, the first deliveries expected in December."[11] Peking broadcast this report without comment, and on the next day reprinted the entire *Pravda* editorial of November 5 in *People's Daily*, again without comment. Significantly, no comparable publicity had been accorded the October 25 statement which supported China's position.

With these developments any doubt or debate over the bona fides of Khrushchev's mid-October statements and behavior was resolved to the satisfaction of the anti-Soviet critics in Peking. "More on Nehru's Philosophy" now seemed vindicated in its oblique attack on Soviet policy and its linkages between Indian "reactionary nationalism" and "U.S. imperialism." The combination of external threats which had played so dominant a part in Peking's perceptions and reactions in June reappeared with new evidence to support it as reported by the media. Even the Tibetan insurgents won fresh attention from Radio Peking which claimed that "according to reports received here the Indian authorities are contemplating the use of Tibetan rebels in India 'to fight alongside Indians' " because they were seen as "experienced fighters" and were "acclimatized to the high altitudes on the western sector of the boundary."[12]   Other Indian sources were alleged to advocate "more extensive use" of the rebels "to sabotage" Chinese supply lines in NEFA and the *Hindustan Times* was quoted as advocating that New Delhi "immediately recognize the Tibetan government in exile."

While these developments could be interpreted as posing a threat which had to be dealt with before it became serious, they also added an incentive to denigrate Nehru's prestige by inflicting a military defeat. Whereas the October victories were purely a test between Chinese and Indian forces, the symbolic, if not yet substantive, addition of Soviet and American assistance to New Delhi provided an opportunity to discredit Moscow and Washington as well.

There was no need to spell out the implications of Moscow's renewed wooing of New Delhi. Peking's laconic reports and the *People's Daily* reprinting of the *Pravda* editorial sufficed. Only in addressing the "Moscow Declaration" of 1957 and the "Moscow Statement" of 1960, wherein relations among the socialist states and communist parties had been hammered out in conference, did the Chinese allude obliquely to Soviet policy and India. Recalling the vocabulary of "More on Nehru's Philosophy," the *People's Daily* editorial of November 15 declared:

> . . . Marxist-Leninists must distinguish between anti-imperialist progressive nationalism and reactionary nationalism which is collaborating with imperialism, and must, while supporting progressive nationalism, struggle against reactionary nationalism. If they do not wage necessary struggles against reactionary nationalism but sympathize with it, chime in and support the reactionary actions of the reactionary nationalists, and become their partners, they will be running counter to Marxism-Leninism, running counter to proletarian internationalism and falling into the quagmire of bourgeois nationalism.[13]

On November 15, one day before the second and final PLA offensive, Chou En-lai dispatched a bulky "letter" to heads of various Afro-Asian governments, presenting the main historical and documentary support for China's case, including an appendix of thirteen maps from such diverse sources as the Office of the Surveyor General, Calcutta (1862), the Survey of India (1917), and the *Encyclopedia Britannica* (14th ed., 1929).[14] The collection was climaxed by photostatic copies of "the original map of the illegal McMahon Line," both in original scale and in enlargement, clearly showing Dhola (Che Dong) to lie north of that line.

Chou's letter avoided ideological analysis, and focused instead on a seemingly factual appeal to reason, including data not before emphasized in Chinese statements. For instance, it noted that "most of the geographical names here [in NEFA] are in the Tibetan language" and that "up to the time when the British colonialists and the Indians came to this area, the local authorities of China's Tibet region had always maintained administrative organs, appointed officials, collected taxes, and exercised judicial authority." Chou indulged in the rarely employed first person singular to recount his abortive talks with Nehru in April, 1960. However, he carefully avoided any personal invective against the Indian prime minister. He also provided a succinct, if chronologically telescoped, statement of linkage between Indian and American threats, recalling a theme which had rarely appeared in recent Chinese statements:

> . . . Making a series of miscalculations concerning China, India not only turned down China's peaceable proposals, but finally embarked on the road of military adventure. India thought that China's economic difficulties were so grave that it would not be able to overcome them, and that China's southwestern defenses must have been weakened owing to the fact that its national defense forces were tied down by the attempt of the U.S.–supported Chiang Kai-shek clique to invade China's southeastern coastal areas. Therefore India considered the opportunity ripe for launching massive armed attacks along the entire Sino-Indian border.

The plausibility of this linkage was weakened by its being tied directly to the October events, three months after the June crisis in the Taiwan Strait. This, together with the verbatim inclusion of portions of previous notes and statements, suggests the "letter" represented an omnibus effort to include all possible points that might justify China's case against India.

The contrasting public postures of New Delhi and Peking further served China's assertions of peaceful, defensive intent and desire to negotiate as against Indian bellicosity and intransigence. Some of this contrast resulted from Indian rhetoric which compared poorly with the discipline and control manifested by officials and the media in Peking. Informal remarks, amplified in India and abroad, portrayed a determined government mobilizing all its resources for war. At an impromptu airport press conference before Nehru's departure for a three-day visit to Ceylon in mid-October, he remarked, "Our instructions are to free our territory . . . I cannot fix a date, that is entirely for the Army. . . .As long as this particular aggression lasts [at Thag La], there appears to be no chance of talks."[15] The *New York Herald Tribune* titled its editorial comment, "Nehru Declares War on China."[16] Again on October 31, Nehru offered a rambling definition of relations with Peking that invited distortion: "We may not be technically at war, but the fact is that we are at war, though we have not made any declaration to that effect—it is not necessary at the present moment to do so, I do not know about the future."[17] Despite these militant words, India did not break relations with China and continued to support seating the PRC delegate in the United Nations in place of Taiwan's representative.

The Indian government fed the fires of nationalistic fervor with actions appropriate to a prolonged conflict of major proportions.[18] It called for a home guard and a national rifle association and expanded the national cadet corps to enroll all university students. It interned several thousand Indian citizens of Chinese descent as enemy aliens. Slit trenches appeared in Delhi parks and sandbags at the entrance to official buildings. A special defense bond was announced and a national defense fund called for any contribution of money, gold, or jewelry under the slogan "Ornaments for Armaments." At the unofficial level students burned effigies of Mao and Chou and signed pledges of sacrifice with their own blood; mobs ravaged Chinese shops in New Delhi and Calcutta and members of Parliament drilled with rifles after being called back in session ten days early.

On November 12, Lal Bahadur Shastri, Home Minister, publicly declared that "India was now strong enough to repulse the Chinese attackers and was building its military might to drive the invaders from Indian soil."[19] His words reflected a restoration of confidence gained from the three-week lull and the improvement in Indian positions. In NEFA the initial two brigades of early October had grown to two divisions. In the west at Chushul, which controlled access to the main command and support base of Leh, a full brigade now protected the airstrip and village.[20] Actually, the scattering of units among widely separated points in NEFA vitiated much of the reinforcement there, while perimeter defenses were stationed at Chushul, over 14,000 feet in altitude, where the frozen ground combined with treeless slopes to drain the energies of soldiers laboring to carry supplies and build bunkers. Finally, despite the highly publicized arrival of British and American aid, little of this equipment could reach forward Indian positions for immediate use, much less allow time for familiarization and for the systematic stockpiling of spare parts and ammunition.

In short, by mid-November the PLA had completed its preparations for further action and Chinese policy makers had communicated their political case to the fullest extent possible. Meanwhile Indian behavior foreshadowed an imminent counterattack, supported to varying degree by the United States and the Soviet Union. Under the circumstances, a second and final Chinese offensive appeared both necessary and advantageous.

The Second Offensive

By coincidence, on the eve of a coordinated PLA move that was to hit Chushul and NEFA simultaneously, the Indian forces at Walong began an offensive to honor Nehru's birthday on November 14.[21] The Chinese beat back the attack, inflicting heavy casualties, and initiated their own assault at dawn on November 16. By mid-morning the key defenses had fallen and Kaul ordered the brigade to withdraw. PLA ambushes took an additional toll of rear-guard units, but there was no pursuit of the scattered troops which straggled down the Lohit valley toward the Assam plain. This ended the only known instance of Indian offensive action.

Then at Chushul, observers reported a sudden appearance of Chinese infantry units in strength moving into positions on November 17. That night artillery bombarded the outposts, the airfield, and valley targets, followed by an infantry assault on outlying hill positions at dawn the next day. As at Walong, the initial defenses were overrun in a few hours and the PLA threatened the defense perimeter. Chushul itself lay beyond the claim line and was not attacked, although shelling of the airfield continued.[22]

Meanwhile at Se La, the main defenses had been bolstered by five battalions from a new division whose headquarters, along with two additional battalions, were at Dirang Dzong, midway down the thirty-mile road between Se La and the next major defense point at Bomdi La, where another three battalions remained. On November 15, advance elements of Indian units scouting out a bypass to Se La had encountered a PLA battalion and been wiped out. Having stumbled onto the enemy's strategy, the Indian command sent a company to stop the PLA advance but the unit was attacked at noon on November 17 by a force estimated at nearly fifteen hundred Chinese. Combat continued through the afternoon, resulting in the company's destruction. Earlier that same day the Chinese attacked a battalion several miles north of Se La but despite repeated assaults failed to break its resistance.

These skirmishes were only a prelude to the main event. Amidst growing alarm and confusion throughout the NEFA chain of command, orders were given to abandon a key point at Se La. The new defense line behind the pass was barely established when a general withdrawal began on the following night. On the morning of November 18, however, the Chinese entered the abandoned positions from which they fired down on troops moving toward less defensible ground. The coincidence of this assault at Se La with that at Chushul indicated a general offensive had begun. At virtually the same time an outlying company at Dirang Dzong, twenty miles below Se La, came under heavy attack, and machine-gun fire hit divisional headquarters later that morning. Abandoning their two battalions, a squadron of light tanks, one battery of field guns, and several hundred headquarters personnel, the officers fled to Bomdi La, leaving Dirang Dzong virtually defenseless.

The PLA had put its three-week lull to good use, as was dramatically demonstrated at Bomdi La where, within hours of the attack at Se La, three days' march to the north, fierce fighting began. Defenses had been weakened by the dispatch of two companies with supporting tanks and guns earlier that day to the relief of Dirang Dzong and this, combined with repeated Chinese attacks, caused the collapse of Bomdi La by late afternoon. By the night of November 18, all the main prepared defense points in NEFA had fallen. Repeated stopgap efforts to hold back the PLA advance failed. Chinese troops moving down from the adjacent ridges in a succession of roadblocks and ambushes cut up retreating units or captured them in the narrow valley defiles. On the next day, the last organized force attempted to hold at Rupa and then at Chaku, each time falling back before persistent Chinese attacks. By dawn of November 20, no semblance of an Indian army remained in NEFA.

The retreat now turned into a rout. Kaul suddenly ordered his IV Corps headquarters to move from Tezpur to Gauhati, some one hundred miles west, fearing the Chinese would continue unchecked onto the broad Assam plain. Nehru had raised this specter in a nationwide broadcast announcing the fall of Bomdi La: "Now what has happened is very serious and very saddening to us and I can well understand what our friends in Assam must be feeling, because all this is happening on their doorstep, as one might say. I want to tell them that we feel very much for them and we shall help them to the utmost of our ability."[23] These words did not inspire confidence in view of the local behavior of officials in Tezpur whose panic manifested itself in the release of prisoners and asylum inmates, the burning of currency, and the public warning that they were no longer responsible for security.[24] Privately Kaul speculated to visitors that the Chinese might make a paratroop landing at Misamari and would probably attack Tezpur by air. The departing army convoys further crowded the refugee ranks on the highways and heightened the sense of alarm among the populace.

The situation was readily susceptible to "worst case" fears. Not only had the entire NEFA fallen in less than two days but another main PLA force which stood at the head of the Chumbi valley was believed in New Delhi to presage an attack through Sikkim to the narrow link of territory that joined Assam with central India. Ambassador Galbraith stressed this danger both to Washington and to Nehru personally.[25] With less than a hundred miles between Nepal and East Pakistan providing the life-line to Assam, this threat seemed so serious a possibility that New Delhi held major military units at Siligur rather than release them for the defense of NEFA and Assam. In addition, authorities feared that if Chinese bombers made token attacks on Calcutta or Delhi there would be a stampede of these incredibly crowded cities as had occurred with similar Japanese raids in World War II. Galbraith recorded in his diary that November 20 "was the day of ultimate panic in Delhi, the first time I have ever witneesed the disintegration of public morale."[26]

Unilateral Cease-Fire and Withdrawal

In the midst of the Indian debacle, on the night of November 19, Chou En-lai summoned New Delhi's charge d'affaires to inform him that two days later the PLA would halt at the undisputed border of Assam, proclaim a unilateral cease-fire on all fronts, and withdraw from the newly occupied territory in NEFA.[27] Chou amplified his remarks to the charge again the next day, but no word reached top officials in Delhi before the Radio Peking announcement at midnight on November 20–21, exactly one month after the initial PLA offensive of October 20. The PRC statement declared:

> (1) Beginning from . . . 00:00 hours on November 22, 1962, the Chinese frontier guards will cease fire along the entire Sino-Indian border. (2) Beginning from December 1, 1962, the Chinese frontier guards will withdraw to positions twenty kilometres behind the line of actual control which existed between China and India on November 7, 1959.
> In the eastern sector, although the Chinese frontier guards have so far been fighting back in self-defense on Chinese territory north of the traditional customary line, they are prepared to withdraw from their present positions to the north of the line of actual control, that is, north of the illegal McMahon Line, and to withdraw twenty kilometres farther back from that Line.
> In the middle and western sectors, the Chinese frontier guards will withdraw twenty kilometres from the line of actual control. (3) In order to ensure the normal movement of the inhabitants in the Sino-Indian border area, forestall the activities of saboteurs and maintain order there, China will set up checkposts at a number of places on its side of the line of actual control with a certain number of civil police assigned to each checkpost. The Chinese Government will notify the Indian Government of the location of these checkposts through diplomatic channels.[28]

To underscore the seeming reasonableness of China's posture, the statement noted that "after withdrawing the Chinese frontier guards will be far behind their positions prior to September 8, 1962," thereby responding to part of Nehru's demands. However, restoration of the status quo ante was expressly ruled out. The announcement warned that if Indian troops

> (1) . . . . continue their attack after the Chinese frontier guards have ceased fire. . . .(2) . . . again advance to the line of actual control in the eastern sector, i.e., the McMahon Line, and/or refuse to withdraw but remain on the line of actual control in the middle and western sectors; and (3) . . . cross the line of actual control and recover their positions prior to September 8, that is to say, again cross the illegal McMahon Line and reoccupy the Kechliang River [Namka Chu] area north of the Line in the eastern sector, reoccupy Wuje in the middle sector, and restore their forty-three strongpoints for aggression in the Chip Chap River Valley, the Galwan River Valley, the Pangong Lake area and the Demchok area. . . .China reserves the right to strike back in self-defense and the Indian

Government will be held completely responsible for all the grave consequences arising therefrom.

In addition to the unilateral statement of terms governing the disposition of forces, the PRC proposed that the two sides meet "in the various sectors of the Sino-Indian border to discuss matters relating to the twenty-kilometre withdrawal . . . to form a demilitarized zone, the establishment of checkposts by each part on its side of the line of actual control, as well as the return of captured personnel." The reference to "captured personnel," albeit standard, carried an additional cut. Not one Chinese prisoner had been taken, compared with 3,968 Indians captured.

By any measurement, the Chinese victory was overwhelming. According to official Indian calculations, New Delhi lost 1,383 killed and 1,696 missing in action, in addition to almost 4,000 taken prisoner.[29] Slightly different figures offered by Kaul add another 550 wounded.[30] No total Chinese losses were announced but judging from all descriptions of the fighting, they were undoubtedly a fraction of the Indian casualties. The PLA overran 3,750 square miles of NEFA and occupied every foot of contested territory in Ladakh, yet nowhere entered territory not claimed by China as in dispute.

Politically New Delhi's defeat had come amidst total humiliation, dramatically evidenced by Nehru's public appeal to Britain and the United States for direct military intervention at the very moment Peking was transmitting its unilateral cease-fire and withdrawal decision. The gratuitous return of all territory seized in NEFA was followed by the meticulously itemized and maintained inventory of captured equipment, including trucks, guns, and ammunition. Finally, all Indian prisoners were repatriated. These steps further underscored to Asian sensitivities the disparity of power on the Himalayan front. No victory parades in Peking or triumphant announcements by NCNA were necessary. The subtlety of Chinese behavior, Indian self-recriminations, and international reporting were sufficient to make the political point.

Nehru might understandably speculate to the American ambassador that the Chinese cease-fire and withdrawal resulted from "the speed of the American response" in addition to "the unexpected anger of the Indian people when aroused."[31] However, Peking, in full confidence that no significant change could result from American military deliveries before winter closed down the front, had adroitly exploited among the Afro-

Asian neutrals Nehru's turning to Washington. The delay of three weeks between offensives and the timing of the withdrawal were determined by tactical considerations of logistical requirements and winter weather, not by any anticipated consequences of Washington's response. Chou's initial presentation of Peking's decision to halt hostilities came twenty-four hours before Nehru's public appeal for British and American aid, while the NCNA announcement was broadcast shortly before President Kennedy revealed that a high level mission would fly to India to arrange further assistance.[32]

In the broader context, Peking had not only made Washington's role seem irrelevant but it had also scored a stunning victory in contrast with Moscow's humiliating withdrawal from Cuba. Whereas Soviet policy was characterized as "adventurist" through the emplacement of missiles and "capitulationist" in their evacuation under American pressure, China's behavior could not be charged with either error.[33] These considerations were not primary as will be seen in this study's recapitulation of Chinese decision making, but neither were they likely absent from calculations in Peking of the side benefits that accrued from the unprecedented cease-fire and withdrawal.

As announced, the guns fell silent on November 22 and the withdrawal began on December 1. No further clashes occurred, as both sides reserved their activity for a flurry of diplomatic and propaganda exchanges designed primarily for various Afro-Asian intermediaries who tried in vain to mediate the dispute and to bring the antagonists to a conference table. Indian pride had been wounded but not to the point of negotiating on Chinese terms. Chinese prowess had been proven and territorial security ensured, but this did not increase Peking's willingness to compromise its position further. Tacitly however, both sides recognized that the balance of power and interest called for freezing their positions essentially along the boundary of patrol and control that had existed prior to the "forward policy" initiated by India in 1961–62, i.e., along the "line of actual control" denoted in the Chinese statement of November 21. Thus ended China's first historic crossing of the Himalayan frontier.

Why Attack and Why Retreat: The Cuban Calculus

During and after the fighting various explanations of Chinese behavior emerged which can be juxtaposed against the evidence. By examining alternative hypotheses concerning the strategy and tactics which underlay Peking's political and military offensives, as well as the cease-fire and withdrawal, comparisons can be made with other instances of Chinese military behavior, most notably in Korea and Viet Nam, for inferring the implications of consistency and of change.

Soon after the October 20 attack and recurringly in later years, it was suggested that Peking moved at this time because Moscow and Washington were locked in confrontation over Cuba and could not intervene on behalf of New Delhi.[34] While the hypothesis is less argued for the second offensive, it underlies one explanation for the abandonment of NEFA as reflected in Nehru's previously quoted remark. This hypothesis makes Soviet and American behavior primary determinants of Chinese policy. The "Cuban missile crisis" explanation rests on a series of unstated assumptions whose separate identification and evaluation permit the assessment of its plausibility. Taken sequentially, they would appear to take the following course:

1. Before October 20, Peking knew of Soviet missile deliveries to Cuba.

This is almost certainly true in view of the large Chinese presence in Cuba and the likely acquisition of this information through either official Cuban sources or local intelligence.[35]

2. Before October 20, Peking had guessed that American intelligence was aware of Soviet missile deliveries.

This is probably true. In addition to the tendency to overcredit the enemy, Cuban officials could have informed the Chinese of having detected U-2 high altitude reconnaissance aircraft flights on radar. Finally, Peking may have believed that earlier accusations of Soviet missile emplacement made by the Republican opposition, particularly Senator Keating, were based on "leaks" from United States intelligence, regardless of denials by President Kennedy to the contrary.

3. Before October 20, Peking anticipated that a United States–Soviet confrontation would erupt during the next week.

This seems highly unlikely, since it depended not only on knowledge of the previous two factors but also on a correct estimate of the timing and nature of the American response. President Kennedy's ultimatum specifying a naval "quarantine" was not broadcast until the evening of October 22. The previous week saw an increasing awareness among diplomatic and newspaper circles in Washington of an impending crisis focusing on Cuba, but informed opinion did not crystallize until October 20. Moreover this could not have become known immediately in Peking in the absence of direct representation in Washington.[36] Even with these rumors, there was nothing foreordained about the timing of American reaction, much less about the nature and duration of the confrontation.

4. Peking coordinated military actions over widely separated fronts on the Himalayan border with intelligence on developments in Cuba and Washington.

This seems wholly unlikely in view of the preceding events, the disposition of forces, the type of fighting anticipated, and India's logistical distance from the two major powers. The rhythm of strategic moves at monthly intervals, with tactical developments on a weekly basis, is sufficiently consistent to place the PLA attack within a predesigned framework. The fighting at Dhola on September 20, the offensive on October 20, and the cease-fire announcement at midnight on November 20 stand independent of the Cuban chronology, with the first two events additionally linked to the September 13 demand for talks on October 15.

Moreover, given the location and nature of the fighting and the imbalance of force favoring the PLA, the only effective Soviet and American responses could have been diversionary threats against China's borders in Sinkiang and opposite Taiwan. Yet these threats had already been disposed of in June. Strained as were Sino-Soviet relations, they still permitted direct exchanges over India in early October which included at least partial encouragement from Khrushchev to face down Indian preparations for military action.[37] The likelihood of a Chinese Nationalist attack had been sharply reduced by American behavior after the crisis as well as by the oncoming winter monsoon which would complicate an invasion across the Taiwan Strait.

Finally, if "worst case" calculations did seriously credit Moscow or Washington with the possibility of posing a tangible threat during a short border war with India, the gamble would seem too risky to take on the basis of the uncertainties involved with anticipating the course of confrontation in the Caribbean before it had ever begun. The October 20 offensive had to be decided upon for final execution at least several days previous to the attack. This would have been almost a week prior to President Kennedy's ultimatum of October 22 and virtually simultaneous with the United States discovery of the missiles on October 14.

Thus, both logic and evidence argue against the hypothesis that Peking's decision to attack related in any way to the imminent missile crisis.

Subsequently, the PLA halted its offensive on October 25 when the Soviet-American confrontation had yet to be resolved and might well have risen to higher levels, including American air strikes on Russian-manned installations.[38] This further indicates the degree to which Chinese operations were unconnected with Cuban developments. While considerations of Soviet and American policy and prestige in connection with the second attack and cease-fire cannot be excluded, they can be eliminated as factors in the basic planning of the October–November offensives.

The Broader Chinese Calculus

It is inconceivable that the decision to undertake coordinated offensives in NEFA and Ladakh on the scale which emerged in the October–November fighting was arrived at suddenly in the fall of 1962. At the very least contingency planning to make such a final decision possible must have begun during the summer when political uncertainty prevailed with respect to New Delhi's decision on "discussions" without preconditions. Stockpiles of weapons and ammunition, spare parts for vehicles, and additional service personnel were required if the military garrison in Tibet were to take on action beyond that envisaged in its standard posture of internal security and border defense. This in turn required a strengthening of roads and bridges against the natural and manmade disasters endemic in the eastern approaches where steep, narrow routes were vulnerable to rock slides and guerrilla interdiction. Once the war began, the PLA would have to depend primarily on existing stocks, with resupply coming from distant points over rough roads via motor transport.

It is possible that discussion of war with India arose as early as June in overall assessments of threat perceived in the Taiwan Strait, Tibet, and to a lesser extent, Sinkiang. Certainly the crisis atmosphere which prevailed in Peking at that time upgraded the Indian problem from its previous status. It has been seen how Ch'en Yi's press conference and other Chinese references linked the Himalayan and Taiwan situations. In this context, strengthening of PLA forces in Tibet would have been dictated by defensive rather than offensive needs, but once set in motion the reinforcement could meet additional purposes. The July confrontation in the Galwan valley followed by actual fighting in the Chip Chap valley accelerated the strengthening of communications and logistics lines, thereby serving potential offensive as well as actual defensive needs.

This study has emphasized the evidence of deterrence and diplomacy that appeared to dominate the Chinese posture toward India at least until late September and possibly through expiration of the October 15 deadline for negotiations. It has been noted that Peking persistently warned against intransigence on negotiations and against advancing into disputed territory. Such signals in diplomatic and public channels steadily intensified in consonance with visible preparations for combat. The PLA offensive was delayed until the diplomatic and political efforts had clearly failed, despite the uncertainties of winter weather settling over the Himalayan front. Yet other questions must be addressed more systematically and explicitly: how did the Chinese calculus envisage the likelihood of war? Was it seen as inevitable and if so at what time?

Essentially, three different explanations of Chinese decision making exist, although numerous variations could be adumbrated. The first posits a unified Chinese leadership preparing for an inevitable military conflict through the second half of 1962 and meanwhile playing out a political game for the public record.[39] A more sophisticated variant defines the expectation of war as virtually certain but the necessary preparation time was utilized to confirm Indian hostile intentions without any serious hope of avoiding the clash. A second hypothesis posits a united leadership reacting incrementally to rising tensions on the border, ultimately being compelled to fight because deterrence and diplomacy failed to halt the Indian advance.[40] The third explanation focuses on a divided leadership which held differing expectations of "soft" as opposed to "hard" policies, with "reality" determining the ascendancy of one or the other in deciding China's posture at successive points of development.

The implications of the three hypotheses are important not only for understanding the 1962 events but also for a broader understanding of Chinese perceptions, decision making, and behavior in foreign affairs. The first model of a unified leadership anticipating an inevitable clash makes any Indian or other actions essentially irrelevant to the outcome except insofar as they reinforced the leadership's expectations. The second model places virtually the entire responsibility for the conflict on Indian behavior, while the third makes it one of several intervening factors in an ongoing policy dispute with its own internal dynamic.

The strongest evidence for the first hypothesis is the October 27 essay, "More on Nehru's Philosophy," which depicted the confrontation as predetermined by the capitalist class basis of Nehru's government and its dependency on "U.S. Imperialism." According to this analysis there was no way that the war could be averted through deterrence or diplomacy. Instead, their utility lay in providing evidence of Indian perfidy and aggression to be exploited in the "struggle against imperialism and its lackeys" as well as in the "struggle with modern revisionism and reactionary nationalism." Foreign observers who allege that an aggressive design entrapped and brought about the attack of India because of ideological preconceptions in Peking offer this essay as proof. For them it frankly reveals what had underlain Chinese perceptions and policy all year.

One objection to this hypothesis is chronology. The Indians occupied Dhola in June; the PLA did not cross the Thag La ridge in confrontation until September 8 and no outside attention was drawn to Dhola until after the PRC protest of September 16, just prior to the fighting of September 20. Another full month elapsed before the first coordinated attacks at both ends of the border on October 20. The delayed reaction to Dhola and the further slow unfolding of PLA action there and in Ladakh can only be partially explained by the requirements of logistical preparation. A more logical and powerful explanation would appear to lie in the secret diplomacy of July and August which determined Indian intentions with respect to negotiations. Peking's muting of public reporting on the border during this time reinforces the credibility of a serious effort to seek resolution of the dispute by diplomatic rather than military means.

A second objection lies in the importance given by this hypothesis to other audiences and arenas for which Peking was allegedly acting out a shadow play of deterrence and diplomacy to justify its ultimate attack. The Afro-Asian countries and the Sino-Soviet dispute became involved in Chinese statements and actions only during October, in the final weeks before war began. There is no evidence of such considerations determining earlier strategy and tactics. An agreement on the border which secured the Aksai Chin road and Tibet was of far greater importance and deserved serious pursuit as a prior objective as against the attributed goal of lowering Indian prestige in the Afro-Asian world. Moreover, concerning the alleged rivalry for Third-World leadership, there is reason to doubt that Chinese self-perceptions and Chinese perceptions of India in any way correspond to those entertained in New Delhi, and, to a lesser extent, in Washington. Putting aside the failure of the Great Leap Forward, Peking's preeminence in Afro-Asian affairs had been established since Bandung in 1955. In addition Mao's challenge for leadership of revolutionary movements throughout this area made Khrushchev, not Nehru, his acknowledged rival.

A wholly contrary hypothesis eliminates all ideological preconceptions and depicts the government as reacting piecemeal to ongoing Indian behavior, this so as to minimize the possibility of war and maximize some kind of settlement, and only ultimately with great reluctance becoming convinced there was no choice but to fight. However, this explanation ignores the pre-1962 developments as well as the larger context within which perceptions were formed in Peking concerning domestic and foreign events. The 1959 essay, "The Revolution in Tibet and Nehru's Philosophy," had already sketched the ideological outlines of confrontation in terms of class analysis and Indian-American collusion against China.[41] In 1960 Chou En-lai commented to Edgar Snow on the linkage between economic dependence on the United States and Indian intransigence toward China.[42] While these statements did not push the argument to the extreme lengths of the 1962 analysis, they did evidence a prior disposition to suspect the worst of Indian policy on the basis of an ideological view that was authoritatively documented in detail in the October 27 essay.

In the interim Mao had intensified the polemic with Khrushchev, pitting Peking against Moscow as the true interpreter and implementer of Marxism-Leninism. While he was not omnipotent as party chairman, Mao nonetheless remained the prime ideological spokesman, and his view prevailed at the September, 1962 plenum. Under these circumstances it is inconceivable that all Chinese calculations and expectations emerged incrementally in response to successive Indian actions and pragmatically resulted in an estimate of threat wholly based on the material evidence.

The third hypothesis of a divided leadership with differing estimates on the prospects for settlement without the major use of force has been raised at several points in this analysis. The evidence is inconclusive, but it invites speculation and deserves further research within a fuller examination of PRC policy processes. Viewed retrospectively from Cultural Revolution materials and developments, it is intriguing to note the persistent absence in 1962 of Lin Piao, Minister of Defense, from the normal appearance times such as Army Day (August 1), National Day (October 1), and commemoration of the Korean War intervention. In his place, Chief of Staff Lo Jui-ch'ing made most of the speeches. Lo's subsequent purge in 1965 accompanied by Lin's ascendancy as Mao's appointed successor from 1966 to 1971 suggests that a difference of strategy as between Party

Chairman Mao and PRC Chairman Liu Shao-ch'i may have been reflected in the respective absence and prominence of Lin and Lo.

The inconsistencies in *People's Daily* with both "soft" and "hard" line editorials on Nehru and the prospects for a settlement have already been noted. Changes over time could simply reflect intervening events, as suggested in the June-July transition from calm to crisis. Contradictions in closer proximity, however, manifest in the October 27 issue which carried both "More on Nehru's Philosophy" and an editorial praising Chou's latest offer to meet at Nehru's convenience seemed to reflect contrary viewpoints. A fundamental incompatibility existed between diplomatic proposals over Chou's signature and the ad hominem attacks on Nehru as a "liar," "swindler," "double-dealer," and "lackey of U.S. Imperialism." This suggests disagreement within the regime over tactics, if not strategy as well.

To be sure, an organizational duality of approach is traditional in Communist governments where normal diplomatic practices coexist with frankly revolutionary ends and means.[43] Yet the standard explanation does not seem pertinent in this instance because the issue involved a remote border conflict far from the perceptions and interests of revolutionary audiences. In particular there was no prospect that the Indian Communist party, the most obvious target of an ideological line, could play any important role in the near future because it was splintered in factional disputes and miniscule in comparison with the Congress party.[44]

A more plausible interpretation is that factions existed in Peking which espoused contending judgments on the efficacy of deterrence and diplomacy as compared with direct confrontation and the controlled use of force. The most likely division of counsel along these lines was between Mao and Liu with Chou implementing and probably endorsing the more moderate line. While this accords with the general thrust of Cultural Revolution materials so far as Liu is concerned, it has two major shortcomings. First, very little evidence on foreign affairs was made public in the Cultural Revolution documentation and none has been found to bear specifically on the 1962 war, perhaps because its successful outcome precluded its becoming a subsequent source of contention. Further, the emergence of Chou as second only to Mao in eminence and perhaps superior in daily responsibility after 1971 raises obvious problems in defining him as substantially opposed to Mao and agreeing with Liu in 1962.

The scholarly literature on China's leaders and their inner relations is interesting but inconclusive.[45] Certainly Ch'en Yi's secret negotiations with Krishna Menon at Geneva, revealed many years later by Chou, reinforces the hypothesis of serious efforts under his direction to avoid escalation and achieve a settlement. Mao's rumored authoring of the first essay on Nehru in 1959, together with the subsequent attribution to him of the voluminous Sino-Soviet polemics, argues for his holding the ideological confrontation as paramount.[46] Organizational bonds would strengthen the association of Chou and Ch'en Yi with diplomatic solutions as contrasted with the rhetoric of revolutionary values that might characterize writers for *People's Daily* and *Peking Review*. As for the PLA, divided interests could juxtapose a cautious, conservative handling of border defenses locally against a higher level desire to refurbish China's internal and external image of national security with a short but successful war against inferior Indian units. In sum, the inferential ingredients for factionalism coexist with circumstantial evidence of divided counsel to make the third hypothesis the dominant contender.

The Military Options

Regardless of which hypothesis one adopts, reference to the PLA raises questions regarding a subset of decisions required by all three models, namely what specific strategy and tactics should be adopted in the event India refused negotiations and persisted in strengthening its ability to contest China's claims by military force. This issue had to be faced after August 22 at the very latest when Nehru communicated his formal refusal to negotiate under the July formula.

Three choices remained available. First, the PLA could simply stand fast while Indian troops strengthened their positions and retaliate with the minimum force necessary in order to avoid provoking an escalation of hostilities. Second, the Chinese could deliver a sharp blow short of full attack, thereby hoping to deter further advances and to force a tacit, if not explicit, acceptance of the status quo. Third, the PLA could take advantage of the local power balance and attempt to drive Indian forces back to whatever line seemed politically and militarily optimal before winter froze the two sides into position.

These options carried political as well as military implications which can be inferred directly from Chinese statements and actions as well as indirectly from the logic of the situation as seen in Peking. The "least force" choice of standfast with minimal retaliation promised to postpone any serious fighting until the following summer when cooler heads might prevail in New Delhi. It would, however, also provide more time for the Indian acquisition of a better capability through improved roads, a strengthened airlift, and greater firepower. In this regard, the Soviet delivery of transports and helicopters augured ill for the future comparative positions in Ladakh where the only strategic Chinese concern, the Aksai Chin road, could become vulnerable to interdiction. This point was underscored in Peking's demarche to Moscow of October 8 which simultaneously warned of an imminent "massive attack" from India and protested Soviet aircraft supplies.[47] It was also reflected in the consistently greater correlation between allegations of air violations and images of threat reflected in protest notes and *People's Daily* items.

Beyond these purely military considerations, Chinese sensitivity to the implications of minimal resistance against challenges to territorial sovereignty and national security precluded this first option. Manifested in repeated references to Indian misinterpretation of "China's restraint as a sign of weakness," this sensitivity was given a standard formulation, "How could the Chinese people possibly be so weak-kneed and faint-hearted as to tolerate this?"[48] The question took on added weight when applied against the earlier crisis in which the PRC had seen itself facing down the United States. In this regard the shootdown on September 9 of an American-built U-2 high altitude reconnaissance aircraft, piloted by Chinese Nationalists, further heightened the dual sense of external hostility and internal vigilance which together called for more than a minimally necessary response.

Ch'en Yi, speaking at the National Day celebration on October 1, expanded on the language of the Tenth CCP Plenum with the presentation of a graphic image of challenge and response:

> ... *The imperialists, the reactionaries of various countries, and the modern revisionists gloated over the difficulties encountered by our country. They have attempted by every means to vilify, sabotage, and invade our great motherland.* The U.S. imperialists instigated the Chiang Kai-shek gang entrenched in Taiwan to plot vainly an invasion of the coastal areas of our country. They dispatched U-2 planes to engage in war provocation against our country. But they have miscalculated. The criminal activities of the imperialists and

their running-dogs against the People's Republic of China, far from overwhelming the Chinese people, have heightened their revolutionary fervor in building and defending their motherland. *The Chinese people are not to be bullied. Any criminal acts of invading China's mainland, encroaching on China's frontiers and subverting China will surely continue to meet with strong rebuffs.* No force on earth can prevent the advance of the Chinese people.[49]

Ch'en's formulation was easily interpreted by those familiar with the key terminology to mean the United States (imperialists), India (reactionaries), and the Soviet Union (modern revisionists). This defiant language stood in marked contrast with the suggestion reportedly formulated at the beginning of 1962 which had advocated "reconciliation with the imperialists, the reactionaries, and the modern revisionists."

There were strong military and political reasons for rejecting a stand-fast, minimal force option and few arguments in its favor. If these considerations were so weighed in August, they gained increasing validation as events developed to reveal heightened Indian determination to force back the PLA at Thag La ridge.

The second option of a limited attack for deterring further advance and winning acceptance of the status quo could only serve to test Indian responses. Should it succeed in bringing about a settlement, no additional force would be necessary to secure the border. If it failed, however, the consequent Indian reaction to the attack would virtually force adoption of the third choice, namely a major offensive. The promise of a limited attack was questionable in view of the July experience in which a small clash had increased Nehru's interest in compromise while whipping up public bellicosity in parliament and the press. This second option seems to have underlain some of the calculations behind the September 13 demand for discussions and the Dhola attack one week later. Yet prudence required contingency preparations for more serious warfare should limited fighting fail, hence the likelihood that a larger offensive was also included in the initial planning.

The immediate military costs of war in the Himalayan heights were limited because of the terrain, the relatively small size of the respective forces, and the constraint on prolonged fighting imposed by imminent winter weather. The political risks were less certain. While Soviet military assistance to India seemed destined to increase regardless of the border situation (as shown by negotiations for construction of a MIG-21 factory), the United States might also increase its role in developing Indian strength as well as in the subversion of Tibet. These developments could worsen the long-run threat as opposed to whatever short-run gains might be realized through major fighting.

If these considerations argued against the second and third options, they were offset by other factors. The fullest articulation of one such factor was the essay, "More on Nehru's Philosophy," anticipated in some respects by *People's Daily* and *Peking Review* in the previous weeks.[50] Essentially ideological, this view held that Nehru's nonalignment was a transparent fiction which, if not already recognized abroad, should be exposed. India's ruling elite was so dependent on foreign support that "U.S. imperialism" was a determining factor in both domestic and foreign policy, and any closer relationship between New Delhi and Washington would merely reveal what was already secretly operative. Moreover insofar as that relationship became apparent to all, it could be denigrated as a "paper tiger" threat by the successful use of force combined with the proper political strategy and tactics.

The need to challenge, expose, and defeat the coalition of enemies rather than avoid confrontation was put most vigorously by *Red Flag* in an editorial prepared during the November offensive.

> ... If Communists fail to recognize the outwardly strong but inwardly brittle nature of imperialism and the reactionaries of the various countries, are awed by the temporary power of the enemy and overestimate his strength, they will vacillate in the struggle and dare not win victory that can be won. The Right opportunists, that is, the revisionists, grossly exaggerate among the masses the strength of the enemy and underrate the great role of the masses in the struggle. This only adds to the arrogance of imperialism and the reactionaries in the various countries and dampens down the revolutionary struggle of the masses.[51]

Wiping out Indian positions built so laboriously in Ladakh might drive home the conviction that deterrence warnings had failed to communicate, namely Peking's readiness to back its words with action with respect to its territorial integrity. A major attack could end the "forward policy" once and for all. At the worst, New Delhi would have to begin from scratch if it decided to challenge Peking again in the future.

In short, the "soft" line had failed to show results by late August and the risks of a "hard" line were not only low but were more than offset by the gains, particularly when calculated against the consequences of war at a later rather than earlier date. Within the strategic decision to fight, first with a limited attack and then almost certainly with a more extended offensive, the tactical question arose of where and when to mount the casus belli. While the Aksai Chin road was the most salient issue from Peking's perspective, it was the most remote so far as other audiences in the Afro-Asian world were concerned. Moreover it involved the complicated Kashmir dispute through adjacent Ladakh and this was certain to divide support for Peking's claim which itself rested on nebulous historical and cartographic data.

By contrast, the celebrated McMahon Line offered a promising point from which to begin a political offensive against New Delhi. China's willingness to accept the line in establishing the Sino-Burmese border together with its historical repute and general demarcation on widely available maps provided a ready framework within which to exploit the Indian post at Dhola as evidence of "aggression." Moreover the military advantages of focusing the initial attack on Dhola were tempting, as frankly revealed by Kaul in an analysis for Nehru and Menon of October 11:

> (a) If we attacked the Chinese, as things stood then, we were bound to have a reverse. We should therefore pull out of Dhola and go to a more suitable area tactically from where we could fight them better.
> (b) The Dhola area would soon be snow-bound when it would be impossible to maintain it any longer.
> (c) Whatever buildup we might achieve opposite Thag La, the enemy, with their superior resources and approach, could oust us (and in this process weaken other fronts).
> (d) The Chinese were in a better position to build up a superior force due to good communications behind their forward position, an advantage we did not enjoy.[52]

Dhola provided the optimal target, both for the limited attack option to test Indian reaction and for the larger offensive action.

Aside from practical requirements of logistical preparation, the timing of Peking's move was constrained only by the uncertain factor of an early or late winter coming in November or December. This permitted the fall to be utilized for the political preparation of various audiences for the coming hostilities by building a credible record of Indian provocations matched by Chinese efforts at deterrence and negotiation. If these latter efforts succeeded, the offensive would be unnecessary and could be cancelled without public embarrassment. Even after the attack, careful command and control could limit PLA movements according to political need and permit ample "feedback" of military developments for reaction to unforeseen contingencies.

In this context the pattern of Chinese diplomatic, political, and military behavior falls within a recognizable overall strategic and tactical plan. Not all developments could be anticipated at the outset, of course. In particular it is unlikely that Chinese planners foresaw the extent of enemy bungling and the sudden collapse throughout NEFA. Indian officials later estimated that the PLA had utilized only three divisions in NEFA against a slightly smaller, if far more scattered, force.[53] This did not provide the normal three-to-one margin of superiority for offensive action, although superiority was assured in most instances by poor Indian command and deployment. It is quite possible that the overall plan merely determined in advance that a cease-fire would be declared one month after the initial attack regardless of where the PLA advance had reached. This would avoid complications that might result from an early winter with adverse weather hampering support to forward units.

Still the question arises, even if a cease-fire were dictated in advance by a desire to limit the fighting for tactical reasons, why abandon whatever had been won, especially when it included the whole of NEFA? In a curious reversal of the old image, Mao's troops had literally marched down the hill only to march up again, without the slightest pressure or threat against their newly won positions. There was no serious danger of a revolt in their rear to harass extended supply lines which ran among passive hill tribes who had not demonstrated any overriding loyalty to New Delhi. Ahead lay the defenseless Assam plain with an army and populace in manifest panic.

At the time, British and American analysis conjured up a host of reasons for the PLA orders to include the seizure of NEFA. At the minimum, it could be a negotiatory point to be bargained in exchange for Ladakh; at the maximum, it could serve as a forward base for extending Peking's power through the subcontinent.[54] The effect in nearby Bhutan, Sikkim, and Nepal would be to make these tiny mountain kingdoms exclusive protectorates of China instead of India, as hinted in Ch'en Yi's pledge, "Should any foreign power dare to attack Nepal, the Chinese government and people . . . will stand forever at the side of Nepal."[55] This in turn would furnish a protective buffer against further subversion by Tibetan refugees and foreign agents. In addition ethnically related groups in these feudal states could be penetrated and eventually absorbed into the Tibetan Autonomous Region with no fear of serious resistance by the small ruling elites.

Control over the sub-Himalayan escarpment, expanded from NEFA, would provide ready access to the Indian plains through the low jungle foothills. Overt assistance to the three small principalities could develop an infrastructure of communications facilities if the PLA wished to move southward in force. Covert activity could fan minority separatist sentiment in India, already manifest among the Nagas of Assam, while strengthening indigenous Communist movements in East Pakistan and West Bengal. A separate sweep beyond NEFA into the eastern plain would isolate Burma, raise China's stature in the eyes of Pakistan, and crush Indian pretensions in the subcontinent. Assam itself held possible strategic interest with the Digboi oilfields and access to the Indian Ocean.

These prospects, logical enough from the conventional military emphasis on "worst case" analysis of capabilities rather than on intentions, underlay the concern of Sandhurst-trained Indian officers and West Point graduates in the Pentagon.[56] Such calculations, however, apparently played no part in the planning of Chinese strategists whose primary concern was stabilization of the border in order to stop the "forward policy" in general and secure the Aksai Chin plateau in particular. During the November offensive, such additional considerations as enhancing China's prestige while denigrating that of Nehru, "unmasking" the collusion of Moscow and Washington in Indian designs, and winning points among Afro-Asian governments were secondary, albeit reinforcing goals. Basically China was moving from self-perceived weakness to enhance its sense of security and was not exploiting its power for maximum advance in the subcontinent.

Under this calculus, therefore, the retention of NEFA might conceivably enhance the likelihood of a negotiated settlement, but the Indian record to date made this a remote possibility. Without negotiations NEFA's retention would merely provide New Delhi with an argument against "Chinese expansionism," a point which had already proved somewhat difficult to rebut in the western sector. Moreover, NEFA would require more military defense than it was worth should the Indian army and air force be refurbished by Moscow and Washington and return to the attack at some subsequent time. Against these risks the political gains of unilaterally abandoning whatever had been won in NEFA, provided the Indians did not return to their positions north of the McMahon Line, were persuasively in accord with China's pre-attack position on observing "the line of actual control."

American and Indian alarmist speculation over possible Chinese moves included air attacks on Indian cities and invasion through the Chumbi valley and Sikkim to cut off Assam. This completely misperceived Peking's political concern to achieve essential security goals without casting China in the role of a conventional aggressor and to humiliate India without making it the subject of worldwide sympathetic support. These constraints stemmed from the image which PRC policy makers sought to project among Communist allies and revolutionary groups, Afro-Asian neutrals, and assumed or avowed protagonists, i.e., the Soviet Union and the United States. China's successful appeal to world opinion after 1937 through tragic photographs of defenseless civilians killed by Japanese bombs precluded parallel air action as a means of strategy against India.

Similarly, Chinese behavior and statements were consistently sensitive to the political implications of invading contested as opposed to uncontested territory, ruling out a strike through Sikkim. Nearly two thousand Indian troops fled into Bhutan after the first offensive, but the PLA did not pursue them across the boundary.[57] In Ladakh, the limited advance despite the Chinese superiority in force showed an impressive degree of discipline, especially at the abandoned post of Daulet Beg Oldi and the threatened base of Chushul. Only in the case of Chushul airfield, beyond the claimed line but shelled by the PLA, was force projected across an undisputed boundary. Indian charges to this effect were substantiated by foreign visitors but denied by Peking, suggesting the official concern for maintaining a principled posture.

In this general context, the retreat from NEFA was almost certainly agreed upon by civilian and military planners alike, although it ran so counter to western expectation as to prompt one Kennedy aide to remark, "There is no doubt who is in control over there. Can you imagine the difficulty we would have with the Pentagon in pulling back and giving up territory that had cost that many casualties, no matter how great the political end it served?"[58]

Chinese Miscalculations

The successful military and political outcome appears to have minimized recrimination after the event. If indeed two factions did contend, as the author is inclined to believe, each could point to benefits that flowed from its respective posture being implemented without charging disaster to the opposite approach.

This does not mean that miscalculation was absent or carried no consequences. Assuming that there was a genuine desire to avoid war if security could be guaranteed through other means, Chinese policy erred tactically in responding to India's July 26 formula. Whereas Nehru, in contrast with previous statements, avoided any reference to specific pre-conditions for talks, Peking made his self-denial explicit. While it is problematic whether Nehru could have maintained his position in any event against the subsequent storm of protest in the Indian parliament and press, the PRC reply did not help.

In this regard, there seems to have been a basic inability to understand the relatively narrow limits within which Nehru could compromise on the territorial issue, limits which decreased further with each successive attack by *People's Daily*. Under these circumstances, deterrence warnings couched in militant words and actions suffered from three liabilities. At the public level of politics, they appeared provocative and accelerated rather than slowed escalation. At the private level they came too late to affect policy which had already become hostage to bureaucratic inertia and politics. Finally, at the highest level they were discounted because of the overriding conviction that China would not fight. In a fundamental sense then, deterrence and diplomacy were strategically misconceived since India was virtually locked into the "forward policy" by mid-1962.[59]

A further miscalculation exaggerated the degree to which Delhi and Washington were already in active military collusion against China and the propensity of the two governments to so align. Aside from whatever may have been the clandestine cooperation with Tibetan insurgents whose main supplies were air-dropped from bases in Thailand, there was little desire on either side to join hands militarily before the PLA offensive. Contrary to the Chinese interpretation, Nehru's October 26 letter was not a unique request to Kennedy specifically for weapons but a general appeal for "sympathy and support" in a long statement of the Indian case directed to Britain, France, the Soviet Union, and Pakistan, as well as the United States. Peking's initial information was erroneously communicated by

All-India Radio; however, when Nehru issued a clarification it was not reported publicly in China and may well have been missed.[60]

Kennedy's reply was also in general terms. It was not until October 29 that Ambassador Galbraith learned that a more detailed request for arms was coming from Menon and managed to elicit it from Nehru instead.[61] Thus, despite the beginning of the PLA attack on October 20, no official exchange of views on military aid occurred for almost ten days. Nehru's reluctance to seek help from the United States was partly conditioned by his concern over possible Soviet reaction.[62] Kennedy's caution stemmed not only from the prior commitment to Pakistan but also from personal disappointment with Nehru resulting from the prime minister's 1961 visit to Washington, after which "he rather gave up hope that India would be in the next years a great affirmative force in the world or even in South Asia."[63]

In early November the relationship remained limited to the delivery of infantry weapons to supply points in central India. The second assault, however, brought a qualitative change on both sides. On November 19 Nehru privately asked for American air strikes against Chinese troops if they continued to advance on Indian territory. He also asked for fighter protection for the cities in case of raids,[64] and transports to lift arms directly to the front in Ladakh. The next day Galbraith recommended a dozen C-130s with pilots be supplied immediately and as an interim response that "elements of the Seventh Fleet be sent into the Bay of Bengal."[65] An aircraft carrier began this deployment but turned back as a result of the cease-fire announcement.[66] The C-130s and crew arrived almost immediately.

The Harriman mission, in response to Nehru's appeal, landed in Delhi on November 22. It included Paul Nitze, assistant secretary of defense for International Security Affairs; General Paul Adams, commander in chief of the United States Strike Command, "a mobile force of corps strength that would be called upon if United States ground forces should ever be needed in the defense of India"; Carl Kaysen of the White House staff; and Roger Hilsman, director of Intelligence at the State Department, as well as lesser staff aides and specialists.[67] The mission worked with a smaller parallel group from Britain and produced a major military assistance program for the next three years. One result was a joint British-American air exercise in 1963 wherein long-range fighters operated from Indian Air Force bases.[68]

None of this would have eventuated in the absence of the PLA attack; most of it materialized in reaction to the second offensive. To this extent the Chinese analysis of October 27 provides an excellent example of the "self-fulfilling prophecy" whereby the predicted result was realized because of the regime's behavior and not the ineluctable economic forces operating between India and America. Indeed, an effort to soften American policy toward the People's Republic had begun to bear its first fruit by the fall of 1962 when the Sino-Indian war brought this to a halt.[69] Internal Washington analyses to the contrary notwithstanding, the war fueled fresh rhetoric concerning "Communist Chinese aggression" and "the menace of Red China," some of which represented genuine concern at the highest level. As President Kennedy put it the following year, the prospect of China acquiring nuclear weapons with "weak countries around it, seven hundred million people, a Stalinist internal regime, and nuclear power, and a government determined on war as a means of bringing about its ultimate success, [was] potentially a more dangerous situation than any we faced since the end of the Second [World] War."[70]

At the most basic level both India and China miscalculated each other's intent. Persisting throughout discussions in New Delhi and clearly manifest in the desultory implementation of the "forward policy," resulting in the debacle of Ladakh and NEFA, was the express assumption that "China won't fight."[71] So dominant was this view that no amount of warning, diplomatic or political, seemed to shake it. Paradoxically while India entertained a benign misconception, China held a malevolent one, firm in the belief that persistent advances behind PLA outposts represented at least New Delhi's aggressive design and most probably collusion with Moscow or Washington or both. As noted earlier, this perception seems to have crystallized in Peking as a result of the crises in May and June with an apparently panicky assessment of external threat combined with internal weakness in that immediate context. Thereafter selected evidence from Indian statements and behavior served to prove its validity to the satisfaction of those responsible for China's security.

In view of the basic confrontation with Pakistan, there was little possibility of India permanently denying Chinese control of the Aksai Chin, much less Tibet. In addition Peking's vastly larger military base, supplemented by a far more experienced and disciplined command, assured PLA domination in any prolonged contest with the Indian army. Seen from the subjective perspective of the Chinese leadership in 1962, however, no such assurance prevailed. If "worst case" analysis did not describe a clear and present danger, it could predict one for the future that evoked alarm and justified action to prevent its realization. Ironically New Delhi and Peking shared a common assessment of China's weakness; however, where Indian logic argued this would prevent the PLA from fighting, Chinese logic saw it as compelling strong action. New Delhi and Peking also agreed on Indian weakness, but here New Delhi assumed this obviously made its behavior harmless, although Peking saw it as necessitating some larger, hidden design, aided and abetted from outside.

It is clear that mutual miscalculation resulted in a war that neither side wanted. The actual military costs were marginal for both sides, but the political reverberations were far-reaching. Nehru lost his pretensions of leadership in the Afro-Asian world as well as his illusions of "understanding" China. China lost its underdog role as a mere victim of imperialist diplomacy and projected a sense of power which reinforced the threatening image projected by American spokesmen. The complex historical claims of each side, the legal and moral disputes, and the attempt to weigh relative blame continued to spawn studies for years thereafter. The fact that China had crossed the Himalayas in military force for the first time in modern history was a fact of overriding political importance whose implications were to be felt throughout Asia for at least the rest of the decade.

Chapter 6

Indochina and PRC Deterrence

Vietnam: The Air Threat

Before incorporating the Indian case study into a broader framework of analysis, some attention should be given to the Indochina conflict as another case of the Chinese use of force in order to deter a perceived threat. While China's troops did not participate openly in the fighting, Peking's aircraft shot down at least nine American planes and Chinese anti-aircraft divisions in North Vietnam took an additional, albeit unknown, toll. Moreover from 1965 to 1968, approximately 50,000 PLA troops were stationed in the Democratic Republic of Vietnam (DRV) in direct war support and deterrence posture. They built a massive military complex and airfield northwest of Hanoi. They strengthened and repaired transportation routes and bridges under repeated attack by American bombers. Their presence signaled to North Vietnamese and Americans alike a Chinese willingness to suffer casualties and risk retaliation in air attack or ground invasion.

Chinese reactions emerged in the context of a threefold threat to North Vietnam. First, from the spring of 1964 to early 1965 Washington indicated it would bomb the North if DRV support continued for Communist guerrillas in the South. Second, from 1965 to 1968, American air attack against the North threatened to cut the supply lines from China to Vietnam. This possibility reoccurred in 1972 when President Nixon resumed the bombing of railroads and bridges below the Sino-Vietnamese border and mined Haiphong harbor to interdict sea supplies. Third, beginning in the summer of 1965, the massive buildup of 500,000 American ground forces in South Vietnam raised the prospect of an invasion of the DRV. This could pinch off the lower panhandle so as to cut infiltration

170

routes into Laos and across the Demilitarized Zone or it could strike up the Red River Delta at Hanoi's industrial and agricultural heartland.

China's interaction with the Vietnam war deserves a separate study to reconstruct the signals, perceptions, and reactions of both sides in the same detail with which the 1962 Indian border conflict was considered. It is useful here, however, to examine briefly that evidence which pertains to the specific use of force in deterrence in order to compare the Korean and Indian cases of failure with the Vietnam case of partial success. This study will not analyze the other dimensions of the policy arguments associated with the Indochina conflict, particularly the complex interlock in 1965 of domestic disputes and foreign involvement. The coincidence of Mao's preparation for the Cultural Revolution with United States escalation in Vietnam compels a much more encompassing effort to test all the interrelationships and their implications for China's internal and external politics at this time.[1]

The analytical problem is highlighted by the purge of Lo Jui-ch'ing, chief of staff, in November, 1965, in an apparent controversy over planning defense needs in the context of American escalation. Whatever may have been the domestic inputs to policy, there is still the output of military behavior as a basis for inferring perceptions and the ensuing strategy. This will not identify which alternatives were rejected, much less for what reasons, but it does indicate within relatively fixed parameters of operational requirements what policies were adopted with their attendant commitments and constraints.

The role of Chinese military participation, particularly within an explicit deterrence framework, has been almost wholly ignored because it was largely covert.[2] By comparison considerable academic analysis has been devoted to Peking's pronouncements for evidence of domestic and foreign aspects of decision making in 1965.[3] This literature is rich in detail but inconclusive in its findings, with sharply varying interpretations based on virtually identical statements. Several shortcomings hamper an exclusive content analysis approach. The Sino-Soviet polemic reached a state of open confrontation during the Indochina conflict, adding rhetoric and argument for audiences in Moscow, Hanoi, and elsewhere to statements which required more care and consistency if they were to affect American behavior in Indochina. In addition hortatory prose for boosting morale and resistance in North Vietnam was an inherent part of China's self-defined role as patron and protector of the "national liberation forces in their struggle against U.S. imperialism and all its running-dogs." Both the Sino-Soviet polemic and the "big brother" posture inflated Peking's language and devalued its credibility as a deterrence signal to Washington.

A more serious objection to exclusive preoccupation with Chinese statements, however, lies in the omission of military activity as an operational indicator of decisions and intentions. This activity was carried out in such a manner as to be certain of detection by United States intelligence but not by general audiences at home or abroad. It therefore is of particular interest as a signal that combined maximum private credibility with minimum public embarrassment or provocation for the United States.

Soon after the assassination of President Kennedy on November 22, 1963, proposals to threaten Hanoi with attack won increasing consideration as revealed in press rumors and authorized interpretations of presidential remarks.[4] These were quickly reflected in Chinese media, albeit without undue attention or alarm. On March 4, under the reassuring title "U.S. Aggressors Heading for Complete Defeat in South Vietnam," *People's Daily* noted " 'leaks' . . . in the press that the Administration was considering 'carrying the war to North Vietnam'—including commando raids, bombing, sabotage and subversion, sea blockade and a march to the north."[5]

On March 26 these indirect indicators of American intentions won official confirmation from Secretary of Defense Robert McNamara who warned that "initiation of military actions outside of South Vietnam, particularly against North Vietnam" was under study.[6] As was later reliably reported, "The State Department passed the word to Hanoi, through East European diplomats, that the U.S. 'meant business.' "[7] The transfer of General Maxwell Taylor from chairman of the Joint Chiefs of Staff to ambassador in South Vietnam on June 23 amplified the growing chorus of hints and speculation that Washington was seriously preparing to expand the war.

Actually an expanded American involvement was already under way in Laos where on May 21 the United States began reconnaissance flights over Communist positions, soon followed by the delivery of T-26 fighter-bombers to the Royal Lao air force.[8] With the shootdown of two reconnaissance planes on June 7–8, Washington added armed escorts authorized to attack "if fired upon." This brought American air power into the Laotian war. On June 9 United States aircraft bombed the Pathet Lao headquarters in Khang Kay, inter alia hitting the PRC mission, killing one person and injuring others. For the next month Peking exploited these developments to issue its first official warnings against American escalation. While ostensibly addressed to the confrontation in Laos, the Chinese statements became intelligible only in the larger context of Washington's oblique threats against Hanoi. Although they evoked the leitmotif of earlier deterrence warnings used for Korea and India, they paralleled the American threats in ambiguity as to the specific courses of action which might be anticipated on either side.

In calling for the Geneva Conference to be reconvened, Peking focused on the military prospects should diplomacy fail to halt recent trends. On June 24 Foreign Minister Ch'en Yi declared:

> . . . The United States is continuing its wanton bombings in Laos and stepping up preparation for new military adventures in south Vietnam. It has openly boasted that it would extend the war in Indochina. . . . It must be pointed out that Indochina lies alongside China. . . . The Chinese people absolutely will not sit idly by while the Geneva agreements are completely torn up and the flames of war spread to their side.[9]

On July 1 *People's Daily* editorialized on the "300th serious warning" against the alleged American "intrusion into China's territorial waters and airspace" by linking the earlier United States–Chinese Nationalist activities with recent developments in Indochina. Its defiance was bluntly worded:

> . . . U.S. military and administrative chiefs from Johnson down have repeatedly made a show of force and cried out for war. Some have even openly advocated expanding the aggressive war to the Democratic Republic of Vietnam and the People's Republic of China. The U.S. propaganda machine openly stated that the Johnson Administration was involved in "an exercise in brinksmanship that could conceivably end in war between the United States and China."
> We would like to ask the U.S. policy-makers: What is your intention? Do you hope to cow the Chinese people by force of arms? . . . Do you intend to embark on an adventure such as extending the war? We would like to ask the U.S. rulers: Have you pondered carefully what consequences such an adventure would bring about?[10]

Peking increased its signal on July 6 with a formal letter from Ch'en Yi to his DRV counterpart, Xuan Thuy, declaring inter alia, "U.S. imperialism is openly clamouring for an extension of the war to the DRV and threatening to subject northern Vietnam to air and naval blockade as well as bombing. . . . China and the DRV are fraternal neighbors closely related like the lips and the teeth. The Chinese people cannot be expected to look on with folded arms in the face of any aggression against the Democratic Republic of Vietnam."[11] *People's Daily* echoed Ch'en's words editorially, adding "The Chinese people will certainly not allow the U.S. imperialists to play with fire right by their side."[12] A new deterrent hint came in an official PRC statement on the tenth anniversary of the 1954 Geneva Accords:

> . . . Despite the fact that the United States has introduced tens of thousands of its military personnel into southern Viet Nam and Laos, China has not sent a single soldier to Indochina. However, there is a limit to everything. The United States would be wrong if it should think that it can do whatever it pleases in Vietnam and Indochina with impunity. We would frankly tell the United States: the Chinese people will by no means sit idly by while the United States extends its war of aggression in Vietnam and Indochina. . . .[13]

The intent of this succession of signals soon met its first test. On August 2 three DRV torpedo boats attacked two American destroyers on an electronic intelligence mission in the Gulf of Tonkin concurrent with clandestine South Vietnamese attacks on nearby DRV islands.[14] One destroyer received two holes in its superstructure from machine-gun fire; one DRV vessel was sunk and others were damaged. The next day President Johnson announced that the naval patrols would continue with a "combat air patrol" to counter any force that attacked the patrols "with the objective of not only driving off the force but of destroying it."[15] On August 4 a second DRV attack was reported, albeit under circumstances which never wholly confirmed the report. The United States claimed to have sunk two enemy boats without suffering any damage.

Disregarding Peking's warnings, President Johnson on August 5 sent American bombers over six DRV naval bases and associated facilities, inflicting heavy damage in what was expressly identified as a retaliatory raid. According to Secretary McNamara, sixty-four sorties destroyed twenty-five vessels and several oil storage depots, with only two planes lost and two damaged. PRC deterrence had clearly failed. After several months of warning, Washington had made good its threat to bomb the North, thereby signaling further eventual escalation regardless of the justification and disclaimers specifically associated with the Gulf of Tonkin incidents.

As might be expected, Chinese reactions included the full gamut of speeches, editorials, and mass demonstrations, all of which repeated the earlier themes but with one significant addition. The official PRC statement of August 6 declared, "U.S. imperialism went over the 'brink of war' and made the first step in extending the war. . . . Aggression by the United States against the Democratic Republic of Viet Nam means aggression against China."[16] While "aggression" was susceptible to many meanings, some amplification emerged in the closing paragraph:

> Whenever the U. S. imperialists invade the territory, territorial waters or airspace of the Democratic Republic of Viet Nam, the Chinese people, without hesitation, will resolutely support the Vietnamese people's just war against the U.S. aggressors. The Chinese Government has served serious warnings on the U.S. Government on many occasions that should it dare to launch an attack on the Democratic Republic of Viet Nam, the Chinese people will absolutely not stand by with folded arms or sit idly by without lending a helping hand.

This formulation was well chosen on two counts. First it recalled the Korean War deterrence warning by use of the "will not stand idly by" phraseology. Second, it was less threatening and therefore more credible a commitment of Chinese involvement through the operational phrase "lending a helping hand." The only American threat being one of air strikes and not of invasion, this suggested more than a passive response but less than an immediate, direct intervention by China.

A series of overt and covert military moves soon signaled more specifically the range of action implied by "a helping hand." The first such move was initially revealed by Washington on August 10 with the announced detection of MIG-15s and MIG-17s in North Vietnam, as had been "expected for some time because of known preparations such as lengthening of runways of airfields in the Hanoi area."[17] Other "preparations" had included the training of North Vietnamese pilots in China and presumably detailed negotiations between Peking and Hanoi that specified how the two countries would react under the contingency of American bombing signaled that spring.

One squadron of MIG fighters was no threat to the hundreds of

American aircraft being deployed to Southeast Asia for carrier and land basing. However, it did imply a logic of further assistance, at the very least in replacing parts and aircraft as necessary and at most in offering support from Chinese bases, as sanctuary for North Vietnamese pilots and planes and for direct air cover over North Vietnam. These possibilities were strengthened by two new developments. First, in an area extending roughly three hundred miles above the Vietnamese border, Peking began a systematic reinforcement of its air power, both by increasing the number of aircraft and by concentrating its relatively few MIG-19s which had previously rotated between Northeast and East China. Second, it undertook the construction of three new airfields immediately above Indochina, with only one appearing to fill a normal defensive need of covering a prospective enemy route for attack against the interior.[18]

The two other airfields became visible to overhead reconnaissance in the early stages of construction. By October an airfield was sighted at Ningming, within twelve miles of the railroad junction of Ping-hsiang where vital supplies were shipped across the border from standard to narrow-gauge track. A second airfield was discovered further west at Peitun-Yunnani, duplicating an existing facility which it adjoined. The Ningming field violated all standard operating procedures for defense against external attack by its forward position, in maximum proximity to the Gulf of Tonkin where American carriers provided the main air threat. Conceivably it could be used against the carriers themselves, but this was so certain to invite nuclear retaliation as to be ruled out by any prudent planner in Peking. Normal fighter bases are sited to afford maximum distance from enemy launch points so as to give an advantage to the defending aircraft on the basis of comparative fuel reserves and to limit an enemy attack on the bases by constraining his time over the target through the need to conserve fuel for the return trip. In addition, they are located to cover strategic avenues of approach or vital targets. All of these criteria were met by already existing facilities. The unique advantage provided by Ningming lay in extended protection over North Vietnam and the adjacent border.

Peitun-Yunnani was located more than a hundred miles behind the western end of the border, far from American bases but nearer likely targets in the DRV. The only logic in adding a new base complex to one already existing was in its use by a different air force where a separate language would be necessary for command and control of flights as well as ground facilities. At a minimum, this foreshadowed its availability to Hanoi for the rest and recuperation of pilots and the repair of aircraft. However, it could provide a refuge for the North Vietnamese air force to use against American bombers who could quickly destroy the half dozen military fields within the DRV but who might stop at "hot pursuit" across the border, observing the Chinese sanctuary as they had done in the Korean War.

Peking could be confident that knowledge of these developments would soon reach Washington. Nationalist pilots systematically flew over eastern and southern China in reconnaissance missions that were regularly tracked by PLA radar and intermittently hit. On July 7 the third U-2 shootdown evoked an official tabulation which claimed "in recent years" a total of ten such victories, including "one RB-57A, one RB-57D, one B-17, three P2V-7's, one RF-101C, and three U-2's."[19] Aerial photography could identify the number and type of aircraft deployed at airfields as well as new construction and, in addition, communications intercepts monitored the movement of air units from one point to another. Therefore, these contingency preparations for possible intervention could also serve deterrence purposes which might obviate the need to intervene.

A more explicitly focused activity emerged in January, 1965, when Chinese and North Vietnamese fighters conducted joint air exercises against a hypothetical enemy in an area extending approximately twelve miles below the border.[20] This limited coverage suggested that protection of cross-border communications was of mutual interest. In addition it might foreshadow a possible joint air cover for the nearby complex of Hanoi, Haiphong, and the Red River delta, containing the heart of North Vietnam's industry and agriculture. Subsequently DRV grid patterns were redesigned to accord with Chinese grids, permitting a uniform radar system in both countries to provide common coverage above the seventeenth parallel.

Throughout this period speculation in American newspapers about plans to escalate the war against North Vietnam increased, particularly after the November presidential election. Such speculation was reflected in an "Observer" commentary of December 12:

> ... The U.S. press has made many disclosures about the new White House plans for aggression. All indicate that these envisage "a limited expansion of the war." The *Washington Evening Star* has given the most comprehensive and detailed account of what is in

mind. There will be three steps, it says, in "a gradual increase of escalation." The first step is to use the south Vietnamese puppet air force for "air strikes . . . against . . . the . . . trail which cuts from north Vietnam through Laos into south Vietnam." In the second step American pilots would take a direct part and "the targets would be airfields and other military bases in the north." In the third step U.S. "planes would hit refineries, power plants, factories."[21] (Eliding in original.)

An endless stream of Chinese statements countered the flow of official and unofficial American hints of escalation, reiterating the pledges of July and August to "not stand idly by" and the formulation of "lips and teeth."[22] More important, however, were the secret air defense activities which gave substance to these statements.

Chinese deterrence again failed to halt American escalation. On February 7, ostensibly in response to a guerrilla attack on American troops and aircraft at Pleiku, United States and South Vietnamese planes struck "in joint retaliatory attacks" against training and staging areas in the southern DRV.[23] Further raids occurred on February 8 and 11, with systematic attacks beginning on March 2. In open defiance of Peking's threat that "aggression against the Democratic Republic of Vietnam is aggression against China," Washington gradually unleashed its air power over the next three years, dropping a greater tonnage of bombs on North Vietnam than had been dropped on Japan in World War II.[24] Yet no overt Chinese military intervention resulted at any time.

The Sino-American interaction did not end as quickly or decisively as this simple summary might suggest, nor did Chinese signals cease in March, 1965. In addition to further statements of resolve to support Hanoi, most of which sounded hollow in the absence of visible deeds to match the words, the Chinese air force began a series of actions to warn Washington that it was prepared to accept the risks of retaliation and escalation by engaging aircraft that strayed over Chinese territory. On April 9, 1965, Peking announced that "eight U.S. military planes in two groups intruded over China's Hainan Island. Panicking when Chinese planes took off to meet them, the U.S. planes fired two air-to-air missiles at random and fled. In the confusion, one U.S. plane was hit by a missile fired by another and crashed in the area of Hainan."[25]

The decision to scramble MIG fighters under circumstances that did not otherwise presage an American attack carried the risk of provoking an engagement, but it also offered an opportunity to communicate an important signal. Peking's prompt announcement of the incident and its careful explanation of the shootdown indicated its sensitivity to the provocative implications and its desire to deny Washington an excuse to retaliate. Nonetheless, a precedent was established where Chinese aircraft followed a random pattern of reactions involving varying degrees of risk in order to remind American planners and pilots they could not exclude the possibility of clashes if they chose to approach the border.

Peking claimed to have shot down a total of nine American aircraft during the Vietnam War, with another two reportedly damaged.[26] As shown on the following table, only two losses were officially confirmed by Washington with another two listed as "possible." In addition the aforementioned aircraft were admitted to have been downed over Hainan under circumstances never officially explained by American sources. For its part Peking claimed to have lost one MIG-17 in action with American aircraft over China on May 12, 1966; no confirmation came from Washington.

This did not exhaust the PLA inventory of reactions. As American aircraft approached they were tracked by Chinese radar which in turn was monitored by the United States, thereby providing an initial signal of alert.[27] Sometimes overflight would result in the scrambling of MIGs with

Chinese and U.S. Claims on PRC Shootdown of
U.S. Piloted Aircraft

Date	PRC Claim	U.S. Claim
September 20, 1965	1 F104 downed	Confirmed
October 5, 1965	1 F104 downed	
April 12, 1966	1 A-3B downed	Confirmed
September 9, 1966	1 F105 damaged	Admitted "possible"
September 17, 1966	1 fighter damaged	Admitted "possible"
April 24, 1967	1 F-4B downed	
May 1, 1967	2 A-FB downed	
June 26, 1967	1 F-4C downed	
August 21, 1967	2 A-6 downed	

no effort at attack. On other occasions attack would be attempted but was frustrated by quick exit from Chinese airspace. On one occasion an American plane was pursued a dozen miles into North Vietnam where it was finally downed by Chinese fighters. Significantly Radio Peking credited the victory to Hanoi (which duly seconded this version of the account) and thereby attempted to ensure against any reciprocal reaction.[28] These various PLA responses were not always announced by Peking. This minimized the appearance of open challenge and provocation, although their occurrence was certain to become known to the United States military command.

An alternative to direct air intervention was the DRV use of Chinese bases. Sensitive to the Korean precedent, Secretary of State Rusk warned in mid-1965 against any "assumption" of "sanctuary" and virtually pledged "hot pursuit" in combat even if this meant overflying China. [29] All sides sought to avoid this point of confrontation, however, while exercising their power to the maximum. Hanoi's pilots and planes regularly used Peitun-Yunnani for rest and repair but landed in North Vietnam en route to or from combat, after or before going across the border. [30] Reciprocally until mid-1967, American aircraft never destroyed all DRV bases at once but systematically left one capable of use so as to avoid pressing Hanoi to the final choice of quitting the air completely or raising the sanctuary question directly. As argued by one high level adviser, "I think we have gone far enough to hurt and not far enough to drive the aircraft to Chinese fields, which I think could be very dangerous."[31] More specifically the main base near Hanoi was singled out as particularly sensitive: "As to the Phuc Yen airfield, we believe there is a significant chance that this attack would cause Hanoi to assume we were going to make their jet operational airfields progressively untenable. This could significantly and in itself increase the chances of their moving planes to China and all the interacting possibilities that then arise."[32]

Finally in August, 1967, multiple political pressures in Washington forced President Johnson to lift his prohibition against attacks within the Hanoi-Haiphong sanctuaries and the Chinese border zone. As shown by the above table, PLA shootdowns had already claimed four aircraft from April to June; nevertheless, new attacks were sanctioned within eight miles of the boundary.[33] On August 21 two American planes that had strayed over the border fell to Chinese MIGs. Potentially more serious was the publicly unreported development in which North Vietnamese pilots appeared to sortie directly to or from Chinese bases while engaging in combat.[34] Occurring on three occasions in the fall of 1967, these instances came as the United States struck at DRV bases in unprecedented simultaneous sweeps, hitting Phuc Yen for the first time.

The use of PRC "sanctuary" made real the contingency first signaled in 1964 which seemed to accept the threat of "hot pursuit" with the attendant risks of combat over Chinese territory and attacks on Chinese bases. This prospect became more threatening in the larger context of Cultural Revolution violence which included the sacking of the British chancery in August and the kidnapping of a British official on the Hong Kong border.[35] Under the circumstances any attempt to determine the limits of Chinese risk taking was hazardous, and Washington soon abandoned attacks near the border, reinstating the buffer zone. In March, 1968, President Johnson announced the suspension of all raids above the twentieth parallel. When President Nixon resumed them in May, 1972, to "deny the aggressor the weapons of war" he mined Haiphong harbor but left the border sanctuary inviolate.[36]

So far as the prolonged massive American bombing of North Vietnam was concerned, Chinese deterrence was a prominent failure. The physical destruction devastated DRV industry, crippled transportation, and virtually wiped out entire towns and villages. However, deterrence was a partial success in determining both the pace and the limits of escalation. While gradual escalation aimed in part at facilitating Hanoi's capitulation to American demands by threatening greater damage should it resist, it was also predicated on avoiding the threshhold of likely Chinese responses. The deliberate pattern initially limited attacks to targets below the nineteenth parallel, incrementally expanding in April and May, 1965, to the twentieth and then the twenty-first parallel. Finally a twenty-five to thirty-mile buffer zone below the border was excluded from attack under a restriction which lasted until August, 1967, despite Hanoi's continued resistance to American demands. In addition a sanctuary ring was observed around Hanoi and Haiphong for most of this period and permanently around the Red River dikes.[37]

These restrictions were defended by key decision makers, among themselves and before others, as a precaution against PRC reactions. On April 1, 1965, McGeorge Bundy noted in a "Key Elements for Discussion" memorandum for President Johnson, "Hanoi has shown no signs of give, and Peiping has stiffened its position within the last week. We still believe that attacks near Hanoi might substantially raise the odds of Peiping coming in with air."[38] The president reportedly used more colorful language to explain his strategy to congressional visitors:

> . . . As for Communist China, he was watching for every possible sign of reaction. Employing a vivid sexual analogy, the President explained to friends and critics one day that the slow escalation of the air war in the North and the increasing pressure on Ho Chi Minh was seduction, not rape. If China should suddenly react to slow escalation, as a woman might react to attempted seduction, by threatening to retaliate (a slap in the face, to continue the metaphor), the United States would have plenty of time to ease off the bombing. On the other hand, if the United States were to unleash an all-out, total assault on the North—rape rather than seduction—there could be no turning back, and Chinese reaction might be instant and total.[39]

Although restricted bombing clearly failed to accomplish the stated aims of forcing Hanoi to negotiate and of decreasing DRV infiltration into the south, Secretary of Defense McNamara nonetheless cautioned the president on July 30, 1965, "The bombing program—especially as strikes move toward Hanoi and toward China and as encounters with Soviet/Chinese SAMs/MIGs occur—may increase the risk of escalation into a broader war."[40] In August Secretary McNamara testified before senatorial critics, "An attack on the Haiphong petroleum [dumps] would substantially increase the risk of Chinese participation" while targeting power plants in addition would require hitting SAM sites and Phuc Yen. "I had better not describe how we would handle it but it would be one whale of a big attack . . . this might well trigger, in the view of some, would trigger Chinese intervention on the ground. . . . This is what we wish to avoid."[41]

Multiple benefits accrued to Hanoi by these limitations which resulted from Chinese deterrence. Graduated escalation provided time to evacuate material and people from important target areas, particularly in Hanoi and Haiphong. An extensive shelter program was combined with relocation to cut casualties far below what they would have been otherwise. By limiting attacks on DRV bases and by providing rest and repair facilities across the border, Peking sustained Hanoi's ability to maintain an indigenous air defense, thereby improving morale of the DRV under intensive bombing. When the MIGs, together with Soviet-supplied SAMs, impeded American attacks and on occasion shot down American planes, the victories were fully exploited in North Vietnamese propaganda.

Most important, deterrence prevented any attempt to interdict supplies at the border, a major source for weapons and ammunition destined for use in the south. Peking's pledge that "China provides a vast rear" proved meaningful. By early 1966 the Communist forces in South Vietnam had been completely reequipped with Chinese weapons up to the level of mortars, in contrast with their previous potpourri of captured French, Japanese, and American equipment supplemented with crude handmade devices.[42] The buffer zone permitted a vast stockpiling of supplies which were delivered to the border and transferred there to countless small storage dumps for overland shipment through Laos and by sea to South Vietnam. Yet the inability of fast aircraft to attack in this narrow area and turn sharply enough to avoid overflight of Chinese territory precluded such raids so long as the PLA made credible its willingness to engage such overflights.

It would be misleading to conclude that these restrictions made a critical difference in Hanoi's will and ability to resist. No such limitations had existed in North Korea but that regime did not surrender. In January, 1969, the Joint Chiefs of Staff estimated "that a minimum of 6,000 sorties per month would be required against the two rail lines from China [and] even at this level of effort, the North Vietnamese could continue to use the rail lines to shuttle supplies if they were willing to devote sufficient manpower to repair and transshipment operations."[43] But within the limited context of Washington's *political* goals and Hanoi's reaction thereto, Chinese behavior significantly deterred conduct of the air war.

Invasion of the North?

The third area of deterrence concerned the prospects of an invasion of North Vietnam. Retrospective analysis has viewed the dispatch of 3,500 marines to Danang in March, 1965, as the first deliberate step in committing regular ground forces to combat as distinguished from the prior role of "advisers."[44] However, the deployment was not portrayed as such at the time in Peking, where an official statement called it "a grave move to further expand the war" but dismissed the prospect of "a few U.S. warships, several hundred U.S. planes, and some tens of thousands of U.S. ground forces" as being unable to "frighten the Vietnamese people."[45]

As Hanoi persisted in its course despite the steady increase in coverage and intensity of United States bombing, American press speculation turned to the possibility of major ground force commitments in South

Vietnam. On June 1, "Observer" noted in *People's Daily,* "Large numbers of U.S. troops have already been sent to south Vietnam and the number is growing. They have risen from 23,000 at the end of last year to more than 50,000 today. Some reports say that in the next few months they will be increased to 75,000. Other reports claim that they will go up to 100,000, 200,000, 300,000, or even 500,000."[46] Claiming that Washington, "really wants to escalate the war of aggression against Vietnam into a Korean-type local war," the author noted, "[raises] a hue and cry that DRV troops are entering south Vietnam and talks about massive concentrations of Chinese troops on the Sino-Vietnamese border.... Is all this not a dramatic change? And is it not an indication that the Johnson administration . . . is preparing to extend the war from Indochina to Southeast Asia and even to China?"

"Observer" did not enlarge on this allegation nor did he make clear how it was linked with the increase of troops in South Vietnam. He concluded with an expansion on the standard formulations of support to hint elliptically at a possible parallel response by Peking should the American role continue to expand:

> . . . Since the United States, in defiance of the Chinese people's many warnings, has not only sent large numbers of its own troops but also has mustered troops of its satellite countries to invade Vietnam, China's fraternal neighbor, the Chinese people have secured the right to do all in their power to aid the Vietnamese people in hitting back at the U.S. aggressors. . . . The United States raises a howl about how China is assisting Vietnam. Why all the fuss? The United States, all the way from the other side of the ocean, has sent troops to China's neighboring country, threatening China's security daily. Why should socialist China not give all-out support to socialist, fraternal Vietnam? . . . Now that U.S. imperialism is sending large numbers of reinforcements to south Vietnam, expanding air raids in the north, and more and more seriously threatening China's security, the Chinese people all the more have the right to take every additional measure that is necessary.

Contrary to the implications of this article, no major campaign followed to mobilize greater support for Hanoi much less signal a PLA equivalent to Washington's latest moves. Articulated concern over American intentions, however, heightened after an alleged American violation of Yunnan airspace in the course of an attack on Lao Cai, an important rail juncture across the river. This violation of the buffer zone prompted *People's Daily* to respond in an editorial on July 13:

> ... On the same day the U.S. aircraft intruded into the Hokow area in Yunnan province, Dean Rusk was saying that the concept of "sanctuary" in the Vietnam war no longer existed. This is clearly meant to intimidate China. ... We have made a full estimation of the madness of U.S. imperialism and are well prepared with regard to its war adventure plan. The Chinese People's Liberation Army now stands ready, in battle array. We will not attack unless we are attacked; if we are attacked, we will certainly counter-attack.[47]

This wording excluded any ground combat with American troops unless and until American troops crossed the border. The implication was reinforced by a curious juxtaposition of remarks on July 15 by Hoang Van Hoan, leader of a DRV friendship delegation, and P'eng Chen, mayor of Peking and member of the Politbureau. Hoang declared that "large numbers of men of the Chinese People's Liberation Army and Chinese youth have volunteered to go to Vietnam and take part in the fighting there," while P'eng did not mention this or any other specific means of implementing his pledge "to give the Vietnamese people whatever support and aid they need."[48] Thus, if Chinese policy makers anticipated a qualitative as well as quantitative change in American escalation manifested by the incremental increase in ground forces in South Vietnam during the spring of 1965, they failed to signal any consistent concern or to threaten any serious reaction. They may well have been uncertain as to how fast and how far Washington intended to go, and after having failed to prevent the bombing they undoubtedly differed over the timing, nature, and consequences of further deterrence efforts.[49]

Any uncertainty over American intentions in terms of a massive ground commitment, whatever its purpose, was resolved on July 28 when President Johnson formally announced he was increasing American troop strength in Vietnam from 75,000 to 125,000 and doubling the monthly draft calls, indicating further forces would be sent as necessary.[50] On August 7, the PRC issued an official statement in response, vowing, "We, the 650 million Chinese people, have repeatedly pledged to the Vietnamese people our all-out support and assistance, up to and including the sending, according to their need, of our men to fight shoulder to shoulder with them to drive out the U.S. aggressors. We warn the U.S. aggressors once more: We Chinese people mean what we say!"[51] Within two months PLA deployments into the DRV reinforced the seriousness of these words, just as the deployment of planes, the construction of bases, and joint air exercises had seemed to signal intervention in the earlier confrontation over the threatened bombing of the North. But when that threat material-ized no intervention had occurred. How then could this signal be made credible and what was it designed to deter?

Five aspects of the PLA deployment deserve attention in this regard. First, it was not conducted under maximum security against detection by the United States. On the contrary, the use of normal communications patterns permitted the outside location and identification of engineer, railroad construction, and antiaircraft divisions, although the concealment of such information was well within Peking's capability.[52] Furthermore the troops wore regular uniforms and made no pretense of being civilian or "volunteer" groups, thereby enhancing the likelihood of an eventual American awareness through observer reports, as indeed occurred. The logical conclusion is that the PLA presence was deliberately made known in a manner so as to be credible without appearing provocative by publicly confronting the United States.

Second, the deployment was sizable. Between September and Decem-ber, 1965, approximately 35,000 Chinese military personnel crossed the border, a number which expanded to nearly 50,000 by the early spring of 1966. These forces remained in roughly the same disposition until Presi-dent Johnson stopped the massive bombing of the North in March, 1968, after which they gradually returned to China. The only quantitative change detected during this time was an increase from two to three antiaircraft divisions in 1967 concurrent with heavier attacks on Hanoi, Haiphong, and the border area. Routine changes in personnel occurred with the regular six-month rotation of these antiaircraft units, apparently to provide maximum opportunity for experience under fire.

The implications of size were twofold. The troops posed a logistics burden of resupply which, considering the damage to North Vietnam by air attack, had to be assumed by Peking. This in turn made the troops a hostage against the interdiction of transport lines from China, providing Washington with a highly credible token of PLA determination to keep those lines open regardless of the attendant risks in escalation. These Chinese ground forces were living proof to the North Vietnamese that PRC pledges would be honored even at the loss of life. Officially their presence remained publicly unacknowledged. Only in 1968 was a single small item found in DRV media reporting tribute to the "sacrifices" borne by these troops. Nevertheless, their presence and their participation in defense against air attack were widely known in the North. This served to bolster morale and strengthen resistance to American demands and pressure.

A third feature of importance was the fact that the PLA did not remain in passive reserve but engaged in combat, inflicted losses, and suffered casualties. The antiaircraft divisions fired on American planes and were bombed in return. Engineer and railroad construction battalions, the bulk of the deployment, worked to keep communications routes open despite repeated attack. This behavior indicated a willingness not only to take casualties but also to risk an escalatory reaction. Alternative tactics could have been adopted to minimize these consequences. The PLA propensity for underground structures and extensive tunneling was amply demonstrated during the two-year stalemate in Korea when the entire battle zone was honeycombed with subterranean storerooms, hospitals, and shelters connected by a labyrinth of tunnels estimated to extend many miles behind the front.[53] A similar approach, to the extent permitted by the different terrain and topography, would have reduced both visibility and casualties. More important, refraining from attempts to shoot down attacking planes would have removed the danger that American losses might bring retaliation against the PRC.

The awareness on both sides of the dangers in provocation and escalation resulted in the curious anomaly whereby Washington was the sole official source to acknowledge the PLA presence in North Vietnam, with no confirmation from Peking or Hanoi. However, American officals carefully counched their revelations in such a manner so as to minimize attention and reaction in congressional and press circles where concern about a possible Sino-American war was acute.[54] In this way Peking accepted a modest propaganda loss while the visible and dramatic use of Russian surface-to-air missiles prompted foreign comment to disparage Chinese pledges of support, claiming Peking was prepared to fight but only to the last Vietnamese. The Chinese leadership apparently appreciated the difference between credible deterrence and a provocative "lock-in" of enemy escalation. Under the circumstances a low profile was preferable to publicity. For its part, the Johnson administration had no desire to arouse American concern over the prospects of war with China and had no intention of stumbling inadvertently into that war.[55] Its unobtrusive release of information revealing the PLA presence avoided alarm while alerting Peking it was aware of Chinese activity in the DRV and intended to abide by its implications.

A fourth point of significance was the PLA construction of a large base complex at Yen Bai in the DRV northwest.[56] This grew to nearly two hundred buildings and a large runway with attendant facilities, protected by antiaircraft guns revetted into caves on railroad tracks that permitted a prompt response against American aircraft reported from radar stations to the south. The purpose of Yen Bai was ambiguous, perhaps intentionally so. It could become a DRV redoubt in the event of an invasion overrunning Hanoi and Haiphong. Proximity to China and the surrounding jungle offered a viable refuge on home territory for continued resistance, in contrast with the plight of the North Korean regime after fleeing Pyongyang. However, the Korean precedent raised the possibility of Yen Bai serving a massive Chinese intervention should this become necessary. Before crossing the Yalu River in mid-October, 1950, no preparations had been made for PRC entry into the war in the form of prepositioned supplies, strengthened logistical lines, and advance base development. Now in 1965–66 Chinese engineers were building a network of roads to improve transport facilities across the border, widening and reinforcing bridges, and in addition creating the Yen Bai complex.

Public speculation concerning the prospects for Chinese ground intervention remained preoccupied with its possible role in South Vietnam and properly discounted this as unlikely for several reasons. The National Liberation Front remained insistent on its indigenous image to the point of concealing regular DRV units fighting on its side, thereby hoping to maximize its appeal to South Vietnamese and to exploit sentiment against foreign, i.e., American intervention. Chinese participation could not be similarly concealed and would vitiate these tactics. Moreover Chinese troops would inordinately complicate command and control of the fighting because of language differences and a total unfamiliarity with the country. The need to traverse Laos and North Vietnam would not only expose the PLA to heavy casualties before entering combat but could also threaten Hanoi's control over developments in these areas during and after the war. This political hazard might prove necessary as a last resort, but until then it presumably would be unacceptable given the vivid memory of Chinese conquest and domination preserved by Vietnamese museums, statues, and folklore. As a final consideration, the National Liberation

Front (NLF) needed firepower and protection from bombing. Its manpower was sufficient to cope with the larger enemy through small guerrilla forces which could elude, harrass, and intermittently defeat conventional American and South Vietnamese units. In short there was no logic to Chinese intervention in the South.

The only credible PLA role was in the North. Here two threats might be warded off by the anticipated use of deterrence; should deterrence fail, the threats could be coped with through massive Chinese intervention. An American invasion up the Red River could seize the industrial and agricultural heartland of North Vietnam. Another possibility was a combined attack on infiltration routes whereby an amphibious landing at the nineteenth parallel would cut across the narrow panhandle to deny access to the main passes which provided entry to the "Ho Chi Minh" trail in Laos. Either of these contingencies would strain North Vietnamese defenses, already complicated by increasing commitments in Laos and South Vietnam, unless the PLA could take on all rear echelon responsibilities in the upper half of the DRV and perhaps in Laos as well. Under "worst case" circumstances, of course, massive intervention could help to block an advance on the border, as in Korea. Short of this, however, less dramatic options open to the United States still raised major problems for Hanoi, as evidenced by repeated Saigon threats to "march North" as well as by American press speculation.

As a fifth and final consideration, the PLA deployment into North Vietnam was accompanied by growing indications of Chinese concern over a possible Sino-American war. The most overt manifestation of this came on September 29 in a press conference by Ch'en Yi. The foreign minister's defiant rhetoric reduced his credibility abroad; however, in the context of other evidence his fervor may have reflected a high level consensus on the likelihood of escalation involving China. Expanding on a question concerning Hong Kong, Ch'en launched into an extended, rambling reply which repeatedly returned to the prospect of war:

> ... The Chinese Government considers the question not only one of using Hong Kong as a base for aggression against Vietnam but also of preparing to use it in future as a base for aggression against China. . . . It is possible that the United States may extend the war to China's mainland. . . . If the war should spread to China, she will put up staunch resistance and will be determined to defeat U.S. imperialism. . . . It is up to the U.S. President and the Pentagon to

decide whether the U.S. wants a big war with China today. . . . If the U.S. imperialists are determined to launch a war of aggression against us, they are welcome to come sooner, to come as early as tomorrow. . . . Should the U.S. imperialists invade China's mainland, we will take all necessary measures to defeat them. By then, the war will have no boundaries.[57]

Ch'en's words were reinforced by an announcement of special emergency conditions for southern and coastal provinces and Sinkiang.[58] Less public evidence of war preparations came through letters and from travellers in these areas who told of civil defense lectures, air raid drills, films on nuclear weapons, and the earmarking of factories for dismantling and evacuation inland.[59] Foreign sources of blood plasma were queried about emergency stockpiling, although no large orders resulted at this time.[60]

These indicators were not publicized as part of a general mobilization campaign or in open challenge to "U.S. imperialism." Their implications were taken at face value locally, however, as reflected in anxious and alarmed views reaching relatives in Hong Kong and overseas Chinese communities. Finally in January, 1966, a major Communist newspaper in Hong Kong ran a month-long series of articles which systematically addressed various aspects of an "inevitable" Sino-American war in so detailed and unprecedented a fashion as to suggest it represented study materials utilized by authorities in South China for briefing cadres and citizens on the situation.[61] This series deserves examination as a unique statement of how and why the war might escalate to China and as an apparent reflection of judgments at higher policy levels.

The main message was that war between the PRC and the United States was near at hand, as illustrated by the following excerpts:

> . . . U.S. moves to increase troop strength deployed in Vietnam to 300,000 and to shift key military bases for carrying out aggression in Vietnam from Okinawa to Taiwan furnish proof that the U.S. is prepared at any time to attack China on a massive scale. *Fighting early and on a big scale appears inevitable.*[62]
> . . . The enemy is sharpening his knife, and we are also sharpening our knife. U.S. imperialism proclaims loudly that it can attack China at any time, and China also declares that she is prepared to meet the war resolutely. *An early war, and a large scale war between China and the United States seems to be inevitable.*[63]
> . . . However fierce may be the internal dispute of the U.S. ruling class, it exactly reflects one thing: that the United States wants to

attack China, that the United States wants to go to war with China. The fiercer the argument, the more exposed is the fact that *the plans for war are being pushed forward, the steps for war are being intensified, and the time of fighting is coming nearer.*[64]

... The *United States must finally attack China, war between China and the United States finally cannot be averted.* . . . The problem is one of time, whether they will fight later or fight earlier.[65] (Italics added.)

These formulations in their categorical assertions went beyond anything that had been issued in major PRC media. However, they were anticipated by a more qualified alert voiced by Chou En-lai the previous month. Speaking on December 20 at a rally celebrating the fifth anniversary of the NLF, he described a series of probable escalatory measures allegedly aimed at "a watertight blockade on South Vietnam [to] render the South Vietnamese people isolated and helpless."[66] He then warned,

> ... If it [U.S. aggression] still fails to achieve its aim—and it certainly will fail—it is possible that, in accordance with the objective laws governing the development of aggressive wars, U.S. imperialism will go a step further and extend its war of aggression to the whole of Indochina and to China. Indeed, U.S. imperialism is now making preparations to meet this eventuality which may emerge.
> ... The Chinese people have been long prepared. Should U.S. imperialism insist on going along the road of war expansion and on having another trial of strength with the Chinese people, the Chinese people will resolutely take up the challenge and go along with it to the very end. Come what may in the future, the Chinese people will unswervingly side with the fraternal Vietnamese people and contribute all their efforts to the defeat of U.S. imperialism, until final victory.

Chou's linkage of a "trial of strength" with support for Vietnam was expanded on in the Hong Kong series to explain why a Sino-American war would emerge at this time. The analysis summarized earlier American efforts in South Vietnam and noted, "after the failure of its 'special warfare,' the U.S. sent its own troops to the battle-fields. When these are again defeated, the U.S. wants to save the situation by means of escalation. It wants to vent its frustration against the Chinese and tries to stop China from supporting the Vietnamese people. . . . The U.S. is still dreaming that it can force the Chinese to do this by threatening them with war."[67]

In part the escalatory process was depicted as inexorable and not by American design. The writer claimed, "The development of war is governed by this objective law. Unless one side can overwhelm the other, the war will become increasingly intense and get out of control. In South Vietnam, Johnson has repeatedly increased his stake. The present scale of war is obviously larger than what he had originally intended. . . . So even supposing that Johnson did not want to escalate the war too much, he would still find it impossible to prevent this from happening."[68] In part the war was shown to be the culmination of American policy since 1950, flowing from the needs of a monopoly capitalist class that determined the course of American imperialism and saw China as its primary opponent leading the world revolutionary movement. The former interpretation implied an unwitting enemy blindly escalating toward war; the latter stressed his purposeful behavior. But both converged in their conclusion that war was inevitable.[69]

The series argued defensively against the proposition that Chinese policy was provocative in its support of Vietnam and unyielding in its opposition to discussing American peace proposals. The repeated linkage of Peking's posture on Vietnam with the likelihood of war, coupled with the preparations and anxieties manifest in southern cities, suggests the degree to which anticipation of war hinged on Indochina. In this context, the PLA presence in North Vietnam took on added importance. As a token of credible commitment, it increased the likelihood of escalation to the extent that the provocative role of the PLA might outweigh its deterrent role. Yet despite this acknowledged risk, Peking committed the force on behalf of Hanoi.

Not only did the PLA presence impede American air attacks and help repair the damage therefrom, but it countered American pressures on Hanoi to accept Washington's terms or suffer intolerable destruction. This was increasingly at issue in December, 1965, as the Johnson administration began an intensive "peace campaign," correctly rumored in advance to include a "bombing pause" in January ostensibly to permit Hanoi to respond without duress. Drawing both on past precedent and recent American press speculation, *People's Daily* forecast that the "peace hoax" would end with a further escalation and expansion of the war.[70] If Hanoi needed any persuasion to persist without responding to the "pause," the only credible deterrent against the "worst case" prospects of all-out bombing and an American invasion was Chinese intervention. Whatever may have been the earlier disappointment or disagreement over providing air cover, the PLA ground units met a more serious, if not yet more immediate, threat.

Peking did not publicly define the precise course of American escalation after the "pause" or depict how a Sino-American war would eventuate. As the Hong Kong analysis admitted, "We are not the 'red-whiskered counselor' of the United States and we do not know in advance the time and the date when the United States will launch its attack."[71] However, the consequences of such an attack were not dismissed lightly: "War is bound to bring destruction but destruction makes re-construction on a larger scale possible. Pyongyang was reduced to ruins during the Korean War. It is now one of the newest cities in the Far East. If the people of our generation yielded to U.S. imperialism for fear of sacrifice, then our posterity would have to pay a heavy price."[72] Aside from the unconvincing "better than ever" postwar picture portrayed in these remarks, their example of Pyongyang as "reduced to ruins" was a realistic forecast of the results of further escalation.

In sum, Peking's posture in the fall and winter of 1965 signaled a willingness to increase the risk of war with the United States by open statements, by unpublicized war preparations in south China, and by the covert deployment of troops to the DRV for construction and combat against American bombing. The signals were consistent and credible and, insofar as they addressed a willingness to help in the event of an American invasion, they communicated a feasible Chinese response, underlined by repeated allusions to a "Korean-type war." In addition their implications of possible intervention to protect border communications and vital targets in Hanoi-Haiphong further cautioned against expanding United States raids beyond existing limits.

The general principles of Peking's posture were summarized by Chou En-lai in April, 1966. Speaking with a Pakistani correspondent, he declared:

> (1) China will not take the initiative to provoke a war with the United States. . . .
> (2) The Chinese mean what they say. In other words, if any country in Asia, Africa, or elsewhere meets with aggression by the imperialists headed by the United States, the Chinese Government and people definitely will give it support and help. Should such just action bring on U.S. aggression against China, we will unhesitatingly rise in resistance and fight to the end.
> (3) China is prepared. Should the United States impose a war on China, it can be said with certainty that, once in China, the United

States will not be able to pull out, however many men it may send over and whatever weapons it may use, nuclear weapons included. . . .

(4) Once the war breaks out, it will have no boundaries. Some U.S. strategists want to bombard China by relying on their air and naval superiority and avoid a ground war. This is wishful thinking. Once the war gets started with air or sea action, it will not be for the United States alone to decide how the war will continue. If you can come from the sky, why can't we fight back on the ground? That is why we say the war will have no boundaries once it breaks out.[73]

The consistency of verbal deterrence from Ch'en Yi in September to Chou in April, reiterated through numerous government statements and editorials, was materially reinforced by the 50,000 PLA troops in North Vietnam. While not taking any "initiative to provoke a war," their activity and its implications showed "the Chinese mean what they say," that Peking would help Hanoi even "should such just action bring on U.S. aggression against China." Together with smaller PLA units located in Nam Tha and Phong Saly provinces in Laos, these troops building roads reaching from Yunnan toward North Vietnam and Thailand provided meaning to how "once the war breaks out, it will have no boundaries."[74] American attacks on China "from the sky" would be answered "on the ground" in Laos, Thailand, and if necessary, South Vietnam.

All this was not without effect in Washington. One of the staunchest advocates of escalation and an early proponent of American ground forces in Indochina was Walt W. Rostow. As head of the National Security Council, he conceded in May, 1967, "With respect to Communist China, it always has the option of invading Laos and Thailand; but this would not be a rational response to naval and air operations designed to strangle Hanoi. A war throughout Southeast Asia would not help Hanoi; although I do believe Communist China would fight us if we invaded the northern part of North Vietnam."[75] His implication that invasion below "the northern part" was safe won a tacit rebuttal from Secretary McNamara: "To U.S. ground actions in North Vietnam, we would expect China to respond by entering the war with both ground and air forces."[76]

The final examination of this option came from the State Department's Assistant Secretary for Far Eastern Affairs, William P. Bundy. Writing in the immediate aftermath of the sweeping Communist "Tet offensive" of February, 1968, which triggered requests from General William B. Westmoreland in Saigon for increasing American troop levels from 520,000 to 700,000, Bundy concluded:

5. *U.S. Invasion of North Vietnam*

Chinese reaction would depend on the scale of U.S. moves, on North Vietnamese intentions and on Peking's view of U.S. objectives. If it became evident that we were not aiming for a rapid takeover of North Vietnam but intended chiefly to hold some territory in southern areas to inhibit Hanoi's actions in South Vietnam and to force it to quit fighting, we would expect China to attempt to deter us from further northward movement and to play on our fears of a Sino-U.S. conflict, but not to intervene massively in the war. Thus, if requested by Hanoi, Peking would probably be willing to station infantry north of Hanoi, to attach some ground forces to North Vietnamese units further south, and to contribute any "volunteers" contingent that North Vietnam might organize. At home, China would probably complement these deterrents by various moves ostensibly putting the country on a war footing.

If the North Vietnamese, under threat of a full-scale invasion, decided to agree to a negotiated settlement, the Chinese would probably go along. On the other hand, if the Chinese believed that the U.S. was intent on destroying the North Vietnamese regime (either because Hanoi insisted on holding out to the end, or because Peking chronically expects the worst from the U.S.), they would probably fear for their own security and intervene on a massive scale.[77]

While there were other inhibitions against an invasion of North Vietnam, the available documents make explicit the prominent role of Chinese deterrence in foreclosing this choice of action. On balance, the debatable effects of air attack as against the certain victory attainable through invasion and occupation made this success for deterrence of greater significance in the Indochina struggle than its earlier failure.

Chapter 7

Chinese Deterrence:
Korea, India, and Vietnam

The Basis for Comparison

Any effort to determine deterrence strategies and to compare their effectiveness encounters significant analytical obstacles, even apart from the fundamental problem of access to documents that reveal policy assumptions and goals.[1] A longitudinal study of one country such as China deals with a developing society whose capabilities as well as leadership composition change over time. As capabilities change so may perceptions and goals. In addition the type of threat, both in origin and in manifestation, often differs from one situation to another. The opponent's power will change as will the stakes involved in confrontation. A third variable, the international context, can alter the relationship with other countries whose posture may range from ally to potential enemy.

Despite these obstacles, it is necessary to construct and test generalizations from different case studies with respect to the behavior of one country over time and hopefully for eventual cross-cultural hypotheses that will apply to a number of countries. This study has focused on three major instances when the PRC deployed military force across its boundaries in situations where deterrence had been an objective of policy: Korea, 1950; India, 1962; and Vietnam, 1965. The first two efforts failed to affect enemy behavior as desired and war resulted. In Vietnam success was partial and at least sufficient to avoid open conflict.

At first glance, the dissimilarities among these three case studies discourage comparison. China's domestic capabilities changed markedly over the fifteen years between Korea and Vietnam, particularly with respect to the military. In 1950 the People's Republic was wholly dependent on Soviet deliveries for air power and most ground equipment. The army had just emerged from a prolonged civil war and was in the process of absorbing recently defeated Nationalist forces into a national military system. The PLA had never fought on foreign soil. By 1962 China produced MIG-19s and its arsenals could supply all needs short of sophisticated electronics systems and nuclear weaponry. A unified and modernized military organization had not only successfully thrown the United Nations forces back from the Yalu River but had fought them for more than two years to a stalemate at the thirty-eighth parallel.

In the civilian sector, equally impressive changes had occurred. The People's Republic entered the Korean War within a year of declaring itself the victor in the Chinese civil war; however, large pockets of resistance remained. The residual chaos of three decades without an effective central government but with almost twenty years of foreign invasion and civil war had led to rampant inflation, a totally stagnant economy, and widespread destruction of the industrial sector with its supporting infrastructure. By 1962, organized resistance had long since disappeared; the central administration had extended control over all sectors of society, and a major social and economic transformation had laid the foundations for a modern industrial system with the potential for regional dominance and global influence. The disasters of Great Leap Forward experimentation, natural calamities, and withdrawal of Soviet aid had grave short-run effects, but by the Vietnam war these had been overcome and better rates of growth could be anticipated.

The second dimension, enemy capabilities and the stakes at issue, also varied considerably among the three cases under examination. In Korea and Vietnam, the United States confronted China with an overwhelming superiority in conventional and nuclear weaponry, whereas in the border dispute India could mount a credible threat only to the most remote and peripheral portion of the People's Republic. Furthermore "U.S. imperialism" could add the threat of invasion from Taiwan with 600,000 Nationalist troops and an indeterminate potential among mainland dissidents. By comparison the Tibetan guerrillas had shown their peak capability in the abortive 1959 revolt, posing merely an interdiction and nuisance threat thereafter.

In Korea and Vietnam the stakes were nothing less than the existence of neighboring regimes bound by ties of ideology and propinquity, the support of which was essential to Chinese claims of leadership in both Communist and Asian affairs. Beyond this, passive acquiescence in enemy conquest would bring "U.S. imperialism" literally to China's land borders as compared to containing it on Taiwan, separated from the mainland by one hundred miles of water. No strategic stakes were threatened in the disputed Himalayan territory, however, except for the Aksai Chin road. In short, not only was the punitive power of the enemy vastly greater in 1950 and 1965 as against 1962, but the stakes were also far greater in Korea and Indochina than in the border dispute.

The international context within which these crises emerged also differed considerably over time. In 1950 the recently concluded Sino-Soviet Treaty of Friendship, Alliance, and Mutual Assistance pledged Russia's assistance in the event China were attacked by "Japan or any state allied with it."[2] Although Russia had only tested its first nuclear weapon in 1949 and could not yet match the United States in this area, Soviet military capabilities in Europe, particularly around Berlin, posed a strong counterthreat to American involvement on the Asian continent. By 1962, however, Sino-Soviet relations had deteriorated so badly that Moscow was actually providing India with the military capability to threaten Chinese claims in Ladakh. In 1965 Moscow and Peking waged open political warfare at the expense of North Vietnam's need for joint military assistance and deterrence of American escalatory threats. Meanwhile the Cuban missile crisis had shown how Soviet strategic inferiority compelled backing down before an American ultimatum in the closest confrontation ever to emerge between the two nuclear powers. On all these counts China's position in relation to major third countries had steadily weakened, although its internal military, political, and economic power had grown.

One minor difference pertinent to the focus on deterrence concerns communications between China and its opponents. The absence of diplomatic relations with the United States precluded the normal channels available in the case of India. Although Sino-American ambassadorial meetings occurred in Warsaw during the Indochina war, they were known to be monitored by one or more governments.[3] China wanted the DRV to fight; the United States wanted it to halt insurgency. Meanwhile the Soviet Union wanted to enhance its own influence at the expense of both. Therefore anything uttered at Warsaw that would undermine Peking's pledges of support or Washington's threats of increased pressure might be communicated to Hanoi via Russian or East European channels on the basis of monitored Sino-American exchanges. This prevented the Warsaw talks from going beyond the positions communicated by both sides elsewhere.

Important objective differences can be identified in China's capabilities, the power of opponents, the importance of the stakes at issue, and the international context attending these three crises. However, as viewed from Peking, important similarities in these factors made the three crises comparable. In the eyes of Chinese leaders both in 1950 and in 1962 internal vulnerability invited external exploitation. While the earlier situation included armed resistance in the context of remnant civil war, malnutrition and disaffection in the wake of Great Leap Forward disasters were seen to pose the most serious threat to authority since 1950, as evidenced in the secret PLA journal, *Kung-tso T'ung-hsün.*[4]

A more complicated situation attended the Vietnam war. In 1964–65 there was no mass discontent; tensions did exist at the elite level, resulting primarily from policy differences, but only Mao viewed them as serious enough to require confrontation. In 1967, however, as American escalation brought the war closer to China's borders, the Cultural Revolution shook China's political system to its foundations. Armed violence wracked a dozen cities while the PLA teetered on the brink of civil war with splits within the army and between ground and air forces.[5] Although the initial period was not comparable with 1950 and 1962, the events of 1967–68 produced still another combination of internal crisis with external threat.

Despite the gross capability differences between the United States and India, Chinese perceptions linked Washington and New Delhi together with Taipei through Tibetan insurgency and the coincidence of Nationalist invasion threat with Indian troop advances. In addition a growing possibility of Soviet-Indian collusion was suspected on the basis of Russian military deliveries and the proximity of dissident Sinkiang groups to the Soviet border. Sinkiang's security was linked with that of western Tibet. As a result, the 1962 confrontation appeared in Peking as comparable, although obviously not identical, to those which directly involved one of the two major powers.

According to Chinese perceptions, one similar issue at stake in all three crises was territorial security. During the Korean and Indochinese wars, the first concern was the survival of neighboring allies threatened by a common enemy. Their occupation, actually realized in the Korean case, would bring that enemy to China's borders where, in collusion with the civil war foe on Taiwan, serious threats could be mounted against major parts of the country. In 1950 American troops reached the Yalu River boundary; in 1965–68 American bombers repeatedly crossed the frontier. However, in 1962 the area threatened by Indian claims was essentially irrelevant to military, economic, and political needs except in Aksai Chin. Clearly, the symbolic, if not the substantive, problem of border security and territorial integrity was common to all three situations.

Another similarity in the three crises was that issues emerged within an unanticipated context that unfolded through several months of enemy behavior. On the one hand, the element of surprise prevented the regime from reacting according to previous plans. New decisions were required to meet changed circumstances, including preparation for "worst case" contingencies. On the other hand, the time gap between the initial perception of threat and its final realization provided an opportunity to test the efficacy of deterrence for modifying enemy behavior and perhaps removing the threat of advance. Despite the pre-June, 1950 absence of an American commitment and presence in South Korea, Washington responded to the North Korean attack with full intervention.[6] The UN forces did not counterattack until August and threatened to invade the North only in late September. While the prospective threat to PRC interests was serious and initially unanticipated, there was ample time for policy planning and implementation to attempt deterrence and if that failed to intervene directly.

Somewhat similar although less dramatic was the change in New Delhi's "forward policy" from a verbal posture in 1959–61 to military advances in 1962. The coincidence of threatened invasion from Taiwan gave this sudden prominence in Peking, but Indian strength grew only incrementally through the summer and fall and provided an opportunity for deterrence and defense moves in reaction. An even longer time elapsed between the first American hints of threatened air attack against North Vietnam in early 1964 and the systematic bombing in 1965. In short, none of these crises emerged from long-standing confrontation with "lock-in" effects, but neither did they require an instant response.

Finally, the uncertain Sino-Soviet relationship provided Chinese calculations with still another element of continuity. As early as 1950 Mao's celebrated emphasis on "self-reliance" pertained insofar as China lay immediately exposed to conventional and nuclear air attack by the United States with no prospect of Soviet retaliation against American cities and little likelihood of a Russian reaction in the region.[7] Although Moscow could guarantee Peking weapons and technical assistance, it provided no overt, effective protection for the northeast industrial base or the "Volunteers" in Korea. In short, the risks of American retaliation and Chinese troop casualties existed despite the treaty of February, 1950. The absence of Soviet deterrence against American air attack was relevant in both the Korean and the Indochina conflict.

Problems of comparability are endemic to case studies as well as to larger quantitative data-based approaches, but they must be coped with if hypotheses of general applicability are to carry understanding beyond the idiosyncratic explanation of unique events. While the balance between similarities and differences among the independent variables or policy inputs as perceived from Peking is arguable, the dependent variable—policy outputs which involve the use of military force—is sufficiently identical in all three cases to warrant broader generalization with respect to the role of force in Chinese deterrence policy. Some observations may pertain to the Korean and Indian situations or the Korean and Vietnam events, but not to all three. Changes in patterns of behavior as well as consistency will be noted and analyzed. For example, in 1950 and 1965 China faced the same opponent, the United States. This raises the possibility of adaptation and learning as factors which might induce change. At a minimum, however, careful comparison should permit the formulation of explicit hypotheses concerning the Chinese perception of and reaction to external threat. These may then be juxtaposed against hypotheses generated elsewhere to test for broader comparability between China and other countries.

The Calculus of Deterrence

To speak of "the calculus of deterrence" is to attempt to infer what general strategy underlies persistent patterns of behavior aimed at persuading a perceived opponent that the costs of his continuing conflictual activity will eventually prove unacceptable to him because of the Chinese response. This does not identify the origins of the calculus in terms of individuals or organizations. There is no assumption of its representing the view of Mao Tse-tung, Chou En-lai, or Lin Piao per se, or that it emanates from central organs of the People's Liberation Army and the Ministry of Foreign Affairs as agreed upon within the State Council or the Central Committee of the Chinese Communist party. If patterns do persist over considerable time, their point of origin may be of interest but it is not essential to analysis.

A second caveat concerns the theoretical origins of Chinese political-military strategy, a subject to which several scholars have contributed insights but one which remains largely unexplored in a systematic manner that incorporates post-1949 developments.[8] There is no attempt here to explain deterrence behavior either in terms of the classical strategist, Sun Tzu, or his modern counterpart, Mao Tse-tung.[9] It is insufficient to explain contemporary Chinese military behavior by simply correlating it with quotations from Mao. While his writings became increasingly prominent after 1938 in the indoctrination of political and military personnel, independent experience and analysis by his colleagues who continued to fight separate campaigns undoubtedly modified Mao's maxims in application, albeit without public claims of innovation. Moreover those maxims were expressly rooted in a revolutionary war fought against a foreign invader and had no clear relevance for the types of situations China confronted after 1949. Strategists in Peking probably developed a consensual core of perceptions and behavior which both converged with and diverged from Mao's military writings, perhaps with the tacit or even explicit sanction of the chairman himself.

At the risk of substituting a "cookbook" of his own for one of Sun Tzu or Mao, the author has attempted a modest codification of deterrence principles that reflect the patterns of perception and behavior manifest in the crises under examination.

Threats and Their Deterrence as Seen from Peking

1. The worse our domestic situation, the more likely our external situation will worsen.
   a) A superior power in proximity will seek to take advantage of our domestic vulnerability.
   b) Two or more powers will combine against us if they can temporarily overcome their own conflicts of interest.
   c) We must prepare for the worst and try for the best.
2. The best deterrence is belligerence.
   a) To be credible, move military force; words do not suffice.
   b) To be diplomatic, leave the enemy "face" and a way out.
   c) To be prudent, leave yourself an "option."
   d) If at first you don't succeed, try again but more so.
3. Correct timing is essential.
   a) Warning must be given early when a threat is perceived but not yet imminent.

b) The rhythm of signals must permit the enemy to respond and us to confirm the situation.

c) We must control our moves and not respond according to the enemy's choice.

At first glance some of these propositions might appear to be the product of common sense and undeserving of categorization. To the extent this is true, it is nonetheless worth attention. The parameters of successful behavior in politics and in war have relatively few alternative configurations. These have been systematically examined and explicated, not only in China but elsewhere, for several thousand years. There are no wholly innovative or unique approaches to universal problems. Moreover to discover patterns of rationality and behavior in the PRC common to other regimes advances understanding beyond assumptions of totally idiosyncratic behavior that cannot be submitted to analytical comparison or predictability.

When examined more closely, it becomes clear that not all of these guidelines are universally shared or identically implemented. For example, the first proposition and its subunits highlight the far greater degree of anxiety in Chinese estimates of linkage between internal vulnerability and external threat than would be found elsewhere, for instance, in Japan or India. This perception is rooted in classical as well as modern experience as exemplified by one PRC study which claimed, "China's history shows that no matter what feudal dynasty ruled, 'danger from without' generally coincided with 'trouble from within'."[10] This traditional tendency to expect the worst from the outside when the situation had deteriorated on the inside is reinforced by Communist assumptions of capitalist cum imperialist behavior and international class conflict. The first proposition therefore gives a uniquely Chinese contextual framework for deterrence perceptions and behavior.

An excellent illustration of this proposition in operation is found in the 1962 Taiwan Strait crisis. While the crisis does not fully parallel the other situations in that the principal actor, the United States, had no intention of supporting an invasion from Taiwan and therefore objectively could not be "deterred," the contrary subjective estimate in Peking permits its reintroduction at this point. In addition the Nationalist indicators of intent gave credibility to Communist perceptions of threat (proposition 1 above), thereby justifying inclusion of the crisis in the deterrence framework.

Having concluded that the United States would support an invasion to exploit the economic discontent in China (1 *a*), the PLA deployed to meet the attack (1 *c*) and to manifest a deterrent posture (2 *a*) in conjunction with a secret demarche at Warsaw (2 *b*). Once successful in halting the Nationalists by deterring the Americans, it was but a single step to assume collusion between the United States–Nationalist threat and Indian activity in the Himalayas (1 *b*). Prima facie evidence for such collusion lay in the external support of Tibetan insurgency and was reinforced by contemporary Indian press speculation on a "two-front war." The sharper PLA responses in July as compared with the pre-June period suggests this reasoning resulted from the Taiwan Strait crisis and the attendant reevaluation of Indian intentions (1 *c*). When these intentions became less susceptible to change through military deterrence and diplomatic probes in July–August, additional suspicion may have focused on Soviet as well as American collusion (1 *b*, 1 *c*), as evidenced by Russian military aircraft deliveries and the prospective sale of a MIG factory.

The full implications of this "worst case" assumption arise in connection with the second proposition which posits belligerence as the best means of deterrence. If a Chinese defensive move is misunderstood as signaling offensive intent, an opponent's heightened posture in response will only confirm the initial expectation (1 *c*) and trigger additional military moves (2 *d*). The escalatory spiral will lock both sides into mutually reinforcing behavior likely to end in war. Fortunately this did not happen in June, 1962, because the United States did not match the additional PLA deployments with comparable naval and air movement into the Taiwan Strait. Instead the crisis was resolved immediately upon the credible transmission, private and public, of American assurances against a Nationalist invasion. Should similar situations arise in the future along with political or economic tension in China, evidence of PLA belligerence must be carefully examined for possible defensive, deterrent intent as well as for possible offensive, aggressive design.

The assumption of collusion between threatening regimes (1 *b*) applies to the Indian case but not to Korea or Indochina. Examining Sino-Indian relations in isolation as a conventional study of interaction would make incomprehensible Chinese expressions of alarm, particularly in July, 1962. This conventional approach explains much of the miscalculation in New Delhi concerning the likely consequences of continued "forward movement." Seen in conjunction with circumstantial evidence of a Moscow-

Delhi-Washington linkage, the Indian military and diplomatic behavior becomes intelligible as triggering alarm in Peking over future intentions and capabilities.

This cautions against analyzing and forecasting Chinese behavior on the basis of an exclusively bilateral focus. Particularly in northeast Asia where the interaction of the Soviet Union, Japan, and the United States juxtaposes the multilateral interplay of major powers in a semicircle around China, the appearance of collusion (1 *b*) can undermine separate efforts at avoiding tension unless consciously guarded against by all concerned parties.

The admonition to "prepare for the worst, try for the best" (1 *c*) introduces a two-sided component into PRC policy. It permits the use of military force simultaneously for prehostility deployment and for deterrence that may make fighting unnecessary. In 1950 PLA movements toward Korea facilitated intervention, but their visibility to American intelligence, together with diplomatic and propaganda warning postures, might have halted the U.N. advance and thereby avoided war. In 1962 the daily strengthening of positions opposite Dhola warned of an impending attack, but as in 1950, the regime did not commit itself irrevocably for some time thereafter. In 1965–68 the PLA presence in North Vietnam provided an advance staging area for more massive deployment in the event of an American invasion but did not precipitously provoke or openly challenge Washington.

Thus, while the "worst case" syndrome manifest in the first proposition and its several subcomponents casts Chinese perceptions in a pessimistic light, there is no "inevitability of war" assumption to make the outcome a foregone conclusion. True, the general tenor of both these initial propositions places the burden of restraint on an opponent to determine the intent behind Chinese military behavior as well as to disprove Chinese perceptions of his own intentions. However, the admonition to "try for the best" does leave open the possibility of a confrontation ending with little or no fighting, as in Indochina, rather than in war as with Korea and India.

Chinese Signals

The second set of propositions focuses on the need for credibility associated with military movement (2 *a*), sensitivity to enemy needs to retain "face" and to reserve an avenue of reatreat (2 *b*), flexibility amidst belligerence (2 *c*), and persistence through strengthened signals of deterrence (2 *d*). These postulates reveal an inner tension between a posture of firmness and force, on the one hand, and flexibility for one's opponent as well as one's self, on the other hand. The task of maintaining these somewhat contradictory postures in proper balance while assuring their correct perception by the enemy is an exceptionally delicate and difficult matter. Bureaucratic inputs and interactions are not uniform in their impact, as for instance between military movement and media statements, nor are they equally susceptible to daily control. Moreover genuine differences within the regime, whether personal or factional, can make implementation of these propositions inconsistent at best and self-defeating at worst.

In identifying the separate elements of Chinese deterrence behavior it is necessary to abstract an ideal model of rational, purposeful decision making from a dynamic, multifaceted and multilayered bureaucratic system. [11] The possible divergence from reality must be acknowledged in advance of evidential analysis. However, this does not preclude comprehension of the basic design which underlies PRC actions and reactions in these crises.

Chinese leaders rarely refer to past deterrence efforts but one such allusion to the Korean case emerged in May, 1962, on the very eve of PLA deployment toward the Taiwan Strait. In an illuminating reference Foreign Minister Ch'en Yi recalled, "At the time of the Korean War, we first warned against crossing the thirty-eighth parallel but America ignored the warning. The second time, we warned again, but America occupied Pyongyang. The third time, we warned once again, but America aggressed close to the Yalu River and threatened the security of China." [12] These references drew an implicit parallel with the impending effort in 1962 to warn Washington against an invasion from Taiwan. The parallel became explicit a month later at Warsaw.

Ch'en Yi's words implied confidence that each "warning" had been perceptible and credible and that Washington had acted in willful defiance. Specifically the verbal signals had included a secret demarche by Chou En-lai to Ambassador Panikkar on October 2 prior to the U.N. crossing, a public Ministry of Foreign Affairs statement on October 10 before seizure of the North Korean capital, and the formal acknowledgment by Peking on November 11 that Chinese "volunteers" were in Korea. The acknowledgment was made after initial contact with U.N. forces but more than two weeks prior to General MacArthur's "end the war" offensive to the Yalu River.[13]

Chinese warnings did not rest on words alone, however. In accordance with the dual need to "prepare for the worst" (1 *c*) and to "move military force" for credible deterrence (2 *a*), beginning in late August, 1950, the PLA strength in northeast China increased from 180,000 to at least 320,000 troops.[14] This deployment was correctly assumed to become known to American intelligence at the time. Foreign diplomats reported seeing troop trains passing through Peking.[15] Chinese Nationalist reconnaissance flights over the mainland provided additional information. Finally military communications which could have been kept silent maintained regular patterns that were known to be monitored abroad and permitted the identification of headquarters and subordinate units throughout the deployment. Thus military movement backed up verbal warnings (2 *a*) while not challenging the United States to open confrontation (2 *b*). Even after attacking U.N. forces briefly near the Yalu in early November, the PLA disengaged for three weeks to permit General MacArthur time to accept the Chinese position at face value and to change his course of action (2 *b*).

Similarly in 1962 the PLA buildup in Tibet came under systematic scrutiny by Indian reconnaissance planes, but no effort was made to shoot them down. This would have denied New Delhi information that made deterrence credible, namely preparations for combat in the event Indian troops continued their advance. This design was particularly obvious at Dhola, as has already been noted. Likewise in September, 1965, the PLA deployment to North Vietnam utilized regular communications procedures that could be monitored by the United States while the 50,000 troops wore regular uniforms that permitted identification by ground and air observers. In short, secrecy was operative for public audiences at home and abroad, but official American knowledge of troop movements was desirable in order to deter an American invasion of the North. Finally, there is the Taiwan Strait deployment in 1962 which was so visible to American intelligence as to be "leaked" to American newspapers a week before the crisis was publicly revealed by Peking.

In contrast with this pattern of deliberate revelation it is worth calling attention to instances of deliberate and successful secrecy that demonstrate the aspect of conscious choice in Chinese behavior. During the "pause" in November, 1950, and again in November, 1962, the PLA covertly infiltrated along and behind enemy lines of communication, effectively trapping the American and Indian armies. Whereas precombat detection by enemy intelligence might deter, subsequent secrecy could prepare for surprise attack should further fighting occur. The clandestine deployment during the two November pauses in combat served tactical military purposes, while other indicators in Chinese media signaled every intention of resuming the battle if necessary. If the enemy persisted, tactical surprise would increase the chances of victory. If he desisted, further warfare could be avoided because tactical secrecy had avoided commitment to action.

It is difficult to demonstrate credibility with military force (2 a) while allowing the enemy to retain "face" (2 b) and preserving a prudent option (2 c). The risks of provocation and "lock-in" are juxtaposed against the risk of being discounted as bluffing. In Korea the PLA did not cross the Yalu River before mid-October and it maintained secrecy thereafter until initial combat with South Korean units began on October 26. Peking's failure to deploy troops into North Korea before mid-October undermined the credibility of the threat to intervene. This was to remain a serious problem in American perceptions during the three-week PLA disengagement in November. In September, 1962, however, the alternate tactic of establishing credibility earlier through token combat backfired when small clashes heightened intransigence in New Delhi and political pressures locked Nehru into "throwing Chinese troops out of every inch of sacred Indian soil."

Only in Indochina did the PLA make its moves early enough to be credible but covertly enough to avoid public provocation and confrontation. Although the air defense activity of 1964–65 did not deter American attacks against North Vietnam, it did secure the border against interdiction bombing. Moreover the ground deployments in 1965–66 contributed significantly to American decisions against invasion of the North.

One of the most impressive patterns of Chinese deterrence signals is the concern for establishing consistency, with changes in strength dictated by enemy failure to respond as desired (2 d). This is particularly evident in the Korean and Indian cases. On August 20, 1950, Chou En-lai initiated Peking's diplomatic intervention with a low-key cable to U.N. Secretary General Trygvie Lie, declaring "The Chinese people cannot but be concerned about the solution of the Korean question."[16] This formal declaration came in response to the American UN ambassador's speeches of

August 10 and 17 which had called for UN control over "the whole of the Korean peninsula," implying an eventual invasion and conquest of the northern half.

Then on September 22 the PRC officially admitted General Mac-Arthur's accusation of four days previous which charged that "substantial if not decisive military assistance" had gone to North Korea. Peking stated flatly that China "will always stand on the side of the Korean people." Following an informal demarche made by General Nieh Jung-chen to Ambassador Pannikar, Chou En-lai on September 30 publicly declared, "The Chinese people . . . will not supinely tolerate seeing their neighbors being savagely invaded by the imperialists." To cap this series of statements, Chou formally declared to Pannikar on October 2 that "the South Koreans did not matter but American intrusion into North Korea would encounter Chinese resistance."[17] Thus, Chinese warnings carried a steady, authoritative signal of interest and intervention with increasing emphasis and more explicit content as the crisis heightened and deterrence seemed closer to failure.

The Sino-Indian crisis invited a different approach with direct diplomatic communication between the two capitals and a longer precrisis period. Under these circumstances the Ministry of Foreign Affairs carefully graduated its protests to communicate varying degrees of concern. From August 1 to mid-September only one "strongest protest" was sent to New Delhi. In the last two weeks of September, however, the MFA identified four notes as "strongest protest." It employed harsher language than had been used theretofore, with two notes described as "most serious, strongest protest." These precise changes in formal vocabulary accompanied more bellicose military and media postures as the October 15 deadline for talks expired without Indian acquiescence to Peking's demands.

Just as the MFA protests became more strident and frequent as the crisis intensified from Peking's perspective so too did NEFA become the chief point of focus as a threatened "tit for tat" response to the Indian position on Ladakh. Several points in this chronology deserve attention. The threat to NEFA was first hinted at on August 4 in a significantly delayed protest over moves that had allegedly occurred between May 18 and 22. This appears to have been a pretext for raising the question of NEFA in low-key fashion, along with formal acceptance of New Delhi's proposal for talks, but at the same time explicitly reiterating there would be no

Ministry of Foreign Affairs Protests to India

Date	Area	Warning
July 22	Ladakh	"The Chinese Government *can by no means sit idle* while its frontier guards are being encircled and annihilated by aggressors."[18]
August 27	Ladakh	"The Chinese side *will have to resort to self-defense.*"[19]
September 5	Ladakh	"seriously urges the Indian Government to give careful consideration to the grave consequences that may arise from such acts of playing with fire. . . . One should be aware that *whoever plays with fire will hurt himself.*"[20]
September 13	Ladakh	"*He who plays with fire will eventually be consumed by fire.* . . . Chinese border defense forces are duty-bound to defend their territory."[21]
September 21	NEFA	"The situation is extremely dangerous and *flames of war may break out there.*"[22]
September 25	NEFA	"in the face of the increasingly frantic armed attacks by the aggressive Indian troops, the Chinese frontier guards cannot but take resolute measures of self-defense."[23]
October 3	NEFA	"*Whenever India attacks, China is sure to strike back.*"[24]
October 11	NEFA	"*Should the Indian side still not rein in before the precipice but continue to spread the flames of war,* the Indian Government must bear full responsibility for the resulting casualties on both sides and all other consequences that may ensue."[25] (Italics added.)

preconditions. Exactly one month later, on September 4, Peking reintroduced the McMahon Line in a belated protest of a move on July 18. After a third mildly worded note of September 16 referring to "recent" Indian activity, the campaign moved into high gear. Thus, whereas Ladakh represented Peking's main strategic interest and had provided the arena for most of the maneuvering by both sides, NEFA came to receive the sharpest focus of PRC attention, as illustrated by the unprecedented warning of September 21, "the flames of war may break out there."

This colorful figure of speech was more than stylistic in design. The subtle escalation of language strengthened the deterrence signal from the ex cathedra reminder that "whoever plays with fire will hurt himself" (September 5) to the threat of the far worse fate of being "eventually consumed by fire" (September 13). Similarly, while the "flames of war" might simply "break out" spontaneously on September 21, by October 11 "another stern warning [from] the Chinese Government" warned "the Indian side not [to] . . . continue to spread the flames of war." As additional fuel to this inflamatory verbiage, PLA attacks on September 20 and October 10 had an impact which went beyond the force of words alone.

Verbal imagery might seem an inadequate basis for inferring perception and policy, but an interesting analogue from the Korean situation is worth recalling at this point. In July, 1950, before a Sino-American confrontation loomed on the Korean horizon, the celebrated author, Mao Tun, had scornfully depicted the United States as "a greedy and stupid hog, incapable of correcting its mistakes even though its snout bleeds from wounds received in Korea."[26] By the end of August indicators of an American intention to invade the North, combined with an apparent air attack on Chinese villages adjoining Korea, changed the image from one of blind incapacity to ferocious threat. In Mao Tun's words:

> This mad dog seizes Taiwan between its hind legs while with its teeth it violently bites the Korean people. Now one of its forelegs has been poked into our Northeast front. Its bloodswollen eyes cast around for something further to attack. All the world is under its threat. The American imperialist mad dog is half beaten up. Before it dies, it will go on biting and tearing.[27]

Another aspect of credibility concerns the specificity of the threatened response to enemy behavior. During the Korean War, a key phrase was used with such consistency and emphasis as to suggest it was seen in Peking as suitably evocative in meaning. General Nieh, as paraphrased by Ambassador Panikkar, warned that China would *not sit back with folded hands* and let the Americans come up to the border."[28] Chou publicly declared, "The Chinese people will *not supinely tolerate* seeing their neighbors being savagely invaded," with this sentence subsequently singled out by Chinese media as "the most important" portion of his speech, "above all with respect to the Korean War."[29] On October 10 the MFA warned, "Now that the American forces are attempting to cross the thirty-eighth parallel on a large scale, the Chinese people *cannot stand idly by* with regard to such a serious situation created by the invasion of Korea."[30] (Italics added.)

The American disregard of Chinese warnings may retrospectively have appeared to result in part from the ambiguity of this formulation. In 1962, its appearance early in the signaling process purposefully recalled the Korean precedent, but it was subsequently replaced by the more explicitly worded warnings cited above. On May 19 the MFA declared, "The Chinese Government *will not stand idly by* seeing its territory once again unlawfully invaded and occupied" and on July 22 sounded this tocsin once again, affirming that China "*can by no means sit idle* while its frontier guards are being encircled and annihilated by aggressors." (Italics added.) New Delhi's July 26 response was implicitly compromising, but its later hardening proved this phraseology to be insufficient.

By the time of the Indochina crisis Chinese failures at deterrence through the graduated strengthening of verbal signals reached global prominence with wide-ranging American air attacks against the DRV despite repeated protestations of opposition from Peking. The second phase of American intervention which threatened an invasion of the North saw a steady decline in the strength and frequency of overt Chinese warnings at the same time that PLA deployments to the DRV provided a more tangible, albeit more risky, token of commitment. This shift of emphasis may reflect learning from past experience. Future crises may prove less susceptible to open analysis than was possible, for instance, in the Sino-Indian confrontation if greater reliance is placed on secret military moves as compared with public statements. In any event such evidence as appears which shows a consistently strengthened signal deserves attention as a possible reflection of threat perception and the failure of enemy responses to meet earlier deterrence efforts.

The Importance of Timing

At different points in the examination of Chinese diplomatic and military moves vis-à-vis India this study has noted how regular intervals of a week or a month suggested planned initiatory behavior rather than unanticipated reactive steps. These deserve reexamination in the broader context of deterrence patterns codified under the third general principle, "correct timing is essential." More specifically this includes the need for early warning (3 *a*), intervals to permit enemy response and Chinese reassessment (3 *b*), and avoidance of responding in accordance with enemy plans but instead maintaining the initiative and self-control (3 *c*).

The dynamic interaction of deterrence "signals" and "feedback" of enemy response requires some preplanned rhythm of activity and passivity if crises are not automatically to end in war (3 *b*). The specific contingency for which plans are prepared may prove to be modified in reality, lessening the need for some actions and increasing the risks for others. In maintaining a rhythm, ongoing reassessment of the situation and corresponding adjustments in plans must be made. There is no utility in maintaining an option (2 *c*) if it has no opportunity to be considered and adopted. Moreover as long as deterrence has any possibility of success (1 *c*), the enemy must be permitted ample opportunity to change behavior in the desired fashion (2 *b*).

In keeping with the principle of "prepare for the worst, try for the best," nondeterrent needs argue for the regular timing of key moves in a crisis context where the contingent outcome is war. Standard bureaucratic procedures often pattern behavior to weekly and monthly benchmarks because they provide easily chosen and readily remembered intervals for scheduling, communicating, and implementing a policy design. This is especially important to minimize mistakes and misunderstanding where planning involves a number of sequential moves by various units of government and where enemy detection or surprise is not an inhibiting consideration. Even after the "point of no return" is passed and the two sides are locked in combat, the desire for recurring reassessment and maximum command and control over subordinate units may warrant "fail-safe" benchmarks to reconfirm previous orders in new contexts.

Because of these nondeterrent, standard operating procedures it is difficult to determine from timing alone when discernible patterns simply reflect systemic behavior and when in addition they are in pursuit of conscious political objectives. However, by juxtaposing the specific content of diplomatic and military actions against patterns of timing, certain logical inferences may be drawn pertinent to the hypotheses presented by this study on Chinese deterrence strategy.

Chinese Diplomatic and Military Moves:
Korea and India

*Korea, 1950**

September 25 — PRC chief of staff informally tells Indian ambassador China will intervene if American forces approach her border

October 2 — Chou En-lai formally tells Indian ambassador China will intervene if the United States crosses 38th parallel

October 26 — PLA attacks South Korean forces near Yalu River

November 2 — PLA attacks American forces near Yalu River

*India, 1962**

September 13 — PRC proposes talks on October 15

September 20 — First fighting in NEFA

October 20 — PLA attacks in NEFA, Ladakh

November 20–21 — PRC announces cease-fire and withdrawal

*Broken line indicates one-week interval; solid line shows monthly interval.

Unplanned reactions occur randomly. The regularity and rhythm manifest in this chronology suggest deliberate design. Moreover the logic of a relationship between certain moves strengthens the appearance of planning. Precisely one month separated Chou's formal demarche against the American entry into North Korea from the initial attack on American troops. Similarly, one month after the first fighting at Dhola the PLA offensive came at both ends of the border, followed again in one month by announcement of the unilateral cease-fire and withdrawal.[31]

During the month between Chou's 1950 warning and the attack on American forces, Washington might have responded so as to make Chinese intervention superfluous or unwise, either by halting its invasion far below the border or by some wholly unanticipated act which made intervention too dangerous (3 *b*). This period left the enemy "face" (2 *b*) and China options (2 *c*). Likewise the month between the small clash at Dhola and simultaneous attacks in NEFA and Ladakh allowed New Delhi time to moderate its posture (2 *b*) while leaving Peking the chance to avoid further combat if the situation there or elsewhere suddenly worsened more than had been anticipated (2 *c*). Again, the month between attack and cease-fire also permitted a change in Indian behavior (3 *b*) while notifying the PLA in advance of the temporal limit on military action so that undesirable or unanticipated consequences could be avoided. In sum, Chinese behavior in the Korean and Indian crises gave ample opportunity for functional "feedback" by preserving important options for both sides.

The content as well as the timing of monthly intervals suggests the care with which planners in Peking moved armed forces across their borders. After credibly communicating its intervention in Korea by first attacking the South Koreans and later the Americans, the PLA broke off all contact for three weeks. Between November 7 and November 20, 1950, Peking strengthened its position with secret deployments while watching the United States–UN response. When General MacArthur ordered his final all-out offensive to the Yalu, the PLA counterattacked on November 26 with a massive assault that drove the American armies completely out of North Korea. Similarly in 1962 the PLA halted its attack against India around October 25, monitored New Delhi's reaction for approximately three weeks while infiltrating behind its forces in NEFA, and then struck both there and in Ladakh on November 18 to eliminate all Indian positions in contested territory.

In neither case was deception the primary motive behind the hiatus in Peking's offensive since ample evidence of its intention to resume action if the enemy persisted was communicated during the lull (2 *d*). In 1950 a full-throated mass campaign mobilized the populace under the slogan, "Resist-America, Aid-Korea." In 1962 the military buildup and the blasting of roads in NEFA clearly signaled intent. While the lull was covertly utilized to tactical advantage, it was also employed overtly to signal the enemy and to provide time for evaluating his behavior for clues to his further intentions (3 *b*).

This deliberate timing of strategic moves adds an element of flexibility at the top as well as command and control over subordinate units, both of which are important for deterrence under crisis conditions. By establishing a "fail-safe" benchmark for the issuance of final orders to confirm or cancel contingency plans, confusion at lower levels is minimized when actions are terminated or instructions reversed at a predesignated time. In addition this timing permits the enemy to reconsider his course of action.

The importance of timing in Chinese moves is highlighted by the way in which tactical actions occur at weekly intervals within the strategic monthly framework. In 1950 Chief of Staff Nieh Jung-chen's September 25 dinner conversation with Ambassador Panikkar provided a preliminary signal to Washington. This was sufficient for a situation in which American troops had not reached the thirty-eighth parallel and the UN had not authorized its crossing (3 *a*). However, once the South Korean troops had crossed the parallel with express UN sanction, a stronger signal was required (2 *d*). Precisely one week later Chou summoned Panikkar to a dramatic midnight meeting at the Ministry of Foreign Affairs to deliver a carefully worded casus belli focused on the question of American forces. Similarly the initial clash with South Korean units gave token witness of Peking's resolve (2 *a*), but it was greatly enhanced one week later when the PLA first engaged American troops (2 *d*). In both cases, tactical moves preceded strategic moves by one week.

In 1962 the weekly benchmarks were more numerous. One week separated the September 13 proposal for talks from the first serious fighting in NEFA on September 20 which provided an additional incentive to accept the proposal (2 *a*). On October 3 Peking declared that India had agreed to the talks, although in fact it had completely rejected PRC terms and imposed its own, on October 10 the second clash occurred at Dhola. Under the circumstances, this may not have been accidental. Again, one week after the October 20 offensive *People's Daily* published the 15,000 word attack on "Nehru's Philosophy. " Finally, a two-week interval separated Chou En-lai's letter to Nehru conveying the October 24 proposal and the November 7 publication of the entire Chou-Nehru correspondence.

It would be a mistake to infer Chinese intent exclusively from the timing of strategic and tactical moves. Preplanning is mandatory for offensive as well as for defensive purposes. However, the deterrent nature of these particular sequences has been demonstrated both by the context and the content of the actions. The care and calculation with which they were scheduled strengthens the plausibility of a deterrence hypothesis.

The Efficacy of Chinese Deterrence

In attempting to identify the reasons for complete failure in the cases of Korea and India and partial failure in the case of Indochina, the calculus which appeared operative in these crises should be compared with propositions of deterrence based on the behavior of other states. This will permit an examination of the premise that PRC failure resulted from too great a degree of Sinocentric, idiosyncratic behavior for effective interaction with a non-Chinese world.

Among the various writers on contemporary political-military strategy, Alexander George and Thomas C. Schelling have systematically codified propositions of conflict management and conflict behavior which are particularly germane to this inquiry.[32] George presents a list of seven "criteria or requirements for controlled, measured use of force and effective crisis management," six of which appear applicable to Chinese behavior as indicated by the parenthetical references to parallel propositions:

1. [Not relevant.]

2. *Pauses in military operations*: . . . Time must be provided for the opponent at each point to assess the actions already taken, to receive and reflect upon the signals and proposals addressed to him, and to decide whether he will call a halt or open up negotiations. . . . [3 *b*] Must control and eliminate actions and statements that might have given confusing signals regarding his demands and offers, and how he proposes to act if the opponent rejects them.

3. *Clear and appropriate demonstonstrations*: . . . Military and other actions taken should together constitute a consistent signal. [2 *a*] . . . They should not suggest . . . objectives more ambitious than proclaimed or . . . much less.

4. *Military action coordinated with political-diplomatic action*: . . . Military actions should be coupled with—that is, preceded, accompanied, or followed by—those political and diplomatic actions, communications, consultations, and proposals that are an essential part of the overall strategy for persuading the opponent to alter his policy and behavior in the desired direction. [2 *a*, 2 *d*]

5. *Confidence in the effectiveness and discriminating character of military options*: . . . It is often preferable that tactical objectives be accomplished with relatively small increments of force.

6. *Military options that avoid motivating the opponent to escalate*: . . . Must not confront the opponent with an urgent requirement to escalate the conflict himself in order to avoid or compensate for the military or political damage inflicted upon him. [2 *b*)

7. *Avoidance of impression of resort to large-scale warfare*: . . . [otherwise] this would indicate to him the . . . abandoning [of] efforts to resolve the dispute by diplomatic means and relying largely on a military strategy to achieve objectives.[33]

George presents this as a viable guide to "special political-military requirements [which] military capabilities must meet in order to constitute usable options in controlled crises." While his propositions are not explicitly or exclusively designed for deterrence, their content is sufficiently similar and their intent sufficiently parallel to juxtapose against those the author has postulated for Chinese behavior. The similarities between the two sets of propositions argue against stress on the unique aspects of Chinese perceptions and policy. At the same time they support the rationality of Peking's deterrent posture, indicating that failure must be explained by other factors.

Schelling offers two propositions which coincide less with PRC practice than those of George but which nonetheless form an interesting parallel. His "being a little impulsive or unreliable" holds that a state should "get into a position where [it] cannot fail to react as it said it would—nor where [it] would be obliged by some overwhelming cost of not reacting in the manner [it] had declared."[34] This "calculated irrationality" accepts the risk of greater physical damage than can be inflicted on the enemy. China's willingness to risk war with the United States in both Korea and Indochina would appear to exemplify this proposition. Although the risk was lessened somewhat by the use of "volunteers" in Korea and covert deployment in Indochina, the positive actions taken show that the risk was accepted rather than avoided by all means.

Schelling expands on this concept in what he calls "relinquishing the initiative" by making "commitment credible because it is inescapable" through "a political involvement to get a nation's honor, obligation, and diplomatic reputation committed to a response."[35] He warns that "the hardest part is communicating intentions . . . to keep from sounding like bluff" and he sees the preservation of options as running this risk in contrast with "getting into a position where the initiative is up to the enemy and it is he who has to make the awful decision to proceed to a clash."[36]

It has been noted how the preservation of options (2 *c*) may have undermined the credibility of PRC deterrence when the PLA failed to cross the Yalu before UN forces crossed the thirty-eighth parallel. Schelling's precepts, however, would seem applicable to the open combat with UN forces, to the accompanying panoply of public statements, and to the national mobilization to "Resist-America, Aid-Korea," These actions combined to make China's "honor, obligation, and diplomatic reputation committed to a response." Deterrence clearly failed, as evidenced by General MacArthur's "home by Christmas" offensive in late November. Similarly Peking pinned its prestige to the public wall in September and October, 1962, through its diplomatic and media postures together with broadcast accounts of the "frontier guards" funeral in Lhasa. But once again the final fighting came as a shock to the enemy.

Indochina illustrates the relevance of "relinquishing the initiative" instead of preserving options as a better means of deterrence. Sino-Vietnamese air defense activity in 1964–65 remained secret from all public audiences and from much of the United States government. This left open the option of limiting China's response to American bombing of the DRV, an option which American escalation pressed up to the border sanctuary. The result evinced the failure of deterrence and discredited Peking's express assertion issued in the Gulf of Tonkin crisis, that "an attack on the Democratic Republic of Vietnam is an attack upon China."

By contrast with the virtual abandonment of all but a fraction of North Vietnam to air attack, the PLA presence made commitment against invasion credible because, in Schelling's words, it was "inescapable." Unlike the air defense preparations which were secret and therefore could be abandoned without public embarrassment, the PLA engineer batallions working on major roads and railroads were widely visible to the North Vietnamese. The troops could not be withdrawn so long as the United States pressed its attack on the North because the local populace would interpret withdrawal as betrayal and abandonment. Moreover a second backdown in the face of "U.S. imperialist aggression" would eliminate any future deterrent credibility for the PRC so far as friend and foe were concerned. Moscow would exploit this politically if not militarily as well. Chinese Nationalist hopes might be revived for American support in further invasion planning. As a final consideration, the 50,000 troops required rotation and replacement in addition to supplies, thereby serving as a hostage against China's permitting the cutting of communications lines across the border. These circumstances made "inescapable" the PLA commitment to defend the DRV against both invasion and the interdiction of transport lines from China.

The parallel between the set of propositions in the literature of George and Schelling and that set which characterizes Chinese deterrence behavior suggests Peking's calculus was both national and shared elsewhere. Nevertheless, the United Nations commanders repeatedly rejected PRC warnings, New Delhi persisted to the end in its "forward policy," and the United States bombed most of North Vietnam from 1965 to 1968. Beyond the rationality of a deterrence strategy, then, other factors may reduce its effectiveness and account for failure in these instances. The opponent must recognize deterrence signals for what they are. Flawed perception impeded both American and Indian acceptance of Chinese signals on two counts. First, neither Washington nor New Delhi saw their own actions as sufficiently threatening to Peking's interests to warrant the alarm and anxiety communicated by PRC behavior. Their self-perception simply did not accord with the perceptions entertained by Chinese decision makers. Neither Washington nor New Delhi took seriously Peking's expressed concern. Second, in 1950 and in 1962 China was believed to be so weakened by internal problems as to be unwilling, if not incapable, of engaging in external hostilities. American estimates completely discounted the PLA's capability against American firepower and assumed that the only rational decision for Peking was to avoid combat. General MacArthur assured President Truman that should the PRC intervene, there would be "the greatest slaughter."[37] In the second case, Indian officals discounted China's expressed willingness to fight because of Peking's parlous economy, dramatically evidenced by the mass exodus into Hong Kong. Thus, what appeared credible and feasible in Peking was not seen as such in Washington and New Delhi.

No such liability afflicted American perceptions in 1964–65. The United States understood the Chinese definition of security and interest and recognized the Chinese capacity to defend its interests. Air attack avoided challenging these interests, recognizing that their legitimacy backed by sufficient defense made unwise the risk of an enlarged war that might attend a demonstration of American air superiority.

In addition to recognizing deterrence signals, the opponent must be willing to reverse policy. This places a premium on early deterrence, before bureaucratic and political pressures make reversal difficult if not impossible. In Korea PLA movements into the northeast appeared insignificant until September, by which time the momentum of policy in Washington and counterattack in the peninsula was well under way. Theoretically the "point of no return" was reached only with the UN crossing of the thirty-eighth parallel in October, but actually the advance was a foregone conclusion in late August.[38] MacArthur's initial orders to enter North Korea were conditioned on the express proviso "that at the time of such operations there has been no entry into North Korea by major Soviet or Chinese Communist forces, no announcement of intended entry, nor a threat to counter our operations militarily in North Korea."[39] But even after all three contingencies had been realized, including combat between Chinese and American forces, Washington still did not change direction. As the then Secretary of State Dean Acheson later admitted, "I was unwilling to urge on the President a military course that his military advisers would not propose." In short, the system was locked in. It was too late to change fixed goals and too humiliating to do this in public confrontation.

Similarly in 1962 the "forward policy" had advanced Indian positions since the previous fall; Peking only began its truly serious warnings in July. By the time of the PRC diplomatic ultimatum and NEFA clashes in September, the issue had become a cause célèbre in New Delhi. Reversal under public pressure was a political impossibility for Nehru and his associates. From their perspective Chinese deterrence threatened too little and too late to halt advancing patrols and to silence the demand to "expel the invaders from every inch of sacred Indian soil."

In 1964–65, however, Chinese airfield construction, fighter movements, and joint air defense preparations with North Vietnam were all conducted outside the public spotlight and at a time when the United States had not yet decided upon, much less initiated, its full escalatory design. This minimized the chance of sensed embarrassment, challenge, or provocation which would force the very response which deterrence sought to avoid. The timing and nature of the signals found the United States able and willing to adapt its policy, at least partially, to accord with PRC deterrence objectives. After the bombing began, PLA reactions and Peking's public handling of them continued to avoid too overt a challenge, while at the same time persisting in the attempt to influence the pattern of future air strikes. Washington remained willing to restrain its attacks on Hanoi, the Red River dikes, and the border zone.

Similarly in 1965–66, when major American ground deployments raised the possibility of an eventual invasion of the DRV, the PLA counterdeployment occurred long before invasion could become a feasible policy option. Chinese restraint in revealing this move allowed Washington to keep silent or to define the situation publicly in any way it chose rather than respond to a direct open challenge. Although invasion was intermittently argued for, it was steadfastly rejected on the basis of China's likely response.

The Indochina interactions differ sufficiently from the Korean and Indian situations to suggest a conscious change in Chinese deterrence behavior as a result of previous experience. The outcome is particularly impressive in view of the duration and cost of the American effort in Indochina which greatly exceeded that of Korea by every measurement. It is true that Washington tested the full limits of Peking's commitment in the air. Had either side lost command and control of its military forces or its public information policy the risk of war would have increased considerably. This was most hazardous when Chinese antiaircraft units went into action below the boundary and when American efforts to interdict supply lines neared the boundary. But whatever unintentional incidents occurred, they remained so minor or secret as to permit China and the United States to approach but avoid the brink of war in Vietnam.

Just as Peking adapted its behavior on the basis of past experience, so too did Washington endeavor to learn from its mistakes. Military actions were closely controlled by the White House in order to minimize the possibility of local field commanders willfully or inadvertently violating sensitive political boundaries. American pilots flying over North Vietnam were tracked from the south by radar. When they threatened to stray into prohibited areas near or over China, the pilots were warned in readily monitored English transmissions so as to alert Chinese defenses of a possible unauthorized overflight which should not be misinterpreted as a deliberately hostile act. Evidence of the PLA presence in North Vietnam was publicly revealed so as to let Peking know of Washington's awareness that this signal had been received, but not exploited in any way which would prejudice the chances of avoiding a wider war.

These measures carried costs and raised risks. The gradual American escalation with semipermanent sanctuaries provided time for Hanoi to improve its defenses and evacuate likely target areas, and allowed Peking to counter efforts at interdiction and isolation of the DRV. Alerting Chinese defenses to oncoming American planes facilitated shooting them down. Revealing the PLA activity in North Vietnam, including the presence of antiaircraft divisions, increased the risk of a Sino-American conflict from extremist pressures to reject all limitations on the fighting, including war with China if necessary.

Yet despite these possible consequences, some hypothetical and some real, they were accepted in preference to the miscalculation and misperception that had spawned the Korean tragedy. That both sides interacted so belligerently without stumbling into war cannot be wholly fortuitous. On the contrary, the evidence suggests that the deliberate exercise of deterrence and the carefully calculated responses thereto succeeded in avoiding major Chinese involvement and an expansion of the war beyond the Indochinese borders.

There is no certain way to avoid the complicating effects of such nonrational phenomena as bureaucratic determinants, idiosyncratic behavior, misinformation, and domestic pressures. These can obstruct successful communication between nations. Deterrence theory, whether Chinese or another sort, can be simplistic, if not naive, in its assumptions about governments and their interaction. This does not, however, negate its value as an instrument of policy for avoiding conflict and for managing crisis. It is in this context that Chinese behavior in the Korean, Indian, and Indochinese conflicts provides insights from the past that may lessen the likelihood of miscalculation in the future.

Chapter 8

Retrospect and Prospect

At this point a step back must be taken from detailed analysis of the evidence for a more reflective overview of the past and a more speculative look to the future so as to elucidate such phenomena in Chinese foreign policy as the question of rationality, the use of force, and the degree of risk taking. In addition to drawing on this study's intensive examination of the Sino-Indian war and the more general comparison with the Korean and Vietnam conflicts, intuitive and hypothetical constructs derived from observation of the first twenty-five years of the People's Republic as a major actor in the world arena will be introduced and discussed.

Several limitations must be recognized at the outset. Scholarly documentation seldom exists for the inner assumptions and workings of the policy process in governments, particularly one as remote from direct examination as that of China. Instead hypotheses must be initially based on logical or impressionistic foundations and then submitted to a more systematic test on the basis of past and future behavior. Illustrative examples are intended to provide plausibility but not proof for such hypotheses. In no case can they be taken as confirmed or conclusive.

It goes without saying that any attempt to project the future is subject to the hazards of unforeseeable events and change. In this regard, two areas deserve special mention: the decision-making process and China's nuclear weapons capability. Given the paucity of information on the contribution of individual figures in the formulation and implementation of foreign policy, it is uncertain how leadership change will affect future policy. The direct evidence concerning Mao's specific role in foreign affairs is largely confined to Cultural Revolution documents dealing with the 1958 Quemoy crisis and Sino-Soviet relations. The volumes, *Mao Tse-tung ssu-hsiang wan-sui* (Long Live Mao Tse-tung's Thought), are tantalizingly suggestive but fragmentary.[1] Chou En-lai's more visible presence in foreign relations generated more speculation on his role with even less original evidence at hand.

However, whether the focus is on Mao or Chou, it probably distorts the policy process because a personalized approach runs counter to most scholarly analysis, professional experience, and common sense concerning governmental systems. Large complex organizations are seldom mere putty in the hands of one individual. Instead, a congeries of bureaucratic sub-units with different interests interact in the shaping and implementation of policy, frequently independent of the leader's own will.[2] The socialization process and routinization of organizational procedures result in the handling of most problems in a standardized bureaucratic manner. Only when these procedures break down under the pressure of a crisis is the personal element likely to play an important role as the circle of participants in the policy process narrows and rises to the highest levels.[3] Even here any single individual's more idiosyncratic contribution—except for a uniquely endowed figure such as Mao—will still be heavily constrained by prior bureaucratic and policy-making procedures, interests, and capacities.

Thus, a basic continuity is probable in Chinese foreign policy with only incremental change on the assumption that standardized procedures and bureaucratic processes that have evolved through twenty-five years of the PRC will prevail over individual leadership changes in the near future. Chou En-lai's professional cohorts in the foreign ministry and its overseas branches may reflect his personal views and style, but they have presumably institutionalized their perspectives so as to survive his passing with relatively little effect.[4] The expansion of foreign trade and investment in foreign technology have similarly developed a growing core of interests that will engage the policy debate from a particular point of view. Military planning and intelligence analysis have matured into professional occupations with large staffs following patterns established by their predecessors.[5] These and other components in the decision-making process offset the personalized element.

A relatively stable continuity of foreign policy output can be identified despite changes in the power positions of the components which comprise the dominant coalition at different times. Between 1968 and 1971, for instance, the role of the party was appreciably less than it had been prior to the Cultural Revolution of 1966–68, and conversely the PLA occupied more prominent positions of authority.[6] By 1974 these roles had been reversed, with the party ascendant and the military subordinate.[7] Yet no major change in foreign policy occurred during this time that correlated in any discernible way with changes in the bureaucratic balance of power.

This is not to suggest that PRC foreign policy remains wholly immune to alteration by one faction as opposed to another. The temporary seizure of control over foreign affairs by an extremist faction in May, 1967, resulted in dramatic differences in the handling of international relations as compared both with the previous eighteen years of the regime and with the period after the faction's ouster that same August. The uniqueness of this short-lived development, however, argues for a model of basic continuity with incremental change rather than one of total unpredictability with wide fluctuations in behavior.

A second hazard in projecting future PRC policy from the past is the transformation of China into a nuclear power. As China advances from a token first-generation missile capability into a global strike posture based on seaborne as well as landbased systems, its offensive strength compared with all except the two superpowers will change dramatically. The relevance of this for any concern with the role of force and risk taking is obvious, yet it is not possible here to go beyond a few general observations of a highly speculative nature. An additional dimension of uncertainty lies in the quadrilateral interaction of the United States, the Soviet Union, Japan, and China in Northeast Asia. To project the behavior of any single state in isolation from that of the other three, whether on nuclear or other matters, is a perilous undertaking at best. Nevertheless the following frankly speculative construct is offered as a stimulus, insightful or provocative, to further reflection and research.

Rationality in PRC Foreign Policy

Central to any plausible forecasting of Chinese foreign policy is an assumption of rationality. This assumption must be reexamined periodically because contrary assumptions exist abroad which receive at least token reinforcement from selected aspects of PRC behavior. A 1966 television documentary entitled "China: The Roots of Madness," seemed particularly appropriate in 1967 with the Cultural Revolution's more extreme manifestations of internal violence and xenophobia.[8] Images of "human wave" attacks by "Chinese hordes" in the Korean War were conjured up again by Soviet propaganda in the wake of border clashes in 1969.[9]

One of the Chinese statements most widely quoted abroad as purportedly proving that an irrational view prevails in Peking declared that should the United States start "war by using atomic and nuclear weapons . . . on the debris of a dead imperialism, the victorious people would create very swiftly a civilization thousands of times higher than the capitalist system and a truly beautiful future for themselves."[10] Coupled with the fact that China may have a population of nearly one billion by 1985, such words seem to mock standard formulas of nuclear deterrence, striking a posture both dangerous and unpredictable. In short, the true Chinese attitude could critically determine world peace and survival.

Rationality in an initiatory policy was defined earlier as the pursuit of likely attainable goals through available means where perceived costs are outweighed by anticipated gains. In a reactive policy against perceived threat, rationality is the attempt to deter an enemy with a credible counterthreat of costs which he will find unacceptable if he persists in conflictual behavior. Unfortunately definition is easier than confirmation. Without access to primary sources that explicitly reveal the assumptions which underlie policy decisions, the matter must be approached largely through policy outputs with both domestic and foreign inputs being indirectly inferred. Unless there are powerful indications to the contrary, this analytical process of logical inference tends a priori to favor a rational actor model.

As a result this approach eliminates contrary impulses in the policy process which have already been identified as extant in large, complex organizations, namely organizational processes, bureaucratic politics, and factional struggles.[11] The Cultural Revolution provided a vivid reminder that sharp differences may exist behind the public facade of unity, with outcomes that by definitions used in this study are irrational. A few highlights from the crisis which gripped Hong Kong from May to September, 1967, will suffice to illustrate the point.

In December, 1966, local radicals in Macao had succeeded in winning important concessions from a newly installed Portuguese governor in key areas of military and police authority by means of strikes, demonstrations, and threatened violence.[12] During the next spring parallel tactics were applied by extremist groups in Hong Kong who confronted the colonial government with demands that would have virtually surrendered control over law and order to an avowed "anti-imperialist" faction within the local Communist party. In the midst of this rapidly deteriorating situation marked by daily confrontations between riot police and militant demon-

strators, the Chinese Ministry of Foreign Affairs suddenly issued a statement which fully supported the militants. On May 15, 1967, the PRC
demanded "in all seriousness" that Great Britain order the Hong Kong
government to:

> . . . immediately accept all the just demands put forward by
> Chinese workers and residents in Hong Kong; immediately stop all
> fascist measures; immediately set free all arrested persons (including
> workers, journalists, and cameramen); punish the culprits responsible
> for these sanguinary atrocities, offer apologies to the victims and
> compensate for all their losses; and guarantee against the occurrence
> of similar incidents.[13]

If these demands were not accepted "immediately and unconditionally"
the British authorities would "be held responsible for all the grave consequences arising therefrom."

Except for the legal nicety of its being termed a "statement" and
therefore technically not requiring formal acknowledgment or reply, the
document was a virtual ultimatum. The vulnerability of the colony extending only fifteen miles from the Chinese border underscored the implications of "the grave consequences" which might follow a refusal to
comply. Evidence that this was not the product of a normally functioning
political system in Peking was revealed in the inability of the British charge
d'affaires there to receive the MFA statement for more than a day because
Red Guard rioters had seized the foreign ministry building and were
ransacking its contents.[14] An additional clue of divided counsels emerged
later that week when a high official admonished a mass rally in Peking to
support "our oppressed compatriots in Hong Kong" but made no reference to the contentious demands.[15] Years later an informed Chinese
authority claimed that Mao had immediately revoked the MFA "statement" when he learned of its contents after it already had been issued.[16]

This did not end the problem, however. Confrontation continued to
ebb and flow in Hong Kong with indiscriminate bombing of public
thoroughfares and violence at the border. Although the PRC foreign
ministry was nominally restored to order, extremist elements remained in
charge until late August when a mob sacked and burned the British
chancery, beating and abusing its staff in the process.[17] Only then was the
trend reversed. Chou En-lai personally apologized for the terrorism, indicating that a small but powerful group had usurped foreign policy direc-

tion during the previous months. In 1971 one alleged ringleader was reportedly executed for "ultra-left" activities.[18]

The Hong Kong crisis came as a surprise to British official and commercial circles which had previously relied on Chinese rationality to guarantee the colony against radical disturbances. A prime source of foreign exchange, Hong Kong annually earned more than 600 million American dollars in convertible currency which covered nearly one-third of the PRC imports in 1966.[19] Any disruption of the colony's commerce or threat to its security would jeopardize this irreplaceable aid to trade, as proven by the sudden flight of capital during the 1967 crisis. However, in the Cultural Revolution context, politics temporarily took priority over economics, thereby lifting the chief constraint against "anti-imperialist struggle" in Hong Kong while inhibiting counterarguments based on rational considerations.

This brief ascendancy of extremists permitted the pursuit of political gains that were outweighed by economic losses. The result was a policy that was both short-lived and irrational for China, as well as threatening for Hong Kong. This exceptional case is sufficient to weaken but not nullify the rationality model.

Two other weaknesses in the model which appear more frequently to characterize PRC policy also deserve attention, namely the comprehension of other political systems and the assessment of intentions on the part of perceived enemies. Such problems are not uniquely Chinese, but they must be evaluated for their impact on rationality. Although there is little firsthand evidence which pertains to these questions, certain patterns of behavior are sufficiently consistent to suggest some tentative hypotheses.

Conventional Chinese public commentaries on foreign affairs draw heavily on standard Marxist-Leninist concepts amended by Mao and depicting international relations primarily in terms of "class struggle" and "contradictions." Alternatively, however, stress is often placed on the role of specific personalities. Thus, in 1961 President Kennedy was anathematized as "worse than Eisenhower," without regard for the prominence of such Democrats as Adlai Stevenson and Chester Bowles who argued for changes in American China policy to improve relations with the PRC.[20] This analysis may have heightened apprehension over American intentions in the Taiwan Strait the following year. At a less dramatic level it could explain the Chinese failure to respond positively to President Kennedy's hint that American wheat was available to meet the PRC food crisis.

In a different context, Chou En-lai's muffling and manipulation of Nehru's opposition to the Aksai Chin road in 1958 was followed by a propaganda backlash against the Indian prime minister in 1959 in the aftermath of the Tibet revolt when refuge was given the Dalai Lama and border clashes flared. Chinese media paid little attention to the influence of Indian parliamentary politics and press opposition as constraints on Nehru's posture. Again, a personal focus may have raised unrealistic hope of agreement before Chou's 1960 trip to New Delhi. Some quarters persisted in this personalistic policy down to September, 1962, despite all logic and evidence to the contrary. Then Chinese media analysis suddenly attacked Nehru as an individual enemy, resuming a theme first articulated in 1959 but muted in the interim.

This personalized approach fails to plumb the intricacies of pluralistic political systems, although on occasion it may coincide with an idiosyncratic situation wherein certain individuals are indeed a determining factor. Such a coincidence between Chinese perception and reality occurred in the Sino-American rapprochement of 1971–72 which turned uniquely on the activity of Henry Kissinger as special assistant to President Richard Nixon.[21] In general, however, the approach seems better suited for an authoritarian system in which the symbolic leader may hold considerable substantive power as well. Thus Peking's persistent attack on Nikita Khrushchev as the source of "revisionism" appeared plausible until his downfall in October, 1964. But thereafter it was both impolitic and illogical to tar his opponents with the brush of "Khrushchev's revisionist successors" so far as Sino-Soviet relations were concerned.

In short, while much of the material in Chinese media may be routinely propagandistic, the persistence of analysis which is either simplistically ideological or misleadingly personalized raises the possibility of similar flaws in the leadership's perception of other political systems. Whatever the extent to which this may have been true in the past, it should diminish as PRC representatives extend their presence abroad through political, economic, scientific, and cultural contacts. Continuous diplomatic association in international organizations and foreign capitals will provide a steadily widening stream of information and analysis to policy officials in Peking, limited only by the constraints imposed through domestic politics in China. These constraints could be serious in periods of acute conflict if contesting factions utilize ideological arguments to impugn the loyalty of opposing views. Under such circumstances the pressure to conform to preconceived postulates of class struggle may distort analysis of other governments and their intent. With more normal conditions, however, this apparent weakness in the rationality model should lessen in importance over time.

While examples which have so far been presented have included misunderstanding of political systems coinciding with miscalculation of enemy intent, the two errors can and do occur separately. Comprehending a political system does not guarantee a correct estimate of regime intentions as the system is more readily discernible than the intent. It should not be assumed that a "worst case" bias always distorts PRC perceptions. In this regard, it is interesting to note how Chinese estimates erred in opposite directions concerning the United States during the 1960s. On the one hand, Peking overestimated Washington's willingness to back a Nationalist invasion and consequently responded with a higher military and diplomatic deterrent posture than was necessary. On the other hand, Mao's sanguine remarks to Edgar Snow in January, 1965, showed no anticipation of massive American combat troop deployment to Indochina later that year or a prolonged air bombardment of the DRV over the next eight years.[22]

It is more difficult to assess estimates of Indian intention since some of the PRC calculus concerned the future consequences of continued passivity in the face of a "forward policy" based on Soviet-supplied air power. At the very least, Chinese exaggeration of American intent in the Taiwan Strait crisis of June, 1962, contributed to an overestimation of the degree to which Indian policy resulted from hostile collusion with the United States or the Soviet Union, or both. This in turn evoked a more militant PLA border stance in July, which had a "self-fulfilling prophecy" effect in triggering an equally militant upsurge of nationalistic fervor in the Indian parliament and press. The resulting bind on Nehru's ability to compromise eliminated all possibility of a negotiated settlement, while the steady reciprocal hardening of military postures in the disputed border areas brought on a conflict which planners in New Delhi had not anticipated at the beginning of 1962.

The miscalculation of a potential enemy's intent is so universally commonplace as to scarcely require attention here except as a caution against assumptions of a too simplistic rationality model. On the positive side, it should be remembered that Chinese Nationalist indicators of invasion planning were substantial while the behavior of Indian troops in the Galwan Valley supported a qualitative as well as quantitative change in military policy. As for underestimating American intervention in Indochina, even highly placed American officials failed to foresee the length and depth of involvement of the United States prior to the commencement of regular air attacks against the DRV in February, 1965.[23] Thus, while PRC calculations can be faulty, they are usually not without some basis in evidence or logic.

In this regard, the 1969 Sino-Soviet border clashes deserve brief mention. In subsequent years, considerable debate persisted abroad over whether proclaimed fear of a Soviet attack was genuine or fabricated for internal and external political purposes. There was debate also over the actual Soviet calculations behind a major military buildup around China's border which became manifest in 1968–69. Both questions need much more systematic examination than can be given here. However, the plausibility is greater that Chinese fear was genuine than that the Soviets had deliberately planned an attack on China. Thus, it is possible that Peking was guilty of a major miscalculation of Moscow's intentions.

The combination of a perceived enemy on the border and serious internal crisis increases the likelihood of a "worst case" analysis in Peking. The 1962 confrontations in the Taiwan Strait and the Himalayan mountains juxtaposed evidence of imminent external attack with continued domestic economic discontent. Similarly, discovery of the Russian buildup in 1968–69 followed two years of political struggle which had reached the highest levels of authority. These circumstances favored an alarmist estimate of Soviet intent, whereas the logic of the situation made a Russian invasion unlikely.

This analysis raises the prospect of future tensions arising between the PRC and neighboring powers when internal political or economic tensions combine with prima facie evidence of external threat. Japan, for instance, may become more susceptible to Chinese misperception should it acquire a more formidable military capability to extend its power beyond the home islands. Against this prospect is the increased sense of self-assurance and security that should accompany economic growth and political consolidation in a post-Mao regime. On balance, this weakness in the rationality model is likely to be less important in the future than it has been in the past, but its recurrence cannot be ruled out.

In sum, reliance on a modified rationality model for projections of Chinese foreign policy seems justified. It may prove misleading in unique situations and it probably underestimates the impact of bureaucratic and factional politics, but it can provide a guide to the parameters which constrain as well as the calculations which determine policy choice.

The Controlled Use of Force

PRC foreign policy has not eschewed the use of force in less threatening situations than those just examined. The PLA occupied contended territory in Burma in 1955–56, it fired on Himalayan outposts during the brief Pakistan-Indian war of 1965, and it ousted South Vietnamese forces from the disputed Paracel Islands in January, 1974. Recourse to force has not been reckless or adventuristic but rather has remained subordinate to foreign policy principles which frequently violate standard military considerations in pursuit of political goals.

For example, in the Korean War no advance preparations in the peninsula paved the way for PLA intervention, and the massive Chinese troop crossing of the Yalu River was subjected to intensive aerial bombardment without corresponding air cover. These circumstances resulted in far heavier casualties than might otherwise have occurred. Yet, for the sake of political objectives determined in Peking, the PLA persisted in the war for almost three years, without any hope of breaking the military stalemate. Similarly in 1965–68 the PLA exposed some 50,000 troops to American air attack, with no protection from Chinese fighters, in order to strengthen North Vietnamese logistics and morale. Some analysts hold that the ouster of Lo Jui-ch'ing as chief of staff in November, 1965, climaxed a policy debate during the previous months over the degree to which Chinese interests required the acceptance of risks which might be reduced by closer military collaboration with the Soviet Union.[24] Certainly Mao's adamant opposition to any joint Sino-Soviet effort on behalf of Hanoi placed the PLA presence there in greater jeopardy.

The political command and control over the military was dramatically demonstrated with the abandonment of NEFA in the face of a totally demoralized enemy. A different type of reversal occurred in 1958 when the blockade of Quemoy was broken by United States–Nationalist efforts, but the military humiliation was heightened by the political decision to continue a token shelling of the island on alternate days. A more basic question surrounds the design behind the Quemoy bombardment and blockade which risked public defeat by having no capability of coping with the possible contingency of American intervention.[25] In addition to these strategic decisions, the tactical use of measured military force was manifest in both conflicts. Despite the fact that localized movement and fighting occurred at both ends of the long, undemarcated Himalayan front, only the shelling of Chushul airfield extended PLA power into undisputed Indian territory. Similarly, throughout the six-week Quemoy crisis PRC ships and planes carefully maneuvered so as to avoid hitting their American counterparts while engaging the Chinese Nationalists in combat. The most dramatic demonstration of this self-control came on the first day that the American navy convoyed supplies from Taiwan to Quemoy. Hundreds of artillery pieces which had shelled the island for two weeks fell silent as the Nationalist ships ran the last three miles unescorted to Quemoy. On the next day, Communist guns effectively zeroed in on this strip of water so as to destroy the Nationalist ships without hitting any American vessels in the adjacent area.[26]

Besides the controlled use of force, its coordination with diplomatic and political moves is an important characteristic of Chinese policy. This was seen in connection with the prominence of monthly intervals for strategic moves and weekly benchmarks for tactical timing. Beyond timing, however, the content of diplomacy and propaganda, both domestic and foreign, is carefully orchestrated in concert with military activity. The period October–November, 1962, exemplifies this overall coordination. The warning to Moscow as early as October 8 of forthcoming hostilities, and the attention to border affairs with Pakistan and Burma, coincided with a diplomatic offensive toward governments throughout Asia and Africa. At the same time no domestic campaign appeared to suggest that China was mobilizing for war on its own initiative, even as the PLA prepared for the October 20 offensive.

The general pattern raises questions about China's failure to follow through with a joint Sino-Vietnamese air defense system, which was anticipated in the winter of 1964–65 by airfield construction in south China, joint air exercises over North Vietnam, and linked radar systems. At least three alternative explanations arise. First, simple bluff was used to deter American air attacks on the DRV with no intention of further action if deterrence failed. Second, a capability was developed to provide operational options for an eventual decision which ultimately proved very limited in scope. Third, a genuine deterrence effort aborted and the initial decision to defend the DRV by air was modified, if not reversed. The second and third hypotheses raise the possibility of differing views in Peking, although how the lines of division cut among military and civilian officials is impossible to determine without further evidence. The positions of Moscow and Hanoi need examination as likely inputs, particularly since Soviet involvement increased significantly after Khrushchev's removal in October, 1964. Despite these uncertainties, the example is worth noting as another possible instance of political considerations overriding military preparations.

Except for a single Cultural Revolution accusation that Lo Jui-ch'ing acted for his own political purposes and without authorization to provoke minor naval clashes with the Chinese Nationalists, there is no direct evidence linking his ouster in November, 1965, as chief of staff with a military-civilian confrontation. However, as noted earlier it does appear that his fall resulted in part from differences over China's military needs during the Indochina conflict. In any case his removal confirmed the supremacy of civilian authority, more specifically that of Mao. Many decades of insistence that "the party commands the gun" has cemented a tradition of politics prevailing over military affairs.

As China expands its acquisition of nuclear weapons, the question of their unauthorized or accidental use arises. In this regard the regime's command and control over the nature and timing of PLA activity offer reassurance against the likelihood of deliberate military insubordination. Moreover the disciplined behavior of pilots and ship commanders in successive confrontations suggests that accidental clashes which might unwittingly escalate into larger hostilities are virtually ruled out both by training and by communications procedures under potential combat conditions.

Another relevant concern in a nuclear confrontation is the danger of "lock-in" effects which compel escalation to higher levels of violence. Here the demonstrated PRC willingness to sacrifice military "face" for political flexibility at both the strategic and tactical levels argues against "lock-in" providing any greater hazard than for other nuclear nations. Abandonment of the 1958 Quemoy blockade and the 1962 withdrawal from NEFA showed the ability of decision makers in Peking to take embarrassing and unorthodox measures in order to avoid continuation or escalation of conflict if it seemed unwise.

Chinese Risk Taking

Against these reassurances of civilian command over military force the fact remains that the PLA has repeatedly projected its power across China's borders, at times increasing the risk of war. Major conflict resulted in Korea and in India. In the Taiwan Strait the express enemy was Chiang Kai-shek but his American support raised the possibility of greater hostilities in 1954–55 and again in 1958. Between 1964 and 1972 the PLA moved upwards of 15,000 troops into the adjacent provinces of Laos to counter parallel covert Thai deployments under American direction in support of the Royal Lao against the Pathet Lao.[27] Although Chinese forces never entered combat, the accompanying antiaircraft units shot down Royal Lao and Air America planes and the potential for escalation was heightened by their presence. Similarly the activity of 50,000 Chinese troops in North Vietnam from 1965 to 1968 confronted American military and political pressure on Hanoi with risks that could not be wholly controlled by Peking. In March, 1969, Chinese border troops clashed with Soviet forces and triggered reactions which posed a near-war situation for months.

To be sure, various steps were adopted to lessen the risk of escalation, but they were minor by comparison with actions that heightened the risk. In Korea the PLA nomenclature was replaced by "Chinese People's Volunteers," ostensibly disassociating the PRC from official involvement in the war. Peking never publicly acknowledged the Chinese military presence in Laos and Vietnam. On the contrary, Chou En-lai and other officials consistently claimed that "China does not have a single soldier stationed outside its own borders." Besides these verbal defenses against enemy retaliation, temporary disengagement after initial combat in Korea and India provided an opportunity to reassess the risks and to permit the enemy to reverse course.

The risk of war was increased by actions which placed the PLA in a belligerent forward posture as opposed to a passive role of remaining behind the PRC border or withdrawing from positions of potential conflict. This risk taking was especially noteworthy when the enemy possessed an overwhelming military superiority in conventional and nuclear weapons, as with the United States in Korea, the Taiwan Strait, and Indochina, and with the Soviet Union in the 1969 border clashes.

Indeed, the Sino-Soviet clash on March 2, 1969, may constitute the most dramatic evidence of Chinese risk taking in reaction to perceived threat. Although some of the facts remain uncertain, it appears that after the invasion of Czechoslovakia in August, 1968, PRC estimates of Soviet intentions manifested in a Russian military buildup around China concluded that an attack was possible. The regime reacted by alerting the country to the threat of war and by strengthening its defensive posture vis-à-vis the Soviet Union. Seen in this context, the fighting on the Ussuri River may have arisen as part of a heightened deterrent posture in accord with the precepts examined earlier. While the developments cannot be traced in detail, a brief summary will illustrate the plausibility of this hypothesis.[28]

A qualitative and quantitative increase in Soviet military capability around China's borders had been underway since 1965, and an awareness of this was evident in Peking as early as January, 1967.[29] The matter may have evoked relatively little high level attention prior to mid-1968 for two reasons. First, the Cultural Revolution was of immediate urgency as domestic turmoil shook the political system from top to bottom with recurring waves of public denunciation and urban violence from May, 1967, to August, 1968. Second, the Indochina conflict offered a continuous threat of escalation across China's borders until March, 1968, when President Johnson restricted American bombing in North Vietnam to the lower quarter of that country.

The Chinese may not have been able to fully appreciate the dimensions of the Soviet buildup until the winter of 1968–69, when electronic intelligence was able to detect newly-placed units in areas where predeployment preparations required considerable advance construction. The PRC had no overhead reconnaissance capability to monitor these earlier developments. Ground observation could report shipments over the Trans-Siberian railroad, but the building of local roads and barracks, the construction of additional airfields, and the establishment of new missile bases could not be detected until regular military groups occupied these facilities and communicated with distant headquarters by radio messages that could be intercepted and identified as to source and location.[30]

The Czech crisis may have had a heightened impact through a reevaluation of intelligence pertaining to Soviet military strength which revealed a major increase in the number of Russian divisions, supplemented later that winter by the discovery of new airfields in the People's Republic of Mongolia and a ring of Soviet medium-range nuclear missiles around northeast China.[31] It should be noted that prior to the invasion of Czechoslovakia, no alarm was sounded over the prospect of a Russian attack. On the annual PLA anniversary on August 1, 1968, regime statements routinely warned against war preparations aimed at China but did not single out the Soviet Union as specifically threatening an attack.[32] In the first official reaction to "the Soviet military occupation of Czechoslovakia" three days after the event, Chou En-lai gave a wide-ranging attack on recent Russian moves but again made no mention of a threat to China.[33]

The change in Peking's assessment of the situation first emerged on September 16 in an official MFA protest that sounded an initial albeit oblique alert. Alleging "119 cases" of Soviet overflight during "the past year," the note declared,

> ... However, it is rare that within a short space of twenty-one days, the Soviet side should have committed such concentrated, frequent, bare-faced and flagrant military provocations over China's air space in one area. In particular, it should be pointed out that these intrusions by the Soviet minatory aircraft took place around August 20 when the Soviet Union sent its troops for aggression into Czechoslovakia. And this is in no way accidental.[34]

The actual chronology cited in the note did not back up the general charge, however, nor were any fresh intrusions alleged for the three weeks preceding the MFA statement.[35] This indicates the note was not actually triggered by recent overflights but instead was designed to lay the groundwork for a more serious charge based on the reinterpretation of military intelligence in the aftermath of Czechoslovakia.

On October 1, 1968, Chou En-lai in his National Day address for the first time explicitly linked "Soviet revisionism" with the possibility of "invasion":

> U.S. imperialism and Soviet revisionism are capable of any evil. We must heighten our vigilance, intensify our preparations against war and be ready at all time to *smash any invasion launched by U.S. imperialism, Soviet revisionism,* and their lackeys, whether individually or collectively. *Should any enemy dare to invade our great motherland,* the 700 million Chinese people ... will definitely wipe them out resolutely, thoroughly, totally and completely.[36] [Italics added.]

Three days later Chief of Staff Huang Yung-sheng charged that the Soviet Union "has sent large numbers of troops to reinforce its forces stationed along the Sino-Soviet and Sino-Mongolian frontiers and has intensified its armed provocations against China."[37] Meanwhile the Sinkiang command defiantly asserted that its forces were "maintaining sharp vigilance, strengthening preparations against war, consolidating frontier defense, and defending the motherland. Should the Soviet revisionists dare to attack us, we would wipe them out resolutely, thoroughly, wholly and completely."[38] In the short space of two months PRC officials had moved from total silence on the threat of a Soviet invasion to explicit, authoritative alarms keyed to this specific contingency.

Under the circumstances, prudence dictated the utmost precaution against providing any pretext for a Soviet attack with specific instructions to guarantee that frontier guards conduct themselves accordingly. The deterrence schema, however, posits the need to "prepare for the worst and try for the best" by behavior that demonstrates "the best deterrence is belligerence." Chinese sources acknowledged later that patrols at Damansky Island had previously engaged in hostile physical contact, albeit without firing, on sixteen occasions between December, 1967, and the end of February, 1969.[39] They also reported Russian warnings on February 25 that any further Chinese presence would be fired upon. Nevertheless on March 2 additional troops, concealed from Soviet view, reinforced the standard group. With nearly a hundred men on each side a fierce gun fight resulted in at least thirty-one Soviet dead and fourteen wounded as against twenty Chinese killed with thirty-four wounded. Regardless of which side fired the first shot, there is no question that the Chinese sought the confrontation.

Peking may have underestimated the number of Soviet casualties that would result and almost certainly miscalculated the magnitude of Russian reaction. Moscow Radio first broke the news and for the next months maintained the propaganda initiative to mobilize domestic and foreign opinion on a global basis. Yevgeny Yevtushenko's poetry recalled the "hordes" of Genghis Khan, while photos depicted mutilated bodies purportedly gathered by Soviet forces after the clash. Undaunted, the Chinese persisted in their effort to control Damansky Island. An even larger clash erupted on March 15, 1969, which involved Soviet tanks and artillery and resulted in much larger casualties.

The legal question of ownership of this uninhabited island was not of sufficient moment to justify the risks involved in confronting superior Soviet force, particularly under the attendant circumstances of a major military buildup throughout the territory adjacent to China. Seen in the larger context, the PLA forward posture reflected a fundamental policy which places a premium on deterrent action against a threat to vital interests even when that threat comes from a markedly stronger military power.

In contrast with this willingness to incur high risks in reaction to perceived threat, a more conservative calculus constrains initiatory actions. For instance, once the United States Seventh Fleet was interposed between Taiwan and the mainland in June, 1950, no further preparations were made for an invasion across the Strait. This caution was particularly striking because the simultaneous American intervention in the Korean War completely absorbed all existing American force in the West Pacific. Meanwhile on Taiwan a wholly demoralized and ill-equipped Nationalist army offered little potential for resistance against attack. Peking did not develop an amphibious capacity for mounting a serious invasion, and tacitly accepted the American intervention while refusing publicly to forswear the use of force in its pledge to "liberate Taiwan."[40]

Again, during the attack on Quemoy in 1958, the timing of PRC moves revealed a deliberate design to minimize the risks of escalation. After the garrison refused to surrender in response to locally broadcast demands, President Eisenhower and Secretary of State Dulles on September 4 signaled their willingness to intervene in an undefined but threatening posture. Shortly after the American position became known in Peking, Chou En-lai publicly proposed resumption of the Sino-American ambassadorial talks which had been suspended since the previous spring. The promptness with which his proposal was issued after the Eisenhower-Dulles statements suggests it was a prearranged response, planned for the possible contingency of American intervention.[41] This hypothesis is strengthened by the fact that on the very next day Premier Khrushchev first announced formal Soviet support for Peking's position in a letter to Eisenhower warning, "An attack on the People's Republic of China . . . is an attack on the Soviet Union."[42] Exactly one month after Chou's proposal, on October 6, Minister of Defense P'eng Teh-huai announced a one-week suspension of the bombardment, ostensibly to permit the resupply of Quemoy on the express proviso that no more American convoys accompany the Nationalist ships. The proviso was observed, and one week later P'eng extended the cease-fire for two weeks. On October 25, nine weeks after the shelling began, he declared that shelling would continue only on odd-numbered days.

This chronology reveals preplanning in the standard pattern of strategic moves at monthly intervals with tactical developments scheduled at weekly points. Once Washington entered the action it was necessary to back off from confrontation to avoid a major war while trying to preserve a semblance of control over the outcome. The month between the proposal of renewed talks at Warsaw and the first suspension of bombardment was to permit a fortuitous collapse of the island's defense, but in the absence of this unlikely outcome the month would end with the status quo ante and the defeat of Peking's initial objectives.

Initiatory action developed from a different source in the 1967 Hong Kong crisis to which this study has already alluded, but here too Peking displayed a desire to minimize the risk of escalation. After the first wave of riots and demonstrations had subsided in the center of the colony, trouble arose at the frontier. On July 8 automatic weapons fire from both sides of the border pinned down a British police post for six hours, resulting in five dead and eleven wounded.[43] The guns were almost certainly in the hands of radical militia or Red Guards but the PLA made no move to suppress the attack and instead merely watched from observation posts. When British Ghurka troops finally moved into position the firing stopped and the weapons simply vanished.

Although nothing this serious occurred afterward, the border remained disturbed by demonstrations, rail service was interrupted at Lowu, a British police officer was kidnapped by militants in open confrontation, and a Communist police group seized oystermen from the Hong Kong side of Deep Bay. Coincident with these developments, rallies in Canton pledged thousands of Red Guards to march on the colony to liberate their compatriots suffering under "fascist oppression." This posed a formidable threat in conjunction with rioters at the border and terrorists in Hong Kong, against which stood a lightly-armed Chinese police force under British direction and a few Ghurka battalions.

PLA behavior revealed an illuminating mixture of constraints against both supporting the radicals and suppressing them. On July 8 it stood by and passively watched the British snuff out a highly incendiary situation. With recurrent violence sweeping Chinese cities and the political balance in

Peking tipping back and forth between moderates and radicals, the local commander apparently felt inhibited by the Cultural Revolution environment and failed to interfere with the ambush of the police post or to deter the British moves against the armed attack. After the Canton rallies, however, the PLA quietly proliferated checkpoints to restrict movement toward the colony, and patrols fired on persons attempting to cross the border illegally at night. In effect, the PLA unobtrusively provided a shield for Hong Kong without openly declaring its opposition to the militants.

In the reversal of policy following the mob assault on the British chancery, an MFA official privately hinted that local negotiations might further reduce tensions at the border. That fall, prolonged secret talks between the Hong Kong authorities and PLA officers at Lowu resulted in agreements that defused the explosive situation. In this way the PRC moved from a neutral position, which neither supported nor suppressed a threat to the colony, to a positive posture which protected Hong Kong against external attack.

It is unlikely in the context of the Cultural Revolution that the crisis, at least so far as PLA involvement was concerned, ended because of economic considerations. At that time economics was too bourgeois a perspective to advance as an argument against revolutionary support for the liberation of Hong Kong as a heritage of imperialism. A more telling argument, however, lay in the threat of possible American reaction to external pressure on Hong Kong. The United States Seventh Fleet continued to visit the colony throughout the crisis with aircraft carriers whose planes previously had been bombing targets daily in North Vietnam, only a few hours distant. Washington cautioned tourists against visits during the peak of terrorist activity but did not stop the the influx of American servicemen from Vietnam or advise its citizens to leave Hong Kong. In short, the risk of American retaliation against external support rendered to revolutionaries in the colony far outweighed the prospective gains of "liberation." This appears to have been the primary factor affecting PLA behavior and the ultimate PRC decision to end the confrontation.

Finally, despite the limitations involved, some assessment must be made of the effects the acquisition of strategic nuclear weapons is likely to have on China's risk-taking propensity. On the initiatory side, the PRC pledge not to use nuclear weapons first was so ritualistically reiterated throughout its first decade of weapons testing and acquisition as to gain considerable political credibility.[44] Certainly this is a logical position to adopt with respect to the vastly superior retaliatory capacity of the nuclear superpowers. On the reactive side, however, China's possession of an assured second strike capability seems likely to increase the propensity for belligerent deterrence. As an ancillary aspect, the massive tunnel and shelter program of 1968–73 permits the prompt evacuation of major urban centers to dispersed points and affords modest protection against thermal effects and fall-out. This would further induce the defiant acceptance of risks in order to deter perceived threats.

There is no basis for anticipating change in the cautious posture adopted in situations where the PRC initiates action, but there is reason to believe increased risk-taking will occur in reactive situations as China improves its second-strike nuclear capability. This in turn suggests that the sheer threat of superior power will not cause Chinese compliance where vital interests are at stake.

The Future: Dim But Not Dismal

The use of force is not a paramount characteristic of Chinese foreign policy as manifested in the behavior of the People's Republic over the past quarter of a century. The attention given to it by this study has been intentionally selective, however, for three reasons. First, the revolutionary rhetoric of Peking projects an image of bellicosity which at times has been taken literally by outside observers to reflect a fundamentally aggressive regime. Second, China's military engagement in the Korean War and the Sino-Indian conflict reinforced this bellicose image, particularly in the perception of certain American and Asian leaders. Third, the growing power of the People's Republic, most dramatically manifested in its acquisition of a long-range nuclear weapons capability, adds a potential for combat which, combined with the world's largest population, justifies careful and continuous examination.

One important group of situations wherein the PLA was employed in action between 1949 and 1974 involved perceived threats to China's territorial security. It is impossible to exaggerate the psychological importance of past events in determining both this perception and the means adopted to deter or defeat the threats. China's "century of shame and humiliation," beginning with the Opium War of 1840, was an unbroken record of foreign incursion and invasion which nibbled away at the periphery of the "Middle Kingdom" from all sides. No point, coastal or inland, was safe from foreign penetration and control, whether by leased concessions forced on China with gunboats, by subversion of non-Chinese peoples in Mongolia, Sinkiang, and Tibet, or by outright attack as in the case of Manchuria. Small wonder that the newly-established Communist regime which already saw itself figuratively at war with world capitalism headed by the United States watched any foreign approach toward its borders with apprehension and alarm.

Moreover China's response to foreign pressure and penetration between 1840 and 1937 rarely included outright military resistance. Instead reliance on alternative means, including diplomacy, international law, appeals to world opinion, and passive non-resistance characterized the effort to preserve territorial integrity under conditions of increasing internal weakness and growing external threat. The end result, however, consistently left China a second-class power whose sovereignty and territorial integrity depended more on the will of other nations than of itself. The most pointed and ironic instance of this phenomenon was the Yalta agreement of 1945 whereby the United States and Great Britain agreed that the Soviet Union should have special economic and military rights in Manchuria in return for Russia's entering the war against Japan. Despite the fact that China was an ally of the "Big Three" and had been fighting Japan since 1937, she was excluded from the negotiations and was only informed afterward of the pact.

This cavalier treatment of Chinese sovereignty was particularly bitter for Communist and Nationalist alike who recalled the shame and humiliation of 1931–32.[45] When Japan moved to detach Manchuria under the pretext of a fabricated incident, Nanking's posture of "non-resistance" and appeals to the League of Nations had proven a total failure. The League spent more than a year investigating and debating "the facts" of Japanese aggression. Finally it chastised Tokyo by adopting the sanctimonious but impotent policy of "non-recognition," first announced by the United States, concerning the puppet state of Manchukuo. However, no economic sanctions or other punitive measures followed. China's passivity and military weakness led to further Japanese encroachments in north China. Not until establishment of a united front between the Nationalists and Communists, forced on Chiang Kai-shek when he was kidnapped in December, 1936, did Japan face the need to wage all-out war to pursue its goals on the continent.

Against this background, it is understandable that any situation involving China's territorial integrity is certain to arouse concern in Peking. In addition, it is likely to evoke a determined response designed to deter or defeat an opponent before he can pose a more serious threat. Fortunately for China as well as its neighbors, most adjacent countries have negotiated an agreement on their boundary with the People's Republic and none of these have the will or the power to change the status quo. However, until the boundaries with India and the Soviet Union are actually demarcated, contention can recur between China and these two countries. The Sino-Russian frontier is particularly volatile with major military concentrations, intense political confrontation, and local cross-border economic activity.

China has also felt its territorial security threatened along its seacoast where rival claims of ownership include remote islands, their adjacent waters, and the underwater seabed. Here the potential exists for clashes primarily with the Republic of Korea and Japan, and to a much lesser extent with the Philippines and the Republic of Vietnam.[46] The importance of such areas is heightened by the prospect of offshore oil which is believed to exist in vast amounts throughout East Asia. The fact that China's competitors are all allied with the United States further complicates the problem.

China's past border settlements indicate a willingness to compromise rather than exert the full strength of its powerful bargaining position.[47] Since this was the case where the PLA possessed military superiority, it should also apply in situations of inferiority which might confront the PLA, for instance, in the East China Sea. Peking's navy is growing rapidly as a long-range submarine force and a short-range surface fleet of limited attack craft, principally destroyer escorts and torpedo boats.[48] Against present American, potential Soviet, and possible Japanese capability, however, the PRC will be in no position to strike an aggressive naval posture for many years. Although it will vigorously press its claims to distant islands there is little likelihood the regime will use force to attempt the unilateral closure of access to large portions of the ocean and seabed.

Past conflicts also arose through the interaction of Communist and non-Communist states under the protection of the larger powers, as in Korea and Indochina. The experience of all the participants, however, argues against replaying these events. The gradual withdrawal of American forces from Southeast Asia combined with the partial détente between Peking and Washington provides one hopeful trend. The future may not be wholly peaceful for the indigenous inhabitants of that area but at least it will not see China and the United States involved directly in armed confrontation.

Korea offers further potential for major power involvement with both North and South formally pledged to receive help from allies in the event of war. Fortunately, during the more adventuresome activities of Pyongyang, such as seizure of the *Pueblo* in 1968 and the shootdown of an EC-121 aircraft in 1969, the PRC showed no inclination to heighten tensions. Moreover when the Sino-American détente emerged in 1971–72, Pyongyang's posture visibly relaxed in response to consultation with Peking.

The last matter of concern to the PRC during the years of 1949–74, namely the acquisition of Taiwan and its associated islands, seems least likely to evoke the use of force. Except for the islands of Quemoy and Matsu which lie within easy striking distance of the mainland, the Chinese Nationalists are invulnerable to an invasion by the PLA.[49] Peking's ability to blockade the offshore islands is appreciably greater than in 1958 but a third attempt would not be worth the risk of reintroducing Sino-American confrontation. Only in conjunction with a sudden deterioration of Nationalist control on Taiwan might pressure on Quemoy and Matsu seem promising as part of a larger effort to collapse morale and to negotiate a final end to the longstanding civil war.

China's relations with the Soviet Union will always offer the possibility for friction and tension. Historical rivalry in Mongolia and Central Asia and traditional mistrust bordering on mutual xenophobia combine to sow the seeds of potential conflict.[50] Similarly China's experience at the hands of Japan from 1870 to 1945 leaves a rich store of bitter memories on which to draw for anticipation and interpretation of Japanese intentions. In addition to these sources of hostile perception, the willingness of Chinese leaders to utilize external enemies for internal political purposes has been amply demonstrated over the past half-century, from the Boxers to the Red Guards. As a final source of potential conflict, the express support for "revolutionary war and national liberation movement" articulated by Chinese officials and implemented with varying degrees of material aid beyond PRC borders leaves ample room for anxiety among China's neighbors concerning the course of future relations.[51]

Against this negative record stands a stronger basis for reassurance, if not genuine relaxation. Mao Tse-tung's fundamental antipathy to better relations with the Soviet Union was not wholly shared by his colleagues and therefore the prospects of a Sino-Soviet rapprochement should improve after he leaves power. This in turn will lessen the ability of Hanoi and Pyongyang to exploit Sino-Soviet conflict to their own advantage in pursuing policies of confrontation with other countries. While rivalry between Moscow and Peking is likely to continue at some lesser levels, it will not jeopardize their basic common interest in avoiding any conflict, bilateral or through third parties, that could involve nuclear weapons.

Pivotal to northeast Asian developments, of course, is Japan and its ally, the United States. Here the future is far more hopeful in comparison with the past. The establishment of diplomatic relations between the People's Republic and Japan in 1972, followed by liaison missions in Peking and Washington in 1973, ended an era of mutual isolation and confrontation. It is true that the growing bonds of economic interaction are far outweighed by China's ability to reverse course and attempt complete self-reliance. However, Sino-American and Sino-Japanese trade provides at least some basis of argument in Peking for giving priority to domestic economic development as against external postures of political hostility. To the degree that Chinese xenophobia stems from resentments and humiliation, future relations of equality and mutual benefit should mitigate, if not eliminate, the wellsprings of hatred and distrust that have exploded as genuine grievances or have been exploited by various factions for manipulative purposes.

As for the future use of force in support of revolution abroad, aside from the remote possibility of an extremist factional ascendancy, extrapolation from past behavior furnishes little cause for concern. During its first twenty-five years, the regime gave so little help to "national liberation wars" as not to provide a single success anywhere except Indochina where the fight was primarily against a foreign government, initially the French and subsequently the United States. The Chinese role in insurgency in India, Burma, Thailand, Malaya, the Philippines, and Indonesia shows no willingness on the part of the Chinese to furnish the support necessary to assure victory against a local government.[52] The consistency of this behavior is confirmed by the fact that it applied to a wholly nonaligned country such as Burma, with no American commitment to threaten retaliation, as well as to Thailand, center of the Southeast Asian Treaty Organization.

By contrast, at the height of the Cultural Revolution, extremism in Peking spilled over into neighboring countries, arousing formal protests and informal counterdemonstrations in Rangoon, Phnom Penh, and even

Hanoi.[53] A post-Mao succession struggle might find a similar group temporarily in the ascendancy with voluble repercussions in Chinese media at home and abroad. Yet the passive PLA posture in 1967 provides considerable reassurance against the prospect of military force moving to support "national liberation war." The potential for such deployment admittedly has been enhanced by the construction of roads to previously difficult or inaccessible points on and across China's borders, most notably in Laos, Nepal, and Pakistan.[54] Against this development stands the continually reiterated doctrine of "self-reliance" advocated for "revolutionary struggles," as well as the heretofore unbroken record of PLA noninvolvement in such situations.

On balance, then, the positive prospects outweigh the negative causes for concern. This provides small comfort for those whose basic responsibility lies in securing the defense of their own or allied states. They remain compelled to calculate "worst case" contingencies on the basis of capabilities rather than intentions, remembering that probability is not certainty and human behavior is never wholly predictable for a single specific future instance. It is for these reasons that in this study an attempt has been made to evaluate past Chinese perceptions and patterns of behavior in terms of rationality, the use of force, and risk-taking. True, the past does not predict the future, but neither is the future wholly discontinuous from the past. With a regime as self-consciously directed as that of the People's Republic, change coexists with continuity. Adaptation through learning is accompanied by repetition from a repertoire of behavioral routines. Past experience provides a perceptual framework for interpreting the present and forecasting the future. Indeed, far from being unstable or inscrutable, the People's Republic of China has enjoyed more stability and continuity of decision making in foreign policy over the past twenty-five years than any other major power in the world, thereby enhancing its susceptibility to diagnosis and prognosis.

In short, understanding China's international behavior is both possible and essential. Understanding is not sufficient to guarantee peace, but misunderstanding increases the risk of war. As a quarter of humanity faces the two superpowers in nuclear competition, the perils of ignorance and miscalculation increase accordingly. Korea, India, and Indochina testify to the blunders of past decisions. Hopefully they will serve to instruct future decisions.

Notes

Preface

1. Originally published by Columbia University Press, 1954; republished by Stanford University Press, Stanford, California, 1968.
2. Coauthored with Sheng Shih-ts'ai, Michigan State University Press, East Lansing, Michigan, 1958.
3. For evidence of the accuracy of State Department intelligence analyses during the Vietnam War, see *The Pentagon Papers*, 4 vols. (Boston: Beacon Press, 1971), especially vol. II, p. 690, RFE-59, December 3, 1962, and p. 770, RFE-90, October 22, 1963.
4. Originally published by the Macmillan Co., 1960; republished by Stanford University Press, 1968.
5. See John Kenneth Galbraith, *Ambassador's Journal* (Boston: Houghton Mifflin, 1969), pp. 499–500. He notes "the London telegram . . . just before the last push which promised no further action" as reportedly reflecting the INR estimate.
6. Because of their highly technical nature and length these data papers were not included in this book. See Kuang-sheng Liao and Allen S. Whiting, "Chinese Press Perceptions of Threat: The U.S. and India, 1962," *The China Quarterly* (January–March, 1973), pp. 80-97.

Introduction

1. Neville Maxwell, *India's China War* (New York: Pantheon Books, 1970), p. 425.
2. John E. Coon, "The PLA and Chinese Power Abroad," in William W. Whitson, ed., *The Military and Political Power in China in the 1970's* (New York: Praeger, 1972), p. 346. For a detailed reconstruction of the tactical combat situations, albeit heavily favorable to one side, see Major Sita Ram Johri, *Chinese Invasion of NEFA* (Lucknow: Himalaya Publications, 1968) and *Chinese Invasion of Ladakh* (Lucknow: Himalaya Publications, 1969).

3. Maxwell, op. cit., p. 424.

4. Maxwell's book continued to evoke Indian criticism for several years after its appearance. Peking responded by granting him visas in 1971 and 1973, including an interview with Chou En-lai on the first occasion and an exclusive visit to the site of Sino-Soviet border clashes on the second trip.

5. Among the more important are Lt. Gen. B. M. Kaul, *The Untold Story* (Bombay: Allied Publishers, 1967); Brig. J. P. Dalvi, *Himalayan Blunder* (Bombay: Thacker and Co., 1969); S. S. Khera, *India's Defense Problems* (Bombay: Orient Longmans, 1968); B. N. Mullik, *My Years with Nehru: The Chinese Betrayal* (Bombay: Allied Publishers, 1971); and P. V. R. Rao, *Defense Without Drift* (Bombay: Popular Prakashan, 1970).

6. A scholarly argument to this effect is presented by Margaret W. Fisher, Leo E. Rose, and Robert A. Huttenback, *Himalayan Battleground: Sino-Indian Rivalry in Ladakh* (New York: Praeger, 1963).

7. B. M. Kaul, *Confrontation with Pakistan* (New Delhi: Vikas Publishers, 1971), p. 276, notes that the Indian post at Dhola was established when it was "raining" on the basis of "maps not absolutely accurate" and later admits, p. 293, that "our maps were not entirely accurate and showed Thagla Ridge incorrectly." Kaul omitted these observations from his first book, *The Untold Story.* For a balanced assessment of the conflict's origins see Harold C. Hinton, *Communist China in World Politics* (Boston: Houghton Mifflin Co., 1966), pp. 296—302.

8. In addition to Maxwell, op. cit., see Alastair Lamb, *The McMahon Line: A Study in the Relations Between India, China and Tibet 1904 to 1914* (London: Routledge and Kegan Paul, 1966); Dorothy Woodman, *Himalayan Frontiers* (New York: Praeger, Inc., 1969); also M. W. Fisher et al., op. cit.

9. Maxwell, op. cit., devotes only thirty pages of his book to "the view from Peking," although he includes valuable and insightful material on this aspect throughout the work.

10. After the Tibet portion was completed in draft, the author's attention was called to a parallel effort by Steve Weissman, "Last Tangle in Tibet," *Pacific Research and World Empire Telegram*, no. 5 (July—August, 1973), pp. 1—18. Weissman's research is impressive as is his analysis and deserved more prominent publication.

11. J. Chester Cheng, ed., *The Politics of the Chinese Red Army* (Stanford, Calif.: Hoover Institute, 1966), translated from *Kung-tso T'ung-hsün* (Bulletin of Activities), nos. 1—30, no. 9 missing (January—August, 1961).

12. The best critique of this model is in Graham Allison, *Essence of Decision: Explaining the Cuban Missile Crisis* (Boston: Little, Brown and Co., 1971), chap. 1.

13. Allen S. Whiting, *China Crosses the Yalu* (Stanford, Calif.: Stanford University Press, 1968). Robert C. North and his associates applied their conceptual framework to several case studies, the results of which are available in the *Stanford Studies in International Conflict and Integration,* mimeographed (Stanford, Calif.: Stanford University, v.d.). One such paper by North and Nazli Choucri analyzes the articulated perceptions of the Indian and Chinese governments during October 22–31, 1962.

14. For an elucidation of organizational processes and bureaucratic politics as variant models of decision making see Allison, op. cit. A later elaboration is in Graham T. Allison and Morton H. Halperin, "Bureaucratic Politics: A Paradigm and Some Policy Implications," in Raymond Tanter and Richard Ullman, eds., *Theory and Policy in International Relations* (Princeton, N.J.: Princeton University Press, 1972), pp. 40–79.

15. Thomas C. Schelling, *The Strategy of Conflict* (Cambridge, Mass.: Harvard University Press, 1960), and *Arms and Influence* (New Haven, Conn.: Yale University Press, 1966); Alexander L. George, David K. Hall, and William E. Simons, *The Limits of Coercive Diplomacy: Laos, Cuba, Viet Nam* (Boston: Little, Brown and Co., 1971).

16. *Notes, Memoranda and Letters Exchanged and Agreements Signed Between the Governments of India and China: White Paper,* 10 vols. (New Delhi: Ministry of External Affairs, Government of India, 1959–63); vols. I–VIII; hereafter cited as *White Paper.*

17. *The Sino-Indian Boundary Question* (Peking: Foreign Languages Press, 1962).

18. Dalvi, op. cit., commanded a brigade while Kaul, op. cit., directed corps operations.

19. B. N. Mullik, op. cit., p. 195, asserts, "there was no lack of intelligence and no blind spot about Chinese preparations in Tibet," but from his account the problem would appear to have been a surfeit of "intelligence," most of which was erreoneous. For instance, he recounts a dispute with Defense Minister Krishna Menon over whether or not Russia had supplied MIG-21s to China, noting "Subsequently it was revealed that the Chinese had, in fact, a large number of MIG-21 fighters prior to 1962, and so the information given to us was correct," p. 351. Mullik is wrong, nonetheless, at least so far as "a large number" was concerned. On p. 366, he claims that "in June, the Chinese had clearly declared their intention of throwing out by force Indian troops who had encroached into their territory," although his alleged evidence, p. 330, includes a *People's Daily* article which, from its description, actually appeared in October. Interesting challenges to accepted fact may be correct but cannot be substantiated by his account. Thus, on p. 196, he denies Chou En-lai's claim of 1960 that the PLA entered western Tibet in October 1950 via the Aksai Chin

route, asserting, "There is irrefutable evidence that the Chinese did not enter western Tibet until June, 1951. These troops came not through Aksai Chin but from Khotan. . . . This route at no point passed within one hundred miles of the northeastern frontier of Ladakh."

20. A critical assessment of its utility in World War II is provided by Alexander L. George, *Propaganda Analysis* (Evanston, Ill.: Row Peterson, 1959). The earliest clues to the Sino-Soviet rift emerged through content analysis done within the Central Intelligence Agency as reflected by one of its staff members after leaving government service, Donald S. Zagoria, *The Sino-Soviet Conflict, 1956–1961 (Princeton,* N.J.: Princeton University Press, 1962). Similar success in analysis of Soviet domestic and foreign politics is shown by Myron Rush, *The Rise of Khruschev* (Washington, D.C.: Public Affairs Press, 1958).

Chapter 1

1. A lucid synthesis of the complex historical, political, and legal background may be found in Neville Maxwell, *India's China War* (New York: Pantheon Books, 1970), pp. 17–64. More detailed studies include Alastair Lamb, *The China-India Border: The Origins of the Disputed Boundaries* (London: Oxford University Press, 1964); Alastair Lamb, *The McMahon Line: A Study in the Relations Between India, China and Tibet 1904 to 1914* (London: Routledge and Kegan Paul, 1966); Dorothy Woodman, *Himalayan Frontiers* (London: Barrie and Rockliff, 1969); Margaret W. Fisher, Leo E. Rose, and Robert S. Huttenback, *Himalayan Battleground: Sino-Indian Rivalry in Ladakh* (New York: Praeger, 1963).

2. Tieh-tseng Li, "The Legal Position of Tibet," *American Journal of International Law* (April, 1956), pp. 394–404, presents a meticulously researched brief based on British and Chinese archives to support Chinese sovereignty claims. See also his *Tibet Today and Yesterday* (New York: Bookman Associates, 1960).

3. This portion is based on Karunakar Gupta, "The McMahon Line, 1911–1945: The British Legacy," *The China Quarterly* (July–September, 1971), pp. 521–45.

4. Allen S. Whiting and Sheng Shih-ts'ai, *Sinkiang: Pawn or Pivot?* (East Lansing, Mich.: Michigan State University Press, 1958).

5. Cited by Gupta, op. cit., p. 525.

6. Ibid., p. 525.

7. Ibid., p. 527, quotes Caroe and H. E. Richardson, "the last British— and the first Indian—representative in Tibet" in agreement on this point.

8. Ibid., p. 536. Two copies escaped destruction; one is in the Harvard University Library, the other is in the India Office Records.

9. For the involvement of secret American agents in probing logistic possibilities in Tibet, Tibetan requests for radio transmitting equipment, and Washington's refusal to challenge Chinese claims, see *Foreign Relations of the United States, 1943, China* (Washington, D.C.: Department of State, 1967), pp. 620–45. An excellent examination of subsequent secret United States involvement with Tibet has been carefully pieced together by Steve Weissman, "Last Tangle in Tibet," *Pacific Research and World Empire Telegram* (July–August, 1973), pp. 1–18. Weissman fails to utilize Chinese sources but otherwise provides detailed footnotes for tracing the labrynthine associations between Tibetan insurgent activities, exploitation abroad thereof, and United States government agents.
10. Li, op. cit.; also Weissman, op. cit.
11. A concise reliable survey is offered by Theodore Shabad, *China's Changing Map* (New York: Praeger, Inc., 1972), pp. 319–31.
12. J. P. Mills, "a British adviser on tribal affairs" noted, "The tribes to be incorporated [in India] belong naturally more to Tibet than to India. In race and in language they are Mongoloid. They all speak Tibeto-Burmese languages which have nothing in common with the Assamese of the plains. It follows therefore that what one might call the cultural and social pull is towards Tibet. . . .The [McMahon Line] therefore suffers from the disability that though it may look well on the map . . . it is in fact not the natural boundary, whereas the frontier along the plains is the natural one." J. P. Mills, "The Problem of the Assam-Tibet Frontier," *The Royal Central Asian Journal* (April, 1950), pp. 152–61.
13. Chiang Kai-shek, *China's Destiny* (New York: Roy Publishers, 1947), p. 34.
14. Edgar Snow, *Red Star Over China* (New York: Modern Library, 1944), p. 96.
15. Whiting and Sheng, op. cit., pp. 104 ff.
16. Ibid., pp. 142–43.
17. Ibid., pp. 144–46.
18. M. W. Fisher et al, op. cit., pp. 7–8.
19. George Patterson, *Tragic Destiny* (London: Faber and Faber, 1959) provides a firsthand account of developments at this time from excellent sources among various Tibetan groups; a solid scholarly study is offered by George Ginsburgs and Michael Mathos, *Communist China and Tibet* (The Hague: M. Nijhoff, 1964).
20. Ginsburgs and Mathos, op. cit., p. 98.
21. Maxwell, op. cit., p. 87. The following portion draws heavily from his work.
22. For the convenience of English-language readers the Western terminology used on maps will be employed first, followed by transliteration of Chinese names in parentheses.

23. Maxwell, op. cit., pp. 96 ff.
24. Ibid., pp. 159—61.
25. *White Paper* (New Delhi: Government of India, v.d., 1959—63).
26. The most informative version so far as clandestine activities and intelligence analysis are concerned is the so-called "Senator Gravel Edition," *The Pentagon Papers*, 4 vols. (Boston: Beacon Press, 1971). See especially vol. II, pp. 643—49.
27. Lowell Thomas, Jr., *Out of This World* (New York: The Greystone Press, 1950), p. 239.
28. Patterson, op. cit., p. 44, quoting *The Statesman* of Calcutta, August 6, 1950, report of a New China News Agency (NCNA) dispatch whereby "General Liu Po-chen [Po-ch'eng], Chairman of the South-West China Military Affairs Commission," declared "that the People's Liberation Army would soon enter Tibet with the object of wiping out British and American influence there."
29. Anna Louise Strong, *When Serfs Stood Up in Tibet* (Peking: New World Press, 1960), p. 43.
30. Patterson, op. cit., pp. 82ff. This account conflicts with that of the Dalai Lama's brother, Thubten Jigme Norbu, as told to Heinrich Harrer, *Tibet Is My Country* (New York: E. P. Dutton and Co., 1961). Patterson claims they met in Kalimpong; Norbu, p. 244, places it in Calcutta. Norbu makes no reference to the plan for the Dalai Lama's escape, the alleged role of the United States, etc., all of which is told in considerable detail by Patterson. Patterson's other accounts, while egocentric and tinged with religious mysticism, are credible and at least one instance was backed up by photographic evidence. He had personal differences with Harrer as recounted in his book, pp. 88—89. Alternatively Harrer may have chosen to omit this portion of Norbu's account because of its political sensitivity.
31. Based on firsthand knowledge. See also Steve Weissman and John Shoch, "CIAsia Foundation," *Pacific Research* (September—October, 1972), pp. 3—4.
32. Patterson, op. cit., p. 85.
33. Ibid., pp. 92, 98.
34. Ibid., p. 98.
35. Ibid., pp. 101—2.
36. Ibid., p. 109.
37. George Patterson, *Tibet in Revolt* (London: Faber & Faber, 1960), p. 93.
38. Allen S. Whiting, *China Crosses the Yalu* (Stanford, Calif.: Stanford University Press, 1968). chaps. 6—7.
39. Memorandum from Brig. Gen. Edward G. Lansdale to Gen. Maxwell D. Taylor, "Resources for Unconventional Warfare, S. E. Asia," undated but apparently July, 1961, *The Pentagon Papers*, vol. II, pp. 643—49.

40. The *New York Times*, October 21, 24, 1954.

41. Strong, op. cit., p. 65.

42. Ibid., p. 67.

43. Anna Louise Strong, *Tibetan Interviews* (Peking: New World Press, 1959), pp. 94−95.

44. The author lived in Taiwan and Hong Kong between December 1953 and March 1955 as a Foreign Area Fellow under a grant from The Ford Foundation. On Taiwan the so-called "Western Enterprises Corporation" was readily identifiable as a CIA "cover" for clandestine operations against the mainland. In Hong Kong recreation facilities for young American males who arrived in unmarked khaki uniforms for brief sojourns aroused local speculation, amplified by newspaper allegations concerning "U.S.-Chiang agents."

45. Report of Saigon Military Mission, headed by Edward G. Lansdale, undated, *The Pentagon Papers*, vol. I, pp. 573−83.

46. Lansdale to Taylor, op. cit., p. 649.

47. The *New York Times*, April 3, 1967.

48. Ibid., April 7, 1960.

49. New China News Agency (NCNA) dispatch of September 17, 1960, in The *New York Times*, September 18, 1960.

50. Ibid.

51. The *New York Times*, February 17, 18, and 24, 1961, also March 4, 1961.

52. Quoted in George Patterson, *Peking Versus Delhi* (London: Faber and Faber, 1963), p. 298.

53. Ibid., pp. 137−38.

54. L. Fletcher Prouty, "Colorado to Koko Nor," *Empire Magazine, The Denver Post*, February 6, 1972. See also his *The Secret Team: The CIA and Its Allies in Control of the United States and the World* (Englewood Cliffs, N.J.: Prentice-Hall, 1973).

55. Ibid.

56. David Wise, *The Politics of Lying* (New York: Random House, 1973), chap. 8 tells of the bus accident in detail.

57. CIA involvement in the Burma-Thai-Laos region is summarized in Lansdale to Taylor, op. cit., and Roger Hilsman, *To Move A Nation* (Garden City, N.Y.: Doubleday and Co., 1967), chap. 10. At the Geneva Conference on Laos in mid-August, 1961, the Chinese delegate formally charged, "the United States is supporting remnant Chiang Kai-shek troops in their interventionist activities in Laos," and won help from the British delegate who declared, "We want to see all Chiang Kai-shek troops withdrawn"; see Arthur Lall, *How Communist China Negotiates* (New York: Columbia University Press, 1968), pp. 147, 279, quoting from restricted verbatim records. Lall was head of the Indian delegation.

58. General surveys of the period may be found in Peter S. H. Tang,

Communist China Today (Washington: Research Institute on the Sino-Soviet Bloc, 1961), vol. I, pp. 357–75; Stanley Karnow, *Mao and China* (New York: Viking Press, 1972), chaps. 5–6, incorporates later material from the Cultural Revolution. Analysis of the Great Leap Forward's impact is woven throughout the study by Alexander Eckstein, *Communist China's Economic Growth and Foreign Trade* (New York: McGraw-Hill, 1966).

59. J. Chester Cheng, ed., *The Politics of the Chinese Red Army* (Stanford, Calif.: Hoover Institution, 1966). This is a complete translation of twenty-nine issues of the secret military journal, *Kung-tso T'ung-hsün* (Bulletin of Activities), January 1–August 26, 1961, published by the General Political Department of the Chinese People's Liberation Army (PLA), classified as "secret" and distributed only to regimental and higher commanders of the People's Liberation Army. One issue, no. 9 for February 7–19, 1961, was missing from the series, apparently because it was classified "top secret" and distributed only at higher levels.

60. The fact that this classified military publication was captured in a Tibetan guerrilla ambush of a PLA convoy illustrates the linkage between clandestine United States activity and threats to Chinese security extant in early 1962. Presumably this raid became known in Peking.

61. Frank Robertson, "Refugees and Troop Moves—A Report From Hong Kong," *The China Quarterly* (July–September, 1962), pp. 111–15; Ezra Vogel, *Canton Under Communism* (Cambridge, Mass.: Harvard University Press, 1969), pp. 292–95.

62. Edward E. Rice, *Mao's Way* (Berkeley, Calif.: University of California Press, 1972), chaps. 11–13, reconstructs the confrontation on the basis of Cultural Revolution materials.

63. A chronological account of the Sino-Soviet split is offered by Donald S. Zagoria, *The Sino-Soviet Conflict, 1956–1961* (Princeton, N.J.: Princeton University Press, 1962). A topical arrangement of documentary excerpts which emerged later to throw light on this period may be found in John Gittings, *Survey of the Sino-Soviet Dispute* (London: Oxford University Press, 1968).

64. A foreign observer resident in China at the time declared that the euphoria of Great Leap Forward claims so overwhelmed the judgment of senior officials of long experience that the collapse of 1960 triggered an equally exaggerated negative reaction which verged on panic over fear of losing control.

65. Cheng, op. cit., pp. 579–85.

66. Ibid., pp. 743–50.

67. Ibid., pp. 279–80, report of February 10, 1961.

68. Ibid., p. 284, report of January 30, 1961.

69. Ibid., p. 287.
70. Arthur G. Ashbrook, Jr., "China: Economic Policy and Economic Results, 1949–71," *People's Republic of China: An Economic Assessment*, A Compendium of Papers submitted to the Joint Economic Committee, Congress of the United States, May 18, 1972 (Washington: U.S. Government Printing Office), pp. 3–51, statistics selected from table 3, p. 5.
71. Karnow, op. cit., pp. 104–5.
72. Ashbrook, op. cit., p. 23.
73. Alva Lewis Erisman, "China: Agricultural Development 1949–71," *People's Republic of China: An Economic Assessment*, p. 127.
74. Cheng, op. cit., pp. 117–23, 137–45.
75. Ibid., pp. 117, 566.
76. Ibid., p. 190.
77. Ibid., p. 191.
78. Ibid., p. 192.
79. Joseph Alsop, "On China's Descending Spiral," *The China Quarterly* (July–September, 1962), pp. 21–38.
80. Vogel, op. cit., p. 292. The following account draws on his reconstruction of events.
81. Ibid., p. 296.
82. See contemporary accounts in *Time, Newsweek,* The *Washington Post,* and The *New York Times.*
83. Interview with well-informed Soviet official.
84. George Patterson, *The Unquiet Frontier* (Hong Kong: International Studies Group, 1966), pp. 8–10. According to an authorized Soviet account, 67,000 Soviet citizens left Sinkiang illegally between April 22 and June, 1962; see O. B. Borisov and B. T. Koloskov, *Sovetsko Kitaiskie Otnosheniia, 1945–1970* (Moscow: Izdat, Mysl', 1972), p. 275.
85. Gittings, op. cit., p. 161.
86. Patterson, op. cit., p. 9.
87. Interviews with Soviet officials familiar with this situation.
88. Ibid.; Borisov and Koloskov, op. cit., report the first Chinese protest accusing the Soviet Union of organizing the exodus as August 30, 1962.
89. Whiting and Sheng, op. cit., pp. 104–10.
90. Cheng, op. cit., p. 487. The date of publication in the "Bulletin" is April 25, 1961; the abortive invasion of Cuba referred to in the text occurred April 17–18.
91. Ibid., p. 483.
92. Ibid., p. 585. The date of publication in the "Bulletin" is June 1, 1961.
93. Ibid., pp. 738–40.
94. Ibid., p. 484.

95. Richard H. Solomon, *Mao's Revolution and the Chinese Political Culture* (Berkeley, Calif.: University of California Press, 1971), pp. 419—20. For a fuller treatment of the domestic debates and meetings at this time, see Byung-joon Ahn, "Adjustments in the Great Leap Forward and Their Ideological Legacy, 1959—62," in Chalmers Johnson, ed., *Ideology and Politics in Contemporary China* (Seattle, Wash.: University of Washington Press, 1973), pp. 257—300. According to one Cultural Revolution version, Liu claimed the "three reconciliations and one reduction" was "put forward . . . in a rough draft and was not brought up at any Central Committee meeting. At the time I did not know about this proposal," quoted by Solomon from "The Third Confession of Liu Shao-ch'i" in *Chinese Law and Government* (Spring 1969), pp. 78—79. However, another account has Liu presiding over the conference wherein the proposal was openly advanced; the author is indebted to Parris Chang for calling this to his attention on the basis of *Mainichi Shimbun* (Tokyo), January 28, 1967.
96. Cheng, op. cit., p. 487.
97. Lall, op. cit., chap. 14, traces the gradual evolution of compromise between the United States and Chinese positions at Geneva between September and December 1961; Hilsman, op. cit., p. 139, notes how the State Department put pressure on General Phoumi Nosavan to compromise, first by halting cash payments to his troops in February, 1962, and then moving to replace all American officials who were personally friends of Phoumi. Phoumi had been backed by the CIA. W. Averill Harriman was simultaneously Assistant Secretary of State for Far Eastern Affairs and head of the American delegation at the Geneva Conference.
98. *Jen Min Jih Pao (People's Daily)*, February 14, 1962, in *Peking Review,* no. 7, February 16, 1962.
99. *Pravda,* February 14, 1962, in *Current Digest of the Soviet Press,* no. 7, March 14, 1962.
100. The editorial omitted, however, all reference to the specific Taiwan Strait crisis of 1958 which had prompted this statement.
101. For summary analysis of this period see Alexander Dallin, ed., *Diversity in International Communism* (New York: Columbia University Press, 1963), pp. 651—53.
102. Edgar Snow, *The Long Revolution* (New York: Random House, 1972), p. 186, recounts an interview with Chou En-lai wherein the Premier told of being besieged by Red Guards "for more than two days and nights . . . in his offices in the Great Hall" in August, 1967. Although Foreign Minister Ch'en Yi was heavily attacked in Red Guard posters and pamphlets, his patron, Chou, was only criticized by indirection.

Chapter 2

1. Lt. Gen. B. M. Kaul, *The Untold Story* (Bombay: Allied Publishers, 1967), p. 299.
2. From an official source.
3. The technical talks were agreed to in the joint Nehru-Chou communiqué of April 25, 1960. Meetings took place in Peking from June 15 to July 25, 1960; nineteen sessions occurred in New Delhi from August 19 to October 5. A third series occurred in Rangoon, November 7 to December 12. Both sides presented their findings in a joint publication, *Report of the Officials of the Government of India and the People's Republic of China on the Boundary Question* (New Delhi: Government of India, 1961).
4. For an extremely detailed analysis of the conflicting claims, albeit clearly favorable to India, see Margaret W. Fisher, Leo E. Rose, and Robert A. Huttenback, *Himalayan Battleground: Sino-Indian Rivalry in Ladakh* (New York: Praeger, 1963), chap. 11. The map presented by the Chinese side in 1960 added some 2,000 square miles of Ladakh to that claimed in the 1956 map, partly in the Ladakh-Sinkiang boundary near the Karakoram Pass but largely in the Ladakh-Tibet boundary near the Pangang and Spanggur lakes. Both lines were claimed to be valid by Foreign Minister Ch'en Yi in December, 1961; ibid., pp. 129–30. Construction of an additional southern spur to the Aksai Chin road probably accounted for the change.
5. For an excellent and concise analysis of these developments see Harold C. Hinton, *Communist China in World Politics* (Boston: Houghton Mifflin, 1966), pp. 315–16 and pp. 321–22.
6. Neville Maxwell, *India's China War* (New York: Pantheon Books, 1970), pp. 211–14.
7. These reports circulated within the United States government at that time.
8. See chapter 1, Military Affairs Commission (MAC) directive, January 16, 1961.
9. Maxwell, op. cit., pp. 205, 221.
10. Ibid., pp. 221–23. Maxwell won access to an unpublished copy of this directive through an authoritative source in New Delhi.
11. Chapter 1, MAC directive, January 16, 1961.
12. Maxwell, op. cit., pp. 179–225.
13. Kaul, op. cit., p. 280.
14. Ibid., pp. 280–81.
15. *White Paper*, VI, p. 4.
16. Ibid., p. 10.
17. Maxwell, op. cit., p. 226.
18. Kaul, op. cit., p. 339. Because the PLA documents were seized

through an ambush in Tibet their contents might have been made known to Indian officials.

19. Maxwell, op. cit., pp. 226–32.
20. Ibid., p. 230, quoting Nehru press conference of December 28, 1961.
21. Ibid., p. 230, quoting Shastri statement of early February, 1962.
22. *White Paper,* VI, p. 188.
23. Ibid., VI, pp. 189–90.
24. Ibid., VI, pp. 10–13.
25. Ibid., VI, p. 18.
26. For an English summary with some notes in full see *Peking Review* no. 16, April 20, 1962.
27. *White Paper,* VI, pp. 21–25.
28. Maxwell, op. cit., pp. 232–33.
29. *Peking Review,* no. 17, April 27, 1962.
30. *White Paper,* VI, pp. 37–39.
31. Ibid., VI, pp. 133–36.
32. Ibid., VI, pp. 139–41.
33. The *New York Times,* April 2, 15, and May 3, 4, 1962.
34. Maxwell, op. cit., p. 235.
35. Ibid., p. 237.
36. The closest coincidence of time and location for an encounter reported in the published protests shows a more easily defused confrontation. According to the Indian protest, "On 6th May 1962, at 0930 hours, approximately 20 Chinese soldiers came within 150 yards of the Indian post at $78°07'E$, $35°28'N$. They were supported by a party of another 100 Chinese soldiers, who were approximately 1,000 yards away. When the 20 Chinese soldiers moved up closer to the Indian post, the Indian post commander walked up to within 100 yards of the Chinese party and asked them to withdraw." From this wording it appears that nothing further occurred. *White Paper,* VI, p. 42.
37. *White Paper,* VI, p. 54.
38. Ibid., p. 44.
39. Ibid., p. 46.
40. Allen S. Whiting, *China Crosses the Yalu* (Stanford, Calif.: Stanford University Press, 1968), p. 115; text from Radio Peking, Chinese International Service in English, October 11, 1950.
41. K. M. Panikkar, *In Two Chinas* (London: Allen and Unwin, 1955), p. 108.
42. Ibid., p. 110.
43. *Peking Review,* no. 23, June 8, 1962.
44. *White Paper,* VI, p. 179.
45. Ibid., pp. 203–5.
46. Ibid., p. 43.
47. Ibid., pp. 56–57.

48. Ibid., p. 60.
49. "Quarterly Chronicle and Documentation," *The China Quarterly* (July–September, 1962), pp. 253–54.
50. The *New York Times*, May 24, 1962.
51. Interview of May 29, 1962, between Vice Premier Ch'en Yi and five Japanese newspapermen as reported in *Tokyo Journalist*, June 26, 1962, translated in *Foreign Broadcast Information Service*, August 13, 1962.
52. The *New York Times*, March 30, 1962, in Roger Hilsman, *To Move a Nation* (Garden City, N.Y.: Doubleday, 1967), p. 310.
53. Information available to the author while in the United States government. During the June crisis Chinese Nationalist officers were informed the invasion was about to begin. Senior commanders acquiesced but junior commanders reportedly refused to begin preparations in the absence of American military assistance in the invasion.
54. Nationalist negotiations proceeded without American approval but became known in Washington.
55. The *New York Times*, March 31 and May 6, 1962.
56. *Peking Review*, no. 26, June 29, 1962.
57. Ibid.
58. Hinton, op. cit., p. 271.
59. Hilsman, op. cit., p. 141.
60. *Peking Review*, no. 21, May 25, 1962.
61. Ibid.
62. Ch'en Yi interview, *Tokyo Journalist*.
63. *Peking Review*, no. 21, May 25, 1962.
64. Ch'en Yi Interview, *Tokyo Journalist*.
65. Information available to the author. The diplomat spoke with high officials in early June.
66. The author is indebted to Parris Chang for calling this to his attention on the basis of a Red Guard publication, *Peking Commune*, January 28, 1967.
67. Hilsman, op. cit., p. 318, suggests 500,000 PLA troops were involved; contemporary press "leaks" give lower estimates; see also Frank Robertson, "Refugees and Troop Moves–A Report From Hong Kong," *The China Quarterly* (July–September, 1962), pp. 111–15. The author was responsible for collating and assessing intelligence on these developments at the time.
68. The initial "leak" of the troop movements appeared in Joseph Alsop's columns which had previously analyzed the Hong Kong exodus as "proof" of his conclusion concerning the regime's parlous state.
69. Hilsman, op. cit., p. 318; The *New York Times*, June 21, 1962.
70. *Peking Review*, no. 26, June 29, 1972.
71. The *New York Times*, June 24, 1962. This "leak" occurred in Warsaw

and was an extraordinary instance of behavior by one of the two sides, under the circumstances presumably the Chinese. The author handled the receipt of Ambassador Cabot's cable in Washington.

72. Kenneth T. Young, *Negotiating With The Chinese Communists* (New York: McGraw-Hill, 1968), p. 250, based on State Department sources.
73. The *New York Times*, June 28, 1962.
74. Central News Agency in English to the United States, June 13, 1962, in *Foreign Broadcast Information Service (FBIS)*, June 14, 1962.
75. Taipei Domestic Service, June 8, 1962, in *FBIS*, June 12, 1962.
76. *People's Daily*, July 21, 1962 in *Peking Review*, no. 30, July 27, 1962.
77. Singapore, Agence France Presse in English, June 17, 1962, in *FBIS*, June 18, 1962.
78. *Hsin Sheng Pao* as quoted in Taipei Domestic Service, June 17, 1962, in *FBIS*, June 18, 1962.
79. Information provided to the author by Dr. William W. Whitson.
80. Radio Peking to Taiwan, June 13, 14, and 16, 1962, as summarized by *FBIS* at the time.
81. The *New York Times*, May 24, 1962. For background on the United States move by a participant in policy at the time see James C. Thomson, Jr., "On The Making of U.S. China Policy 1961–69: A Study in Bureaucratic Politics," *The China Quarterly*, no. 50 (April–June, 1972), pp. 220–43.
82. Ch'en Yi interview, *Tokyo Journalist*.
83. Information available to the author at the time.
84. *FBIS* summary analysis at the time.
85. For different statements of this hypothesis and testing of its relevance on other situations see Raymond Tanter, "Dimensions of Conflict Within and Between Nations," *Journal of Conflict Resolution* (March, 1966), pp. 48–64; Jonathan Wilkenfeld, "Domestic and Foreign Conflict Behavior of Nations," *Journal of Peace Research* (1968), pp. 56–59; Lewis Coser, *The Functions of Social Conflict* (New York: The Free Press, 1969), pp. 87–94.
86. A more rigorous test of this hypothesis, employing quantitative measurements in content analysis, found it basically inapplicable in 1962. See Kuang-sheng Liao, *Internal Mobilization and External Hostility in The People's Republic of China, 1960–62 and 1967–69*, Ph.D. thesis, University of Michigan, Department of Political Science, 1974.
87. A topical recapitulation of these and other issues together with supporting documentation may be found in John Gittings, *Survey of the Sino-Soviet Dispute* (London: Oxford University Press, 1968).
88. Ibid., p. 111; see pp. 112–15 for documentary excerpts of Soviet and Chinese views on the border crisis as allegedly exchanged at the time but recapitulated in the polemic of 1963.

89. Ibid., p. 115.
90. Ibid., p. 115. The Chinese claimed, "In a verbal notification to the Central Committee of the CPC on February 6, 1960, the Central Committee of the CPSU stated that 'one cannot possibly seriously think that a state such as India, which is militarily and economically immeasurably weaker than China, would really launch a military attack on China and commit aggression against it,' that China's handling of the question was 'an expression of a narrow nationalist attitude' and that 'when shooting was heard on the Sino-Indian border on the eve of N.S. Khrushchev's trip to the United States the whole world considered this to be an event that could hamper the peace-loving activity of the Soviet Union.' On June 22, 1960, Khrushchev said to the head of the delegation of the Chinese Communist Party during the Bucharest meeting, 'I know what war is. Since Indians were killed, this meant that China attacked India.' He also said, 'We are Communists, for us it is not important to know where the frontier line runs.' . . ." See "The Truth About How the Leaders of the CPSU Have Allied Themselves With India Against China," *People's Daily*, November 2, 1963, in *Peking Review*, no. 45, November 8, 1963.
91. Gittings, op. cit., pp. 110–11 notes that "In July 1959 the Soviet Union more than doubled her aid so far to India by offering credits worth over US $375 million." Arthur Stein, *India and the Soviet Union: The Nehru Era* (Chicago: University of Chicago Press, 1969), p. 125, calculates the total pledged by mid-1960 as $500 million.
92. Stein, op. cit., p. 126.
93. Ibid., p. 131, quotes Nehru's reply of March 30, 1962, as guaranteeing "adequate precautions to see no secret information would leak" to the Soviet pilots.
94. Ibid., p. 126, and Maxwell, op. cit., p. 285.
95. Ian C. C. Graham, "The Indo-Soviet MIG Deal and Its International Repercussions," *Asian Survey* (May, 1964), pp. 823–32; see also Kaul, op. cit., pp. 342–44.
96. A summary of these developments may be found in Alexander Dallin, *Diversity in International Communism* (New York: Columbia University Press, 1963), p. 652.
97. Information available to the author.

Chapter 3

1. Neville Maxwell, *India's China War* (New York: Pantheon Books, 1970), p. 241.
2. Ibid., pp. 235–36.
3. Ibid., p. 235, statement by Nehru of June 20, 1962.
4. Lt. Gen. B. M. Kaul, *The Untold Story* (Bombay: Allied Publishers), p. 354.
5. *White Paper*, VI, p. 78.

6. *Peking Review,* no. 28, July 13, 1962.

7. *White Paper,* VI, p. 81.

8. Ibid., pp. 79–80.

9. Maxwell, op. cit., p. 238, drawing on private interviews as well as on the published Indian note.

10. "The Afterthoughts of Premier Chou," interview with Neville Maxwell, the *Sunday Times,* December 19, 1971.

11. *White Paper,* VII, p. 133.

12. *Peking Review,* no. 29, July 20, 1962. The spokesman could not have known at that time of the July 13 Nehru-Pan conversation.

13. Ibid.

14. Ibid., no. 30, July 27, 1962.

15. *White Paper,* VI, p. 92, for the Indian note; ibid., VII, p. 1, for the Chinese.

16. Maxwell, op. cit., p. 239.

17. *White Paper,* VII, p. 1.

18. Ibid., VII, pp. 3–4.

19. "The Afterthoughts of Premier Chou," the *Sunday Times.* This is confirmed in part by Arthur Lall, in a review of the Maxwell book wherein he refers to "the three most important talks which Krishna Menon and I had with Ch'en Yi, Chang Han-fu, and Chiao Kuan-hua at Geneva towards the end of July 1962. Ch'en Yi was pleased with the way the talks developed. At their conclusion he proposed that a joint communique be issued. Owing to technical failures, this was not done, a lapse which caused suspicion and annoyance on the Chinese side. This technical failure together with the failure to follow up the talks, proved to be a significant link in the chain of events which led to the senseless war three months later." *The Asian Student,* November 27, 1971.

20. Maxwell, op. cit., p. 243.

21. See chapter 2.

22. This appears to be the most critical year of policy debate between 1959 and 1965. For illuminating analyses, see Richard H. Solomon, *Mao's Revolution and The Chinese Political Culture* (Berkeley, Calif.: University of California Press, 1971), pp. 416ff.; Byung-joon Ahn, "Adjustments in The Great Leap Forward and Their Ideological Legacy, 1959–62," in *Ideology and Politics in Contemporary China,* Chalmers Johnson, ed. (Seattle, Wash.: University of Washington Press, 1973), pp. 257–300; and Stuart R. Schram, "The Cultural Revolution in Historical Perspective," in Stuart R. Schram, ed., *Authority Participation and Cultural Change in China,* (Cambridge: Cambridge University Press, 1973), pp. 1–108.

23. Solomon, op. cit., and Merle Goldman, "The Unique Blooming and Contending of 1961–62," *The China Quarterly* (January–March, 1969), pp. 57–84.

24. Goldman, op. cit., p. 81.
25. Ibid.
26. Solomon, op. cit., p. 443. Schram, op. cit., pp. 65–68, details the building of a "Mao-cult" by Mao and Lin Piao in 1959–60.
27. Indirect corroboration of this hypothesis is suggested by the delay in Peking's protest to Moscow over the Sinkiang events of May, an official note only emerging on August 30, 1962; see O. B. Borisov and B. T. Koloskov, *Sovetsko-Kitaiskie Otnosheniia, 1945–1970* (Moscow: Izdat, Mysl', 1972), p. 275. This was after Sino-Indian negotiatory prospects had ended.
28. Maxwell, op. cit., p. 244 quoting the *Hindustan Times*, August 8, 1962.
29. *White Paper*, VII, pp. 17–18.
30. Ibid., pp. 14–16.
31. Maxwell, op. cit., p. 245.
32. Ibid., p. 249.
33. Chang Chi, "The Sino-Indian Boundary Question," *Peking Review*, no. 33, August 17, 1962.
34. *White Paper*, VII, p. 26.
35. Ibid., p. 29.
36. Ibid., pp. 32–37.
37. Chang Chi, op. cit.
38. Maxwell, op. cit., p. 248.
39. The impasse in Geneva over issuing a joint communiqué confirming agreement to hold discussions without preconditions may be relevant here, although Chou's account dates the conversation there July 26 with implementation to occur after Menon's return to New Delhi. The failure of that implementation is blamed for the diplomatic breakdown by both Chou and Lall, yet it would seem unlikely to have been realized as definite by August 4, the time of Peking's reply to the July 26 note. See n. 19.
40. Chou, in his 1971 interview with Maxwell, "The Afterthoughts of Premier Chou," the *Sunday Times*, declared, "The Soviet revisionists told India: 'China will not fight back.' Why did the Soviet Union say that? Because they had got a lot of our people from Sinkiang but nevertheless we maintained the status quo according to our past practice, and our men did not cross the border to fight them." It is unclear when in 1962 this Soviet advice was allegedly given. Moreover it is difficult to determine how and when Chinese officials were apprised of this since relations with both New Delhi and Moscow were so strained as to make them unlikely sources. However, this is an interesting reconstruction and at the very least would appear to reflect policy divisions in Peking over the consequences of "reconciliation" as opposed to militant confrontation, with the "soft line" approach subsequently being indirectly blamed for the war.

41. See Samuel B. Griffith, II, *The Chinese People's Liberation Army* (New York: McGraw-Hill, 1967), p. 282; Arthur Huck, *The Security of China* (New York: Columbia University Press, 1970), p. 43; P. V. R. Rao, *Defense Without Drift* (Bombay: Popular Prakashan, 1970), p. 139; also information available to the author.

42. William W. Whitson with Chen-hsia Huang, *The Chinese High Command: A History of Communist Military Politics, 1927–71* (New York: Praeger Publishers, 1973), pp. 465–68, discusses military geography and regional defense; Rao, op. cit., pp. 139ff. discusses PLA logistical problems in Tibet. Rao was Defense Secretary prior to 1967.

43. Major Sita Ram Johri, *Chinese Invasion of Ladakh* (Lucknow: Himalaya Publications), p. 84. Whitson, op. cit., p. 489, claims "two Chinese corps—the 54th in Chengtu and the 18th in Lhasa" were involved in the October-November war, supplemented by "commanders and possibly elements of only one other corps . . . [the] 46th which then occupied a garrison in Manchuria . . . [and] proved to be remarkably effective against General Kaul's Indian 4th Infantry Corps." The movement of one regiment of railroad engineers was detected between the Kunming and the Tibet Military Regions during August and additional moves may have occurred between the Sinkiang and Tibet Military Regions. The failure of the Indians to take any prisoners of war during the fighting prevented an accurate reconstruction of PLA moves as had been possible in the Korean conflict.

44. *White Paper*, VII, pp. 42, 54, 55, 69 for Chinese protests of August 27, September 4, 5, 13, 1962 respectively.

45. Ibid., VII, p. 55.

46. Maxwell, op. cit., p. 253.

47. *White Paper*, VII, p. 51.

48. Ibid., p. 67–68.

49. Maxwell, p. 297. The Chinese for "our river and mountain" also means "our country."

50. Ibid., pp. 292 ff.

51. Brig. J. P. Dalvi, *Himalayan Blunder* (Bombay: Thacker and Co., 1969), pp. 153–54.

52. Ibid., pp. 97–98, 121, 173.

53. Ibid., p. 217.

54. Ibid., p. 166.

55. Ibid., pp. 166–209; Kaul, op. cit., pp. 354–60.

56. *White Paper*, VII, p. 74.

57. Dalvi, op. cit., p. 218.

58. Ibid., p. 208.

59. *White Paper*, VII, p. 75.

60. Dalvi, op. cit., p. 216.

61. *White Paper*, VII, pp. 83–84.

62. Dalvi, op. cit., pp. 211–12.

63. Ibid., p. 214.
64. Ibid., pp. 213–14.
65. *White Paper,* VII, pp. 80–81.
66. *People's Daily,* September 22, 1962.
67. *White Paper,* VII, pp. 88, 90, 92 for protests of September 25, 26, 29.
68. Dalvi, op. cit., pp. 210–11.
69. Radio Lhasa, Domestic Service in Mandarin, September 28, 1962, in *Foreign Broadcast Information Service (FBIS),* October 1, 1962.
70. Radio Peking, New China News Agency (NCNA) in Chinese, September 29, 1962, in *FBIS,* October 1, 1962.
71. *Peking Review,* no. 39, September 28, 1962.
72. Radio Peking, Domestic Service, September 26, 1962, in *FBIS,* September 27, 1962.
73. *Peking Review,* no. 39, September 28, 1962.
74. Radio Peking, NCNA in English to Asia and Europe, September 28, 1962, in *FBIS,* September 28, 1962.
75. Kaul, op. cit., p. 362.
76. Ibid., op. cit., p.363.

Chapter 4

1. *White Paper,* VII, pp. 98–99.
2. *White Paper,* VII, pp. 100–102.
3. Brig. J. P. Dalvi, *Himalayan Blunder* (Bombay: Thacker and Co., 1969), p. 218.
4. For Chinese protests and accounting down to September 30 see enclosure to note of October 17, 1972, *White Paper,* VII, p. 149.
5. Dalvi, op. cit., p. 219.
6. Neville Maxwell, *India's China War* (New York: Pantheon Books, 1970), p. 329.
7. Lt. Gen. B. M. Kaul, *The Untold Story* (Bombay: Allied Publishers, 1967), p. 366.
8. Dalvi, op. cit., p. 226.
9. Ibid., p. 239.
10. Maxwell, op. cit., p. 331; Dalvi, op. cit., p. 239.
11. Dalvi, op. cit., p. 280.
12. Ibid., p. 222.
13. Ibid., p. 234.
14. Maxwell, op. cit., pp. 332 ff.; Kaul, op cit., pp. 374 ff.; Dalvi, op. cit., pp. 282 ff.
15. Dalvi, op. cit., p. 293, gives 800; Kaul, op. cit., p. 381, gives 509.
16. *White Paper,* VII, pp. 117–20, the Indian protest of October 16, 1962, replying to earlier Chinese protests, simply cites Indian losses as "seventeen casualties."
17. Ibid., pp. 105, 108, 113.

18. Dalvi, op. cit., pp. 299–300.
19. Editorial Department of *People's Daily*, "The Truth About How The Leaders of the CPSU Have Allied Themselves with India Against China," *People's Daily*, November 2, 1963, in *Peking Review*, no. 45, November 8, 1963.
20. Dalvi, op. cit., p. 299.
21. Kaul, op. cit., p. 383.
22. Dalvi, op. cit., p. 312, quoting *The Statesman*, October 13, 1962.
23. *Peking Review*, no. 41, October 12, 1962.
24. Radio Peking, NCNA in English, October 10, 1962, in *Foreign Broadcast Information Service (FBIS)*, October 11, 1962.
25. Ibid.
26. Radio Peking, NCNA in English, October 12, 1962, in *FBIS*, October 15, 1962.
27. Radio Peking, Domestic Service in Mandarin, October 6, 1962, in *FBIS*, October 11, 1962.
28. Radio Peking, NCNA in English, October 12, 1962, in *FBIS*, October 15, 1962.
29. A good treatment of the situation is John Rowland, *A History of Sino-Indian Relations* (Princeton: D. Van Nostrand, 1967), pp. 188 ff.; for fuller details of the diplomacy, see S. M. Burke, *Pakistan's Foreign Policy* (London: Oxford University Press, 1973), especially pp. 290 ff.
30. See Burke, op. cit., pp. 290 ff.
31. Chien Po-tsan, vice-president of the China-Burma Friendship Association, Peking, NCNA in English, October 13, 1962, in *FBIS*, October 15, 1962.
32. *People's Daily*, October 14, 1962, in *Peking Review*, no. 42, October 19, 1962.
33. Dalvi, op. cit., p. 308.
34. Ibid., pp. 321–22, 315.
35. Ibid., pp. 321, 362.
36. Ibid., p. 315.
37. Ibid., p. 336.
38. Ibid., p. 364.
39. Kaul, op. cit., p. 430.
40. Dalvi, op. cit., p. 376.
41. Radio Peking, NCNA in English, October 20, 1962, in *FBIS*, October 22, 1962, for timing on NCNA release.
42. *Peking Review*, no. 43, October 26, 1962.
43. *White Paper*, VII, pp. 123–24.
44. Radio Peking, NCNA in English, October 20, 1962, 2100 GMT, in *FBIS*, October 22, 1962.
45. Ibid.
46. *Peking Review*, no. 43, October 26, 1962.

47. Ibid.
48. *Peking Review,* no. 45, November 9, 1962.
49. Ibid., no. 43, October 26, 1962.
50. *Peking Review,* nos. 44 and 45, November 2 and 9, 1962.
51. Radio Peking, NCNA in Chinese, October 25, 1962, in *FBIS,* October 26, 1962.
52. *White Paper,* VIII, pp. 4—7.
53. *Peking Review,* no. 44, November 2, 1962.
54. Ibid.
55. For comparison see documentation in Dallin, op. cit.; William E. Griffith, *The Sino-Soviet Rift* (Cambridge, Mass.: The M.I.T. Press, 1964); and John Gittings, *Survey of the Sino-Soviet Dispute* (London: Oxford University Press, 1968).
56. Dallin, op. cit., pp. 253—89, gives the *Red Flag* articles; Griffith, op. cit., pp. 33—43, offers analysis.
57. Donald S. Zagoria, *The Sino-Soviet Conflict, 1956—61* (Princeton, N.J.: Princeton University Press, 1962); also Dallin and Griffith.
58. *People's Daily,* November 2, 1963, quoted in Gittings, op. cit., p. 178.
59. Maxwell, op. cit., p. 365, citing Kuldip Nayar, *Between The Lines* (Bombay: Allied Publishers, 1969), p. 152.
60. Radio Moscow, TASS, in English to Europe, October 25, 1962, in *FBIS,* October 25, 1962.
61. Maxwell, op. cit., p. 366.
62. *People's Daily,* November 2, 1963, in Gittings, op. cit., p. 179.
63. Griffith, op. cit., pp. 51—55.
64. Ibid., p. 55; according to Borisov and Koloskov, op. cit., p. 277, the actual decision to close all Soviet consular and trade offices in September, 1962, was made by Moscow in response to alleged Chinese harassment and not in response to a formal demand by Peking.
65. Gittings, op. cit., p. 186, quoting Chinese official statement, August 15, 1963.
66. Ibid.
67. Maxwell, op. cit., p. 270.
68. Although considerable difference of opinion exists among scholars concerning exactly what transpired at the Tenth Plenum, there is a general consensus that it muted the dispute which had raged over the previous year, to the benefit of Mao's general position. See Solomon, op. cit., pp. 428—30; Ahn, op. cit., pp. 292—94.
69. Radio Peking, NCNA in English, October 24, 1962, and October 26, 1962, in *FBIS,* October 25, 1962, and October 29, 1962.
70. Radio Peking, NCNA in English, November 5, 1962, in *FBIS,* November 6, 1962.
71. Summary of October 30, 1962, broadcasts in *FBIS,* October 31, 1962.

Chapter 5

1. Neville Maxwell, *India's China War* (New York: Pantheon Books, 1970), p. 388.
2. Radio Peking, NCNA in English, October 27, 1962, quoting the *New York Herald Tribune*, in *Foreign Broadcast Information Service* (*FBIS*), October 29, 1962.
3. Radio Peking, NCNA, October 29, 1962, in *FBIS*, October 30, 1962.
4. Ibid.
5. Radio Peking, NCNA, November 4, 1962, in *FBIS*, November 5, 1962.
6. *White Paper*, VIII, pp. 7–11.
7. Ibid., VIII, pp. 62–64.
8. *Peking Review*, no. 45, November 9, 1962.
9. *People's Daily*, November 11, 1962, in *Peking Review*, no. 46, November 16, 1962.
10. *Pravda*, November 5, 1962, in *FBIS*, November 5, 1962.
11. Radio Peking, NCNA, November 10, 1962, in *FBIS*, November 11, 1962.
12. Radio Peking, NCNA in English, November 2, 1962, in *FBIS*, November 11, 1962.
13. *People's Daily*, November 15, 1962, in *Peking Review*, nos. 47–48, November 30, 1962.
14. *Peking Review*, nos. 47–48, November 30, 1962.
15. Nehru statement of October 14, 1962, in Maxwell, op. cit., p. 342.
16. Ibid., p. 344.
17. Ibid., p. 383.
18. Ibid., pp. 380 ff.
19. Ibid., p. 387.
20. Ibid., p. 395.
21. Ibid., pp. 393 ff.
22. *White Paper*, VIII, p. 64.
23. Maxwell, op. cit., p. 409.
24. Ibid., pp. 412 ff.
25. John Kenneth Galbraith, *Ambassador's Journal* (Boston: Houghton Mifflin, 1969), pp. 463–71.
26. Ibid.
27. *White Paper*, VIII, p. 24; Maxwell, op. cit., p. 417. Unfortunately Maxwell's cited source, S. S. Khera, *India's Defense Problems* (Bombay: Orient Longmans, 1968), p. 185, gives no further details of this key communication.
28. *Peking Review*, nos. 47–48, November 30, 1962. The announcement is dated "Peking, 00:00 hours, November 21, 1962," proclaiming the cease-fire will begin "00:00 hours, November 22, 1962."
29. Maxwell, op. cit., p. 424.

30. Lt. Gen. B. M. Kaul, *The Untold Story* (Bombay: Allied Publishers, 1967), p. 433.

31. Galbraith, op. cit., pp. 490–91, recounting conversation with Nehru of November 21, 1962.

32. Roger Hilsman, *To Move A Nation* (New York: Doubleday and Co., 1967), p. 327. The author took part in this mission and was present at its final Washington meeting which was interrupted by the first monitored broadcast of the cease-fire announcement.

33. Speech of Chinese delegate to the XII Congress of the Communist Party of Czechoslovakia, December 8, 1962, Radio Peking, NCNA in English, December 14, 1962, in Alexander Dallin, et al., *Diversity in International Communism* (New York: Columbia University Press, 1963), pp. 664 ff.

34. Kaul, op. cit., pp. 434–35. See also Girilal Jain, "The Border Dispute in Perspective," *China Report* (November–December, 1970), pp. 56–63: "The Chinese pressed the attack when the two superpowers were immobilized. . . .The Chinese withdrew as the Cuban crisis was brought under control and Washington and Moscow were relatively free. . . .They apparently took some quick decision when the Cuban crisis overshadowed every other dispute in the world. They moved with lightning speed and consolidated their hold in Aksai Chin. . . ."

35. According to the then Hungarian charge d'affaires in Washington, the Hungarian ambassador to Cuba had been informed by the Chinese ambassador in July or August "that according to information he had received from private sources the Soviet Union was delivering surface-to-surface ballistic missiles to Cuba and that Soviet military advisers had come to Cuba not as instructors but as members of Soviet special rocket force units to operate these missiles." Ambassador Beck reported "his Chinese friends had complained of Soviet unwillingness to disclose any details and had asked Beck whether he knew anything more about the whole affair." Janos Radvanyi, *Hungary and the Superpowers* (Stanford, Calif.: Hoover Institution, 1972), p. 124.

36. For a reconstruction of the speculation and diplomatic analyses on the eve of the crisis, October 19–20, see Arthur M. Schlesinger, Jr., *A Thousand Days* (Boston: Houghton Mifflin, 1965), pp. 809–10. As late as 9 P.M. on Saturday, October 20, Max Frankel of the *New York Times* personally called at the author's home to eliminate the possibility that whatever crisis was brewing concerned Asian problem areas such as India, Laos, and Vietnam.

37. See chapter 4.

38. Graham T. Allison, *Essence of Decision* (Boston: Little Brown and Co., 1971), pp. 64–65, recounts the October 27 developments which included an explicit United States warning that unless the Soviet Union committed itself immediately to withdrawal of the missiles the

United States would mount an air strike or an invasion within two or three days. Robert F. Kennedy, brother of the president, who communicated the message to Soviet Ambassador Dobrynin recalled, "Saturday, October 27 was the most serious time." See Robert F. Kennedy, *Thirteen Days: A Memoir of the Cuban Missile Crisis* (New York: W. W. Norton, 1969), p. 24.

39. This characterizes most Indian analyses of the 1962 conflict.
40. This is essentially the position of Peking, best argued independently by Neville Maxwell's volume.
41. *People's Daily,* May 6, 1959, in *Peking Review,* no. 19, May 12, 1959.
42. Edgar Snow, *The Other Side of the River* (New York: Random House, 1960), p. 74.
43. For a systematic examination of the differing organizational perspectives and consequent policy differences manifest in the first Communist government, see Allen S. Whiting, *Soviet Policies in China, 1917–1924* (Stanford, Calif.: Stanford University Press, 1968).
44. For a good contemporary analysis of the Indian Communist Party in the larger context of Sino-Soviet polemics see William E. Griffith, *The Sino-Soviet Rift* (Cambridge, Mass.: The M.I.T. Press, 1964), pp. 56–59. A much more detailed treatment is offered by Harry Gelman, "The Communist Party of India: Sino-Soviet Battleground," in A. Doak Barnett, ed., *Communist Strategies in Asia* (New York: Praeger, 1963), pp. 101–47.
45. The interested reader might begin by perusing *The China Quarterly* since 1968 to sample the range of analysis and available evidence. Selected essays in the series published under the auspices of the Joint Committee on Contemporary China of the American Council of Learned Societies and the Social Science Research Council are also suggestive, as noted in the foregoing footnotes of this study. As of 1974, however, no definitive, comprehensive study was able to delineate the persons and their respective policy positions that dominated the decision-making process in Peking during the pre-Cultural Revolution period.
46. On the 1959 essay, see Maxwell, op. cit., p. 264.
47. See chapter 4.
48. *People's Daily,* October 14, 1962, in *Peking Review,* no. 42, October 19, 1962.
49. *Peking Review,* no. 40, October 5, 1962.
50. See, for instance, the *People's Daily* editorials of October 10 and October 14, 1962.
51. *Red Flag,* no. 22, in *Peking Review,* nos. 47–48, November 30, 1962.
52. Kaul, op. cit., pp. 385–86.
53. Maxwell, op. cit., p. 425.
54. For American speculation, see Galbraith, op. cit., p. 478 and Hilsman,

op. cit., p. 324. Maxwell, op. cit., p. 419, offers the authoritative British view.

55. Radio Peking, Domestic Service in Mandarin, October 6, 1962, in *FBIS,* October 11, 1962.

56. The author participated in interagency meetings in Washington and New Delhi where these views were expressed by military analysts.

57. Galbraith, op. cit., p. 482.

58. Hilsman, op. cit., p. 339.

59. This is the basic conclusion reflected by the Maxwell volume.

60. For details see Khera, op. cit., pp. 176 ff.

61. Galbraith, op. cit., pp. 444–45.

62. Ibid., p. 445.

63. Schlesinger, op. cit., p. 526.

64. Maxwell, op. cit., p. 410.

65. Galbraith, op. cit., p. 487.

66. Maxwell, op. cit., p. 487.

67. Hilsman, op. cit., p. 327.

68. Maxwell, op. cit., p. 435.

69. James C. Thomson, Jr., "On the Making of U.S. China Policy, 1961–69: A Study in Bureaucratic Politics," *The China Quarterly* (April–June, 1972), pp. 227–28. The author participated in a series of meetings and moves designed to change opinion within the United States government as a prelude to change in American policy.

70. President John F. Kennedy, press conference of August 1, 1963, in Hilsman, op. cit., p. 339.

71. The books by Maxwell and Kaul amply reflect this assumption.

Chapter 6

1. The best survey of alternative hypotheses based on a preliminary examination of Chinese sources is Harry Harding and Melvin Gurtov, *The Purge of Lo Jui-ch'ing: The Politics of Chinese Strategic Planning* (Santa Monica, Calif.: The Rand Corp., R-548-PR, February, 1971).

2. Harold C. Hinton, *Communist China in World Politics* (New York: Houghton Mifflin Co., 1966), pp. 355–67 offers one of the best factual summaries with analysis.

3. Tang Tsou, ed., *China in Crisis* (Chicago: University of Chicago Press, 1968), vol. II; David P. Mozingo and Thomas W. Robinson, *Lin Piao on 'People's Wars': China Takes a Second Look at Vietnam* (Santa Monica, Calif.: the Rand Corp., RM 4814-PR, 1965); Donald S. Zagoria, *Vietnam Triangle* (New York: Pegasus, 1967); Michael Yahuda, "Kremlinology and the Chinese Strategic Debate, 1965–66," *The China Quarterly* (January–March, 1972), pp. 32–75; Donald S. Zagoria, "On Kremlinology: A Reply to Michael Yahuda," and Uri

Ra'anan, "On Kremlinology: A Second Reply," *The China Quarterly* (April–June, 1972), 343–50.

4. *The Pentagon Papers,* 4 vols., (Boston: Beacon Press, 1971) vol. III, pp. 150 ff., in particular the statements by President Lyndon B. Johnson at the University of California, Los Angeles, on February 21, 1964, and his press conference on February 29, 1964.

5. *Peking Review,* no. 11, March 13, 1964, p. 20.

6. Marvin Kalb and Elie Abel, *Roots of Involvement: The U.S. in Asia, 1784–1971* (New York: Norton and Co., 1971), p. 167.

7. Ibid., p. 168.

8. Ibid., p. 169.

9. *Peking Review,* no. 27, July 3, 1964, p. 13.

10. Ibid., p. 8.

11. Ibid., no. 28, July 10, 1964, p. 24.

12. Ibid., p. 25.

13. Ibid., no. 30, July 24, 1964, p. 5.

14. The author's office was responsible for coordinating and assessing intelligence on the crisis for the Department of State.

15. The *New York Times,* August 4, 1964.

16. *Peking Review,* no. 32, August 7, 1964, p. ii.

17. The *New York Times,* August 11, 1964.

18. The author was responsible for supervising the analysis of this intelligence data within the Department of State.

19. *Peking Review,* no. 28, July 10, 1964, p. 23.

20. Information available to the author from official data.

21. *Peking Review,* no. 51, December 18, 1964, p. 5.

22. A comprehensive review and analysis of all "lips and teeth" references is in "Sino-Vietnamese Relations, 1954–70," Brian Carl Joseph Shaw, Ph.D. thesis, University of Hong Kong.

23. The *New York Times,* February 8, 1965. Actually the raids were preplanned on the basis of the author's forecast that a Communist assault would be mounted against an American installation during the visit of McGeorge Bundy, special assistant for National Security Affairs.

24. *The Pentagon Papers,* op. cit., vol. IV, p. 216.

25. *Peking Review,* no. 16, April 16, 1965.

26. Information available to the author from officially compiled data.

27. This section is drawn from data compiled by the author while in the Department of State.

28. This was the only detected instance of deliberate deception on the part of Peking concerning alleged air incidents.

29. The *New York Times,* July 12, 1965.

30. From data compiled by official sources.

31. *The Pentagon Papers,* op. cit., vol. IV, p. 156, memorandum by

William P. Bundy, assistant secretary of state for Far East Affairs, undated but apparently May, 1967.

32. Ibid., p. 168, memorandum of William P. Bundy, May 8, 1967.
33. Ibid., p. 198.
34. From officially compiled data.
35. For details on the August events, see Edward E. Rice, *Mao's Way* (Berkeley, Calif.: University of California Press, 1972), pp. 364–81. Rice was the United States consul general in Hong Kong at this time.
36. The *New York Times*, May 9, 1972.
37. *The Pentagon Papers*, op. cit., vol. III, pp. 29–30 for details on the 1965 limits; see ibid., p. 198 for the changes in 1967. Although some dikes were damaged in 1972 there was no evidence this resulted from deliberate orders or systematic attack.
38. Ibid., vol. III, p. 346, memorandum by McGeorge Bundy.
39. Ibid., p. 354, quotation from column by Rowland Evans and Robert Novak, undated.
40. Ibid., p. 388, memorandum by Robert P. McNamara, secretary of defense, July 30, 1965.
41. Ibid., vol. IV, p. 31.
42. From officially compiled data.
43. The *New York Times*, April 26, 1972, from text of National Security Study Memorandum no. 1, prepared on the basis of memoranda submitted by the United States government agencies within ten days of an initial request by the White House on January 21, 1969.
44. David Halberstam, *The Best and the Brightest* (New York: Random House, 1972), pp. 538–47, provides the best political-military reconstruction and analysis of this development. See also Kalb and Abel, op. cit., pp. 185 ff.
45. *Peking Review*, no. 12, March 19, 1965, official statement of March 12, 1965.
46. *Peking Review*, no. 23, June 4, 1965.
47. Ibid., no. 29, July 16, 1965.
48. Ibid., no. 30, July 23, 1965.
49. For deep-seated differences of interpretation over basically identical evidence see exchanged views among Michael Yahuda, Donald S. Zagoria, and Uri Ra'anan, *The China Quarterly*, op. cit.
50. The *New York Times*, July 29, 1965.
51. *Peking Review*, no. 33, August 13, 1965.
52. The bulk of the following section draws primarily upon data available to the author while in the Department of State.
53. General Mark W. Clark, *From the Danube to the Yalu* (New York: Harper and Bros., 1954), p. 96, reported "underground defense works as much as twenty-five miles deep . . . from one coast of Korea to the

other . . . impervious to air and even artillery attack." General Matthew B. Ridgeway, *The Korean War* (Garden City: Doubleday, 1967), p. 187, described "tunnels as much as 1,000 yards long to take quick shelter from bombardment."

54. The *New York Times,* December 1, 1965, contained the fullest public summary of intelligence reports to date.

55. Halberstam, op. cit., talks intermittently throughout his book of the problems President Johnson faced in maintaining congressional support for domestic programs and his anxiety not to jeopardize them by increased costs of the Vietnam War; see especially pp. 603–10.

56. From data available to the author while in the Department of State.

57. *Peking Review,* no. 41, October 8, 1965.

58. *Washington Post,* November 24, 1965.

59. Information available to the author. See the *New York Times,* December 3, 1965, for reports of economic activity associated with war preparations.

60. Information available to the author at the time.

61. Hong Kong *Wen Hui Pao,* January 26–February 24, 1966; a much briefer series with parallel themes appeared in Hong Kong *Ta Kung Pao,* January 24–28, 1966. The authoritative nature of these two newspapers as representative of Chinese Communist views makes the simultaneous and unprecedented public discussions of these themes of particular interest.

62. Hong Kong *Wen Hui Pao,* January 26, 1966.

63. Ibid., January 27, 1966.

64. Ibid., February 14, 1966.

65. Ibid., February 14, 1966.

66. Chou En-lai at National Liberation Front rally, December 20, 1965, in *Peking Review,* no. 52, December 24, 1965.

67. Hong Kong *Ta Kung Pao,* January 24, 1966.

68. Ibid., January 27, 1966.

69. While these analyses appeared intermittently in both series, the most complete statement is in Hong Kong *Wen Hui Pao,* February 14, 1966.

70. *People's Daily,* December 14, 1965, in *Peking Review,* no. 51, December 17, 1965.

71. Hong Kong *Wen Hui Pao,* January 27, 1966.

72. Hong Kong *Ta Kung Pao,* January 28, 1966.

73. *Peking Review,* no. 20, May 13, 1966.

74. For a good summary of the Laotian road developments see John E. Coon, "The PLA and Chinese Power Abroad," in William W. Whitson, ed., *The Military and Political Power in China in the 1970's* (New York: Praeger Publishers, 1972), pp. 343–45.

75. *The Pentagon Papers,* op. cit., vol. IV, p. 163, memorandum of May 6,

1967, by Walt W. Rostow, special assistant to the president for National Security Affairs.

76. Ibid., vol. IV, p. 173, draft presidential memorandum of May 19, 1967, prepared in the office of secretary of defense Robert S. McNamara.

77. Ibid., vol. IV, pp. 245–46, memorandum by William P. Bundy, undated but approximately March 1, 1968.

Chapter 7

1. The major stimulus for this chapter came from Daniel I. Okimoto whose theoretical focus is broad and sharp. The author is also indebted to Alexander George for his sharing of various drafts and papers associated with his long-standing interest in deterrence and the use of force.

2. The text of the 1950 Treaty of Friendship, Alliance, and Mutual Assistance is in *People's China*, no. 5, March 1, 1950, pp. 25–26.

3. James C. Thomson, Jr., "On the Making of U.S. China Policy, 1961–69: A Study in Bureaucratic Politics." *The China Quarterly* (April–June, 1972), p. 228.

4. J. Chester Cheng, ed., *The Politics of the Chinese Red Army* (Stanford: Hoover Institute, 1966).

5. For authoritative accounts of this period see Edward E. Rice, *Mao's Way* (Berkeley: University of California Press, 1972), chaps. 20–24; also Stanley Karnow, *Mao and China: From Revolution to Revolution* (New York: Viking, 1972), chaps. 10–17.

6. The best survey of the period is Foster Rhea Dulles, *American Policy Toward Communist China, 1949–1969* (New York: Thomas Y. Crowell, 1972), chaps. 4–7. The most detailed reconstruction of the Washington reaction to Korean events is Glenn D. Paige, *The Korean Decision, June 24–30, 1950* (New York: The Free Press, 1968).

7. For specific Chinese domestic preparations against possible air attack, including references to nuclear weapons, see Allen S. Whiting, *China Crosses the Yalu* (Stanford: Stanford University Press, 1968), pp. 134–36.

8. Among the better works in English are Scott A. Boorman, *The Protracted Game: A Wei-ch'i Interpretation of Maoist Revolutionary Strategy* (London: Oxford University Press, 1969); and William W. Whitson with Chen-hsia Huang, *The Chinese High Command* (New York: Praeger, 1973), especially chap. 11.

9. Ibid.; see also Lionel Giles, *Sun Tzu on the Art of War* (London: Lucac and Co., 1910); Samuel B. Griffith, *The Chinese People's Liberation Army* (New York: McGraw-Hill, 1967), chap. 14; Scott A.

Boorman, "Deception in Chinese Strategy," in William W. Whitson, ed., *The Military and Political Power in China in the 1970's* (New York: Praeger, 1972), pp. 313—38; Mao Tse-tung, *Selected Military Writings* (Peking: Foreign Languages Press, 1963).

10. Hu Sheng, *Imperialism and Chinese Politics* (Peking: Foreign Languages Press, 1955), p. 9.

11. For various perspectives on this problem see Whitson, ed., op. cit., particularly Joseph Heinlein, "The Ground Forces"; Glenn G. Dick, "The General Political Department"; and Paul Elmquist, "The Internal Role of the Military."

12. Ch'en Yi interview of May 29, 1962, *Tokyo Journalist,* June 26, 1962, in *Foreign Broadcast Information Service (FBIS),* August 13, 1962.

13. For a detailed reconstruction see Allen S. Whiting, *China Crosses the Yalu* (Stanford: Stanford University Press, 1968), chaps. 6—7.

14. Ibid., especially table A, p. 119, and map 8, p. 120.

15. K. M. Panikkar, *In Two Chinas* (London: Allen and Unwin, 1955), p. 107.

16. Whiting, op. cit., p. 79.

17. Ibid., p. 190. Panikkar, op. cit., p. 110, provides a paraphrase within inverted commas that imply a direct quote although it does not parse grammatically.

18. *White Paper,* VII, p. 1.

19. Ibid., p. 43.

20. Ibid., p. 55.

21. Ibid., p. 68.

22. Ibid., p. 84.

23. Ibid., p. 88.

24. Ibid., p. 96.

25. Ibid., p. 108.

26. Whiting, op. cit., p. 99, quoting *People's Daily,* July 28, 1950, Radio Peking in English Morse to North America, July 28, 1950.

27. Ibid., p. 99, quoting *People's Daily,* August 30, 1950, Radio Peking in English to North America, August 30, 1950.

28. Panikkar, op. cit., p. 108.

29. Whiting, op. cit., p. 108, quoting *Hsüeh Hsi* (Study), October 16, 1950.

30. Ibid., p. 115, quoting Radio Peking, Chinese International Service in English, October 11, 1950.

31. The announcement was officially dated "00.00 hours, November 21, 1962" and was broadcast just before midnight.

32. Alexander L. George, David K. Hall, and William R. Simons, *The Limits of Coercive Diplomacy* (Boston: Little, Brown and Co., 1971),

especially pp. 1—35; Thomas C. Schelling, *Arms and Influence* (New Haven: Yale University Press, 1966).

33. George, op. cit., pp. 9—11.
34. Schelling, op. cit., p. 43.
35. Ibid., p. 49.
36. Ibid., pp. 44, 35.
37. Whiting, op. cit., p. 191, footnote 40, summarizes military estimates of the period; for fuller evidence see *Military Situation in the Far East, Hearings Before the Committee on Armed Services and the Committee on Foreign Relations,* Eighty-Second Congress, First Session (Washington, D.C.: 1951).
38. Dean Acheson, *Present at the Creation* (New York: Norton, 1969), p. 445.
39. Ibid., p. 453.

Chapter 8

1. For analysis of these materials see articles by Stuart R. Schram, John Gittings, and Allen S. Whiting in *The China Quarterly,* nos. 57, 60, and 62.
2. A convenient synthesis of the theoretical literature on this question with respect to foreign policy may be found in Graham T. Allison, *Essence of Decision* (Boston: Little, Brown, and Co., 1971), chaps. 3 and 5. See also Morton H. Halperin, *Bureaucratic Politics and Foreign Policy* (Washington: Brookings Institution, 1974).
3. For one case study of this phenomenon see Glenn D. Paige, *The Korean Decision* (New York: The Free Press, 1968); a more theoretical treatment is offered by Charles Hermann, *Crises in Foreign Policy* (New York: Bobbs-Merrill, 1969).
4. Donald Klein, *The Chinese Ministry of Foreign Affairs,* Ph.D. dissertation, Columbia University, 1974.
5. William W. Whitson, ed., *The Military and Political Power in China in the 1970's* (New York: Praeger, 1972), especially part 3, "The Organization of Military Power in China," pp. 135—268.
6. Parris Chang, "Changing Patterns of Military Roles in Chinese Politics," ibid., pp. 47—67; also Paul Elmquist, "The Internal Role of the Military," ibid., pp. 269—90.
7. For summary information on the Tenth Party Congress of 1973 and the shuffle of regional military commanders shortly thereafter, see *The China Quarterly* "Chronicle" for issues no. 56 and 57, October—December, 1973, and January—March, 1974.
8. *China: The Roots of Madness,* narrated by Theodore H. White, distributed by Films Incorporated, Wilmette, Ill.; for 1967 developments

see Edward E. Rice, *Mao's Way* (Berkeley: University of California Press, 1972), especially chaps. 22 and 23.

9. See *Current Digest of the Soviet Press* for March and April, 1969.

10. "Long Live Leninsim," by the editorial staff of *Red Flag*, in *Peking Review*, no. 17, April 26, 1960.

11. In addition to Allison, op. cit., see Andrew Nathan, "A Factionalism Model for CCP Politics," *The China Quarterly*, no. 53 (January–March, 1973), pp. 34–66.

12. The author was United States deputy consul general in Hong Kong at this time; the following account draws on his personal knowledge; see also Rice, op. cit., chapter 22.

13. Rice, op. cit., p. 368.

14. Melvin Gurtov, "The Foreign Ministry and Foreign Affairs During the Cultural Revolution," *The China Quarterly*, no. 40 (October–December, 1969), pp. 65–102.

15. The speech by Hsieh Fu-chih was broadcast live to Hong Kong through loudspeakers mounted on the Bank of China, an unprecedented pattern of communication between Peking and local Communist followers.

16. Personal interview given to the author in 1974.

17. Rice, op. cit., pp. 375–78.

18. The *New York Times*, June 21, 1971, reporting foreign diplomats in Peking on the mass public trial and subsequent execution of Yao Tseng-shan, former charge d'affaires in Indonesia and identified in 1967 as directing the radical line in foreign affairs.

19. Estimate of the United States Consulate General, Hong Kong, including remittances from overseas Chinese.

20. Chester Bowles, *Promises to Keep: My Years in Public Service, 1941–1969* (New York: Random House, 1971), chap. 11.

21. For a detailed analysis of the Sino-American rapprochement during 1968–71, see Allen S. Whiting, "The Sino-American Detente: Genesis and Prospects," in Ian Wilson, ed., *China and the World Community* (Sydney, Australia: Angus and Robertson, 1973), pp. 70–96.

22. Edgar Snow, *The Long Revolution* (New York: Vintage Books, 1973), p. 218, reported that Mao believed fighting would go on perhaps for one to two years after which time American troops would leave; the interview occurred January 9, 1965, and was cleared by Chinese officials for publication but without the use of direct quotation.

23. David Halberstam, *The Best and the Brightest* (New York: Random House, 1971).

24. Uri Ra'anan, "Peking's Foreign Policy 'Debate,' 1965–1966," and Donald S. Zagoria, "The Strategic Debate in Peking," in Tang Tsou, ed., *China in Crisis* (Chicago: University of Chicago Press, 1968), vol. II, pp. 23–71 and 237–68.

25. See Allen S. Whiting, "Quemoy, 1958: Mao's Miscalculations," *The China Quarterly*, no. 62 (April–June, 1975).

26. For details see Harold C. Hinton, *Communist China in World Politics* (Boston: Houghton Mifflin Co., 1966), chap. 10.

27. A reliable resume of Chinese troop activity in Laos may be found in *The Washington Post*, April 8, 1974. An earlier report is in *Laos: April 1971*, staff report prepared for the use of the Subcommittee on U.S. Security Agreements and Commitments Abroad of the Committee on Foreign Relations, United States Senate, Washington, D.C., August 3, 1971.

28. For a systematic but inconclusive examination of alternative explanations for Chinese behavior, see Thomas W. Robinson, "The Sino-Soviet Border Dispute," *The American Political Science Review*, December, 1972, pp. 1175–1202. An authoritative presentation of the Chinese side which includes an eyewitness description of the disputed island is offered by Neville Maxwell, "The Chinese Account of the 1969 Fighting at Chenpao," *The China Quarterly*, no. 56 (October–December, 1973), pp. 730–39.

29. See Mao Tse-tung's alleged statement in January, 1967, that Soviet "ground forces are on the move," *Current Background*, no. 892, October 21, 1969, p. 50. This purportedly comes from an "Instruction to the People's Liberation Army" as "relayed by Vice Chairman Yeh Chien-ying, January 27, 1967."

30. The wording of Mao's alleged statement that "ground forces are on the move" suggests it was based on electronic intelligence.

31. Contrary to later public estimates which posited a tripling of Russian divisions between 1968 and 1971, other information showed that the bulk of the buildup already had doubled 1965 Soviet strength by mid-1969, with only an increase of another one-third thereafter. Presumably PRC estimates were based on the same source as this information. The former reports are contained in the annual publication by the Institute of Strategic Studies, London, *The Military Balance*. For a fairly accurate reflection of the 1968–69 situation see the columns of Joseph Alsop in July and August, 1969.

32. See, for instance, the joint *People's Daily, Red Flag, Liberation Army Day* editorial which called upon the country to "strengthen preparedness against war, exercise full vigilance against sabotage, subversion, and aggression carried out by class enemies abroad against our proletarian state power" and "go all out and be sure to destroy the enemy intruders"; *Peking Review*, no. 32, August 9, 1968. Chief of Staff Huang Yung-sheng, ibid., p. 13, identified "U.S. imperialism and its accomplices" as those who "dare to impose war" while merely accusing "U.S. imperialism, Soviet revisionism and the Indian and other reactionaries [as] intensifying their efforts . . . to create border ten-

sion by frequently encroaching on our territorial waters and air space."

33. *Peking Review,* no. 34, August 23, 1968, supplement.

34. *Peking Review,* no. 38, September 20, 1968.

35. Thus within the "twenty-one days" twenty alleged sorties occurred between August 9–12 but only four between August 20–24, i.e., after the Czech invasion. Moreover alleged penetration of Chinese airspace was "three kilometres at the farthest and the longest distance covered was five kilometres," hardly sufficient to cause alarm in Peking.

36. *Peking Review,* no. 40, October 4, 1968. No such language appeared in Chou's previous speeches of October 1, 1967, and May 1, 1968.

37. Huang Yung-sheng on October 4, 1968, at a mass rally in Peking for an Albanian party and government delegation, *Peking Review,* no. 41, October 11, 1968.

38. Wang En-mao, political commander of the PLA, Sinkiang Military Area Command and vice-chairman of the Revolutionary Committee of the Sinkiang Uighur Autonomous Region, addressing the Albanian delegation on October 8, 1968, *Peking Review,* no. 42, October 18, 1968.

39. The following details are drawn from Maxwell, op. cit.

40. Ellis Joffe, "The People's Liberation Army," in Wu Yuan-li, ed., *China, A Handbook* (New York: Praeger, 1973), pp. 263–65; Frank E. Armbruster, "China's Conventional Military Capability," in Tang Tsou, op. cit., vol. II, pp. 165–66.

41. Considering the twelve-hour time difference between Peking and Washington, it is likely that less than a day elapsed between the actual receipt of Dulles's words at decision-making levels and the approval of Chou's response. The standard time lapse for official Chinese reaction to unanticipated events of international importance appears to be three days.

42. Hinton, op. cit., p. 268.

43. The following account draws on the author's experience in Hong Kong. For a more detailed account see *Hong Kong, Report for the Year 1967* (Hong Kong: Hong Kong Government, 1968), chap. 1.

44. Jonathan D. Pollack, "Chinese Attitudes Towards Nuclear Weapons, 1964–69," *The China Quarterly,* no. 50 (April–June, 1972), pp. 244–71.

45. I wish to thank Professor Tang Tsou who argued this point forcefully in correspondence.

46. Choon-ho Park, *Continental Shelf Issues in The Yellow Sea and the East China Sea,* Law of the Sea Institute, University of Rhode Island, Occasional Paper, no. 15, September, 1972; also his *Fisheries Issues in the Yellow Sea and the East China Sea,* Occasional Paper, no. 18, September, 1973. For more recent statements of the PRC position consult *Peking Review.*

47. Hinton, op. cit., chaps. 11–12.
48. John R. Dewenter, "China Afloat," *Foreign Affairs* (July, 1972), vol. 50, no. 4, pp. 738–51.
49. Earl C. Ravenal, "Approaching China, Defending Taiwan," ibid. (October, 1971), vol. 50, no. 1, pp. 44–58.
50. For a survey of the pre-PRC interaction, see O. Edmund Clubb, *China and Russia: The "Great Game"* (New York: Columbia University Press, 1971), chaps. 1–26.
51. A comprehensive survey, although somewhat dated, is offered by A. M. Halpern, ed., *Policies Toward China: Views From Six Continents* (New York: McGraw-Hill Book Co., 1965).
52. Monographic studies of selected countries and time periods include Daniel D. Lovelace, *China and "People's War" in Thailand, 1964–1969* (Berkeley: University of California, 1971), Center for Chinese Studies Research Monograph, no. 8; Melvin Gurtov, *China and Southeast Asia—The Politics of Survival* (Lexington, Mass.: D. C. Heath, 1971); and Peter Van Ness, *Revolution and Chinese Foreign Policy* (Berkeley: University of California, 1970).
53. Gurtov, "The Foreign Ministry," op. cit.
54. John E. Coon, "The PLA and Chinese Power Abroad," in Whitson, ed., op. cit., pp. 339–57.

Bibliography

Acheson, Dean. *Present at the Creation.* New York: Norton, 1969.

Allison, Graham. *Essence of Decision: Explaining the Cuban Missile Crisis.* Boston: Little, Brown and Co., 1971.

Alsop, Joseph. "On China's Descending Spiral." *The China Quarterly.* July–September, 1962, pp. 21–38.

Ashbrook, Arthur G., Jr. "China: Economic Policy and Economic Results 1949–1971." *People's Republic of China: An Economic Assessment.* A Compendium of Papers Submitted to the Joint Economic Committee, Congress of the United States, May 18, 1972. Washington: U.S. Government Printing Office, 1972, pp. 3–51.

Barnett, A. Doak, ed. *Communist Strategies in Asia.* New York: Praeger, 1963.

Boorman, Scott A. *The Protracted Game: A Wei-Ch'i Interpretation of Maoist Revolutionary Strategy.* London: Oxford University Press, 1969.

Borisov, O. B., and Koloskov, B. T. *Sovetsko-Kitaiskie Otnosheniia, 1945–1970.* Moscow: Izdat, Mysl', 1972.

Bowles, Chester. *Promises to Keep: My Years in Public Service, 1941–1969.* New York: Random House, 1971.

Burke, S. M. *Pakistan's Foreign Policy.* London: Oxford University Press, 1973.

Cheng, J. Chester, ed. *The Politics of the Chinese Red Army.* Stanford, Calif.: Hoover Institution, 1966. Translated from *Kung-tso T'ung-hsün* (Bulletin of Activities) nos. 1–30 (no. 9 missing), January–August, 1961.

Chiang, Kai-shek. *China's Destiny.* New York: Roy Publishers, 1947.

Clark, General Mark W. *From the Danube to the Yalu.* New York: Harper and Bros., 1954.

Clubb, O. Edmund. *China and Russia: The "Great Game."* New York: Columbia University Press, 1971.

Dallin, Alexander, ed. *Diversity in International Communism.* New York: Columbia University Press, 1963.

285

Dalvi, Brig. J. P. *Himalayan Blunder.* Bombay: Thacker and Co, 1969.

Dewenter, John R. "China Afloat." *Foreign Affairs.* vol. 50, no. 4 (July, 1972): 738–51.

Dulles, Foster Rhea. *American Policy Toward Communist China, 1949–1969.* New York: Thomas Y. Crowell, 1972.

Eckstein, Alexander. *Communist China's Economic Growth and Foreign Trade.* New York: McGraw-Hill, 1966.

Fisher, Margaret W., Rose, Leo E., and Huttenback, Robert A. *Himalayan Battleground: Sino-Indian Rivalry in Ladakh.* New York: Praeger, 1963.

Galbraith, John Kenneth. *Ambassador's Journal.* Boston: Houghton Mifflin, 1969.

George, Alexander L., Hall, David K., and Simons, William E. *The Limits of Coercive Diplomacy: Laos, Cuba, Viet Nam.* Boston: Little, Brown and Co., 1971.

Giles, Lionel. *Sun Tzu on the Art of War.* London: Lucac and Co., 1910.

Ginsburgs, George, and Mathos, Michael. *Communist China and Tibet.* The Hague: M. Nijhoff, 1964.

Gittings, John. *Survey of the Sino-Soviet Dispute.* London: Oxford University Press, 1968.

Goldman, Merle. "The Unique Blooming and Contending of 1961–1962." *The China Quarterly,* January–March, 1969, pp. 57–84.

Graham, Ian C. C. "The Indo-Soviet MIG Deal and Its International Repercussions." *Asian Survey,* May, 1964, pp. 823–32.

Griffith, Samuel B., II. *The Chinese People's Liberation Army.* New York: McGraw-Hill, 1967.

Griffith, William E. *The Sino-Soviet Rift.* Cambridge, Mass.: The M.I.T. Press, 1964.

Gupta, Karunakar. "The McMahon Line, 1911–1945: The British Legacy." *The China Quarterly,* July–September, 1971, pp. 521–45.

Gurtov, Melvin. *China and Southeast Asia–The Politics of Survival.* Lexington, Mass.: D. C. Heath, 1971.

Halberstam, David. *The Best and the Brightest.* New York: Random House, 1972.

Halpern, A. M., ed. *Policies Toward China: Views from Six Continents.* New York: McGraw-Hill Book Co., 1965.

Harding, Harry, and Gurtov, Melvin. *The Purge of Lo Jui-ch'ing: The Politics of Chinese Strategic Planning.* Santa Monica, Calif.: The Rand Corp., R-548-PR, February, 1971.

Hilsman, Roger. *To Move a Nation.* Garden City, N.Y.: Doubleday and Co., 1967.

Hinton, Harold C. *Communist China in World Politics.* Boston: Houghton Mifflin Co., 1966.

Hu Sheng. *Imperialism and Chinese Politics.* Peking: Foreign Languages Press, 1955.

Huck, Arthur. *The Security of China.* New York: Columbia University Press, 1970.

Jain, Girilal. "The Border Dispute in Perspective." *China Report,* November—December, 1970, 56—63.

Johnson, Chalmers, ed. *Ideology and Politics in Contemporary China.* Seattle, Washington: University of Washington Press, 1973.

Johri, Major Sita Ram. *Chinese Invasion of NEFA.* Lucknow: Himalaya Publications, 1968.

————. *Chinese Invasion of Ladakh.* Lucknow: Himalaya Publications, 1969.

Kalb, Marvin, and Abel, Elie. *Roots of Involvement: The U.S. in Asia, 1784—1971.* New York: Norton and Co., 1971.

Karnow, Stanley. *Mao and China: From Revolution to Revolution.* New York: Viking Press, 1972.

Kaul, Lt. Gen. B. M. *The Untold Story.* Bombay: Allied Publishers, 1967.

————. *Confrontation with Pakistan.* New Delhi: Vikas Publishers, 1971.

Kennedy, Robert F. *Thirteen Days: A Memoir of the Cuban Missile Crisis.* New York: W. W. Norton, 1969.

Khera, S. S. *India's Defense Problems.* Bombay: Orient Longmans, 1968.

Lall, Arthur. *How Communist China Negotiates.* New York: Columbia University Press, 1968.

Lamb, Alastair. *The China-India Border: The Origins of the Disputed Boundaries.* London: Oxford University Press, 1964.

————. *The McMahon Line: A Study in the Relations Between India, China, and Tibet, 1904 to 1914.* London: Routledge and Kegan Paul, 1966.

Li, Tieh-tseng. "The Legal Position of Tibet." *American Journal of International Law,* April, 1956, pp. 394—404.

————. *Tibet Today and Yesterday.* New York: Bookman Associates, 1960.

Lovelace, Daniel D. *China and "People's War" in Thailand, 1964—1969.* Berkeley: University of California. Center for Chinese Studies Research Monograph, no. 8, 1971.

Maxwell, Neville. "The Chinese Account of the 1969 Fighting at Chénpao." *The China Quarterly,* October—December, 1973, pp. 730—39.

————. *India's China War.* New York: Pantheon Books, 1970.

Mills, J. P. "The Problem of the Assam-Tibet Frontier." *The Royal Central Asian Journal,* April, 1950, pp. 152—61.

Mozingo, David P., and Robinson, Thomas W. *Lin Piao on "People's Wars": China Takes a Second Look at Vietnam.* Santa Monica, Calif.: The Rand Corp., RM 4814-PR, 1965.

Mullik, B. N. *My Years with Nehru: The Chinese Betrayal.* Bombay: Allied Publishers, 1971.

Nathan, Andrew. "A Factionalism Model for CCP Politics." *The China Quarterly,* January—March, 1973, pp. 34—66.

Norbu, Thubten Jigme. *Tibet is My Country*. New York: E. P. Dutton and Co., 1961.

Paige, Glenn D. *The Korean Decision, June 24–30, 1950*. New York: The Free Press, 1968.

Panikkar, K. M. *In Two Chinas*. London: Allen and Unwin, 1955.

Park, Choon-ho. *Continental Shelf Issues in the Yellow Sea and the East China Sea*. Law of the Sea Institute, University of Rhode Island, Occasional Paper, no. 15, September, 1972.

―――. *Fisheries Issues in the Yellow Sea and the East China Sea*. Law of the Sea Institute, University of Rhode Island, Occasional Paper no. 18, September, 1973.

Patterson, George. *Tragic Destiny*. London: Faber and Faber, 1959.

―――. *Tibet in Revolt*. London: Faber and Faber, 1960.

―――. *Peking Versus Delhi*. London: Faber and Faber, 1963.

Pollack, Jonathan D. "Chinese Attitudes Towards Nuclear Weapons, 1964–1969." *The China Quarterly*, April–June, 1972, pp. 244–71.

Prouty, L. Fletcher. "Colorado to Koko Nor." *Empire Magazine, The Denver Post*, February 6, 1972.

―――. *The Secret Team: The CIA and Its Allies in Control of the United States and the World*. Englewood Cliffs, N.J.: Prentice-Hall, 1973.

Radvanyi, Janos. *Hungary and the Superpowers*. Stanford, Calif.: Hoover Institution, 1972.

Rao, P. V. R. *Defense Without Drift*. Bombay: Popular Prakashan, 1970.

Ravenal, Earl C. "Approaching China, Defending Taiwan." *Foreign Affairs*, vol. 50, no. 1, (October, 1971): 44–58.

Rice, Edward E. *Mao's Way*. Berkeley, Calif.: University of California Press, 1972.

Ridgeway, General Matthew B. *The Korean War*. Garden City: Doubleday, 1967.

Robertson, Frank. "Refugees and Troop Moves—A Report from Hong Kong." *The China Quarterly*, July–September, 1962, pp. 111–15.

Robinson, Thomas W. "The Sino-Soviet Border Dispute." *The American Political Science Review*, December, 1972, pp. 1175–1202.

Rowland, John. *A History of Sino-Indian Relations*. Princeton: D. Van Nostrand, 1967.

Schelling, Thomas C. *The Strategy of Conflict*. Cambridge, Mass.: Harvard University Press, 1960.

―――. *Arms and Influence*. New Haven, Conn.: Yale University Press, 1966.

Schlesinger, Jr., Arthur M. *A Thousand Days*. Boston: Houghton Mifflin, 1965.

Schram, Stuart R., ed. *Authority Participation and Cultural Change in China*. Cambridge: Cambridge University Press, 1973.

Shabad, Theodore. *China's Changing Map.* Rev. ed. New York: Praeger, 1972.

Snow, Edgar. *Red Star Over China.* New York: Modern Library, 1944.

———. *The Other Side of the River.* New York: Random House, 1960.

———. *The Long Revolution.* New York: Random House, 1972.

Solomon, Richard H. *Mao's Revolution and the Chinese Political Culture.* Berkeley, Calif.: University of California Press, 1971.

Stein, Arthur. *India and the Soviet Union: The Nehru Era.* Chicago: University of Chicago Press, 1969.

Strong, Anna Louise. *Tibetan Interviews.* Peking: New World Press, 1959.

———. *When Serfs Stood Up in Tibet.* Peking: New World Press, 1960.

Tang, Peter S. H. *Communist China Today.* Washington: Research Institute on the Sino-Soviet Bloc, 1961.

Thomas, Jr., Lowell. *Out of This World.* New York: The Greystone Press, 1950.

Thomson, Jr., James C. "On The Making of U.S. China Policy 1961—69: A Study in Bureaucratic Politics." *The China Quarterly,* April—June, 1972, pp. 220—43.

Tsou, Tang, ed. *China in Crisis.* Vol. 2. Chicago: University of Chicago Press, 1968.

Van Ness, Peter. *Revolution and Chinese Foreign Policy.* Berkeley: University of California, 1970.

Vogel, Ezra. *Canton Under Communism.* Cambridge, Mass.: Harvard University Press, 1969.

Weissman, Steve. "Last Tangle in Tibet." *Pacific Research and World Empire Telegram,* July—August, 1973, pp. 1—18.

Weissman, Steve, and Shoch, John. "CIAsia Foundation," *Pacific Research,* September—October, 1972, pp. 3—4.

Whiting, Allen S. *China Crosses the Yalu.* Stanford, Calif.: Stanford University Press, 1968.

Whiting, Allen S. and Sheng Shih-ts'ai. *Sinkiang: Pawn or Pivot?.* East Lansing, Mich.: Michigan State University Press, 1958.

Whitson, William W., ed. *The Military and Political Power in China in the 1970's.* New York: Praeger, 1972.

Whitson, William W., with Huang, Chen-hsia. *The Chinese High Command: A History of Communist Military Politics, 1927—1971.* New York: Praeger, 1973.

Wilson, Ian, ed. *China and the World Community.* Sydney, Australia: Angus and Robertson, 1973.

Wise, David. *The Politics of Lying.* New York: Random House, 1973.

Woodman, Dorothy. *Himalayan Frontiers.* New York: Praeger, 1969.

Wu, Yuan-li, ed. *China, A Handbook.* New York: Praeger, 1973.

Yahuda, Michael. "Kremlinology and the Chinese Strategic Debate, 1965—1966." *The China Quarterly,* January—March, 1972, pp. 32—75.

Young, Kenneth T. *Negotiating with the Chinese Communists.* New York: McGraw-Hill, 1968.

Zagoria, Donald S. *The Sino-Soviet Conflict, 1956-1961.* Princeton, N.J.: Princeton University Press, 1962.

———. *Vietnam Triangle.* New York: Pegasus, 1967.

Official Publications and Documents

Notes, Memoranda and Letters Exchanged and Agreements Signed Between the Governments of India and China: White Paper. Vols. 1—8. New Delhi: Ministry of External Affairs, Government of India, 1959—63.

The Pentagon Papers. Vols. 1—4. Boston: Beacon Press, 1971.

Report of the Officials of the Government of India and the People's Republic of China on the Boundary Question. New Delhi: Government of India, 1961.

The Sino-Indian Boundary Question. Peking: Foreign Language Press, 1962.

Periodicals

Numerous articles from the following periodicals were drawn upon extensively in the research for this book.

The China Quarterly (London)
Current Digest of the Soviet Press (Ann Arbor, Michigan)
Foreign Broadcast Information Service (Washington, D.C.)
Jen Min Jih Pao (Peking)
The *New York Times*
Peking Review
Ta Kung Pao (Hong Kong)
Wen Hui Pao (Hong Kong)

Index

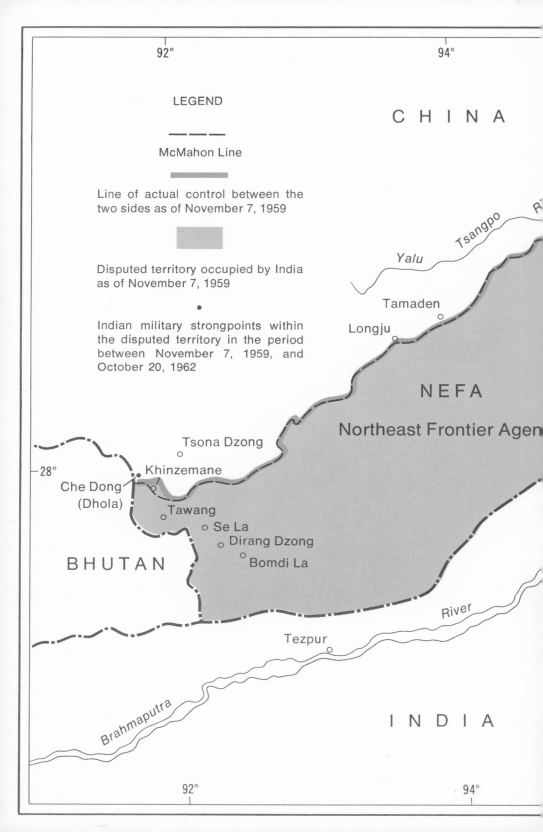